# EUROPEAN COMMUNITY LAW
## AND CIVIL REMEDIES
## IN ENGLAND AND WALES

# EUROPEAN COMMUNITY LAW AND CIVIL REMEDIES IN ENGLAND AND WALES

by

## Rose M. D'Sa

LL.B. (Hons.), Ph.D.
Barrister, Middle Temple
International Relations Consultant,
Edwards Geldard (Cardiff, Wales)

LONDON
SWEET & MAXWELL
1994

Published in 1994 by
Sweet & Maxwell Limited of
South Quay Plaza, 183 Marsh Wall, London E14 9FT.
Phototypeset by LBJ Enterprises Ltd.
of Aldermaston and Chilcompton
Printed and bound in Great Britain by
Hartnolls Ltd., Bodmin.


No natural forests were destroyed to make this product;
only farmed timber was used and re-planted


BRITISH LIBRARY CATALOGUING IN PUBLICATION DATA
A catalogue record for this book is available from the British Library


ISBN 0 421 50550 8


The index was prepared by Patricia Baker

# DEDICATION

To Frank Wooldridge, LL.M., Ph.D.
 Adjunct Professor, University of Notre Dame, London Campus

 my friend and mentor,
 in recognition of his knowledge, insights and contribution to
 legal research.

# PREFACE

European Community law is a rapidly expanding field but remains relatively remote to the vast majority of legal practitioners in England and Wales. In particular, those who qualifed for practice either before the conclusion of the Treaty of Rome in 1972, or before the impetus given to Community law in 1987 by the entry into force of the Single European Act (which amended the Treaty), are likely never to have studied Community law as an academic subject. Yet the topic of remedies for breaches of Community law can be of vital importance to commercial and other client interests.

This book is an introduction to Community law and domestic remedies, primarily for practitioners in England and Wales. It is hoped that, by virtue of my early background as an academic lawyer coupled with my experience of the practice of law, I have been able to explain in a simple and clear way the essential principles of Community law, as well as how to apply those principles in order to obtain domestic remedies. I have tried to summarise and to synthesise the writings of various leading academic writers whilst at the same time adding practical guidance. In this way, the subject is not only put in context but also made relevant to the busy practitioner. Despite its focus on the needs of practitioners, I hope that this work will also be of value to students of law who should find the text readable and concise. In particular, it will be relevant to students on the Law Society's new Legal Practice Course for whom domestic remedies for breaches of Community law will be a growing area of importance when they enter into practice.

In the early chapters, the essential principles of Community law are examined. These may be familiar to those with some knowledge of the subject, but have nevertheless been dealt with in detail because of the need for a clear understanding of the foundations on which remedies are based. The later chapters focus on the availability of, and criteria for, remedies in national law. They are not intended to be exhaustive, but wherever possible examples are given of the use of Community law to illustrate the practical difficulties, both procedural and substantive, which may be experienced.

The early work for the book was undertaken during the tenure of a Visiting Fellowship at the Institute of Advanced Legal Studies, London, during 1991–1992. It partly reflects work undertaken there in association with the project: "The Legal Implementation of the Single European Market at National Level", funded as part of the Economic and Social Research Council's (ESRC) Single European Market Initiative (Grant No. W113251005). The encouragement of the Institute's Director, Professor Terence Daintith, and of Dr Christopher Vincenzi of Huddersfield University is appreciated.

Further impetus for the book was provided when the European Commission approved a continuing vocational training grant to my employers, Edwards Geldard, under the FORCE programme for 1992, to examine "Legal Barriers to Cross-Border Trade in the European Community". My contribution to this project included an examination of State liability for breaches of Community law.

The book was written essentially in my spare time, but I would like to acknowledge the support of my employers, Edwards Geldard, for the provision of some secretarial support and library research facilities. In this connection, I would like to thank my former secretary, Halana Marytsch, for her painstaking and careful typing of some of the earlier drafts and Mary Michell for her efficient library support service. I owe a debt of gratitude to Liesbeth Diaz of the University of Wales, Cardiff, for typing all the final drafts and for keeping me in good humour throughout. I am also grateful for the helpful information provided by Ian Thomson, editor of *European Access*, Peter Armin-Trepte, Barrister, and for the material supplied by Jorgen Hansen, Head of the European Commission's Office in Wales, Helen Deaz of the Single Market Compliance Unit (SMCU) of the Department of Trade and Industry, Saverio Baviera of the Committee on Petitions, European Parliament, Archie McCaffer of the Welsh Office and Paul Lomas of Freshfields.

Peter Duffy, Barrister, is thanked for informal discussions, which have contributed to my insights into this rapidly evolving area of practice. However, I owe my deepest appreciation and gratitude to Dr Frank Wooldridge (to whom this book is dedicated) for having read all the drafts and for his extensive comments on the whole book. The remaining flaws are entirely my own.

I am also grateful to Sweet and Maxwell for all their help.

Finally, thanks are due to the various men in my life for putting up with my neglect of them and for encouraging me, nonetheless. My very special thanks are reserved for my husband, Professor John Matthews, for his extensive general editorial comments, academic insights and encouragement (and for putting up with the other men in my life!).

The book is based on material available from published sources as at March 1, 1994. Some later amendments were possible at proof stage to take account of the House of Lords decision in *R. v. Secretary of State for Employment, ex parte Equal Opportunities Commission: The Times*, March 4, 1994. The judgment of the European Court of Justice in Case C–188/92, *TWD Textilwerke Deggendorf GmbH v. Germany*: March 9, 1994, was not available at the time of going to print. It is therefore only referred to in a foonote at paragraph 3–027. The decision is likely to restrict, in future, the independent right of individuals to challenge by way of a reference from a national court under Article 177 of the E.C. Treaty, the validity of a Community act, such as a decision of the European Commission. It appears from a discussion of the case in the *Financial Times*, March 15, 1994, p. 22 that individuals who are fully aware of their right to challenge such acts by bringing a direct action in the European Court and who do not do so, cannot then later challenge by way of an Article 177 reference to the European Court for a ruling on a preliminary point of law. This is intended by the Court to safeguard legal certainty and avoid delay.

Dr Rose D'Sa
Langstone,
Gwent,
Wales.

# CONTENTS

# TABLE OF CASES

## ALPHABETICAL LIST OF CASES BEFORE THE EUROPEAN COURTS

# EUROPEAN COURT OF JUSTICE

## COURT OF FIRST INSTANCE

## E.C. COMMISSION DECISIONS

# NATIONAL CASES

## Belgium

## Eire

## England and Wales

## France

# Germany

# Northern Ireland

# Scotland

# International Tribunal Cases

# TABLE OF LEGISLATION

## REGULATIONS

# DIRECTIVES

# NOTICES AND GUIDELINES

# COUNCIL DECISIONS

# RULES OF PROCEDURE

# NATIONAL LEGISLATION

## Eire

## Rules of Procedure

## Germany

# INTERNATIONAL TREATIES AND CONVENTIONS

# THE POSITION OF THE INDIVIDUAL IN COMMUNITY LAW: A LITIGANT'S PERSPECTIVE

The aim of this work is first, to explain the principles which govern the **1–001** application of European Community law within the U.K. and secondly, to identify the criteria which govern the availability of remedies in the courts of England and Wales, where there is an alleged infringement of Community law.[1] The book has a commercial focus, in that it concentrates on civil remedies for individuals and businesses, in the course of commercial activities. The present chapter overviews the position of the individual under Community law. It explains the nature of the Community legal order and the role of the European Court of Justice (ECJ) in determining infringements of Community law, and enforcing, compliance. The limited rights of individuals to bring proceedings directly before the ECJ are outside the scope of the book and are referred to in outline only. The importance of national remedies for the enforcement of Community law by the individual litigant is highlighted. Some alternative, non-judicial, remedies are also discussed, as is the Sutherland Report which dealt, *inter alia*, with the possibility of the harmonisation of national remedies.

## SOME IMPORTANT FEATURES OF EUROPEAN COMMUNITY LAW

The entry into force on November 1, 1993 of the Treaty on European **1–002** Union (the Maastricht Treaty)[2] has brought into effect, *inter alia*,

---

[1] See also Sharpston, *Interim and Substantive Relief in Claims under Community Law* (1993); Brearley and Hoskins, *Remedies in European Law* (1994).

[2] In the U.K., ratification was the subject of an unsuccessful legal challenge, by way of judicial review, brought by Lord Rees-Mogg on behalf of the anti-Maastricht campaign, on the grounds that the Government's approach was legally and constitutionally flawed. However, the challenge was rejected at first instance by the High Court; see *R. v. Secretary of State for Foreign and Commonwealth Affairs, ex p. Rees-Mogg* [1993] 3 C.M.L.R. 101, and the U.K. ratified the Treaty on August 2, 1993. A constitutional challenge to the ratification process in Germany was also rejected; see *Europäische Grundrechte Zeitschrift*, 1993, p. 423, and *Brunner* v. *The European Union Treaty:* [1994] 1 C.M.L.R. 57.

substantive amendments to the Treaty of Rome, including a change of name for the latter, from EEC Treaty to E.C. Treaty.[3] The term "E.C. Treaty" is therefore used interchangeably in this book with "Treaty of Rome (as amended)." The use of "Treaty of Rome" or "EEC Treaty" is, however, also retained where the text refers to, or is concerned with, events occurring before the entry into force of the Treaty on European Union.

Unless the contrary is stated, the terms "Community", "European Community" and "European Community law" as used in this book and references to specific E.C. Treaty Articles are intended throughout to encompass any relevant amendments made by the Treaty on European Union.

The new European Union, in accordance with Title I, Article A(3) of the Treaty on European Union, is ". . . founded on the European Communities and supplemented by the policies and forms of co-operation established by this Treaty . . ." By virtue of Title I, Article B, the objectives of the Union also include ". . . to maintain in full the *acquis communautaire* and build on it . . ." The expression "*acquis communautaire*" is an expression which does not have an exact English translation. It is intended to describe the sum of what has been achieved in giving effect to the founding Treaties of the European Communities.[4]

Nevertheless, the legal competences of the new European Union created by the Treaty on European Union are wider than those of the Community *per se*.[5] They include, for instance, in Title V, provisions on a common foreign and security policy and, in Title VI, provisions on co-operation in the fields of justice and home affairs. Such areas fall outside the Community legal system (and are excluded, in Article L (Title VII), from the jurisdiction of the European Court of Justice (ECJ)). They remain, in effect, inter-governmental Treaty obligations binding the Member States of the Union, and are not discussed further in this book.

European Community law poses distinct problems for legal practitioners. It belongs, in a formal sense, to the realm of international law in that it is partly based on treaties concluded between sovereign States. From the view point of its content, however, it is in fact a kind of common internal law within these Member States.[6] In addition, the object of Community rules, unlike that of traditional international law, is

---

[3] See Treaty on European Union, Title II, Article G: [1992] O.J. C191/1, [1992] 1 C.M.L.R. 719. Amendments have also taken effect, in accordance with the Treaty on European Union, to the ECSC Treaty (Title III, Article H) and to the Euratom Treaty (Title IV, Article I), but these are not directly relevant to this work.

[4] See Wyatt and Dashwood, *European Community Law* (1993), 3rd ed., Chap. 23 on "The Treaty on European Union". The phrase can be used to indicate the whole corpus of Community law at a particular time.

[5] For a discussion of the substantive competences of the European Union, see Robert Lane, "New Community Competences Under the Maastricht Treaty" (1993) 30 C.M.L.Rev. 939 to 979.

[6] See Kapteyn and Verloren van Themaat, *Introduction to the Law of the European Communities: After the Coming into Force of the Single European Act* (1989), 2nd ed., p. 36.

not only the regulation of the conduct of national governments, but also the conduct of private persons with respect to the objectives of the Common Market. Consequently, Community law regulates not only the relations between the Community and Member States, but also relations between the Community and private persons, and, most importantly, between these subjects themselves. It therefore also affects relations between private persons.

As a result the Community constitutes:

"A new legal order, for the benefit of which the States have limited their sovereign rights, albeit within limited fields, and the subjects of which comprise not only the Member States but also their nationals."[7]

This affects legal practitioners in England and Wales[8] in a fundamental way. They have to apply English law, but also need to remember the possible application of Community law. A provision of English law may be challenged as being restrictive of a right under Community law and if so, the latter may take precedence. The circumstances when this situation can arise and the legal principles which apply are outlined in this book.

## Role of the European Court of Justice

The Community has also provided its own institutions, including a **1–003** European Court of Justice (ECJ)[9] which exercises sovereign rights derived from Member States. In particular, the Court has extensive powers to ensure that Community law is respected. In terms of jurisdiction, it is without precedent in the law of international organisations.[10] The work of the ECJ is supplemented by the Court of First Instance (CFI) and is discussed further at paragraphs 3–016 and 3–030 below.

The Community has various procedures for determining and enforcing infringements of Community law, and enforcing compliance. For example, Articles 169 and 170 of the Treaty of Rome (as amended)[11] provide a mechanism whereby the European Commission,[12] or a Member State, can bring an action before the European Court against either another Member State or a Community institution, for an alleged infringement of Community law. Clearly, the foundation of the whole Community

---

[7] Case 28/67, *Firma Molkerei-Zentrale Westfalen/Lippe GmbH* v. *Hauptzollamt Paderborn*: [1968] E.C.R. 143 at p. 152, [1968] C.M.L.R. 187.

[8] The general principles of Community law discussed in this book apply equally to Scotland and Northern Ireland.

[9] Also referred to hereinafter as the Court. Some institutional changes have also been made by the Treaty on European Union, such as the establishment of a Committee of the Regions (Article 4(2) E.C. Treaty).

[10] See Kapteyn and Verloren van Themaat, *op. cit.*, p. 28.

[11] Also referred to hereinafter as the E.C. Treaty (formerly EEC Treaty). The change of name was implemented under Title II of the Treaty on European Union (Maastricht Treaty).

[12] Also referred to as the Commission.

system depends on Community solidarity. This is set out in Article 5 of the Treaty of Rome (as amended) which states that:

> "Member States shall take all appropriate measures, whether general or particular, to ensure fulfilment of the obligations arising out of this Treaty or resulting from action taken by the institutions of the Community. They shall facilitate the achievement of the Community's tasks. They shall abstain from any measure which could jeopardise the attainment of the objectives of this Treaty."

A Member State may not raise in its defence, for example, the fact that after the filing of an application by the Commission under the Article 169 procedure, the relevant laws have been changed so as to comply with the relevant directive.[13]

### Sanctions for breach of Community law by a Member State

1–004     However, although the Court has jurisdiction under Articles 169 and 170[14] to give a ruling on breaches of Community obligations by Member States, no sanctions were provided for in the EEC Treaty to compel States to fulfil these obligations. Article 171 EEC merely required Member States to "take the necessary mesaures to comply with the Court's judgments". This situation has been altered by the Treaty on European Union[15] (the Maastricht Treaty) which entered into force on November 1, 1993,[16] following the deposit of the instrument of ratification of the last signatory State, which was Germany.[17] The Treaty makes various amendments to the EEC Treaty (referred to in the text above), including a change of name to "E.C. Treaty".[18] In addition, Article 171 is amended and a new (second) sub-paragraph is added which provides as follows:

> "2. If the Commission considers that the Member State concerned has not taken such measures it shall, after giving that State the opportunity to submit its observations, issue a reasoned opinion specifying the points on which the Member State concerned has not complied with the judgment of the Court of Justice. If the Member State concerned fails to take the necessary measures to comply with the Court's judgment within the time limit laid

---

[13] See Case C–29/90, *Commission* v. *Greece:* judgment of March 18, 1992 not yet reported.
[14] See also certain other E.C. Treaty provisions, *e.g.*, Article 93 concerning breach of the state aid provisions; see also Articles 100a(4) and 225.
[15] For the text of the Treaty on European Union see [1992] O.J. C191/1, [1992] 1 C.M.L.R. 719.
[16] Discussed earlier at para. 1–002 above. For a commentary on the ratification process in the Member States see "Current Survey" (1993) 18 E.L.Rev. 228 and "Current Survey" (1993) 18 E.L.Rev. 541. The European Council has also published a communication on the position of Denmark *vis-à-vis* the Treaty on European Union: [1992] O.J. C348/1–4.
[17] The instruments of ratification were deposited with the government of the Italian Republic.
[18] See Treaty on European Union, February 7, 1992, Title II, G: [1992] O.J. C191/1, [1992] 1 C.M.L.R. 719.

down by the Commission, the latter may bring the case before the Court of Justice. In so doing it shall specify the amount of the lump sum or penalty payment to be paid by the Member State concerned which it considers appropriate in the circumstances. If the Court of Justice finds that the Member State concerned has not complied with its judgment, it may impose a lump sum or penalty payment on it. This procedure shall be without prejudice to Article 170."

The Treaty on European Union, therefore, provides for a substantial penalty if, following a judgment of the Court, a Member State does not comply with the judgment. However, it is clear that the State must first be given an opportunity to submit its observations and the Court must issue a reasoned opinion specifying the points on which the Member State has not complied with the judgment of the Court. There is an additional requirement for the Commission to bring a case before the Court in connection with failure to comply with the judgment, in the course of which it must specify the amount of compensation by way of lump sum or penalty payment, which it considers appropriate for the Member State to pay in the circumstances. A further judgment of the Court of Justice imposing a lump sum or penalty payment must then be given before the Member State becomes liable. There is, however, no provision for the Court (or a national court) to impose an injunction in connection with a failure to comply with a judgment of the Court.[19]

It appears that the procedure will be a lengthy process, and would give the Member State concerned ample opportunity to comply with the Court's judgment or for a political or diplomatic solution to be found in each individual case. Nevertheless, the ultimate threat of a financial penalty is a substantial extension of the powers of the Court. However, it may not be sufficient to prevent continuing breaches by a Member State since in particular, it may be difficult to arrive at a figure in respect of the lump sum or penalty payment, which has real deterrent effect. A more effective deterrent would have been a provision to order the suspension of payment of sums due *from the Community* against a recalcitrant State which refused to pay the prescribed lump sum or penalty payment.[20]

Furthermore, these amendments to the Treaty of Rome will not provide directly for a remedy, by way of compensation, for an individual person or private organisation who may have suffered damage as a result of a Member State's breach of Community law. The options currently available are explored further below.[21] It has been suggested by Steiner[22] that the previous lack of provision for financial penalties against Member

---

[19] See further, Curtin, "The Constitutional Structure of the Union: A Europe of Bits and Pieces" (1993) 30 C.M.L.Rev. 17 at p. 33.

[20] Curtin, *op cit.*, pp. 33 to 34.

[21] See Chap. 9, below.

[22] Steiner, "From Direct Effects to Francovich: Shifting Means of Enforcement of Community Law" (1993) 18 E.L.Rev. 3 at p. 6.

States was both a legal and psychological barrier to the introduction of a *general* principle of liability in damages for Member States' failure to fulfil their Community obligations. This situation has substantially altered as a result of Joined Cases C-6 & 9/90, *Francovich and Bonifaci* v. *Italian State*[23] which are analysed in detail below.[24] However, the EEC Treaty as amended at Maastricht appears to leave most of the responsibility for the future development of remedies to the Court, which it appears likely to pursue in its future case law.

## RESTRICTED ACCESS OF INDIVIDUALS TO THE EUROPEAN COURT OF JUSTICE

### Article 173

1–005    The rights of ordinary persons (*e.g.* individuals, institutions or businesses) to bring proceedings before the European Court are restricted. Article 173 of the Treaty of Rome (as amended) provides that:

> "The Court of Justice shall review the legality of acts adopted jointly by the European Parliament and the Council, of acts of the Council, of the Commission and of the ECB, other than recommendations or opinions and of acts of the European Parliament intended to produce legal effects *vis-à-vis* third parties.

> It shall for this purpose have jurisdiction in actions brought by a Member State, the Council or the Commission on grounds of lack of competence, infringement of an essential procedural requirement, infringement of this Treaty or of any rule of law relating to its application, or misuse of powers.

> The Court shall have jurisdiction under the same conditions in actions brought by the European Parliament and by the ECB for the purpose of protecting their prerogatives.

> Any natural or legal person may, under the same conditions, institute proceedings against a decision addressed to that person or against a decision which, although in the form of a regulation or a decision addressed to another person, is of direct and individual concern to the former.

> The proceedings provided for in this Article shall be instituted within two months of the publication of the measure, or of its notification to the plaintiff, or, in the absence thereof, of the day on which it came to the knowledge of the latter, as the case may be."

---

[23] Joined Cases C–6 & 9/90, *Francovich and Bonifaci* v. *Italian State*: [1991] I E.C.R. 5357, [1993] 2 C.M.L.R. 66.

[24] See paras. 8–008 *et seq.* and 9–016 *et seq.* below.

This Article was substantially amended by the Treaty on European Union,[25] but the amendments do not affect the position of individuals under Community law. The amendments, *inter alia*, extended the powers of the Court of Justice to review the legality of acts adopted jointly by the European Parliament and the European Council, as well as the Commission and the proposed European Central Bank (ECB). (The relevant process is one similar to that of judicial review.) The Court is also given an explicit jurisdiction to review the legality of acts of the European Parliament intended to produce legal effects *vis-à-vis* third parties. In addition, the Court is given jurisdiction, under the conditions listed in Article 173, as amended, to hear actions brought by the European Parliament and by the ECB, for the purpose of protecting their prerogatives.[26] (For the earlier case law concerning the power to review the acts of Parliament see, *e.g.* Case 294/83, *Parti écologiste "Les Verts"* v. *European Parliament;* Case 34/86, *Council* v. *European Parliament.*) The converse also applies, namely that if Parliament has an interest, it may bring an action under Article 173: see Case 70/88, *European Parliament* v. *Council* (also known as the *Chernobyl* case reversing the effect of Case 302/87, *European Parliament* v. *Commission* (the *Comitology* case)). This was subsequently confirmed in Case 65/90, *European Parliament* v. *Council of the European Communities: The Times*, November 3, 1992.[27]

The definition of "natural or legal person" in Article 173 refers to private parties and does not include Member States or Community institutions. The private persons usually affected are traders, who may be incorporated persons, *e.g.* a company or trade association.[28] In order for an individual applicant to satisfy the requirements for *locus standi* in Article 173(2) of the Treaty of Rome (as amended), three separate requirements must be satisfied. First, the act must be "a decision" in substance; secondly, the applicant must be individually concerned by it; and thirdly, he or she must be directly concerned by it. Each of these requirements raises separate issues[29] which are outside the scope of this work.

## Article 175

The procedure in Article 173 is essentially for the annulment of illegal **1–006** acts by Community institutions. Article 175 of the Treaty of Rome (as amended) provides a separate remedy for failure to act. Paragraph 3 of Article 175 states that:

---

[25] *Op. cit.*, n. 18.

[26] See further, Bebr, "The Standing of the European Parliament in the Community System of Legal Remedies: A Thorny Jurisprudential Development" (1990) 10 *Yearbook of European Law* 171.

[27] Case 294/83, [1986] E.C.R. 1339, [1987] 2 C.M.L.R. 343; Case 34/86, [1986] E.C.R. 2155, [1986] 3 C.M.L.R. 94; Case 70/88, [1990] I E.C.R. 2041, [1992] 1 C.M.L.R. 91; Case 302/87, [1988] E.C.R. 5615. See further, Emiliou, "Protecting Parliamentary Prerogatives" (1993) 18 E.L.Rev. 56.

[28] See Harding, "Who Goes to Court in Europe? An Analysis of Litigation against the European Community" (1992) 17 E.L.Rev. 105 at p. 109, n. 9.

[29] See further, Hartley, *The Foundation of European Community Law* (1990), 2nd ed., p. 344. See also Sharpston, *op. cit.*, at pp. 117 *et seq.*

"Any natural or legal person may, under the conditions laid down in the preceding paragraphs, complain to the Court of Justice that an institution of the Community has failed to address to that person any act other than a recommendation or/an opinion."

Article 173 therefore provides for a legal remedy in connection with the commission of an act. Article 175, on the other hand provides a remedy for a failure to act, namely an omission.[30] Article 175 has also been amended by the Treaty on European Union so as to include a remedy for failure to act by the European Parliament. The Court of Justice is also given jurisdiction, under the conditions listed in Article 175, as amended, in actions or proceedings brought by the proposed ECB in the areas falling within the latter's field of competence and in actions or proceedings against the latter.

Under Article 176 of the Treaty of Rome (as amended), the consequences of an action before the Court under either Articles 173 or 175 are that:

"The institution whose act has been declared void or whose failure to act has been declared contrary to this Treaty shall be required to take the necessary measures to comply with the judgment of the Court of Justice.

This obligation shall not affect any obligation which may result from the application of the second paragraph of Article 215.

This Article shall also apply to the ECB."[31]

If an individual wishes to challenge the institution's implementation of the judgment, he/she can also do so under Article 173 or Article 175, as appropriate. No further sanctions are provided for non-compliance with the Court's judgment. (See however, the effect of Article 171(2) as amended by the Treaty of European Union, discussed at paragraph 1–004 above.) These restrictions limit the use which can be made by private parties to challenge Member States and/or Community institutions.[32]

---

[30] See further, Hartley, op. cit., pp. 370 et seq.

[31] Article 215(2) provides that: "In the case of non-contractual liability, the Community shall, in accordance with the general principles common to the laws of the Member States, make good any damage caused by its institutions or by its servants in the performance of their duties." The Treaty on European Union amended Article 176 and Article 215(2) and extended them so as to apply to the proposed ECB.

[32] For an analysis of the success or otherwise of this system of challenge under Articles 173 and 175, see Hartley, op. cit. See also, Forster, "Taking on the Commission: Procedural Possibilities for an Applicant Following Submission of a Complaint" [1993] 6 E.C.L.R. 256–262.

# NATIONAL REMEDIES FOR ENFORCEMENT OF COMMUNITY LAW BY INDIVIDUALS

Private parties can also rely on the application of certain provisions of **1–007** Community law in their national legal order. The Court has said that:

"The vigilance of individuals concerned to protect their rights amounts to an effective supervision in addition to the supervision entrusted by Articles 169 and 170 to the diligence of the Commission and of the Member States.[33]

The extent to which individuals can enforce rights and obligations in the domestic legal order both against a Member State, and against other private individuals, is therefore a most important part of the enforcement of Community law.

The Court of Justice has said that the principle of co-operation laid down in Article 5 of the EEC Treaty means that "It is the national courts which are entrusted with ensuring that legal protection which citizens derive from the direct effect of the provisions of Community law."[34]

The principle that individuals have the right to the substantive and effective enjoyment of directly effective Community rights[35] was reaffirmed by the European Court in Case C-213/89, *R.* v. *Secretary of State for Transport, ex parte Factortame*[36] in the following words:

". . . it is for the national courts, in application of the principle of co-operation laid down in Article 5 of the EEC Treaty, to ensure the legal protection which persons derive from the direct effect of provisions of Community law."

The extent to which this is possible, and, in particular, the remedies which may be available to individuals, are the specific subject of this work. The domestic remedies available for breach of Community law are particularly important given the high instance of Member States failing to implement directives in time, in clear breach of their Community obligations. The Commission has considered various measures at the political level, for dealing with this situation. It has maintained a high level of judicial activity against offending Member States. For example, in 1991, 887 letters of formal notice were sent, 412 reasoned opinions and 64 Article 169 infringement proceedings were commenced before the Court of Justice.[37]

---

[33] Case 26/62, *Van Gend en Loos* v. *Nederlandse Administratie der Belastingen*: [1963] E.C.R. 1 at p. 13, [1963] C.M.L.R. 105.

[34] Case 33/76, *Rewe Zentralfinanz eG et al* v. *Landwirtschaftskammer für das Saarland*; [1976] E.C.R. 1989 at p. 1997, [1977] 1 C.M.L.R. 533. For a detailed analysis of Article 5 see Lang, "Community Constitutional Law: Article 5 EEC Treaty" (1990) C.M.L.Rev. 645 to 681.

[35] See further, Ross, "Beyond Francovich" (1993) M.L.R. 55 at p. 56.

[36] Case C–213/89, *R.* v. *Secretary of State for Transport, ex p. Factortame*: [1990] I E.C.R. 2433, [1990] 3 C.M.L.R. 1.

[37] See *Ninth Annual Report to the European Parliament on Commission Monitoring of the Application of Community Law* (1991), COM (92) 136 final, May 12, 1992, p. 75. See also Curtin, "Directives: The Effectiveness of Judicial Protection of Individual Rights" (1990) C.M.L.Rev. 710.

The vast majority of infringement proceedings concern the failure by Member States to implement directives. However, if judgment is obtained against the Member State under the procedures in Article 169, the only sanction is a further action under Article 171 and the disobedient Member State can simply refuse, once again, to implement a judgment given on the basis of the latter Article. This situation has been substantially altered by the entry into force of the Treaty on European Union signed at Maastricht.[38]

On the other hand, the indirect enforcement of Community law by vigilant individuals seeking to enforce provisions of directives before national courts may be more practically effective. Member States may find it difficult to disregard any decision of their own national courts, particularly concerning their liability to individuals for damage caused by their failure to comply with the provisions of directives. It is suggested by Curtin that:

> "the benefit to the individual concerned whose rights are effectively protected in this manner invest the notion of Community citizenship with concrete meaning and provides an efficient and effective paradigm of the much acclaimed principle of subsidiarity."[39]

However, this depends on the readiness of national courts to give effect to Community law and also on the availability of domestic procedures and remedies for the enforcement of rights derived from directives.[40]

Community law may also be directly relevant in legal proceedings brought by private parties against one another. For example, it may form the basis of a civil claim for damages by a plaintiff seeking to rely on a "directly effective" provision of the Treaty of Rome. This is discussed in detail at paragraphs 10–009 et seq. below. It may also be possible to raise a "Euro-defence" in civil proceedings in reliance on Community law providing that the relevant facts are properly pleaded and particularised.[41]

## OTHER FORMS OF REDRESS FOR THE INDIVIDUAL

1–008    Many individuals and businesses discover that the lengthy delays and/ or cost of starting domestic proceedings for breaches of Community law are prohibitive. One alternative is to seek diplomatic/political avenues of redress. Some of the useful alternative forms of redress are discussed below. They may be used in conjunction with each other, in appropriate

---

[38] The relevant amendments have been discussed at para. 1–005 above.
[39] Curtin, op. cit., n.37, p. 713.
[40] See Gráinne de Búrca, "Giving Effect to European Community Directives" (1992) M.L.R. 215 at p. 216.
[41] See further paras. 10–055 et seq. below.

cases, to create the greatest amount of pressure and/or embarrassment to the party alleged to have infringed Community law.

## Single Market Compliance Unit

The Single Market Compliance Unit (SMCU) is part of the U.K.'s **1–009** Department of Trade and Industry (DTI). It advises and assists U.K. companies experiencing illegal barriers to trade in other Member States of the Community. If a company, individual or organisation experiences a problem for which there is a legal basis for complaint, and has evidence to support it, the SMCU can be asked to review the case and advise on the best way to resolve the problem. The U.K. government may be persuaded, for example, to take the case up with the Member State concerned and/or the Commission.

The SMCU may therefore be useful in the case of alleged illegal trade barriers by other E.C. governments. However, the SMCU may not get involved in legal actions brought in the U.K. or other national courts within the Community. It also does not advise U.K. companies disputing U.K. government policies. The SMCU treats information given to it in confidence and company names are not revealed outside U.K. government circles, without consent. This is a recognition of the fact that businesses usually wish to solve problems and it may not always be in their interest to file complaints. The SMCU nevertheless encourages U.K. companies to send it information of breaches of Community law experienced by them, even if no specific action is requested. There is often nothing to lose by referring apparent breaches by other Member States to the SMCU. However, in order to persuade the SMCU to act, cogent evidence should be presented and it may be that legal advice on the presentation and relevance of the available evidence would be helpful in putting together a complaint which the SMCU would be inclined to pursue actively.

It is understood from the SMCU that there is little evidence of deliberate, wide-scale illegal practice by other Member States' authorities, but problems do occur through different interpretation of the rules or patchy enforcement. Illegal trade barriers take months, sometimes years, to be resolved. The SMCU service is, therefore, not to be regarded as a "quick-fix" unit. However, the success rate is improving.[42] Examples of cases investigated by the SMCU are many and varied, and have been included in the Appendix.

---

[42] SMCU enquiries should be passed to the SMCU, telephone: 071-215 6730, Ashdown House, 123 Victoria Street, London SW1E 6RB. Questions about over-implementation of E.C. measures or over-regulation by the U.K. Government should be referred to the Deregulation Unit in DTI, Ashdown House, 123 Victoria Street, London.

## European Parliament

### *Right of petition*

**1-010**    The European Parliament[43] has set up a standing Committee on Petitions to examine matters raised by citizens and, where appropriate, to take action on them. This right of petition was included in the Declaration of Fundamental Rights and Freedoms adopted by the European Parliament in June 1989.[44]

The right of petition is also directly enshrined in the E.C. Treaty (as amended at Maastricht, by the Treaty on European Union) in Article 138d. It states that:

> "Any citizen of the Union,[45] and any natural or legal person residing or having its registered office in a Member State, shall have the right to address, individually or in association with other citizens or persons, a petition to the European Parliament on a matter which comes within the Community's fields of activity and which affects him, her or it directly."

Individuals, as well as relevant companies, organisations or associations may submit petitions. The petition must fall within the scope of the E.C.'s activities and it must relate either to a matter of general concern (*e.g.* the protection of cultural heritage) or to an individual complaint.

The Treaty on European Union signed at Maastricht does not specify any detailed procedure for complaints. The Committee on Petitions has no standard format for the petition but has indicated that it must bear the name(s) of the petitioner(s), give the nationality, occupation and place of residence of the petitioner(s), be written clearly and legibly, and bear a signature or signatures. The petition may include annexes and/or copies of any background documents which the petitioner may have. They may be written in any official working language of the European Community (Danish, Dutch, English, French, German, Greek, Italian, Portuguese or Spanish). Further information about petitions may be obtained from a Member of the European Parliament or the Office of the

---

[43] From 1994, the European Parliament will have 567 members to reflect German unification and achieve overall balance in the enlarged institution. Strasbourg has been officially confirmed as the seat of the Parliament, as a result of decisions taken at the Edinburgh Summit on December 17, 1992, [1992] 12 E.C.Bull. 161. However, additional plenary sessions will continue to be held in Brussels, where the Parliament's committees also meet. The General Secretariat of the Parliament and its departments will remain in Luxembourg.

[44] Article 23, text adopted by the European Parliament on April 12, 1989 of the report by Mr De Gucht. [1989] O.J. C120/51–52 at D. See also, *The European Community and Human Rights*, (1993) European Commission, Luxembourg, at p. 38.

[45] By virtue of Article 8 of the E.C. Treaty (as amended at Maastricht), a Citizenship of the Union is established. "Every person holding the nationality of a Member State shall be a citizen of the Union." See further, Close, "The Concept of Citizenship in the Treaty on European Union" (1992) C.M.L.Rev. 1137 to 1169.

European Parliament in the relevant Member State.[46] Petitions should be addressed directly to the European Parliament in Luxembourg.[47]

## Admissibility of petition

When the petition is received, it is first assessed to decide whether it is **1–011** admissible, *i.e.* whether it falls within the remit of the Committee. The Petition's Committee prepares an Annual Report on its work. The 1990–1991 Report showed that 535 of the 785 petitions received that year were admissible, *i.e.* procedurally in order and falling within the sphere of competence of the Community.[48] In its 1992–1993 Annual Report[49] the Committee noted that the number of petitions had risen significantly in 1992–1993, to 900. Of these, 606 petitions were declared admissible.[50] However, the Committee has stated that it regards as unacceptable the fact that:

> "whilst the number of petitions has risen by over 200% since the Parliamentary year 1986–1987 (from 279 petitions to 900), the Committee Secretariat staff has not increased, and that the rapid and adequate processing of petitions to the European Parliament by Community citizens does not even figure as one of the priorities established in the Report of the Parliament's Secretariat on the assessment and organisation of its services."[51]

## Means of redress

If the petition is admissible, the Committee on Petitions decides what **1–012** type of action should be taken. These may include the following:

(1) The petition may be forwarded to the European Commission. In reply, the latter usually sends a written response to the Committee, which can then give the petition further consideration.

(2) It may be forwarded by the President of the European Parliament to the appropriate national authority.

(3) The petition may be made the subject of a report which will be submitted to Parliament in plenary.

(4) The petition may be forwarded to the Council of Ministers and/or the European Commission, accompanied by an opinion.

(5) It may be referred by the Committee on Petitions to other Committees of the European Parliament for information, for further action or for an opinion.

---

[46] In the U.K. the European Parliament Information Office is at 2 Queen Anne's Gate, London, SW1H 9AA, telephone: 071-222 0411.

[47] To the President of the European Parliament, L–2929, Luxembourg.

[48] Jacobs, Corbett and Shackleton, *The European Parliament*, (1992) 2nd ed., p. 265.

[49] See *Report of the Committee on Petitions, on the work of the Committee on Petitions during the Parliamentary year 1992/93*, Rapporteur: Mr Gil-Robles Gil-Delgado, May 3, 1993, DOC EN/RR/227/227406.

[50] See *Report of the Committee on Petitions, 1992–1993, op. cit.*, p. 9, paras. 6 and 9.

[51] See *Report of the Committee on Petitions, 1992–1993, op. cit.*, p. 13, para. 18.

Since the European Parliament is not a judicial authority, it cannot pass judgment on or revoke legal decisions taken by Member States. It may, however, call on the Commission to refer the case to the European Court of Justice (ECJ).

The Committee on Petitions sometimes advises on the availability of other means of redress at European level, *e.g.* the European Commission of Human Rights or, alternatively, at national level (such as national Ombudsmen or the various committees dealing with petitions in the Member State Parliaments). The Committee on Petitions also liaises closely with these bodies.

Petitioners are informed of decisions taken by the Committee and the reasons for them. Petitions to the European Parliament may be of value in persuading Member States to alter their legislation to conform with Community law. They may also add to pressure on the European Commission to bring infringement proceedings against Member States under Articles 169 and 170. The Parliament can claim some important successes as a result of such petitions, such as the solution of pension problems experienced by individual petitioners moving from one country to another; causing the Commission to bring infringement proceedings against Member States in relation, *e.g.* to the taxation of imported vehicles; persuading Member States to change administrative practices (*e.g.*, Germany modified from 1 to 3 years its deadline for foreigners to change their driving licence); and in helping to obtain refunds in double taxation cases.[52]

Sometimes, a petition can influence the content of Community law before it is enacted. The Parliament has a Standing Committee on Legal Affairs and Citizens' Rights.[53] A reasoned opinion from this Committee, although not legally binding, may carry some persuasive weight when presented to various national authorities, *e.g.* immigration authorities, tax authorities, etc.[54] Letters to Members of the European Parliament are another non-legal form of redress which can result in questions being raised in the Parliament which may be helpful in an appropriate case.

### Inquiries

1–013 As a result of amendments made at Maastricht, the European Parliament's practice of setting up committees of inquiry to enable in-depth investigation of particular issues was given formal recognition[55] and a new Article 138c was added, formally establishing a temporary Committee of Inquiry. Article 138c provides that this Committee may:

". . . investigate, without prejudice to the powers conferred by this Treaty on other institutions or bodies, alleged contraventions or

---

52 See Jacobs, Corbett and Shackleton, *op. cit.*,, n. 48, p. 266.
53 A description of the Committee's powers can be found in Jacobs and Corbett, *op. cit.*, n. 48, particularly Chap. VII.
54 See Burbidge, *1992—the Impact of the Single Market on U.K. Practice* (1992) p. 33.
55 See further, Jacobs, Corbett and Shackleton, *The European Parliament*, (1992), 2nd ed., p. 253.

14

maladministration in the implementation of Community law, except where the alleged facts are being examined before a court and while the case is still subject to legal proceedings.

The temporary Committee of Inquiry shall cease to exist on the submission of its report.

The detailed provisions governing the exercise of the right of inquiry shall be determined by common accord of the European Parliament, the Council and the Commission."

The Committee of Inquiry may, however, only be set up at the request of a quarter of the Parliament's members. It may therefore not be of direct relevance for individual complaints, unless the matter is of E.C.-wide importance and a significant number of the Parliament's members are persuaded to act.[56]

## Ombudsman

However, a new procedure in Article 138e of the E.C. Treaty is of **1–014** potential significance for individuals. It provides for the appointment of an Ombudsman as follows:

"1. The European Parliament shall appoint an Ombudsman empowered to receive complaints from any citizen of the Union or any natural or legal person residing or having its registered office in a Member State concerning instances of maladministration in the activities of the Community institutions or bodies, with the exception of the Court of Justice and the Court of First Instance acting in their judicial role.

In accordance with his duties, the Ombudsman shall conduct enquiries for which he finds grounds, either on his own initiative or on the basis of complaints submitted to him direct or through a member of the European Parliament, except where the alleged facts are or have been the subject of legal proceedings. Where the Ombudsman establishes an instance of maladministration, he shall refer the matter to the institution concerned, which shall have a period of three months in which to inform him of its views.

The Ombudsman shall then forward a report to the European Parliament and the institution concerned. The person lodging the complaint shall be informed of the outcome of such enquiries.

The Ombudsman shall submit an annual report to the European Parliament on the outcome of his enquiries."

The establishment of the Ombudsman (which is intended to take effect following the entry into force of the Treaty on European Union)[57] further

---

[56] See further, *Report by the Committee on Institutional Affairs on parliamentary committees of inquiry*, Rapporteur: Mr François Musso, October 14, 1992, DOC EN/RR/215/215580 and Resolution A3-0302/92 on parliamentary committees of inquiry, December 17, 1992, [1992] O.J. C21/147.

[57] See further at para. 1–002.

strengthens the options available to individuals pursuing diplomatic/ political avenues of redress via the European Parliament. However, a key issue will be the impact of the Ombudsman's reports and the ease with which the Ombudsman will be able to obtain access to essential information and key documents.

The Committee on Institutional Affairs of the European Parliament has prepared a report on the regulations and conditions governing the performance of the Ombudsman's duties.[58] This Report recommends a draft European Parliament Decision, Article 2(2) of which includes a provision whereby the Community institutions and organs:

> "shall be obliged to supply the Ombudsman with the requested information and give him access to the files concerned, *without the right to object on grounds of secrecy*. Officials and other staff of the Community may not refuse to comply with the Ombudsman's requests on the grounds of the imperative of confidentiality by which they would otherwise be bound."[59]

The authorities in the Member States are placed under similar obligations.[60]

## Public right to information

1–015    With regard to the public's right to information, the Parliament is in favour of the widest possible access to Community documents and information, while the Council of Ministers and the Commission appear to want to allow access to non-confidential documents only.[61] The issue of a freedom of information policy which would overturn the current practice which makes all E.C. documents secret until a Community institution or Member State decides to distribute them was also discussed during the adoption of the Treaty on European Union at Maastricht, at which a declaration was made on improved access to public information.[62] The issue was reconsidered at the European Council Summit in Birmingham in December 1992, and again at the European Council Summit in Copenhagen (June 21–22, 1993) where the Council and Commission were encouraged: ". . . to continue this work based on the principle of the citizens having the fullest possible access to information. The aim should be to have all necessary means in place by the end of

---

[58] See Report of the Committee on Institutional Affairs "on the regulations and conditions governing the performance of the European Ombudsman's duties", Rapporteur: Mrs Rosy Bindi, October 14, 1992, DOC EN/RR/215/215009. WP5.

[59] Report of the Committee on Institutional Affairs, *op. cit.*, p. 8 (emphasis added).

[60] *ibid.*

[61] See the Proposal of the Commission on "Public Access to the Institution's Documents" (Communication to the Council, the Parliament and the Economic Social Committee), (93/C156/05) [1993] O.J. C156/05, and *European Report*, (June 8, 1993), 101(SV).

[62] See Proposal of the Commission on "Public Access to the Institution's Documents", *op. cit.*, para. 1.

1993."[63] It is envisaged that the activities of the Committee on Petitions and those of the Ombudsman will complement each other.[64]

## Lobbying

Prevention is very often better than cure. The role of lobbying the **1–016** European Community and its institutions, particularly in connection with proposed Community legislation, is sometimes underestimated or overlooked. However, the art of lobbying appropriate Community institutions, whether on behalf of business or special interest groups, or institutions such as local authorities, may be an important strategic option in certain cases. The interest in lobbying activity within the Parliament has, for instance, prompted its Committee on the Rules of Procedure, the Verification of Credentials and Immunities, to consider in October 1992 whether to introduce a register of lobbyists and a code of conduct for them.[65] Such strategies go beyond the scope of this book.[66] Among the business groups which may be approached in the U.K. in order to advance any particular cause in Europe, are the Confederation of British Industry (CBI), the Institute of Directors (IOD), the Chambers of Commerce and various trade associations as well as professional institutions (*e.g.* the British Medical Association (BMA) or the National Union of Teachers (NUT)). The Law Society of England and Wales also has an office in Brussels. Enlisting the support of trade unions in Europe is another possibility, through lobbying institutions such as the Trades Union's Congress (TUC).

The House of Commons and the House of Lords have parallel systems for scrutinising proposed Community legislation. The House of Commons Select Committee on European Legislation was set up in May 1974 and decides which of the proposals emanating from the European Commission are of sufficient political importance to be referred for special attention by the House of Commons, with or without a debate. However, the Committee does not comment on or offer opinions about the merits of proposed Community legislation.

The House of Lords Select Committee is a larger body with sub-committees covering (A) finance, trade and industry, and external relations; (B) energy, transport and technology; (C) social and consumer

---

[63] Commission's Spokesman's Service; Doc. Ref: DOC/93/3, 23/06/96, Conclusion of the Presidency, European Council in Copenhagen, June 21–22, 1993 at para. 15. See also *Financial Times*, June 11, 1993, p. 4. The Council has since published a Code of Conduct concerning public access to Council and Commission documents, 1990/730/E.C., [1993] O.J. L340/410.

[64] See Opinion of Mr Gutierres Dias on behalf of the Committee on Petitions, annexed to the Report of the Committee on Institutional Affairs, *op. cit.*, pp. 22 *et seq.*

[65] See Jacobs, Corbett and Shackleton, *op. cit.*, n. 48, p. 257 and Thompson, "Bibliographic Snapshot: Pressure Groups, Lobbying and the European Community" (June 1993), No. 3, *European Access*, 38 to 41.

[66] See further, Danton de Rouffignac, *Presenting your Case to Europe* (1991), and Jacobs, Corbett and Shackleton, *op. cit.*, n. 48, p. 256. For an excellent bibliography on various aspects of lobbying see Thomson, *op. cit.*, pp. 38–41.

affairs; (D) agriculture and food; (E) law and institutions; (F) environment. Ad hoc committees are also established. The Committee divides legislative proposals into either the category of non-controversial (in which case they are not considered further) or into a second category whereby the proposal is referred to a sub-committee for further consideration. Of these proposals, some merit the preparation of a special report which may be debated before the full House of Lords. The Committee has, for instance, launched an inquiry into the enforcement of E.C. competition rules by the Commission.[67] Both Committees make extensive use of oral and writen submissions from interested groups[68] and the reports of the House of Lords European Committee are particularly respected for the range and depth of their coverage on European issues.[69]

## SUTHERLAND REPORT

**1–017**  In March 1992, a six-member High Level Group chaired by the former E.C. Competition Commissioner, Peter Sutherland was set up to assess how the Internal Market Programme should be sustained after 1992. The Report of the Group was submitted to the European Commission on October 28, 1992.[70] Its conclusions were welcomed by the Commission and by the European Council at the Edinburgh Summit in December 1992.

### Recommendations

**1–018**  Among its 38 specific recommendations were a number concerning the removal of doubts about Community law. The Group recommended that:

> "(18) The Commission and Member States should, in close liaison, respond to the need to provide informal advice on redress for breaches of Community law to those who request it.
>
> (19) When giving advice, the Commission and Member States should point out the advantages of taking disputes involving the application of Community law before national courts. . . .
>
> (21) The Community needs to review the way in which the rights of individuals to obtain redress for breaches of Community law are provided across the Community. . . .
>
> (25) The Commission should issue an interpretative communication about the implications of the recent *Francovich* and *Bonifaci* judgment for consumers, business and the Member States.

---

[67] *Financial Times*, May 18, 1993 and see para. 3–045 below.
[68] Danton de Rouffignac, *op. cit.*, p. 215.
[69] *ibid.*
[70] See Thomson, "Internal Market Developments, September–November 1992" (December 1992), *European Access*, 17 to 20. The report has not yet been formally published.

(26) The Community needs to initiate progress towards greater comparability of treatment in legal disputes. A way forward could be to consider the implications of the different approaches of the various jurisdictions to the key concepts of 'damage' and 'compensation'. An effort to clarify their meaning, at least for the purposes of Community law itself, could constitute a useful first step.

(29) Judicial co-operation between Member States should aim at an approximation of sanctions in respect of breaches of Community law. Such co-operation should enhance the free movement of goods but avoided benefiting Member States which have the least stringent system of sanctions.

(30) Details of relevant sanctions should be notified by the Member States to the Commission along with the notification of national transposition of Community legislation."

## The Commission's response

The Commission published its initial response to the Sutherland **1–019** Report in December 1992[71] and also promised a fuller analysis at a later date. In relation to matters concerning "access to justice and judicial co-operation" it felt that legal redress was a matter for the Member States. It indicated that it would examine the means of providing satisfactory information on redress, especially to small and medium size enterprises (SMEs). It would also examine the means of providing a training programme for teaching Community law and to undertake analysis of uncertainties over the rights of consumers. With regard to the *Francovich* judgment,[72] the Commission said that it would prepare a statement on compensation for damage caused to individuals by breaches of Community rules.

The Commission felt that deeper analysis of the national legal systems was needed before it could propose harmonisation within the Community, and it would carry out an appropriate study. This would also extend it to matters not directly related to the internal market such as the possible improvement and extension of the operation of the 1968 Convention on the Jurisdiction and the Enforcement of Foreign Judgments in Civil and Commercial Matters (hereon referred to as the Brussels Convention). The Commission stressed, in this context, the importance of rapid implementation of the latter by Spain and Portugal.[73]

There is, therefore, clear recognition of the importance of the role of national remedies for breaches of Community law. The need for clarification, and, if necessary, the harmonisation of such remedies in the different Member States has been highlighted. In addition, the Suther-

---

[71] SEC (92) 2277 of December 2, 1992 and COM (93) 576, November 1993.
[72] Joined Cases C–6 & 9/90, *Francovich and Bonifaci* v. *Italian State*: [1991] I E.C.R. 5357, [1993] 2 C.M.L.R. 66, discussed further at paras. 8–008 *et seq.* and 9–016 *et seq.* below.
[73] See Background Report, "The Internal Market after 1992", March 4, 1993, Commission of the European Communities London Office, ISEC/B7/93 at p. 5.

land Report notes the need to make available much more information to individuals and businesses about the mechanisms for obtaining redress for breaches of Community law, via national courts and by other means.

However, progress on these issues depends on the extent of further political support for the Sutherland Report. It has subsequently been referred to in the Commission's Working Document on a Strategic Programme on the Internal Market which is an important policy document.[74] The issues relating to the role of domestic courts is discussed under the heading "Access to Justice".[75] It is likely that fuller consideration and specific implementation of the key recommendations in the Sutherland Report may take place now that the Treaty on European Union has entered into force.

---

[74] *Working Document of the Commission on a Strategic Programme on the Internal Market: Communication from the Commission to the Council and the European Parliament, "Reinforcing the Effectiveness of the Internal Market"* COM (93) 256 final, June 2, 1993, Brussels.

[75] *Op. cit.,* pp. 17 to 20.

# THE RELATIONSHIP BETWEEN E.C. LAW AND U.K. LAW

The U.K. signed the Treaty of Accession to the European Economic **2–001** Community (EEC) and the European Atomic Energy Community on January 22, 1972. In order to give effect to Community law in the U.K., Parliament enacted the European Communities Act 1972, which was subsequently amended by the European Communities (Amendment) Act 1993. By virtue of amendments made by the European Communities (Amendment) Act 1993, the definition of "the Treaties" and "the Community Treaties" in section 1(2) of the 1972 Act is broadened to include those parts of the Treaty on European Union signed at Maastricht on November 7, 1992 (Cm. 1934) which relate to the European Communities. An exception is made for the Protocol on Social Policy. The Act also does not make provision for those parts of the Treaty which relate to action on an inter-governmental level on common foreign and security policy or on justice and home affairs because they do not give rise to Community rights and obligations. This is also discussed at paragraph 1–002 above. Section 2(1) of the 1972 Act (as amended) provides:

> "All such rights, powers, liabilities, obligations and restrictions from time to time created or arising by or under the Treaties, and all such remedies and procedures from time to time provided for by or under the Treaties, as in accordance with the Treaties are without further enactment to be given legal effect or used in the United Kingdom shall be recognised and available in law, and be enforced, allowed and followed accordingly; and the expression 'enforceable Community right' and similar expressions shall be read as referring to one to which this sub-section applies."

This section is very widely drafted. It provides for all "rights, powers, liabilities, obligations and restrictions" created or arising by or under the Treaties to be incorporated into the law of the U.K. This includes "remedies and procedures". However, it draws a crucial distinction between rights and duties arising under the Treaties which are "without further enactment to be given legal effect" in the U.K., and those which require implementation. The former are to have full and immediate effect. The latter take effect under subordinate legislation enacted under the Act,[1] or by statute, where it is necessary to go beyond the limits

---

[1] See section 2(2) European Communities Act 1972 (as amended).

imposed by the European Communities Act 1972 (as amended).[2] By virtue of section 2(1) of the Act (as amended) *all* E.C. law is *not*, therefore, automatically part of U.K. law.[3]

However, the provisions of the E.C. Treaty itself (and related Treaties) have, by a process of transformation, became part of U.K. law by virtue of the European Communities Act 1972 (as amended).[4] The U.K. courts have acknowledged the principle that the provisions of the Treaty of Rome are part of U.K. law. In *Re Westinghouse Uranium Contract*[5] Lord Denning said that:

> "The EEC Treaty and all its provisions are now part of the law of England: that is clear from Section 2 of the European Communities Act 1972. We have to give force to the treaty as being incorporated lock, stock and barrel into our own law here."[6]

This position is clearly unchanged in respect of amendments made by the Treaty on European Union, insofar as they have been given effect to by the European Communities (Amendment) Act 1993.

## "DIRECTLY APPLICABLE" COMMUNITY LAW

2–002    The primary sources of Community law are the provisions of the Treaty of Rome (as amended) and related Treaties. These are, however, expanded by secondary legislation. The forms of secondary legislation are set out in Article 189 of the Treaty (as amended).

Article 189(1) states that:

> "In order to carry out their task and in accordance with the provisions of this Treaty, the European Parliament acting jointly with the Council and the Commission shall make regulations and issue directives, take decisions, make recommendations or deliver opinions."

With the exception of recommendations and opinions, secondary legislation is legally binding on Member States. Regulations normally have *immediate* binding effects. However, the bulk of Community legislation is issued in the form of directives. They normally give Member States a time period during which the directive must be

---

[2] See Sched. 2 of the Act.

[3] See Collins, *European Community Law in the UK* (1990), 4th ed., p. 45.

[4] In the USA, for example, most treaties are automatically part of the law of the land, without the aid of legislative adoption or transformation. The term "self executing" is used to denote this, and is a term synonymous with that of "direct applicability" in the E.C. context. See further, Winter, "Direct Applicability and Direct Effect: Two Distinct Concepts in Community Law" (1972) C.M.L.Rev. 425 at pp. 428 *et seq*.

[5] [1978] A.C. 547 at p. 564, [1977] 3 All E.R. 703 at p. 711.

[6] See also *Esso Petroleum Co. Ltd. v. Kingswood Motors Ltd.* [1973] 3 All E.R. 1057 at p. 1064.

implemented. This may involve changes to domestic law. Decisions may be addressed either to Member States singly or collectively, or to individuals.

The E.C. Treaty provides in Article 189(2) that "A regulation shall have general application. It shall be binding in its entirety and directly applicable in all Member States." Where the term "directly applicable" is used in the context of Community law, it means that no domestic measures of either adoption or transformation are required to make the relevant provision part of national law. Thus, by virtue of Article 189(2) of the Treaty, Community regulations are part of U.K. law without any need for further implementation. They automatically have this effect, since the Treaty itself has become part of "the law of the land" by virtue of the European Communities Act 1972, (as amended). It should be noted that "directly effective" provisions of Community law, including relevant provisions of the Treaty of Rome, are also "directly applicable" under Community law. However, not all "directly applicable" Community law is "directly effective".[7]

As a general principle, "directly applicable" Community law in the form of a regulation does not therefore require domestic re-enactment. This is in fact prohibited, unless expressly or impliedly required by the regulation itself.[8] In the European Communities Act 1972 itself (as amended), several provisions confer specific powers to issue subordinate legislation relating to "directly applicable" Community law (e.g. European Communities Act 1972, Sched. 4, para. 3(2)(a) with regard to food and Sched. 4, paras. 9(2) and 10 with regard to road transport), and sometimes statutory instruments provide domestic machinery to aid the application of Community law without altering or adding to the directly applicable provision. This is permissible so long as they are justified for the sake of coherence or to make them comprehensible to the addressees of the regulation.[9]

## "DIRECTLY EFFECTIVE" COMMUNITY LAW

The fact that the provisions of regulations are "directly applicable" **2–003** does not mean that they are sutomatically also capable of creating individual rights which U.K. courts must recognise. The latter concept is frequently described as Community law capable of having "direct effects".

In traditional international law, treaties and international agreements cannot, as such, create direct rights and obligations for private individ-

---

[7] See discussion at paras. 2–003 et seq. below.
[8] e.g., Case 34/73, Fratelli Variola SpA v. Amministrazione Italiana delle Finanze: [1973] E.C.R. 981; Case 230/78, Eridania Zuccherifici: [1979] E.C.R. 2749 at para. 34 and Hartley, The Foundations of European Community Law (1990), 2nd ed., p. 197.
[9] See Case 273/83, Commission v. Italy: [1985] E.C.R. 1057 at para. 27, [1987] 2 C.M.L.R. 426.

uals. However, the Community has created a new legal order, in that its subjects are not just a group of States, but also include the citizens of those States.[10] The ECJ has established that some Treaty provisions, as well as certain provisions in regulations, directives or decisions are capable of having "direct effect" in the sense of being capable of conferring individual rights which may be relied upon before national courts by individual litigants.

### Rationale for "direct effect"

**2–004**   In one of the first cases to be referred to the ECJ for a preliminary ruling, Case 26/62, *Van Gend en Loos*[11] the Court of Justice said:

"The objectives of the EEC Treaty, to create a Common Market, the functioning of which directly affects the citizens of the Community – implies that this Treaty is more than an agreement creating only mutual obligations between the contracting State. This interpretation is confirmed by the preamble to the Treaty which, in addition to mentioning governments, affects individuals. The creation of organs institutionalising certain sovereign rights, the exercise of which affects both Member States and citizens is a particular example. In addition the nationals of the States invited into the Community are required to collaborate in the functioning of that Community, by means of the European Parliament and the Economic and Social Council. Furthermore, the role of the Court of Justice in the framework of Article 177, the aim of which is to ensure uniformity of interpretation of the Treaty by the national courts, confirms that the States recognised in Community law have an authority capable of being invoked by their nationals before those courts. We must conclude from this that the Community constitutes a new legal order of international law for whose benefit the States have limited their sovereign rights, albeit within limited fields, and the subjects of which comprise not only Member States, but also their nationals. Community law, therefore, apart from legislation by the Member States, not only imposes obligations on individuals but also confers on them legal rights. The latter arise not only when an explicit grant is made by the Treaty, but also through obligations imposed in a clearly defined manner, by the Treaty upon individuals as well as on Member States and the Community institutions."[12]

The ECJ therefore developed the doctrine of "direct effects" to give practical effect to certain provisions of Community law in the various Member States without the need for national implementing legislation.[13]

---

[10] See Winter, *op. cit.*, n. 4, p. 433.
[11] Case 26/62, *NV and Algemene Transport – en Expeditie Onderneming Van Gend en Loos* v. *Nederlandse Administratie der Belastingen:* [1963] E.C.R. 1, [1963] C.M.L.R. 105.
[12] *Van Gend en Loos, op. cit.*, n. 11, p. 12, [1963] C.M.L.R. 105 at 129.
[13] See further, Gráinne de Búrca, "Giving Effect to European Community Directives" (1992) M.L.R. 215.

Such provisions can be relied upon directly by individual litigants in national courts. For instance, the European Court has established that Treaty articles may have direct effect.[14] This is discussed further in Chapter 4 below.

## Criteria for establishing "direct effect"

Regulations are also capable of direct effect providing that the relevant 2–005 provisions of the regulation are not formulated in vague terms or leave important features to be devised and implemented by Member States.[15] Hartley provides a good illustration of this.[16] Regulation 1463/70[17] is concerned with the introduction of recording equipment (tachographs) in commercial vehicles and Article 4 states that the use of this equipment will be compulsory from a given date. Article 21(1)[18] provides:

> "Member States, shall, in good time and after consulting the Commission adopt such laws regulations or administrative provisions as may be necessary for the implementation of this Regulation. Such measures shall cover, *inter alia,* the reorganisation of procedure for, and means of carrying out, checks on compliance and the penalties to be imposed in case of breach."

It is a provision which specifically requires the enactment of further legislation. Hartley argues[19] that this provision cannot have direct effect with regard to the possible creation of a new criminal offence of driving a commercial vehicle without a tachograph. It is insufficiently precise as to exactly what will consititute the offence, who will be responsible (*e.g.* owner or driver), what the penalties will be and the defences which might be available.

Another example of a regulation in which various provisions are unlikely to be regarded as directly effective, is the Regulation on the European Economic Interest Grouping.[20] However, if the provisions of a regulation are all sufficiently precise to be capable of direct effect and do not require further enactment then the entire regulation is both "vertically" and "horizontally" directly effective.[21]

---

[14] See, *e.g.* Case 43/75, *Defrenne* v. *Sabena (No. 2):* [1976] E.C.R. 455, [1976] 2 C.M.L.R. 98 and discussion at Chap. 4 below.

[15] In *Taittinger* v. *Allbev Ltd.* [1993] 2 C.M.L.R. 741 (C.A.), the English Court of Appeal, held that Article 15(5) of Regulation 832/87 has direct effect and can be enforced at the instance of an aggrieved private party against another private party, by means of an injunction.

[16] Hartley, *The Foundations of European Community Law* (1990), 2nd ed., p. 196. See also Case 32/75, *Cristini* v. *SNCF:* [1975] E.C.R. 1085, [1976] 1 C.M.L.R. 573.

[17] [1970] O.J. Spec.Ed. 482.

[18] Art. 21 was renumbered Art. 23 with effect from June 1, 1978 by Art. II of Regulation 2828/77, [1977] O.J. L334/3.

[19] *Op. cit.*

[20] Reg. 85/2137, [1985] O.J. L199/1.

[21] See further discussion at paras. 2–009 and 2–010 below.

## Direct effect of directives and decisions

**2–006**    Direct effects may also be produced by directives in various areas.[22] This is discussed in detail in Chapter 6. Decisions addressed to Member States may also give rise to direct effects. A decision differs from a directive in that it can be addressed by the Council or the Commission to either an individual or to a Member State. Under Article 189(4) of the E.C. Treaty, a decision "is binding in its entirety upon those to whom it is addressed". Under Article 191(3) decisions take effect upon notification to those to whom they are addressed.

## Rationale for direct effect of decisions

**2–007**    The Court held in Case 9/70, *Franz Grad* v. *Finanzamt Traustein*[23] that decisions can be directly effective as between the Member States and those subject to its jurisdiction. The reasons given are the same as those stated in the subsequent case of *Van Duyn*[24] in relation to directives. The Court said in *Grad*:[25]

> ". . . it would be incompatible with the binding effect attributed to decisions by Article 189 to exclude in principle the possibility that persons affected may invoke the obligation imposed by a decision. Particularly in cases where for example, the Community authorities by means of a decision have imposed an obligation on a Member State or all the Member States to act in a certain way, the effectiveness (*l'effet utile*) of such a measure would be weakened if the nationals of that State could not invoke it in the courts and the national courts could not take it into consideration as part of Community law."

This is regarded as a landmark judgment and was the precursor of the decision in *Van Duyn* on the direct effect of directives.[26] The Court in *Grad* said that in deciding whether or not a provision in a decision had direct effect it was necessary to examine in each particular case whether by its legal nature, background and wording it was capable of creating direct effect. This means that it must be sufficiently clear and precise and unconditional.

---

[22] See for example Case 41/74, *Van Duyn:* [1974] E.C.R. 1337, [1975] 1 C.M.L.R. 1 (freedom of movement); Case 36/75, *Rutili:* [1975] E.C.R. 1219, [1976] 1 C.M.L.R. 140; Case 51/76, *Verbond:* [1977] E.C.R. 113, [1977] 1 C.M.L.R. 413; Case 38/77, *Enka:* [1977] E.C.R. 2203, [1978] 2 C.M.L.R. 212; Case 148/78, *Ratti:* [1979] E.C.R. 1629, [1980] 1 C.M.L.R. 96, (labelling of solvents); Case 8/81, *Becker:* [1982] E.C.R. 53, [1982] 1 C.M.L.R. 499 (VAT); Case 255/81, *Grendel:* [1982] E.C.R. 2301, [1983] 1 C.M.L.R. 379 (VAT); Case 70/83, *Kloppenburg:* [1984] E.C.R. 1075, [1985] 1 C.M.L.R. 205 (VAT); Case 5/84, *Direct Cosmetics:* [1985] E.C.R. 617, [1985] 2 C.M.L.R. 145 (VAT); Case 152/84, *Marshall:* [1986] E.C.R. 723, [1986] 1 C.M.L.R. 688 (sex discrimination).

[23] Case 9/70, *Franz Grad* v. *Finanzamt Traustein:* [1970] E.C.R. 825, [1971] C.M.L.R. 1.

[24] *Op. cit.*

[25] *Op. cit.*, pp. 836 to 7.

[26] See further at Chap. 5 below.

However, dicta in Case 152/84, *Marshall* v. *Southampton Area Health Authority (Teaching)* referred to as *Marshall (No. 1)*,[27] suggest that a decision can impose a directly effective obligation *only on the addressee* and therefore when a decision is addressed to a Member State it cannot be horizontally directly effective. However, Advocate General Reischl in Case 30/75, *Unil-It. SpA*[28] suggests that there is no compelling reason to assume that the Court's earlier case law on direct effect of decisions is limited to obligations on Member States. The distinction between "horizontal" and "vertical" direct effect is discussed further in paragraphs 2–009 and 2–010.

## Enforcement of "directly effective" provisions

If a provision is "directly effective" it is for the national courts to **2–008** decide on its manner of enforcement in each Member State. It should be noted that a provision of Community law can have "direct effect" whether or not it is "directly applicable". Thus, some provisions of the Treaty of Rome (as amended) and associated treaties, provisions of directives addressed to Member States, or decisions, may be capable of being invoked by individuals in the domestic legal order of the Member State in the same circumstances as regulations, *i.e. without* any national implementation. They may thus create rights and obligations which national courts must uphold.

This appears to be another significant difference between Community law and traditional international law. The prevailing international law doctrine in many States (including certain members of the E.C.) is that a treaty rule may never have a self-executing effect if it is not first incorporated (by adoption or transformation) into the municipal legal order.[29] However, the fact that some of the terms of a directive may be capable of direct effect, *i.e.* do not require domestic implementation to be capable of being relied on by individuals in national courts, does not mean that Member States can use this as an excuse for not enacting domestic implementing measures.[30] It is still necessary for Member States to implement directives in a way which fully meets the requirements of clarity and legal certainty, for the benefit of individuals who are the intended beneficiaries of the directives. In Case 236/91, *Re: the Directive on Animal Semen: E.C. Commission* v. *Ireland*,[31] the Commission brought an action before the ECJ under Article 169 EEC for a declaration that Ireland had not implemented Council Directive 87/328 on the acceptance for breeding purposes of pure-bred breeding animals of bovine

---

[27] Case 152/84, *Marshall* v. *Southampton Area Health Authority (Teaching):* [1986] E.C.R. 723, [1986] 1 C.M.L.R. 688.
[28] Case 30/75, *Unil-It.:* [1975] E.C.R. 1419 at 1434, [1976] 1 C.M.L.R. 115.
[29] See Winter, *op. cit.*, n. 4, p. 438.
[30] See Case 102/79, *E.C. Commission* v. *Belgium:* [1980] E.C.R. 1473, [1982] 1 C.M.L.R. 282.
[31] Case C–236/91, *Re: the Directive on Animal Semen: E.C. Commission* v. *Ireland:* [1993] 1 C.M.L.R. 320.

species,[32] which should have been implemented in Ireland by January 1, 1989. In its defence, the Irish government conceded that it had not adopted the legislation needed to implement the Directive but submitted that the Directive was nevertheless observed in practice. The Court held that:

> ". . . mere administrative practices, which by their nature are alterable at will by the authorities and are not given the appropriate publicity, cannot be regarded as constituting that proper fulfilment of a Member State's obligations under the Treaty: Case 168/85, *E.C. Commission* v. *Italy* ([1988] E.C.R. 2945)."[33]

The Court consequently held that Ireland did not, even temporarily, evade the obligation to transpose the Directive by legislative provisions into national law by relying on the application of an administrative practice alleged to be in accordance with the rules laid down by the Directive.

The doctrine of "direct effect" may be used either as a "sword" which gives the individual litigant rights not otherwise provided for under national law, or as a "shield" to protect the litigant against national law which conflicts with a Community rule.[34] It is a concept which is fundamental to the Community legal system. It is also clear from the *Van Gend en Loos* case (*op. cit.*) that obligations may also be imposed on individuals as well as on Member States as a result of directly effective Community law.[35]

## "VERTICAL" AND "HORIZONTAL" DIRECT EFFECT

### *"Vertical" direct effect*

**2–009**    The case law of the Court has established that directly effective provisions of Community law create rights which are enforceable by individuals against Member States. This is known as the concept of "vertical" direct effect. This issue of what constitutes the State or "an emanation of the State" is discussed in detail in Chapter 7. In Case 152/84, *Marshall* v. *Southampton and South West Hampshire Area Health Authority (Teaching), (Marshall (No. 1))*,[36] the European Court confirmed that directives may engender "vertical direct effect" in the national courts. It held that:

---

[32] [1987] O.J. L167/54.

[33] *E.C. Commission* v. *Ireland, op. cit.*, n. 31, para. 6.

[34] See further Ellis, "The Enforcement of EEC Law in the Courts of the Member States: What Does Direct Effect Really Mean?" in *Droit Sans Frontiers* (Hand and McBride, ed. 1991), pp. 265 to 277. See also paras. 10–056 *et seq.* below.

[35] See further para. 2–010 below.

[36] [1986] E.C.R. 723, [1986] 1 C.M.L.R. 688.

"wherever the provisions of a directive appear, as far as their subject matter is concerned, to be unconditional and sufficiently precise, those provisions may be relied upon by an individual against the State where that State fails to implement the directive in national law by the end of the period subscribed or where it fails to implement the directive correctly.

It would in fact be incompatible with the binding nature which Article 189 confers on the Directive to hold as a matter of principle that the obligation imposed thereby cannot be relied upon by those concerned. Consequently, a Member State which has not adopted the implementing measures required by the Directive within the prescribed period may not plead, as against individuals, its own failure to perform the obligations which the Directive entails. In that respect the capacity in which the State acts, whether as employer or public authority, is irrelevant, in either case it is necessary to prevent the State from taking advantage of its own failure to comply with Community law."[37]

This means that provisions in directives which have direct effect can be relied upon by a private individual as against a Member State, where the latter has failed to implement the directive within the requisite time limit (or has not properly implemented the directive) and is seeking to enforce contradictory national measures.

However, the benefit of "vertical direct effect" of directives, may only apply as *against a Member State*. It may not, for example, be relied upon by an "emanation of the State" *against an individual*. In *Wychavon District Council* v. *Secretary of State for the Environment and Another*,[37a] the Queen's Bench Division held that a District Council was not an individual, for the purpose of Community law, and could not rely on the provisions of an unimplemented E.C. directive in the U.K., as against a private individual. In that case, the District Council had submitted a novel proposition, that while acting as a planning authority it could be regarded as an emanation of the State. However, it claimed not to be occupying that role in the context of the case but acting instead for the promotion of the interests of the inhabitants of its area, under section 222 of the Local Government Act 1972. As such, the Council claimed that it was to be treated as though it was an individual and was therefore entitled to benefit from the alleged direct effect of the directive in question. This argument was rejected by the High Court.

## "Horizontal" direct effect

Directly effective Community law may also be enforceable against **2–010** individuals. This is known as the doctrine of "horizontal" direct effect.[38] The question of whether, and to what extent, provisions of the Treaty of

---

[37] Case 152/84, *Marshall (No. 1):* [1986] E.C.R. 723, 1 C.M.L.R. 688 at para. 4.
[37a] *The Times*, January 7, 1994, p. 32.
[38] See Easson, "Can Directives Impose Obligations on Individuals?" (1976) 4 E.L.Rev. 67 to 79 and Collins, *op. cit.*, n. 3, p. 48.

Rome can impose obligations upon individuals (as well as Member States) has been the subject of much academic discussion. The case law of the Court has now established that certain Treaty provisions do have horizontal effect. Their effect is therefore not limited to the relationship between individuals and the State or its agencies.[39] In the *Union Cycliste* case[40] and the *Dona* case,[41] the Court held that Treaty provisions prohibiting discrimination on grounds of nationality between workers or those providing services had horizontal direct effect in that they applied to and were enforceable against private individuals and associations, as well as against the Member States. In the Court's view the provision of Articles 7, 48 and 59 of the Treaty could accordingly be taken into account in judging the validity and effects of the rules of a sporting association.

In Case 15/74, *Centrafarm* v. *Sterling*[42] and Case 119/75, *Terrapin (Overseas) Limited* v. *Terranova*[43] the Court held that Article 30 of the Treaty, concerned with the free movement of goods, enshrined a fundamental principle of the Treaty which is capable of having direct effect and of giving rise to rights enforceable against individuals.[44]

The Court has also held in the second *Defrenne* case, Case 43/75, *Defrenne* v. *Sabena*[45] in which proceedings were brought in the Belgian *Tribunal du Travail* by an air-hostess against her former employer, Sabena, that Treaty provisions in the field of equal pay may also have horizontal direct effect. The Court held that Article 119 of the Treaty created directly effective rights which were enforceable against private employers. The principle of horizontal direct effect has also been successfully invoked before a national court in relation to the competition law provisions in Articles 85 and 86 of the Treaty of Rome.[46]

In *Marshall (No. 1)*[47] the Court indicated *per curiam* that in relation to *directives*, however, these cannot create horizontal direct effect, *i.e.* that a directive may not of itself impose obligations on an individual and that a provision which has direct effect cannot be relied on as such against another private individual. The Court stated that:

> "According to Article 189 of the EEC Treaty the binding nature of a directive, which constitutes the basis for the possibility of relying on the Directive before a national court, exists only in relation to 'each Member State to which it is addressed'. It follows that a directive

---

[39] See Collins, *op. cit.*, n. 3, p. 48.

[40] Case 36/74, *Walrave and Koch:* [1974] E.C.R. 1405, [1975] 1 C.M.L.R. 320.

[41] Case 13/76, *Dona* v. *Mantera:* [1976] E.C.R. 1333, [1976] 2 C.M.L.R. 578.

[42] Case 15/74, *Centrafarm* v. *Sterling Drug:* [1974] E.C.R. 1147, [1974] 2 C.M.L.R. 480.

[43] Case 119/75, *Terrapin* v. *Terranova:* [1976] E.C.R. 1039, [1976] 2 C.M.L.R. 482.

[44] See Easson, *op. cit.*, p. 69. For a detailed analysis of the question of whether Article 30 poses obligations on individuals see Quinn and MacGowan, "Could Article 30 Pose Obligations on Individuals" (1987) 12 E.L.Rev. 163 to 178.

[45] Case 43/75, *Defrenne* v. *Sabena:* [1976] E.C.R. 455, [1976] 2 C.M.L.R. 98.

[46] See *Garden Cottage Foods Limited* v. *Milk Marketing Board* [1984] A.C. 130, [1983] 2 All E.R. 770 (H.L.) and discussion at paras. 10–001 *et seq.* and 10–008 *et seq.* below.

[47] *Op. cit.*

may not itself impose obligations on an individual and that a provision of a directive may not be relied on as such against such a person."[48]

The reasons why directives may not be granted horizontal direct effect are largely political and are discussed in detail in at paragraphs 5–021 *et seq.*[49] However, even though a provision in a directive may not be horizontally directly effective, this does not necessarily mean that it will not have *any* effect on the relationship between private parties. It is possible, by persuading the domestic court to adopt a purposive interpretation of Community law, to achieve an "indirect" direct effect. This argument was, for example, raised but rejected by the High Court in the *Wychavon* case discussed at paragraph 2–009. The circumstances in which "indirect" direct effect may be possible are discussed in detail at paragraphs 6–007 *et seq.* below.

---

[48] *Op. cit.*, p. 725, para. 5.
[49] See in particular the submission of Advocate General Van Gerven in Case C–262/88, *Barber* v. *Guardian Royal Exchange:* [1990] I E.C.R. 1889, [1990] 2 C.M.L.R. 513 and Case C–271/91, *Marshall* v. *Southampton and South-West Hampshire Area Health Authority, (Marshall (No. 2)):* [1993] 3 C.M.L.R. 293, discussed at paras. 9–025 *et seq.* below.

# THE SUPREMACY OF E.C.
# LAW OVER NATIONAL LAW

## COMMUNITY LAW PERSPECTIVE

3–001 Unless Community law can be enforced in domestic courts, the legal basis of the internal market will be undermined. Domestic implementation of Community law and the enforcement of individual rights will be of increasing importance after December 31, 1992, following the completion of the Internal Market. This is because the effect of the new majority voting procedures permitted under Article 100a of the Treaty of Rome (as amended by the Single European Act and the Treaty on European Union), will mean that Member States may be obliged, in the post-1992 era, to implement Community legislation which they originally opposed.[1] In addition, the result of the Court's ruling in Case 300/89, *Commission* v. *Council* (known as the titanium dioxide case),[2] with respect to the interpretation of Articles 100a and 130s of the EEC Treaty means that the concept of the internal market in Article 100a has to be interpreted very widely,[3] and may amount to a general authorisation to legislate in any area which directly or indirectly concerns the internal market.[4] The scope of the relevant domestic legislation, post-1992, is therefore likely to be very wide.

The ECJ has on a number of occasions insisted first, that Community law is paramount and secondly, that national courts must override conflicting national law if it is in conflict with directly effective Community law. This second rule applies irrespective of whether the directly effective Community law is a provision of one of the constitutive Treaties, a regulation, directive, decision or other Community law and irrespective of whether the conflicting national law is that of the constitution,[5] statute, or subordinate legislation.

---

[1] See Ward, "Government Liability in the U.K. for Breach of Individual Rights in European Community Law" (1990) 19 *Anglo-American Law Review* at p. 2.

[2] Case 300/89, *Commission* v. *Council*: [1991] I E.C.R. 2867, [1993] 3 C.M.L.R. 359.

[3] See further, Barents, "The International Market Unlimited: Some Observations on the Legal Basis of Community Legislation" (1993) C.M.L.Rev. 85 at p. 87.

[4] Barents, *op. cit.*, p. 88.

[5] See Case 11/70, *Internationale Handelsgesellschaft mbH* v. *Einführ–und Vorratsstelle für Getreide und Futtermittel*: [1970] E.C.R. 1125 at 1134, [1972] C.M.L.R. 255.

## Application of supremacy rule by national courts

This has required the various national courts of the E.C. to adapt their **3–002** different constitutional rules and traditions to the principle of supremacy of Community law.[6] For example, despite some resistance in France in previous years,[7] the French *Conseil d'Etat* has upheld, in a test case, the principle of supremacy of E.C. directives over French law.[8] In Germany, the German Federal Constitutional Court has also modified its earlier stance. In October 1986, in *Application of Wünsche Handelsgesellschaft*,[9] its earlier position in *Internationale Handelsgesellschaft*[10] was reversed. In Ireland, in *Attorney-General* v. *X*[11] the Irish High Court considered the controversial issue of whether a 14-year-old girl, who had been raped by her friend's father and who had as a result become pregnant, should have an injunction granted against her to restrain her from travelling abroad for the purposes of an abortion; an abortion was unlawful under Irish law. In the Irish High Court it was accepted that Irish courts had to enforce E.C. law even if it conflicted with Irish constitutional law. However, the Supreme Court eventually decided the issues without recourse to Community law and also decided that an Article 177 reference was therefore also unnecessary.[12]

The rule that directly effective Community law overrides conflicting national law applies irrespective of whether the directly effective Community law in question came before or after the national law. In all cases Community law takes precedence over the national law provision.[13] The reasoning behind the principle of supremacy of Community law is simply that without it there cannot be uniform application throughout the E.C., with consequent detriment to Community objectives.[14]

## Doctrine of "pre-emption"

It is suggested by Cross[15] that in more recent cases involving conflicts **3–003** between Community legislation and the national law of Member States, the ECJ no longer necessarily refers to the principle of supremacy, but instead advances various grounds on which national law can be "precluded".[16] In other words, there are various grounds for invalidating national law on the basis of express or implied conflict with secondary

---

[6] See Steiner, *Textbook on EEC Law* (1988) pp. 38–39.

[7] See *Semoules* [1970] C.M.L.R. 395.

[8] *Sté. Rothmans* v. *Sté. Philip. Morris France*, Cons.d'Etat, ass., February 2, 1992, req n. 56776 and 56777; J.C.P. 92 éd. G, Actualités, March 11, 1992.

[9] [1987] 3 C.M.L.R. 225.

[10] [1974] 2 C.M.L.R. 540. See further, Steiner, *op. cit.*, n. 6, p. 38.

[11] [1992] 2 C.M.L.R. 277.

[12] See further, (1992) 41 L.S.Gaz 41.

[13] See Hartley, *The Foundations of European Community Law* (1988), 2nd ed. p. 215; for a succinct survey of the relevant ECJ case law see the Opinion of the Advocate General Reischl in Case 106/77, *Simmenthal*: [1978] E.C.R. 629 at 651 to 652, [1978] 3 C.M.L.R. 263.

[14] See Steiner, *op. cit.*, n. 6, p. 34.

[15] Cross, "Pre-emption of Member State Law in the European Economic Community: A Framework for Analysis" (1992) C.M.L.Rev. 447 to 472.

[16] Cross, *op. cit.*, p. 449.

Community law, though all of these grounds are derived from the principle of the primacy of Community law. Cross suggests that this "pre-emption doctrine" used by the Court is still in the process of development but that it warrants further analysis, particularly in the context of the evolving principle of subsidiarity.[17] The Court has expressed the principle of pre-emption in the following terms:

> "[I]n accordance with the principle of the precedents of Community law, the relationship between provisions of Treaty and directly applicable measures of the institutions on the one hand and the national law of the Member States on the other, is such that those provisions and measures not only render automatically inapplicable any conflicting provision of current national law but – insofar as they are an integral part of, and take precedence in, the legal order applicable in the territory of each of the Member States – also *preclude the valid adoption of new national legislative measures to the extent to which it would be incompatible with Community provisions.*"[18]

### European Convention on Human Rights

3–004 The 1950 European Convention for the Protection of Human Rights and Fundamental Freedoms (hereinafter referred to as the ECHR) is a Treaty concluded within the framework of the Council of Europe (and not the European Community). However, it creates important rights and remedies for both individuals and companies. Although the U.K. has signed and ratified the Convention, it has not directly incorporated its provisions into national law. Nevertheless, the U.K. has accepted the right of petition by individuals, under Article 25 of the Convention, to the European Commission of Human Rights and, under Article 19, to the jurisdiction of the European Court of Human Rights.

The subject of rights and remedies under the European Convention is outside the scope of this book, but the inter-relationship between Community law and fundamental rights (including human rights) is relevant to the issue of supremacy of Community law. Although the Community itself is not a party to the ECHR, there are various rules of public international law which constitute legal obligations to respect fundamental human rights which are binding on all subjects of international law and therefore binding also on the E.C.[19]

The institutions of the E.C. issued a Joint Declaration on April 5, 1977,[20] affirming their adherence to its principles. The Declaration notes that the Treaties establishing the European Communities are based on the principle of respect for the law. It acknowledges that "law"

---

[17] *Op. cit.*, p. 472 and see further paras. 3–047 *et seq.* below.
[18] Case 106/77, *Simmenthal*: [1978] E.C.R. 629 at 643 to 644, [1978] 3 C.M.L.R. 263 (emphasis added).
[19] Schermers, "The European Communities Bound by Fundamental Human Rights" (1990) C.M.L.Rev. 249 at p. 251.
[20] [1977] O.J. C103/1 and see further, Forman, "The Joint Declaration on Fundamental Rights" (1977) 2 E.L.Rev. 210 and Case 44/79, *Hauer*: [1979] E.C.R. 3727, [1980] 3 C.M.L.R. 42 at para. 15.

comprises, over and above the rules embodied in the Treaties and secondary Community legislation, the principles of law and, in particular, fundamental rights, on which the constitutional law of all the Member States is based. In the Declaration, the three Community institutions stress that they attach prime importance to the protection of fundamental rights, as derived from the constitutions of the Member States and the ECHR.

The ECHR is also referred to in the preamble of the Single European Act, and the Treaty on European Union[21] also makes reference in Article F to this Convention. However, unless U.K. domestic proceedings also raise an issue of European Community law, it is not possible to rely *directly* on rights under the ECHR, because the Convention has not been specifically incorporated into U.K. law. Since the Community is not a party to the Convention, neither States nor individuals can lodge a complaint against it to the European Commission of Human Rights.[22]

*Indirect enforcement of Community law by using the ECHR*

However, the procedures under the ECHR can sometimes usefully be **3–005** used as a parallel procedure to domestic proceedings based on Community law. For example, in May 1993, the European Commission on Human Rights held that because of the length of time taken by U.K. courts and tribunals to consider the complaint of Dr Royce Darnell about his dismissal from employment by the Trent Regional Health Authority, the U.K. was in breach of Article 6 of the ECHR. The *Darnell* case[23] involved issues of European Community law under the Equal Pay Act, which was passed in order to give effect to Community law on equal pay. Article 6(1) of the Convention provides that:

"In the determination of his civil rights and obligations or of any criminal charge against him, everyone is entitled to a fair and public hearing within a reasonable time by an independent and impartial tribunal established by law. . . ."

Sir Basil Hall (the English member of the Commission) commented in his concurring opinion that the fact that Industrial Tribunal proceedings took over a year, and there would be a further two years' delay before a hearing in the Employment Appeal Tribunal, was "too long", especially where reinstatement is an issue, in which case "there is particular need that a final determination should be made expeditiously."[24]

---

[21] Also referred to as the Maastricht Treaty. See further para. 1–002 above. For text see [1992] O.J. C191/1, [1992] 1 C.M.L.R. 719.

[22] Schermers, *op. cit.*, n. 19, p. 157. The U.K. government has recently decided to reject the European Commission's proposals on accession to the ECHR: Hansard (H.L.) debate, November 26, 1992, vol. 540, cols. 1113–1117, reply to the debate on the report of the Select Committee on the European Communities, "Human Rights Re-examined", H.L. Paper 10, June 23, 1992: see Lord Anthony Lester, Q.C., "The Crisis Facing Human Rights in Europe" (1993) 8 *Wig and Gavel* 1 to 4.

[23] See the *Darnell* case referred to by Pannick, "Justice Delayed May Mean Justice Denied", *The Times*, March 30, 1993, p. 27; *Darnell* v. *U.K.*, *The Times*, November 24, 1993.

[24] See further Pannick, *op. cit.*

A Chamber of the European Court of Human Rights unanimously held that the U.K. was in breach of Article 6(1) because of the excessive length of civil proceedings involving the applicant. The court also awarded the applicant non-pecuniary damages of £5,000 as compensation for stress and strain caused by the prolonged legal battle, as well as damages for legal costs and expenses.

In the earlier case of *X* v. *France*,[25] the European Court of Human Rights *held, inter alia*, in the circumstances of an applicant who was a haemophiliac, who contracted the HIV virus as a result of blood transfusions and sought compensation from the French government for alleged negligence, the outcome of legal proceedings brought by the applicant was of crucial importance for the applicant, given the incurable disease from which he was suffering and his reduced life expectancy. In these circumstances, exceptional diligence was called for on the part of the administration and judicial authorities. However, the French Administrative Court had not used its powers to speed up the proceedings. The European Court of Human Rights found that a reasonable time had already been exceeded by the time of the judgment of the Administrative Court. In all the circumstances, there had been a violation of Article 6(1) of the ECHR.

The scope for use of Convention procedure has been rapidly increasing in both the quantity and range of cases decided in Strasbourg. Recent cases have, for instance, concerned competition and tax disputes involving companies, planning disputes, care orders, asylum, immigration and prisoners' rights.[26] In view of the substantial growth in the number of cases brought under the Convention procedure, consideration is being given to a reform of the current two-tier structure of a Commission and Court with support from governments for a single tier, full-time court. This is to be created by the adoption of a new Protocol to the Convention to be ready for signature by May 1994.[27] The importance of cases such as *Darnell* is that the Convention procedure may, in an appropriate case, be indirectly used to enforce European Community rights.

## Fundamental rights

3–006    General principles of Community law include fundamental rights and these go beyond the rights included in the ECHR.[28] Where a national

---

[25] *X* v. *France*, 14 E.H.R.R. 483.

[26] See further, Duffy, "European Practice Briefing", (May 1993) S.J. 404.

[27] See further, Duffy, "E.C. Practice Briefing" (February 5, 1993) S.J. 91; Dremczewski, "A Full-Time European Court of Human Rights in Strasbourg", (October 22, 1993) New L.J. 1488 to 1489; Schermers, "The European Court of Human Rights After the Merger" (1993) 18 E.L.Rev. 493 to 505.

[28] On the incorporation of these fundamental Community rights generally see O'Leary, "The Court of Justice as a Reluctant Constitutional Adjudicator: An Examination of the Abortion Information Case" (1992) 17 E.L.Rev. 138 at p. 150, n.36; Case 29/69, *Stauder*: [1969] E.C.R. 419, [1970] C.M.L.R. 112; Case 11/70, *Internationale Handelsgesellschaft*: [1970] E.C.R. 1125, [1972] C.M.L.R. 255; Case 4/73, *Nold*: [1974] E.C.R. 491, [1974] 2 C.M.L.R. 338; Case 44/79, *Hauer*: [1979] E.C.R. 3727, [1980] 3 C.M.L.R. 42; and Case 136/79, *National Panasonic*: [1980] E.C.R. 2033, [1980] 3 C.M.L.R. 169.

rule is adopted to implement a Community legal provision, it may therefore be reviewed by the European Court, on the ground of its compatibility with these fundamental rights.[29]

## Compatibility of national implementing rules with fundamental rights

In Case 5/88, *Wachauf*[30] the ECJ applied fundamental rights principles **3–007** for the first time, to national acts implementing Community legislation.[31] The plaintiff was a tenant farmer in Germany. During the period of his lease he concentrated exclusively on dairy production and obtained a milk production quota. Under Community Regulation 857/84, these milk production quotas were transferred on the sale, lease or inheritance of the land to the person taking over the running of the farm, until the surrender of the quota. If the quota was surrendered to the State, compensation was payable to the milk producer. However, according to the German Order implementing the Community milk compensation scheme in Germany, a tenant farmer such as Wachauf was unable to surrender his quota and claim compensation, without the consent of his landlord. In Wauchaf's case this consent was withdrawn and he faced the situation of not being entitled to compensation despite the efforts he had made to build up the farm as a milk producing concern. The Court held that where a Community provision incorporates the protection of a fundamental right, national implementing rules must also give effect to the provision in such a way as to respect the fundamental rights involved. The German Court was therefore instructed to look again at the primary Community legislation and review the German law in the light of fundamental rights considerations. The German court subsequently came to the conclusion that the relevant section of the German Order was void, as offending against the principle of equal treatment and Wauchaf was awarded compensation.[32]

Another illustration is provided by Case 63/85, *R.* v. *Kent Kirk*,[33] in which the Court held that the principle in Article 7 of the European Convention that penal provisions may not have retroactive effect is among the general principles of law whose observance is ensured by the ECJ. Accordingly, the retroactivity provided for in Article 6(1) of Regulation No. 170/83 could not "be regarded as validating *ex post facto* national measures which imposed criminal penalties, at the time of the conduct at issue, if those measures were not valid."[34]

---

[29] See Joined Cases 60 & 61/84, *Cinéthèque*: [1985] E.C.R. 2605, [1986] 1 C.M.L.R. 365; Case 12/86, *Demirel*: [1987] E.C.R. 3719, [1989] 1 C.M.L.R. 421; Case 5/88, *Wachauf*: [1989] E.C.R. 2609, [1991] 1 C.M.L.R. 328 and Case C–260/89, *ERT*: [1991] 1 E.C.R. 2925.

[30] *Op. cit.*, n. 29.

[31] Coppel and O'Neill, "The European Court of Justice: Taking Rights Seriously?" (1992) C.M.L.Rev. 669 at pp. 674 *et seq.*

[32] Reported as Case 1/2–E62/85, *Re: the Kuechenhof Farm*: [1990] 2 C.M.L.R. 289.

[33] Case 63/83, *R.* v. *Kent Kirk*: [1984] E.C.R. 2689, [1984] 3 C.M.L.R. 522.

[34] *Op. cit.*, paras. 22 and 23 of the judgment.

## Freedom of expression and information

**3–008**     In Case 260/89, *Elleniki Radiophonia Tileorasi (ERT)* v. *Dimotiki Etairia Pliroforissis*,[35] the Court assessed the Greek government's public policy derogations from Community law, on fundamental rights grounds. The case concerned an independent broadcasting company in Greece which challenged the enforcement of a State monopoly on the provision of television services within Greece. Greek law did not permit any party other than the State Television Company to broadcast television programmes within Greek territory. When prosecuted for defying this ban, the defendant company pleaded in its defence that the television monopoly was contrary both to Community law (*inter alia*, on the free movement of goods and services) and Article 10 of the European Convention on Human Rights relating to freedom of expression and information. The Greek government claimed that the television monopoly was a public policy derogation which was permissible under Article 56 and Article 66 of the EEC Treaty.

However, the Court held that:

> "When a Member State invokes Articles 56 and 66 of the Treaty in order to justify rules which hinder the free movement of services, this justification which is provided in Community law, must be interpreted in the light of general principles of law, notably fundamental rights. The national rules in question may only benefit from the Article 56 and 66 exceptions in so far as they are compatible with fundamental rights, the observance of which the Court ensures."[36]

The Court went on to state that the public policy exceptions in Articles 66 and 56 must therefore be understood in the light of Article 10 of the European Convention.

However, in Case C–159/90, *Society for the Protection of Unborn Children* v. *Grogan*[37] although the Court was ready to treat abortion as a service under Community law, it held that the links between the students' association in Ireland, engaged in disseminating information about abortion clinics in the U.K., and the clinics themselves, was too tenuous for the service provided by the association to be brought within the scope of Article 59 of Community law.[38] The dissemination of information was found to be independent of the economic activity which the clinics performed and the Court thereby avoided having to assess the compatibility of Irish law by reference to, in particular, the ECHR. The matter was left to resolution by Irish courts probably because to do otherwise may have led to a constitutional crisis in Ireland. Protocol No. 17 to the Treaty of European Union was subsequently annexed at the request of the Irish government regarding the application in Ireland of

---

[35] Case 260/89, *Elleniki*: [1991] I E.C.R. 2925.

[36] See *ERT* case, *op. cit.*, para. 43. This translation is taken from Coppel and O'Neill, *op. cit.*, n. 31, pp. 677 *et seq.*

[37] C–159/90, *Society for the Protection of Unborn Children* v. *Grogan*: [1991] I E.C.R. 4685, [1993] 1 C.M.L.R. 197.

[38] See O'Leary, *op. cit.*, n. 28, p. 145.

Article 40.3.3 of the Constitution of Ireland.[39] A subsequent referendum in Ireland has led to the approval of an addition to Article 40.3.3 which states: "This sub-section shall not limit freedom to obtain or make available in the State, subject to conditions as may be laid down by law, information relating to services lawfully available in another State."[40]

## Extent of scrutiny by the European Court: competition law cases

These cases suggest an increasing scrutiny by the Court of the action **3–009** of Member States action by reference to fundamental rights. On the other hand, the general Community rule has more often than not prevailed against claims of violation of fundamental rights.[41] It is suggested by Clapham that:

> "[Al]though the Court has increasingly referred to the [European] Convention, the European Social Charter, international treaties and constitutional principles and traditions, the rights contained therein have hardly been developed by the Court, and they have rarely been relied on to give concrete protection to an individual."[42]

Nevertheless, in the field of Community competition law, the Court has developed principles embodied in the ECHR to create specific rights for individuals. For instance, in Case 374/87, *Orkem* v. *Commission*[43] the Court went beyond the application and scope of Article 6 of the ECHR and inquired whether "certain limitations on the [European] Commission's powers of investigation are implied by the need to safeguard the rights of the defence which the Court has held to be a fundamental principle of the Community legal order."[44] The Court decided that:

> ". . . Thus, the Commission may not compel an undertaking to provide it with answers which might involve an admission on its part of the existence of an infringement which it is incumbent upon the Commission to prove."[45]

The Court concluded in *Orkem* that by requiring Orkem to acknowledge, in response to certain inadmissible questions, that it had infringed

---

[39] Agence Europe/Documents No. 1759/60, February 7, 1992, discussed by O'Leary, *op. cit.*, n. 28, p. 156.

[40] See further, Andrews and Sherlock, "Information on Abortion Services and Article 10: Case of *Open Door and Dublin Well Woman* v. *Ireland*" (1993) 18 E.L.Rev. 253.

[41] Coppel and O'Neill, *op. cit.*, n. 31, p. 679.

[42] See Clapham in Weiller, Cassese, Clapham (eds), *Human Rights and the European Community* (1991), Vol. I, p. 56. For suggestions about a more ambitious approach see Lenaerts, "Fundamental Rights to be Included in a Community Catalogue" (1991) 16 E.L.Rev. 367 to 390.

[43] Case 374/87, *Orkem* v. *Commission*: [1989] E.C.R. 3283, [1991] 4 C.M.L.R. 502.

[44] *Op. cit.*, p. 3351, para. 32 and see further, Lenaerts, "Fundamental Rights to be Included in a Community Catalogue" (1991) 16 E.L.Rev. 367 p. 381.

[45] *Op. cit.*, p. 3351, paras. 34 to 35.

Article 85(1) of the EEC Treaty, the Commission had undermined the rights of the defence.[46]

In Joined Cases 46/87 & 227/88, *Hoechst* v. *Commission*[47] the Court considered the ambit of Article 8(1) of the ECHR for the purpose of delimiting the scope of the Commission's powers of investigation based on Regulation Number 17/62, the First Regulation implementing Articles 85 and 86 of the EEC Treaty. (This regulation is also discussed at paragraphs 3–032 *et seq.* below). Article 8(1) of the ECHR provides that: "Everyone has the right to respect for his private and family life, his home and his correspondence." Although the Court concluded that Article 8 was concerned with the development of personal freedom and was not, therefore, to be extended to business premises, it nevertheless went on to decide that:

> "Nonetheless, in all the legal systems of the Member States, any intervention by the public authorities in the sphere of private activities of any person, whether natural or legal, must have a legal basis and be justified on the grounds laid down by law, and, consequently, those systems provide, albeit in different forms, protection against arbitraty or disproportionate intervention. The need for such protection must be recognised as a general principle of Community law."[48]

The Court therefore elaborated on what this protection meant in the specific instance of an exercise by the Commission of its powers of investigation under Regulation 17.[49] It has been suggested, nevertheless, that there should be an appeal procedure from the ECJ to the ECHR,[50] but this would only be possible if the Community were party to the European Convention and if it accepted the right of individual petition.

### Approach of the Court to fundamental economic rights

3–010    Certain fundamental economic rights enshrined in the Treaty of Rome have certainly been treated by the Court as being as important as fundamental human rights. For example, the free movement of workers within the Community is one of the basic freedoms underpinning the Community legal order and is enshrined in Article 48 of the E.C. Treaty. It has been cogently argued by Hall[51] that in order to satisfy the demands

---

[46] *Ibid.* at 3353, para. 41 and Lenaerts, *op. cit.*, p. 382. For further discussion of the rights of the defence as a fundamental principle of the Community legal order, see Case 322/81, *Michelin* v. *Commission*: [1983] E.C.R. 3461, [1985] C.M.L.R. 282 and also *Société Stenuit* v. *France*: (1992) 14 E.H.R.R. 509. However, the right to refuse to answer questions in competition cases if to do so might incriminate the individual concerned may not apply to civil cases brought before national courts; see further, Case C–60/92, *Otto B.V.* v. *Postbank N.V.*: judgment of November 10, 1993.

[47] Joined Cases 46/87 & 227/88, *Hoechst* v. *Commission*: [1989] E.C.R. 2859, [1991] 4 C.M.L.R. 410.

[48] *Op. cit.*, p. 2924, paras. 18 and 19.

[49] *Ibid.* at 2925 to 2929, paras. 20 to 38 and see discussion by Lenaerts, *op. cit.*, n. 42, p. 383.

[50] See Schermers, "The European Communities Bound by Fundamental Human Rights" (1980) C.M.L.Rev. 249 at p. 256.

[51] See Hall, "The European Convention on Human Rights and Public Policy Exceptions for the Free Movement of Workers under the EEC Treaty" (1991) 16 E.L.Rev. 466 at p. 488.

of the Community rule of law and in order to achieve real economic integration, as well as to avoid the potentially disastrous political/constitutional problems associated with adopting standards of human rights which are lower than those protected individually within Member States, the Court has in fact gone beyond the minimum standards required by the ECHR.

In Case 41/74, *Van Duyn* v. *Home Office*,[52] Miss Van Duyn was a Dutch national who arrived in the U.K. for the purposes of taking up employment with the Church of Scientology in Britain. She was sent back to the Netherlands by British immigration officials on the basis that the Secretary of State considered it undesirable to give anyone leave to enter the U.K. on the business of or in the employment of the Church of Scientology.[53] This decision was taken pursuant to a policy of the U.K. government which had been declared five years earlier, to the effect that the Church's activities were considered socially harmful. Miss Van Duyn brought a legal action claiming that her right to freedom of movement under Article 48 of the EEC Treaty had been infringed. This case was subsequently referred by the U.K. court to the Court of Justice under Article 177 of the EEC Treaty.

The Court considered the scope of the exceptions to Article 48 provided for in Article 48(3) of the Treaty. These relate to limitations which are justified on grounds of public policy, public security or public health. Both the Court and the Advocate General agreed that is was not possible to proceed on the basis that there was a Community-wide standard of public policy and that therefore judgments on what constituted a threat to public policy could legitimately vary from country to country and from time to time.[54] However, the Court of Justice held that each Member State could not unilaterally determine the scope of restrictions on Article 48 and that permissible limitations must be strictly interpreted. Ultimately, the Court possessed the power to "control" the exercise of measures designed to protect public policy if they exceeded the area of discretion retained by the Member States.[55]

Other cases in which the Court advocates a similar approach are Case 36/75, *Rutili*,[56] Case 30/77, *R.* v. *Bouchereau*[57] and Cases 115 and 116/81, *Adoui and Cornuaille* v. *Belgium*.[58] Thus, for example in Cases 115 and 116/81, *Adoui & Cornuaille*,[59] the Court said with regard to Article 48(3) that:

> "Although Community law does not impose upon the Member States a uniform scale of values as regards the assessment of conduct which may be considered as contrary to public policy, it should

---

[52] Case 41/74, *Van Duyn* v. *Home Office*: [1974] E.C.R. 1337, [1975] 1 C.M.L.R. 1.

[53] *Op. cit.*, E.C.R. p. 1340 and C.M.L.R. p. 6.

[54] See further Hall, *op. cit.*, n. 51, p. 481.

[55] Hall, *op. cit.*, n. 51, p. 481.

[56] Case 36/75, *Rutili*: [1975] E.C.R. 1219, [1976] 1 C.M.L.R. 140.

[57] Case 30/77, *R.* v. *Bouchereau*: [1977] E.C.R. 1999, [1972] 2 C.M.L.R. 800.

[58] Joined Cases 115–116/81, *Adoui* and *Cornuaille* v. *Belgium*: [1982] E.C.R. 1665, [1982] 3 C.M.L.R. 631, discussed in Hall, *op. cit.*, n. 51, pp. 483 *et seq.*

[59] Joined Cases 115–116/81, *ibid.*

nevertheless be stated that conduct may not be considered as being of a sufficiently serious nature to justify restrictions on the admission to or residence within the territory of a Member State of a national of another Member State in the case where the former Member State does not adopt, with respect to the same conduct on the part of its own nationals, repressive measures or other genuine and effective measures intended to combat such conduct."[60]

It is therefore argued by Hall,[61] that the Court has further refined and narrowed the area of discretion available to Member States in deciding what constitutes a genuine and sufficiently serious threat within Article 48. It has thereby extended the principle stated in *Van Duyn* concerning the existence of the requisite threat to public order. This suggests that the Community system does not leave a wide margin of discretion to Member States in an area which concerns fundamental economic rights, such as free movement of persons, which is one of the main goals of the Community.

### Ambit of the Court's review powers

3–011    It is also clear that the Court regards itself as able to review national legislation whenever this operates in an area affected by Community law. This means that national courts will be obliged to give effect to the ECHR (whether or not it is directly incorporated into national law), in relation to all questions which are within the field of Community law. The inclusion of a specific reference to the ECHR in the Treaty on European Union, Article F(2) may further encourage this trend.[62]

However, it is suggested by Coppel and O'Neill that although human rights principles will become applicable to a wider number of cases, the full remit of the ECJ is likely to be that of ensuring closer economic integration in the Community, rather than the protection of human rights as such.[63] However, there may, in appropriate cases, be the possibility of a parallel action brought under the procedures of the ECHR itself.[64]

## ENGLISH LAW PERSPECTIVE ON THE SUPREMACY OF COMMUNITY LAW

3–012    Under U.K. law, the combined effect of section 2(1) and section 3(1) of the European Communities Act 1972 (as amended) is that directly effective Community law must be recognised and enforced in the U.K. However, with regard to statutes passed *after* the European Communities Act, if such statutes are in conflict with Community law, they are subject

---

[60] *Ibid.* at para. 8 of the Court's judgment.
[61] *Ibid.*, p. 486.
[62] Coppel and O'Neill, *op. cit.*, n. 31, p. 691.
[63] *Ibid.*, p. 692.
[64] See discussion at para. 3–004 above.

to the constitutional principle of parliamentary sovereignty. This is a principle under which parliament cannot deprive itself of its power to pass future legislation which overrides Community law.[65] Thus, it remains theoretically possible for the U.K. courts to apply a U.K. statute which is contrary to E.C. law, if the intention was to breach Community obligations.[66] However, in *Macarthys Ltd.* v. *Smith*,[67] Lord Denning M.R. made it clear that:

> "[he] did not however envisage any such situation. Unless there is such an intentional and express repudiation of the Treaty, it is our duty to give priority to the Treaty."

However, the suggestion in Case C–106/89, *Marleasing SA* v. *La Comercial Internacional de Alimentación SA*,[68] is that even if a national parliament expressly repudiates a particular Community law obligation in a directive, national courts would still be obliged to give effect to the latter. This appears to have been accepted by the French Conseil d'Etat in the case of *Rassemblement des opposants à la chasse and others*[69] in which a Ministerial order laying down legislative requirements in disregard of Directive 76/409 on the conservation of wild birds[70] was annulled.[71]

## Factortame (No. 1): conflict with subsequent U.K. statute

The question of conflict between Community law and a subsequent **3–013** U.K. statute arose in the historic case C–221/89, *R.* v. *The Secretary of State for Transport, ex parte Factortame Ltd. (No. 1)* (hereinafter referred to as *Factortame (No. 1)*).[72] This case was referred by the High Court to the European Court under Article 177 of the EEC Treaty, for a preliminary ruling. It concerned the compatibility of various provisions of the EEC Treaty with provisions of the Merchant Shipping Act 1988, which laid down the conditions for the registration of fishing vessels in the U.K. In essence, the Act aimed at ensuring that fishing quotas allocated to the U.K. under the EEC Common Fisheries Policy were only exploited by vessels which had a genuine economic link with the U.K.[73]

The European Court accepted that is was for Member States to determine, in accordance with the general rules of international law, the conditions which must be fulfilled in order for a vessel to be registered and granted the right to fly their flag. However, in exercising that power,

---

[65] See Hartley, *The Foundation of European Community Law* (1988), pp. 242 *et seq.*

[66] See Steiner, *Textbook on EEC Law* (1988), p. 38.

[67] [1979] 3 All E.R. 325 at p. 329.

[68] Case C–106/89, *Marleasing SA* v. *La Comercial Internacional de Alimentación SA*: [1990] I E.C.R. 4135, [1992] 1 C.M.L.R. 305. See further discussion at para. 6–004 below.

[69] [1990] C.M.L.R. 831.

[70] [1979] O.J. L103/1.

[71] See Curtin, "Directives: The Effectiveness of Judicial Protection of Individual Rights" (1990) C.M.L.Rev. 709 to 739, at pp. 725 to 726.

[72] Case 221/89, *R.* v. *Secretary of State for Transport, ex p. Factortame Ltd. and Others* [1991] 3 All E.R. 769, [1991] 3 C.M.L.R. 589.

[73] See Gravells, "Effective Protection of Community Law Rights: Temporary Disapplication of an Act of Parliament" (1991) *Public Law* 180.

Member States must comply with the rules of Community law. (There was found to be no conflict between relevant Community law and the rules of international law).

The Court held, *inter alia*, that the condition in the U.K. statute which stipulates that where a vessel was owned or chartered by natural persons they must be of a particular nationality and where it was owned or chartered by a company, the shareholders and directors must be of that nationality, was contrary to Article 52 of the Treaty which was concerned with freedom of establishment. Such a condition was also contrary to Article 221 of the Treaty, under which Member States must award nationals of the other Member States the same treatment as their own nationals, as regards participation in the capital of companies or firms within the meaning of Article 58. Consequently, the registration system in the 1988 Act and regulations were ineffective in relation to nationals of other Member States.

The Court has consistently held that the fact that a competent domestic authority (in this case, the Secretary of State for Transport), is encouraged to grant exceptions or dispensations to the nationality condition on certain grounds, could not justify a national measure which is contrary to the Treaty, even if the power in question is freely applied. The Court referred in particular to its judgments in Case 82/77, *Openbaar Ministerie of the Netherlands* v. *van Tiggele*[74] and Case 27/80, *Fietje*.[75]

### Factortame (No. 2): the right to an effective interlocutory remedy

**3–014** The European Court was also asked by the House of Lords, in a separate reference under Article 177 arising out of the *Factortame* litigation, Case C–213/89, *R.* v. *Secretary of State for Transport, ex parte Factortame Ltd. (No. 2)*, (hereinafter referred to as Factortame (No. 2)),[76] for a preliminary ruling on the question of whether a national court was under an obligation to provide an effective interlocutory remedy to protect directly effective rights under Community law pending determination of the existence of these rights, and the principles to be applied in deciding whether to grant such relief. The European Court held that a national court was required to set aside a rule of national law which it considered was the sole obstacle preventing it from granting interim relief in a case concerning Community law, if to do otherwise would impair the full effectiveness of Community rights. However, the Court did not fetter the discretion of the national court to determine on the facts whether an appropriate case for the grant of an interim ruling has been made out nor did it specify the nature of the ruling which may be ordered.[77]

---

[74] Case 82/77, *Openbaar Ministerie of the Netherlands* v. *van Tiggele*: [1978] E.C.R. 25, [1978] 2 C.M.L.R. 528.
[75] Case 27/80, *Fietje*: [1980] E.C.R. 3938, [1981] 3 C.M.L.R. 722.
[76] Case 213/89, *R.* v. *Secretary of State for Transport, ex p. Factortame Ltd. and Others*: [1990] I E.C.R. 2433, [1990] 3 C.M.L.R. 1.
[77] See further, paras. 9–035 *et seq.* below.

In the ensuing judgment of the House of Lords in *Factortame (No. 2)*,[78] Lord Bridge confirmed that the decision of the Court of Justice affirming the jurisdiction of national courts to *override national legislation*, if necessary to enable interim relief to be granted to protect rights under Community law, was consistent with the supremacy of Community law and with the doctrine of parliamentary sovereignty. He stated that:

> ". . . the duty of a U.K. court, when delivering final judgment, to override any rule of national law found to be in conflict with any directly enforceable rule of Community law. . . . Thus there is nothing in any way novel in according supremacy to rules of Community law in those areas in which they apply and to insist that, in the protection of rights under Community law, national courts must not be inhibited by rules of national law from granting interim ruling in appropriate cases is no more than a logical recognition of that supremacy."[79]

The effect of the *Factortame* litigation was also to confirm that under U.K. law, in the event of a conflict between directly effective Community law and a provision of national law, even in a subsequent U.K. statute, the former must prevail and the inconsistent national law must be set aside. It was common ground between the parties[80] and implicit in the *Factortame (No. 1)* judgment that Article 52 of the Treaty of Rome (concerning freedom of establishment) had direct effect in the sense of conferring rights on the plaintiffs which the U.K. courts were under an obligation to protect.

## Conflicts with Community directives

However, the situation is more complex where the conflict is between **3–015** a directly effective provision of a *directive* and a provision of national law, even where the latter has been enacted to give effect to the directive. This is because even directly effective provisions of a directive are not *horizontally* effective against other private individuals.[81] However, once national legislation has been enacted in order to implement a directive, national courts are under a duty to interpret that legislation to achieve the results required by the directive. This duty is derived firstly from Article 5 of the E.C. Treaty, under which Member States are required to "take all appropriate measures, whether general or particular, to ensure fulfilment of the obligations arising out of" the Treaty. Furthermore, Member States are obliged under Article 189(3) to achieve the results intended by a directive. Thus, in *Von Colson*[82] the Court stated that:

---

[78] *R. v. Secretary of State for Transport, ex p. Factortame and Others (No. 2)*: [1991] 1 All E.R. 70 at pp. 107 *et seq.*, [1990] 3 W.L.R. 818.

[79] *Ibid.*, 1 All E.R. 108.

[80] See Toth, Case Note on Case C–213/89, *R. v. Secretary of State for Transport, ex p. Factortame Ltd. and Others*, judgment of the Court of June 19, 1990, [1990] C.M.L.Rev. 573 at p. 575.

[81] See paras. 2–010 and 5–021 *et seq.* above.

[82] Case 14/83, *Von Colson v. Land Nordrhein-Westfalen*: [1984] E.C.R. 1891 at p. 1909, [1986] 2 C.M.L.R. 430.

". . . the Member States obligation arising from a directive to achieve the result envisaged by the directive and their duty under Article 5 of the Treaty to take all appropriate measures, whether general or particular, to ensure the fulfilment of that obligation, is binding on all the authorities of Member States including, for matters within their jurisdiction, the courts. It follows that, in applying the national laws specifically introduced in order to implement [the Directive in question], national courts are required to interpret their national law in the light of the wording and the purpose of the directive in order to achieve the result referred to in Article 189(3)."[83]

The principle enunciated in the *Von Colson* case has been accepted by the House of Lords. For example, Lord Templeman in the *Litster* v. *Forth Dry Dock and Engineering Co. Ltd.*[84] cited the *Von Colson* case for the proposition that:

". . . the courts of the United Kingdom are under a duty to follow the practice of the European Court of Justice by giving a purposive interpretation to Directives and to Regulations issued for the purpose of complying with Directives."[85]

The duty of domestic courts to adopt a purposive construction is examined more fully at paragraphs 6–007 *et seq.*

## REFERRAL OF CASES BY NATIONAL COURTS TO THE EUROPEAN COURT OF JUSTICE

3–016   Some domestic cases in which remedies are sought for breach of Community law, will involve the interpretation of Community law. Under Article 177 of the Treaty of Rome (as amended at Maastricht):

"The Court of Justice shall have jurisdiction to give preliminary rulings concerning:

(a) The interpretation of this Treaty;
(b) The validity and interpretation of acts of the institutions of the Community and of the ECB;
(c) The interpretation of the statutes of bodies established by an act of the Council, where those statutes so provide.

Where such a question is raised before any court or tribunal of a Member State, that court or tribunal may, if it considers that a decision on the question is necessary to enable it to give judgment, request the Court of Justice to give a ruling thereon.

Where any such question is raised in a case pending before a court or tribunal of a Member State, against whose decisions there is no

---

[83] *Ibid.*, p. 453 (C.M.L.R.).
[84] *Litster* [1989] 2 W.L.R. 634 at p. 640, [1984] 1 All E.R. 1134 at p. 1139 (H.L.).
[85] *Ibid.*

judicial remedy under national law, that court or tribunal shall bring the matter before the Court of Justice."

By virtue of Article 168a of the Treaty of Rome (as amended) the Court of First Instance (CFI), attached to the ECJ has certain jurisdiction to hear cases at first instance. The jurisdiction of the CFI was extended by a Council of Ministers' decision of June 8, 1993[86] to all direct actions brought by natural or legal persons. The CFI already deals with E.C. competition cases, actions against the European Commission under the ECSC Treaty, and also deals with staff cases from the Community's institutions.[87] However, preliminary references under Article 177 will still only be heard by the ECJ. The entrustment of the CFI with new duties may speed up the time which is taken by the ECJ to decide cases referred to it.

In 1991 the ECJ received 153 requests from national courts for preliminary rulings.[88] The number of cases referred has remained relatively stable since 1989. It appears that there is no Member State that is against the procedure in principle.[89] The Commission does not, however, publish any research on the number of cases where national courts ought to have applied Community rules but did not refer to them.[90]

## Issues which may be referred

Article 177 enables a national court to refer any queston of E.C. law to **3–017** the European Court, for a preliminary ruling. The range of questions which may be referred is wide. References may be made on whether or not a provision of Community law produces direct effect, *i.e.* confers rights on individuals which national courts must protect. It also includes questions not only on the interpretation of the E.C. Treaty itself, but also on amending treaties or on one of the treaties of accession.[91] The questions which may be referred include questions on acts of the Community institutions, and on the effect of legislation in the form of regulations, directives and decisions of Community institutions as well as non-binding measures such as recommendations.[92]

Preliminary rulings may also be made in relation to other international agreements. For instance, rulings may be made in connection with the

---

[86] [1993] O.J. C156/5. See further, ECJ Order September 28, 1993, applying Article 4 of Council Decision 93/350/ECSC/EEC/Euratom of June 8, 1993, [1993] O.J. L144/21, modifying Council Decision 88/591/ECSC/EEC/Euratom establishing the Court of First Instance. See also Decision 94/149, [1994] O.J. L66/29.

[87] See Donaghy, "The European Court of Justice" (1993) 20 *Lawyers in Europe* 15.

[88] See *Ninth Annual Report on Commission Monitoring of the Application of Community Law* (1991) COM (92) 136 final, May 12, 1992.

[89] *Ibid.,* p. 109.

[90] *Ibid.,* p. 112.

[91] Arnull, "Referrals to the European Court" (1990) 15 E.L.Rev. 375 at p. 378.

[92] See, *e.g.* Case C–322/88, *Grimaldi*: [1989] E.C.R. 4416, [1991] 2 C.M.L.R. 265, cited by Arnull, *op. cit.,* p. 378, n. 16.

Brussels Convention,[93] the Rome Convention[94] and the Community Patents Convention.[95]

## Timing of the reference

**3–018**    The request for a preliminary ruling may be made at any stage before the national court gives final judgment. National courts have jurisdiction to make references at the interlocutory stage of proceedings if this is appropriate. In Joined Cases 36 & 71/80, *Irish Creamery Milk Suppliers Association* v. *Ireland*,[96] the European Court made it clear, however, that the national court must "define the legal context" in which the reference was made. For this purpose, it said that:

> "It might be convenient, in certain circumstances, for the facts in the case to be established and for questions of purely national law to be settled at the time the reference is made to the Court of Justice so as to enable the latter to take cognisance of all the features of fact and of law which may be relevant . . . ."[97]

However, the European Court went on to emphasise that:

> "Those considerations do not in any way restrict the discretion of the national court, which alone has a direct knowledge of the facts of the case and of the argument of the parties, which will have to take responsibility for giving judgment in the case and which is therefore in the best position to appreciate at what stage in the proceedings it requires a preliminary ruling from the Court of Justice."[98]

References have been made for example on an application for interlocutory relief[99]; for a stay of preceedings[1]; to strike out proceedings as disclosing no cause of action[2]; and on the grant of leave to apply for judicial review[3] and in a criminal case, at the close of the prosecution case, on a submission by the defendant of no case to answer on the basis that the legislation creating the offence is contrary to Community law.[4]

The decision whether or not to make a reference is that of the national court. It may, for instance, be made even where both parties are opposed to the reference.[5] Usually, one of the parties objects to a reference on the

---

[93] See Convention on Jurisdiction and Enforcement of Judgments in Civil and Commercial matters, [1978] O.J. L304/1, (implemented in the U.K. by the Civil Jurisdiction and Judgments Act 1982).

[94] See Rome Convention on the Law Applicable to Contractual Obligations, [1980] O.J. L266/1.

[95] [1967] O.J. L17/1.

[96] Joined Cases 36 & 71/80, *Irish Creamery Milk Suppliers Association* v. *Ireland*: [1981] E.C.R. 735, [1981] 2 C.M.L.R. 455.

[97] *Ibid.*

[98] *Irish Creamery Supplies Association, op. cit.*, n. 96, p. 748.

[99] *Polydor Records* v. *Harlequin Record Shops* [1980] 2 C.M.L.R. 413; *EMI Records* v. *CBS United Kingdom* [1975] 1 C.M.L.R. 285.

[1] *Rochdale Borough Council* v. *Anders* [1988] 3 C.M.L.R. 431.

[2] *Thetford Corporation* v. *Fiamma SpA* [1987] 3 C.M.L.R. 266.

[3] *R.* v. *Minister of Agriculture, Fisheries and Foods, ex p. FEDESA* [1988] 3 C.M.L.R. 207.

[4] *R.* v. *Plymouth Justices, ex p. Rogers* [1982] Q.B. 863.

[5] See, for example, *Direct Cosmetics Limited* v. *Commissioners of Customs and Excise* [1983] VATTR 194 (VAT Tribunal).

ground that it is not seeking to rely on Community law and/or believes that a reference would be unfavourable to it. If both parties wish a reference to be made, the national court will usually agree. Nevertheless, there must still be a proper foundation for the making of that reference.[6]

It is possible that an Article 177 reference may be pending before the European Court in another case, the outcome of which may be relevant to other domestic proceedings. In these circumstances, it may be possible to obtain a stay of the proceedings until the reference in the other case has been heard by the European Court.[7]

## Discretion whether or not to refer

Article 177(2) draws a distinction between national courts and tri- **3–019** bunals which *may* refer cases to the European Court and those covered by Article 177(3) "against whose decisions there is no judicial remedy under national law." Thus a *final* court of appeal, such as the House of Lords, *must* refer to the European Court questions within the meaning of Article 177(1) raised before it.

However, the application of Article 177(3) is not limited, in the U.K., to the House of Lords. It means any court, even if not the highest court, against whose decisions there is no appeal in the given case.[8] Thus, if the Court of Appeal refuses either to refer or to grant leave to appeal against either the refusal or its substantive decision, then the House of Lords must itself grant leave to appeal. Similar considerations apply where the High Court is considering whether to grant leave to apply for judicial review of a decision from which there is no appeal.[9] However, when a relevant question is raised in interlocutory proceedings for an interim order, a national court is not required to refer the question even if its decision is not subject to appeal, provided that during proceedings on the substance of the case, the same issue may be re-examined and referred to the European Court under the Article 177 procedure.[10]

Courts other than the final court therefore have a discretion whether or not to refer.[11] it should be noted that the German *Bundesgerichtshof* has recently been very reluctant to make references to the ECJ in a number of company law matters. Thus, the question about what limitations the Twelfth Company Law Directive[12] imposed on the rules of German law

---

[6] See Kerr L.J. in *Portsmouth CC* v. *Richards and Quietlynn Ltd.* [1989] 1 C.M.L.R. 673 (C.A.).

[7] However, after examining various reasons why a stay might be beneficial or otherwise, the application for a stay was refused on appeal by the Employment Appeal Tribunal in *Avdel Systems Ltd.* v. *Mrs F Fortune and Others* [1993] 2 C.M.L.R. 246.

[8] See Case 6/64, *Costa* v. *ENEL*: [1964] E.C.R. 585, [1964] C.M.L.R. 425.

[9] See further, *The Supreme Court Practice* (1993), Vol. 1, Part 1 at p. 1614.

[10] See Case 107/76, *Hoffmann La Roche* v. *Centrafarm*: [1977] E.C.R. 957, [1977] 2 C.M.L.R. 334 and Joined Cases 35–36/82, *Morson and Jhanjan* v. *Netherlands*: [1982] E.C.R. 3723, [1983] 2 C.M.L.R. 221.

[11] For guidelines conventionally referred to regarding how this discretion should be exercised see the judgment of Lord Denning in *Bulmer (H.P.) Ltd.* v. *Bollinger S.A.* [1974] 1 Ch. 401, [1974] 2 All E.R. 1226. See also *R.* v. *International Stock Exchange of the U.K. and the Republic of Ireland Ltd., ex p. ELSE (1982) Ltd. and Others* [1993] 2 C.M.L.R. 677.

[12] Council Directive 89/667 of December 21, 1989 on single-member private limited-liability companies, [1989] O.J. L395/40.

governing liability of managers in closely integrated groups of companies, including one-man private companies, was not referred by the *Bundesgerichtschof* to the ECJ in *TBB*[13] despite the controversial character of this question.[14] This raises the issue of when the discretion should be exercised. In Case 166/73, *Rheinmühlen*[15] the Court said that the power to make a reference arises "as soon as the judge perceives either of his own motion or at the request of the parties that the litigation depends on a point referred to in the first paragraph of Article 177."[16] Litigants are not prevented from seeking a reference on appeal, even if they had not chosen to do so at the stage below.[17]

## Criteria laid down by the European Court

**3–020**　Under Article 177(2), national courts and tribunals therefore have a wide discretion in deciding when to make references. Even with regard to the mandatory obligation in respect of Article 177(3), the duty to refer to the ECJ questions concerning the interpretation of Community law, such as the interpretation of directives, is not an absolute duty. In Case 283/81, *CILFIT* v. *Italian Ministry of Health*[18] the Court of Justice made it clear that final courts are in the same position as other national courts. They are not obliged to make a reference whenever a party contends that a question of Community law is at issue. For example, there is no obligation to refer (although there does remain a power) where the point has been adequately covered by a previous Court ruling. There is also no obligation to refer where the correct application of Community law may be so obvious as to leave no scope for any reasonable doubt as to the manner in which the question raised is to be resolved. This is commonly known as the *acte clair* doctrine.[19]

However, before reaching this conclusion, national courts must keep in mind that the matter must be equally obvious to the courts of the other Member States and to the Court of Justice. In that context, the European Court in *CILFIT* made it clear that various factors had to be borne in mind. First, the fact that Community legislation is drafted in several languages and the different language versions are all equally authentic. An interpretation of a provision of Community law thus involves a comparison of the different language versions. Secondly, even where the different language versions are entirely in accord with each other, it must be remembered that Community law uses terminology which is peculiar to it. Legal concepts of Community law therefore do not necessarily have the same meaning as in the law of the various

---

[13] *Zeitschrift Für Wirtschaftsrecht*, 1993, 589.

[14] See also *Ninth Annual Report on Commission Monitoring of the Application of Community Law* (1991) COM (92) 136 final, May 12, 1992, p. 113.

[15] Case 166/73, *Rheinmühlen*: [1974] E.C.R. 33, [1974] 1 C.M.L.R. 523.

[16] *Ibid.*, pp. 38 to 39.

[17] See *R.* v. *The Pharmaceutical Society of Great Britain, ex p. The Association of Pharmaceutical Importers* [1987] 3 C.M.L.R. 951 at p. 954, para. 3.

[18] Case 283/81, *CILFIT*: [1982] E.C.R. 3415, [1983] 1 C.M.L.R. 472.

[19] Weatherill, "Regulating the Internal Market: Result Orientation in the House of Lords" (1992) 17 E.L.Rev. 299 at p. 305.

Member States. Thirdly, every provision of Community law must be placed in its context and interpreted in the light of the provisions of Community law as a whole, regard being had to the objectives thereof and to its state of evolution at the date on which the provision in question is to be applied.

### Application of the criteria in the Freight Transport case

The criteria set out by the Court in the *CILFIT* case are also relevant **3–021** where Article 177(2) applies and may be applied by national courts to properly decline to exercise their discretion to make a reference. These criteria suggest that in very complex cases, the national court ought to refer. In *R.* v. *London Boroughs Transport Committee, ex parte Freight Transport Association*[20] the House of Lords did not do so, and it appears that the Freight Transport Association have complained about the non-referral to the European Commission.[21] In the *Freight Transport Association* case, the House of Lords considered the application of Council Directives 70/157 (the sound level Directive) and 71/320 (the brake Directive). These Directives harmonised, throughout the E.C., the permissible sound levels of vehicles and exhaust systems and laid down the technical requirements for vehicle brakes. The Directives also provided that the sale, registration or use of a vehicle could not be prohibited on grounds relating to its brakes, sound level or exhaust system if the vehicle conformed to the requirements laid down by the Directive.

The traffic regulatory authority for Greater London, (subsequently, the London Borough Transport Committee) made an order under section 6 of the Road Traffic Regulation Act 1984, imposing a ban on heavy goods vehicles using residential streets in Greater London at nighttime without a permit. Permits were granted for vehicles over 16.5 tonnes which were fitted with an air brake noise suppressor. The cost of fitting a noise suppressor to affected vehicles was about £30. The respondents, who were national organisations representing the transport and distribution industries or its members, sought judicial review of the air brake noise suppressor condition imposed by the authority on the grant of permits, on the basis that it was contrary to Community law because it infringed the sound level and brake Directives.

The respondents won at first instance in the Divisional Court of the **3–022** Queen's Bench Division and in the Court of Appeal. The appellants appealed to the House of Lords and succeeded on the grounds that the condition was not contrary to the sound level and brake Directives since it was imposed for the regulation of local traffic and the protection of the environment, whereas the Directives were concerned with the control of vehicles. The House of Lords took the view that the condition was consistent with the express policy of the Commission with regard to the environment and fell within the powers exercisable by the traffic

---

[20] *R.* v. *London Boroughs Transport Committee, ex p. Freight Transport Association* [1992] 1 C.M.L.R. 5.

[21] Weatherill, *op. cit.*, n. 19, p. 318 and see dicussion at para. 3–050 below.

regulation authorities of Member States. The House of Lords did not consider that it infringed Community law and were not willing to make a reference to the Court of Justice for a ruling under Article 177 of the EEC Treaty. Lord Templeman stated that "no plausible grounds have been advanced for a reference to the European Court."[22]

This decision has been severely criticised on the basis that it ignores the guidance given by the Court of Justice in *CILFIT*[23] and may disrupt the uniform development of the Community legal order.[24] The decision in the *Freight Transport Association* case may have been influenced by the House of Lords' views on the principle of subsidiarity and the division of responsibility between Community authorities and Member States authorities.[25] In his judgment, Lord Templeman was conscious that the national authorities, through an imposition of a small burden on traders, had nevertheless achieved substantial benefit.[26] His approach may, in the view of Weatherill[27] reflect a feeling "that national regulatory initiatives deserve protection from the impact of undesirable Community free trade law." However, although the facts of the *Freight Transport Association* case may support his view, it may be a matter which would have been better resolved by the European Court of Justice, in the interests of the Community legal order as a whole.

The European Commission may bring an action under Article 169 against a Member State, for an alleged failure by national courts to give effect to Community law. However, there is no precedent for this and it is more likely that some political pressure will ensue instead, which would indicate to the House of Lords that it should not be too conservative in its approach to referrals to the European Court. However, if the Commission declines to initiate proceedings under Article 169, neither the Court of Justice nor a prejudiced individual litigant can appeal directly against a non-referring court.[28]

*Use of a second reference*

**3–023**     The approach in the *London Freight Transport Association* case may be contrasted with the approach of the House of Lords in *Webb* v. *EMO Air Cargo (U.K.) Limited*[29] which is discussed further at paragraphs 6–016 *et seq*. The *Factortame* litigation[30] also shows a considerable willingness on the part of the Divisional Court and the House of Lords to make use of the Article 177 procedure. That case is somewhat unusual in that two references were made in the same action, the first on the question of compatibility of the Merchant Shipping Act 1988 with Community law. The second *Factortame* case proceeded to the House of Lords on the

---

22 *Op. cit.*, [1991] 3 All E.R. 915 at p. 928, para. b.
23 *Op. cit.*
24 See Weatherill, *op. cit.*, n. 18, p. 305.
25 *Ibid.* at p. 304 and see further below at para. 3–050.
26 See Lord Templeman's judgment, *op. cit.*, p. 920.
27 Weatherill, *op. cit.*, n. 18, at p. 322.
28 *Ibid.*, at p. 318.
29 *Webb* v. *EMO Air Cargo (U.K.) Ltd.* [1993] 1 C.M.L.R. 259, [1992] 4 All E.R. 929.
30 Discussed at paras. 3–013 *et seq.* above.

question of whether the applicants were entitled to interim relief pending the ruling of the European Court in the first reference. In Case 14/86, *Pretore di Salò* v. *Persons Unknown*,[31] the European Court stated that a second reference:

> ". . . may be justified when the national court encounters difficulties in understanding or applying the judgment, when it refers a fresh question of law to the [European] Court, or again when it submits new considerations which might lead the [European] Court to give a different answer to a question submitted earlier."[32]

## *Refusal by the European Court to answer a question referred to it*

However, the referring court must provide sufficient factual and **3–024** legislative information or at least explain the factual circumstances on which the questions are based so that the ECJ can make a useful interpretation of Community law. Otherwise the Court may, pursuant to Article 92 of its Rules of Procedure, order that the reference be manifestly inadmissible.[33] However, as was recognised in Case 104/79, *Foglia* v. *Novello (No. 1)*[34] and in Case 244/80, *Foglia* v. *Novello (No. 2)*,[35] the Court may also refuse to answer a question referred to it. For instance, in a recent decision, Case C–83/91, *Weinand Meilicke* v. *ADV/ ORGA FA Meyer AG*,[36] the Court refused to answer questions which were hypothetical in nature. In Case C–343/90, *Manuel José Lourenço Dias* v. *Director de Alfendega do Porto*,[37] the Court refused to answer the majority of the questions referred to it because they had no connection with the dispute which the national judge was called on to resolve.[38]

## "Courts and tribunals" to which Article 177 applies

The Article 177 procedure is essentially designed to ensure the **3–025** uniform interpretation of Community law.[39] The "courts and tribunals" to which Article 177 applies is itself a question of Community law which has been broadly interpreted by the European Court.

The Court has indicated that a relevant court or tribunal for the purpose of Article 177 should have an element of public or State involvement in the composition or workings of the body so as to be regarded as exercising official authority, and secondly, it must also exhibit judicial characteristics.[40] The body must also be acting in a

---

[31] Case 14/86, *Pretore di Salò* v. *Persons Unknown*: [1987] E.C.R. 2545 at p. 2569.

[32] *Ibid.*, p. 2569.

[33] See Case C–157/92, *Pretore di Genova* v. *Banchero: The Times*, May 20, 1993. See also Joined Cases C–320–322/90, *Telemariscabruzzo SpA and Others* v. *Circostel and Others: The Times*, February 10, 1993.

[34] Case 104/79, *Foglia* v. *Novello (No. 1)*: [1980] E.C.R. 745, [1981] 1 C.M.L.R. 45.

[35] Case 244/80, *Foglia* v. *Novello (No. 2)*: [1982] E.C.R. 3045, [1982] 1 C.M.L.R. 585. See further, Collins, *European Community Law in the U.K.* (1990) p. 170.

[36] Case C–83/91, *Meilicke*: [1992] 1 E.C.R. 4871.

[37] Case C–343/90, *Lourenço Dias*: not yet reported (Portuguese).

[38] See further, Kennedy, "First Step Towards a European Certiorari?", (1993) 18 E.L.Rev. 121 to 128.

[39] See Case 166/73, *Rheinmühlen*: [1974] E.C.R. 33 at 38, [1974] 1 C.M.L.R. 523.

[40] See further Lewis, *Judicial Remedies in Public Law* (1992), p. 478.

judicial capacity in the particular case in which it seeks to make a reference.

One group of tribunals which cannot make Article 177 references are arbitrators appointed pursuant to an arbitration clause in a contract. Although they exhibit many of the requisite features, there is no link between such arbitrators and the State and the parties are not obliged by law to refer a dispute to such a body. Consequently, arbitrators may not refer matters to the European Court despite the possible commercial importance of the arbitration and the finality of the arbitrator's decision.[41] However, the national courts have a duty to ensure that arbitrators observe Community law.[42] For example, in considering whether to grant leave to appeal against an arbitration award, the Court of Appeal held that the fact that an arbitration award raises questions of Community law that were "capable of serious argument" was a relevant consideration in deciding whether to grant leave to appeal.[43]

In the U.K., in addition to references from the usual courts (including magistrates, crown courts and county courts), there have been references from VAT tribunals, the Employment Appeal Tribunal, an Industrial Tribunal, Social Security Commissioners, and the Special Commissioners for income tax.[44]

3–026   In Case C–24/92, *Corbiau* v. *Administration des Contributions*,[45] the Court held that the term "court or tribunal" for the purposes of Article 177 was to be defined in a Community context. By definition, that meant it could only be used in respect of an authority which was a third party in relation to the body or person which had adopted the decision which was the subject of the proceedings concerned. It therefore declared inadmissible a question submitted to it by the *Directeur des Contributions* (Director of Taxation) in Luxembourg. The case concerned an appeal by the applicant, Mr Corbiau, to the *Directeur des Contributions* against the refusal of the Luxembourg tax authorities to repay an alleged excess of tax deducted from him. The court held that as the head of the tax authority, the *Directeur des Contributions* did not have the status of a third party. Instead, he had a clear institutional connection with the services which had made the disputed assessment and against which the complaint before him was directed. This decision was found by the Court to be confirmed by the fact that in the event of an appeal before the *Conseil d'Etat* (State Council), the *Directeur des Contributions* would become a party to the proceedings. It therefore followed that the *Directeur des Contributions* was not a court or tribunal for the purposes of Article 177.

Lewis suggests[46] that there is also a possibility that professional disciplinary bodies such as the Law Society or the General Medical Council may also have the power to refer. He suggests that the presence

---

[41] Case 102/81, *Nordsee, Deutsche Hochseefischerei Gmbh* v. *Reederei Mond Hoschseefischerei Nordstern AG CoKG*: [1982] E.C.R. 1095.
[42] *Ibid.*
[43] *Bulk Oil Zug AG* v. *Sun International Limited* [1984] 1 W.L.R. 147.
[44] See further Lewis, *op. cit.*, n. 40, at p. 480 and Collins, *European Community Law in the U.K.* (1990), p. 147.
[45] Case C–24/92, *Corbiau* v. *Administration des Contributions: The Times*, May 20, 1993.
[46] *Ibid.*

of recourse from such bodies to the ordinary courts (either by way of judicial review or appeal on points of law) does not necessarily preclude these bodies from being brought within Article 177.[47]

However, it may be that the absence of any right of appeal to a national court or tribunal is not the only criterion. In Case 246/80, *Broekmeulen* v. *Huisarts Registratie Commissie*[48] the fact of State involvement with the body in question was a factor in the Court's decision to treat it as fully within Article 177. A professional disciplinary body such as the Law Society is unlikely to be regarded as falling within Article 177 because of its apparent independence from the State, unless a situation arises in which, for example, the Society was directly or indirectly applying, with the consent of Government authorities, Community rules governing, for instance, the right to provide professional legal services in a Member State.[49]

## Some procedural aspects of an Article 177 reference

The Article 177 procedure complements the jurisdiction of the Euro- **3–027** pean Court to review the legality of acts of Community institutions, under Article 173.[50] The typical situation in which this arises in domestic litigation is where a national measure is purportedly based on a Community act, which is itself challenged in a national court on the ground that the Community act is invalid. In this way an individual affected by a Community act has an independent right to challenge the validity of that act by way of an Article 177 action, irrespective of a direct action which may be available before the European Court under Article 173.[51] One advantage of proceeding by way of Article 177, is that the latter does not specify the grounds on which the validity of a Community act may be challenged, though in principle the grounds will be substantially similar under both Articles 177 and 173.[52] For instance, a measure may be invalid because of procedural irregularity, a conflict with a Treaty provision or even conflict with fundamental principles of law which the European Court must recognise, such as fundamental human rights of other "cognate principles" such as the protection of legitimate expectations and of acquired rights.[53]

### *Appeals against decision to make/refuse a reference*

Under the Rules of the Supreme Court[54] the reference by an English **3–028** court to the European Court is not actually transmitted until the time for appealing against that order has expired or, if an appeal is entered within that time, until the appeal has been determined or otherwise disposed of.

---

[47] For a contrary view, see Collins, *op. cit.*, n. 44, at p. 148.
[48] Case 246/80, *Broekmeulen*: [1981] E.C.R. 2311, [1982] 1 C.M.L.R. 91.
[49] See also Case 138/80, *Borker*: [1980] E.C.R. 1975, [1980] 3 C.M.L.R. 638.
[50] The 173 procedure has been discussed at para. 1–005 above.
[51] Arnull, "Referrals to the European Court" (1990) 15 E.L.Rev. 375, at p. 378. But see Case C–188/92, *TWD Textilwerke Deggendorf* v. *Germany*: March 9, 1994.
[52] Arnull, *op cit.*
[53] *Ibid.*, p. 379 and see discussion generally at paras. 3–006 *et seq.* above.
[54] Ord. 114, r. 5; the County Court Rules contain a similar provision; see Ord. 19, r. 11(5).

The Court of Appeal has jurisdiction[55] to entertain an appeal from the decision of a judge at or before the trial, to make or refuse to make a reference to the European Court.[56]

If the judge makes a reference, his decision is deemed to be final and appeal from that decision lies without leave.[57] If, however, the judge refuses to refer, his decision is interlocutory and leave to appeal is therefore necessary either from the judge himself or from the Court of Appeal.[58] A further appeal from the decision of the Court of Appeal against a decision to refer or against a refusal to refer, lies to the House of Lords, but only with the leave of the Court of Appeal or of the House of Lords.

## Form of the reference

3–029    The form of the reference is a matter for the referring court or tribunal and no requirements are laid down by Community law. References from the High Court and Court of Appeal are governed by Order 114. The reference is made by the relevant national court and it may give directions as to the manner and form of the reference.[59] A prescribed form for an order of reference has been adopted.[60]

## The tactics of delay

3–030    Finally, it is important to bear in mind that a reference to the European Court of Justice may delay by around two years a final determination of the case.[61] Partly in response to these pressures, the Court of First Instance (CFI) came into operation in 1989.[62] Despite the existence of the new Court, the workload of cases submitted to both Courts has continued to grow.[63] In 1992, for example, 438 new cases were submitted to the ECJ.[64] The CFI received 166 new applications. The prospect of assession of new Member States in the foreseeable future suggests that the workload of both institutions will continue to grow.

A plaintiff with a strong case will not wish to delay the proceedings by a reference, whereas a defendant with a weaker case may benefit from such a reference. Clearly, the issue may be determined by the importance of the E.C. point raised as well as the attitude of the national court. In the litigation broadly concerned with Sunday trading, some defendants,

---

[55] See the Supreme Court Act 1981, s.18(1)(h).
[56] See *HP Bulmer Limited* v. *J. Bollinger SA* [1974] Ch. 401.
[57] See R.S.C., Ord. 114, r.6.
[58] See the Supreme Court Act 1981, s.18(1)(h).
[59] Ord. 114, r.2(3).
[60] Form number 109, set out in *The Supreme Court Practice 1991* Vol. 2, App. A, para. 110. The Schedule was amended by R.S.C. (Amendment) 1988 (S.I. 1988, No. 298).
[61] Duffy, "Identifying and Using European Law Points", seminar documentation on "Identifying and Using E.C. Law to your Advantage in the U.K.", Tuesday, December 1, 1992, organised by IBC Legal Studies and Services Ltd. at p. 21.
[62] Its jurisdiction was extended by a Council of Ministers' decision of June 8, 1993, [1993] O.J. C156/5 referred to at para. 3–016 above.
[63] See Kennedy, "First Steps Towards a European Certiorari?" (1993) 18 E.L.Rev. 121 at 127.
[64] Kennedy, *ibid.*

in civil proceedings for breach of the Shops Act 1950 sought to rely on the EEC Treaty as a defence. For example, in *Wychavon District Council v. Midland Enterprises (Special Event) Limited*[65] the plaintiff was granted an injunction to prevent trading by the defendants in breach of the Shops Act 1950. The defendants were unsuccessful in seeking to rely on Article 30 of the EEC Treaty. The defendants sought a reference to the European Court, but this was declined. Millett J. declined to refer on the basis that he was not satisfied that the evidence necessary to enable the defendants to succeed, had been established. He went on to say that even if he had reached a different conclusion on this point:

> "Then in my discretion I would still not have referred to the question at this stage to the European Court of Justice, principally for two reasons. In the first case, the paucity of evidence is such that the European Court of Justice would be presented with insuperable difficulties. I would have delayed a reference until the evidence was in such a state that the question could be clearly formulated and the issue squarely raised before the European Court of Justice. Secondly, in all the circumstances, and having regard to the narrowness of the actual issue involved, I am satisfied that the defendants' real concern is to obtain a two-year delay so that they may continue to trade in infringement of the criminal law and at very great profit to themselves in the hope that the answers to these theoretical questions can be long delayed."[66]

In *Commissioners of Customs and Excise* v. *Samex ApS*,[67] a similar point was made by Bingham J. where he said that a reference would not be made where:

> ". . . the question is raised mischievously, not in the bona fide hope of success but in order to obstruct or delay an almost inevitable adverse judgment, denying the other parties his remedies meanwhile."[68]

However, it is relevant to consider whether the position of the party who might be adversely affected by a reference under those circumstances could be adequately protected in some other way such as the granting of an undertaking in damages.[69]

## Costs

The ECJ usually requires E.C. institutions and intervening Member    3–031
States to bear their own costs, but all other costs are normally reserved and determined by the referring English court.[70] In *R.* v. *Intervention*

---

[65] [1988] 1 C.M.L.R. 397 (Ch.D).
[66] *Ibid.*, p. 409. See further discussion at para. 10–057 below.
[67] [1983] 3 C.M.L.R. 194.
[68] *Ibid.*, p. 211.
[69] See further Arnull, *op. cit.*, n. 51, and *Portsmouth CC* v. *Richards and Quietlynn Ltd.* [1989] 1 C.M.L.R. 673 (C.A.).
[70] Duffy, *op. cit.*, n. 61 at p. 21 and see Case 62/72, *Bollman* v. *Hauptzollamt Hamburg-Waltershof*: [1973] E.C.R. 269.

*Board for Agricultural Produce, ex parte Fish Producers' Organisation Limited and Grimsby Fish Producers' Organisation Limited*[71] the Court of Appeal held that there is no *prima facie* reason why the cost of a reference to the European Court should not follow the normal rule applied in the domestic courts for non-EEC cases, *i.e.* that costs should follow the event. It was common ground between the parties that, on the undisputed facts, and in the light of the judgment of the ECJ[72] that the appeal by the Board must be allowed.

However, it was contended for the respondents that the ordinary rule contained in Order 62, rule 3 should not be applied in the circumstances of this case. In particular it was contended that the case of the Fish Producers' organisations had been arguable and of respectable cogency and that the issues raised were of importance to many other producers both in the U.K. and in other EEC countries. It was therefore argued that the resolution of the issues of law, and clarification of the principle by which they were decided, were of benefit to a larger group of interested parties.

However, it was *held* that the fact that it was an issue of European law which fell to be decided was of no significance and that the court's discretion should not be applied differently or in any special way in circumstances where the costs arose in judicial review proceedings. The Court of Appeal held that there was no reason to depart from the ordinary rule in any way and the Board was therefore entitled to its costs.[73] A reference to the ECJ is regarded as a step in the proceedings and accordingly a party to those proceedings who is legally aided is entitled to have the Legal Aid Order extended to cover the reference to the ECJ.[74]

A ruling given by the European Court under Article 177 "is binding on the national court as to the interpretation of the Community provisions and acts in question."[75] This obligation is reinforced in the U.K. by section 3(1) of the European Communities Act 1972.[76]

## CONCURRENT JURISDICTION OF NATIONAL COURTS WITH THE COMMISSION

**3–032**    The rules relating to competition in the E.C. are to be found in Articles 85 to 94 of the E.C. Treaty. In particular, Articles 85 and 86 deal with anti-competitive behaviour and the abuse of a dominant position by "undertakings", which include private individuals and

---

[71] R. v. *Intervention Board for Agricultural Produce, ex p. Fish Producers' Organisation Ltd. and Grimsby Fish Producers' Organisation Ltd.* [1993] 1 C.M.L.R. 707.

[72] Reported in [1990] I E.C.R. 3803, [1991] 2 C.M.L.R. 853.

[73] *Op. cit,* n. 71 at p. 710, para. 13.

[74] R. v. *Marlborough Street Stipendiary Magistrates, ex p. Bouchereau* [1977] 1 W.L.R. 414 (Divisional Court).

[75] Case 52/76, *Benedetti* v. *Munari:* [1977] E.C.R. 163.

[76] See further Chap. 8 below and on the relationship between Community law and national law see generally Chap. 2 above.

organisations. The European Commission is given powers pursuant to Article 87 and Article 89 to deal with infringements of Community competition policy. However, this jurisdiction is not an exclusive one and national authorities may also apply E.C. competition rules. Article 9(3) of Regulation 17/62 implementing Articles 85 and 86 of the Treaty[77] provides that:

". . . as long as the Commission has not initiated any procedure under Articles 2, 3 or 6, the authorities of the Member States shall remain competent to apply Article 85(1) and Article 86 in accordance with Article 88 of the Treaty; they shall remain competent in this respect notwithstanding that the time limit specified in Article 5(1) and in Article 7(2) relating to notification have not expired."

National courts may therefore (subject to Article 9(3) of Regulation 17/62) consider allegations of infringements under either Article 85 or 86 of the E.C. Treaty. This was confirmed by the Advocate General Mayras in Case 127/73, *BRT* v. *Sabam*,[78] to the effect that:

". . . As the prohibitions of Articles 85(1) and 86 tend by their very nature to produce direct effects in relations between individuals, these Articles create direct rights in respect of the individuals concerned which the national courts must safeguard."

The Commission has itself recognised that the task of national courts is thus not merely to decide on the applicability of Articles 85 and 86 in cases brought before them, but also the determination of the effects in private law of these prohibitions. National courts must therefore protect individual rights where Articles 85 and 86 have been infringed. In February 1993, the Commission issued a Notice clarifying the application of EEC's competition rules by national courts.[79] The Notice does not relate to competition rules governing the transport sector, namely, rail, road, inland waterway, maritime and air transportation,[80] nor does it relate to the competition rules laid down in the Treaty establishing the European Coal and Steel Community.[81] It is issued for guidance and does not restrict rights conferred on individuals or companies by Community law[82] and is without prejudice to any interpretation given by the ECJ.[83]

---

[77] [1962] O.J. Spec.Ed. 87, as amended J.O. 1655/62, J.O. 2696/63; [1971] J.O. L285/48.
[78] Case 127/73, *BRT* v. *Sabam*: [1974] E.C.R. 51, [1974] 2 C.M.L.R. 23B at para. 16.
[79] "Notice on co-operation between national courts and the Commission in applying Articles 85 and 86 of the EEC Treaty" [1993] O.J. C39/5.
[80] See Notice, *ibid.* and explanation by Goh, "Enforcing Competition Law in Member States" (1993) 3 E.C.L.R. 114 at p. 116.
[81] See Notice, *op. cit.*, n. 79, para. 45. In Case C–128/92, *H. J. Banks and Company Ltd.* v. *British Coal Corporation*, Opinion of Advocate General Van Gerven delivered on October 27, 1993, not yet reported, the Commission stated at the hearing that the reason for the exclusion of the Notice in relation to the ECSC Treaty is merely because of procedural difficulties (in particular because Regulation No. 17 applies only to EEC cases) between the rules of the EEC Treaty and those of the ECSC Treaty. However, the Commission added that that does not prevent the Notice from extending *mutatis mutandis* to the application of the ECSC Treaty rules; see Opinion of the Advocate General at para. 57.
[82] See Notice, *op. cit.*, n. 79, para. 46.
[83] *Ibid.*, at para. 47.

## Role of the Commission: Protection of the Community interest

**3–033**    However, the intention of the Notice is to encourage national courts to apply EEC competition rules more frequently and encourages a more decentralised policy. The Notice recognises that the administrative resources at the Commission's disposal for the implementation of Community competition policy are necessarily limited. The Commission therefore intends:

> ". . . in implementing its decision-making powers, to concentrate on notifications, complaints and own-initiative proceedings having particular political, economic or legal significance for the Community. Where these features are absent in a particular case, notifications will normally be dealt with by means of comfort letter and complaints should, as a rule, be handled by national courts or authorities."

In other words, the Notice emphasises that the Commission's role is to further and protect the *general* or Community *public* interest.[84] In Case T–24/90, *Automec* v. *Commission*,[85] the Commission considered that there will not normally be a sufficient Community interest in a case when the plaintiff is able to secure adequate protection of his rights before the national courts. In these circumstances, the complaint will normally be filed and no further action taken.[86] National courts, on the other hand, have the task of safeguarding the subjective rights of private individuals in their relations with one another.

The *Automec* case has been described by the Right Hon. Sir Leon Brittan, Q.C. as the basis of the Commission's policy with regard to complaints:

> "Where there is no important Community interest at stake, either in economic terms or in relation to important questions of legal precedent, and redress is available at national level because appropriate legal instruments exist to undertake the necessary fact-finding and order any necessary remedies, the complainant will be referred to the Member State in question."[87]

This policy is, in his view, underpinned by the principle of subsidiary.[88] The requirement in the *Automec* case that the Commission will not take up a complaint if redress is available in the national courts is itself open to legal challenge. In particular, Judge David Edward (now a judge of the ECJ), in his dissenting opinion as Advocate General, pointed out that the Commission is under a duty to take complaints seriously. He suggested that a complainant to the Commission under Regulation 17

---

[84] Riley, "More Radicalism, Please: The Notice on Co-operation between National Courts and the Commission in Applying Articles 85 and 86 of the EEC Treaty" (1993) 3 E.C.L.R. 91 at p. 91. See also Richard Whish, "The Enforcement of E.C. Competition Law in the Domestic Courts of Member States" (January 1994) E.B.L.R. 5, 3 to 9.

[85] Case T–24/90, *Automec* v. *Commission*: [1992] II E.C.R. 2223, [1992] 5 C.M.L.R. 431, paras 91 to 94.

[86] See Notice, *op. cit.*, at n. 79, paras. 14 and 15.

[87] Brittan, "The Future of E.C. Competition Policy" (1993) E.B.L.Rev. 27 at p. 27.

[88] Brittan, *ibid.* and see further paras. 3–046 *et seq.* below.

who was not able to obtain a decision by the Commission, may be able to bring an action for "failure to act" under Article 175, if the Commission failed to proceed to a decision on that complaint.[89]

## The advantage/disadvantage of actions in domestic courts in competition cases

### Commission's view of advantages in national court proceedings

The Notice does not give guidance on the circumstances when **3–034** proceedings will be regarded as having "particular political, economic or legal significance of the Community." It does, however, indicate in the Notice the advantages which national courts have in respect of the application of Community competition law. These are listed in paragraph 16 as follows:

"— the Commission cannot award compensation for loss suffered as a result of an infringement of Article 85 or Article 86. Such claims may be brought only before the national courts. Companies are more likely to avoid infringements of the Community competition rules if they risk having to pay damages or interest in such an event;

— national courts can usually adopt interim measures and order the ending of infringements more quickly than the Commission is able to do;

— before national courts, it is possible to combine a claim under Community law with a claim under national law. This is not possible in a procedure before the Commission;

— in some Member States, the courts have the power to award legal costs to the successful applicant. This is never possible in the administrative procedure for the Commission."

### Some practical disadvantages of national court proceedings

Some of these perceived advantages may be illusory. National judges **3–035** are often ill-equipped for dealing with the economic issues which are often at the heart of competition law cases and may lack information about them. Actual awards of damages in national courts are negligible.[90] The assessment of damages and the difficulty of proving causation, *i.e.* that but for the breach of the duty the damage would not have occurred, are further difficulties. Costs are also rarely awarded on a full indemnity basis.[91] The procedures of discovery and the doctrine of privilege are further obstacles to domestic litigation in the U.K.[92]

Furthermore, as Riley points out,[93] since 1974 when Case 127/73, *Belgishe Radio en Televisi* v. *SABAM*[94] was decided, few cases have in

---

[89] See further, Riley, *op. cit.*, n. 84, at p. 93.

[90] See (Spring 1993), *Competition Law Bulletin*, Linklaters and Paines, p. 9.

[91] *Ibid.*

[92] *Ibid.*, at p. 10.

[93] Riley, *op. cit.*, n. 84, p. 92.

[94] Case 127/73, *Belgishe Radio en Televisie* v. *SABAM*: [1974] E.C.R. 51, [1974] 2 C.M.L.R. 238.

fact been brought before the national courts on the basis of either Article 85 or 86. Riley suggests that one reason for this is the various advantages to a complainant of bringing a complaint to the Commission rather than before national courts. His observations are very pertinent and are quoted below in full:

"A complaint to the Commission can be very cheap. A complaint can be anonymous. Anonymity is of great importance when the complainant is one of a number of small businesses who are threatened by the practices of much larger competitiors. In addition, the Commission has considerable fact-finding powers culminating in its power to carry out on-the-spot inspections under Article 14 of Regulation 17. Often a resolution satisfactory to the complainant can be found quickly as a result of intervention by the Commission, either by making an enquiry or taking interim measures. By contrast, the difficulties that face a plaintiff in the national courts will put off all but the most resilient and wealthy. Clearly, a plaintiff before a national court has no anonymity and, in most Member States, faces considerable cost penalties if he loses the case. As a result, many small and medium-sized businesses, the likely victims of anti-competitive practices, are unable to consider bringing an action before a national court.

The greatest disadvantages facing a plaintiff before national courts relates to evidence and quantum. Evidence is often difficult and sometimes impossible to obtain. Even where discovery procedures exist they are likely to be abused. A defendant is not knowingly going to surrender papers that will result in a fine or an award of damages being made against him, even to his own lawyer. Many of the successful cases before national courts have relied on the official report or decision of a national competition authority or the Commission. Furthermore, the difficulties and uncertainties of assessing a plantiff's loss in a competition action make the bringing of a national court action even more hazardous to a plaintiff. Plaintiffs often face the difficulty of pleading cases before national court judges who are unfamiliar with competition law concepts."[95]

Riley therefore argues persuasively that it will be difficult to see how the Commission will be able to convince complainants that they are better off by bringing legal actions in national courts.[96]

### The absence of a remedy

3–036    However, there may be instances where neither the Commission nor the national court can provide a remedy. In the *Automec* case[97] the plaintiff Automec complained to the European Commission that the conduct of BMW, AG and BMW Italia SpA, was an infringement of Article 85 of the Treaty of Rome. It asked the Commission to adopt two

---

[95] Riley, *op. cit.*, n. 84.
[96] *Ibid.*, p. 93.
[97] *Ibid.*

specific measures against BMW. The first was an order requiring it to give effect to Automec's instructions to supply it with an order for cars, and secondly an order requiring BMW to permit Automec to use certain of its trade marks. By a decision dated February 28, 1990, the Commission rejected these requests pursuant to Article 3(2) of Regulation 17/62.

On appeal to the Court of First Instance, the CFI held, dismissing the application, that although Article 85(1) prohibited certain anti-competitive agreements and practices, it was for national law to define the further consequences which flowed from a breach of Article 85. The contractual freedom of parties was of the utmost importance and, in principle, the Commission could not legitimately be required to use its mandatory powers of suppressing breaches of Article 85, by forcing a party to enter into a contract. In the circumstances of the case, the Commission was not, therefore, empowered to issue specific orders that BMW should supply the applicant with stocks, or allow it to use BMW's trade mark. It is likely that even under English law, for example, although the Court has power in an appropriate case to award damages or grant an injunction, it could not, for instance, require a company to enter into a contract on agreed terms.[98]

## Some advantages of complaints to the Commission

The effect of the Notice is that the existence of a "Community interest **3–037** point", as well as the availability or non-availability of national remedies, will need to be considered before deciding to complain to the European Commission about alleged anti-competitive practices. It may still be possible to persuade the Commission to investigate a complaint where, for example, there may be a number of potential defendants, most of whom are based in jurisdictions other than that of the plaintiff. Alternatively, there may be cases when discovery of relevant documents may be more effectively obtained by the Commission by using its wide investigative powers under Regulation 17/62. These powers may be far more effective than the rules of evidence and principles of discovery usually applicable in civil litigation.[99] A further instance could be where interim orders are required and need to be enforced in a number of Member States. The Notice makes it clear that there is not normally a sufficient Community interest "when the plaintiff is able to secure adequate protection of his rights before the national courts."[1] This implies that national remedies are in fact available. However, there may be occasions when they are not, as discussed above.

## The general principle of non-discrimination

The Notice does reiterate some general principles relevant to the **3–038** question of remedies. In paragraph 11, the Commission confirms that it considers that the principles which govern procedures and remedies for

---

[98] See further *Leyland Daf Ltd.* v. *Automotive Products Plc: The Times*, April 6, 1993, discussed at para. 10–005 below.

[99] Kon and de Souza, "EEC Competition Law: Enforcment by National Courts" (June 1993), P.L.C., 27 at p. 30.

[1] Notice on co-operation between national courts and the Commission in applying Articles 85 and 86 of the EEC Treaty: [1993] O.J. C39/5, at para. 15.

invoking directly applicable Community law applies in the event of breach of the Community competition rules, and that individuals and companies must have access to all procedural remedies provided for by national law on the same conditions as would apply if a comparable breach of national law were involved. This equality of treatment is intended to cover both the application of substantive law, as well as rules of procedure. In particular, the Notice states in paragraph 11 that:

". . . it is the right of parties subject to Community law that national courts should take provisional measures, that an effective end should be brought, by injunction, to the infringement of Community competition rules of which they are victims, and that compensation should be awarded for the damage suffered as a result of infringements, where such remedies are available in proceedings relating to similar national law."

However, this does not resolve the issue which arises where such remedies are not available in national law, but there are nevertheless breaches of Community law. It is also suggested by Riley[2] that more radical action is required to protect effectively the competition law rights of plaintiffs, such as the adoption, by Community regulation if necessary, of common rules of procedure, *e.g.* by introducing legal presumptions against defendants or deeming certain kinds of conduct to be an infringement of the competition rules, subject to rebuttal by the defendant. A tariff system for setting levels of damages for various kinds of anti-competitive behaviour would be a possible solution to issues of quantum of damages. Harmonisation of rules relating to civil procedure such as the obtaining of evidence and the admissibility of evidence as well as the recovery of costs by successful plaintiffs is also necessary.[3]

## Simultaneous application of Community competition rules by national courts

3–039    On the issue of conflict between Community law and national law, the Notice makes clear in paragraph 12 that the simultaneous application of national competition law is compatible with the application of Community law, "provided that is does not impair the effectiveness and uniformity of Community competition rules and the measures taken to enforce them." In particular:

". . . Any conflicts which may arise when national and Community competition law are applied simultaneously must be resolved in accordance with the principle of the precedence of Community law."[4]

---

[2] Riley, "More Radicalism Please: The Notice on Co-operation between National Courts and the Commission in Applying Articles 85 and 86 of the EEC Treaty" (1993) 3 E.C.L.R. 91 at p. 84.
[3] See (Spring 1993) *Competition Law Bulletin*, Linklaters and Paines, p. 11.
[4] The Notice cites Case 14/68, *Walt Wilhelm and Others* v. *Bundeskartellamt*: [1969] E.C.R. 1, [1969] C.M.L.R. 100; Joined Cases 253/78 and 1–3/79, *Procureur de la République* v. *Giry and Guerlain*: [1980] E.C.R. 2327, [1981] 2 C.M.L.R. 99.

The overall effect of the Notice is clearly to increase the opportunities of litigating competition points before national courts either in addition to or as well as referring these matters to the European Commission by way of a complaint. The range of "tactical and procedural options for litigators making or defending competition claims before English courts" is therefore increased.[5]

Some guidance is given in Section IV of the Notice. This makes clear that Articles 85 and 86 may be applied by national courts in various situations. Under paragraph 18, the Notice confirms that:

". . . the direct effect of Article 85(1) and Article 86 gives national courts sufficient powers to comply with their obligation to hand down judgments. Nevertheless, when exercising these powers, they must take account of the Commission's powers in order to avoid decisions which could conflict with those taken or envisaged by the Commission in applying Article 85(1) and Article 86, and also Article 85(3)."[6]

### Establishing the extent of Commission involvement

The first issue which national courts have to consider, is whether the **3–040** agreement, decision or concerted practice infringes the prohibitions laid down in Article 85(1) or Article 86. To answer this, they should first ascertain whether the agreement, decision or concerted practice has already been the subject of a decision, opinion or other official statement issued by the administrative authority and in particular by the Commission. The Notice makes clear that not all procedures before the Commission lead to an official decision, but even a "comfort letter", though not binding on national courts, is nevertheless a statement of the opinion of the Commission and is a factor which the national courts may take into account in determining whether agreements or conduct in question are in accordance with the provisions of Article 85.

However, there is some doubt about the admissibility of comfort letters or Commission opinions as evidence by English courts.[7] It is clear that although parties are usually entitled to rely on comfort letters they do not have any binding effect.[8] In *Intrepreneur Estates Ltd.* v. *Mason*,[9] Mr M. Barnes, Q.C. sitting as Deputy Judge of the High Court was prepared, in accordance with the Commission Notice, to take account of letters written by the Commission but which fell short of being comfort letters.[10] However, he recognised that even on the basis that they could be regarded as comfort letters, there was a real argument as to their status or legal effect in Community law, and therefore in national law.[11] The case was, however, decided on other grounds.

---

[5] See Duffy, "E.C. Practice Briefing" (March 5, 1993), S.J. 196.

[6] The Notice cites Case C–234/89, *Delimitis* v. *Henninger Bräu*: [1991] I E.C.R. 935, [1992] 5 C.M.L.R. 201, para. 47.

[7] Kon and de Souza, "EEC Competition Law: Enforcement of National Courts" (June 1993) P.L.C. 27 at p. 32.

[8] See Case 99/79, *Lancôme*: [1980] E.C.R. 2511, [1981] 2 C.M.L.R. 164 and Notice, *op. cit.*, n. 1, para. 20.

[9] [1993] 2 C.M.L.R. 293 (H.L.) Q.B.D.

[10] *Ibid.*, para. 45.

[11] *Ibid.*, para. 54.

In Case C–128/92, *H.J. Banks and Company Limited* v. *British Coal Corporation*[12] (awaiting judgment by the European Court), the High Court has referred to the ECJ for a preliminary ruling, *inter alia*, the question of the extent to which a national court is bound by a decision of the Commission with regard to the issues of fact and/or law concerning competition law articles of the ECSC and EEC Treaties. In his Opinion, the Advocate General Van Gerven drew a distinction between administrative (or comfort) letters and negative clearance, and formal decisions of the Commission (para. 60). In his view, the latter carry greater significance than administrative letters and negative clearance. In this connection, he referred to the earlier case law of the Court in the 'Perfume' cases where the Court determined that administrative letters:

". . . do not have the effect of preventing national courts, before which the agreements in question are alleged to be incompatible with Article 85, from reaching a different finding as regards the agreements concerned on the basis of the information available to them." (Judgment in Joined Cases 253/78, 1–3/79 *Procureur de la République* v. *Giry and Guerlain*: [1980] E.C.R. 2327, [1981] 2 C.M.L.R. 99 at para. 13.)

However, the Court added:

". . . Whilst it does not bind the national courts, the Opinion transmitted in such letters nevertheless constitutes a factor which the national courts may take into account in examining whether the agreements or conduct in question are in accordance with the provisions of Article 85." (*Giry and Guerlain*, at para. 13.)

The Advocate General went on to consider in *Banks* the extent to which findings of fact and/or of law in formal decisions of the Commission were binding on a national court. He drew attention to the fact that the Commission was a body which supervises compliance with the Community rules of competition and has specialised departments for that purpose. It also has many years of experience, with the result, in his view, that its findings carry a degree of authority, although such authority is not binding (para. 60).

In his view, if, having heard the arguments of the parties, the national court comes to the conclusion that the issues of fact and/or law decided by the Commission are incorrect or insufficient, or, if it has serious doubts in that regard, then in the light of the judgment in Case C–234/89, *Delimitis*,[12a] it must take the following course of action; in the case of findings which carried no weight in the final decision in the Commission and do not therefore underlie the reasoning of the Commission, the national court is at liberty to adopt a different interpretation (para. 60). However, where the findings have had a decisive influence on the final decision arrived at by the Commission, the national court is well

---

[12] Case C–128/92, *Banks* v. *British Coal Corporation*: Opinion of the Advocate General Van Gerven delivered on October 27, 1993, not yet reported. Discussed further at paras. 8–016 *et seq.* and 10–010 below.

[12a] [1991] I E.C.R. 935, [1992] 5 C.M.L.R. 201.

advised, in accordance with the provisions of its national procedural law, to suspend the proceedings in the case and to seek the necessary information from the Commission, or to make a direct reference to the Court for a preliminary ruling concerning the validity of the decision in question or the interpretation of the relevant Community competition rules (para. 61).

The Advocate General concluded in the *Banks* case that the national court is therefore not bound by a Commission decision involving the application of Article 65(1) and/or Article 67(7) of the ECSC Treaty. (These broadly correspond with Article 85(1) and Article 86 of the E.C. Treaty, as amended, although there are some notable differences of wording.) However, he made it clear that in his view, the duty of co-operation contained in Article 86 of the ECSC Treaty, (which corresponds with Article 5 of the E.C. Treaty, as amended), placed the national court under a duty to mitigate as far as possible the risk of a ruling that conflicts with a Commission decision.

If, however, the Commission has not ruled on the same agreement, decision or concerted practice, the national courts should always be guided by the case law of the ECJ and existing decisions of the Commission. This includes Commission Notices, for example, which specify that certain categories of agreements are not caught by the ban laid down in Article 85(1).[13]

## Stay of proceedings in national courts

If the Commission has initiated a procedure relating to the same **3–041** conduct, the national courts may, if they consider it necessary for reasons of legal certainty, stay the proceedings while awaiting the outcome of the Commission's action.[14] A stay of proceedings may also be envisaged where national courts wish to seek the Commission's views in accordance with the Notice itself. However, there is no specific procedure for U.K. courts to refer such points to the Commission, either on points of law or issues of economic analysis. It will therefore be of interest to see whether English courts will be amenable to such a course of action. Finally, where national courts have persistent doubts on questions of compatibility, they may also stay proceedings in order to make a reference under Article 177 to the ECJ.[15]

If, however, the agreement of conduct has been notified to the Commission, and the national court finds, nevertheless, that in effect Article 85(1) or Article 86 are not applicable, the national proceedings may continue on the basis of such a finding, even if the agreement or conduct in question has been notified to the Commission. Where, however, the assessment of the facts shows Article 85(1) or Article 86 do apply:

> ". . . national courts must rule that the conduct at issue infringes Community competition law and take the appropriate measures,

---

[13] See further Notice, *op. cit.*, n. 1, para. 21, n. 4.

[14] Notice, *ibid.*, at para. 22.

[15] Notice, *ibid.*, at para. 22.

including those relating to the consequences that attach to infringement of a statutory prohibition under the civil law applicable."

### Effect of the Commission's sole power of exemption

**3–042**    However, it is important to note that the Commission retains the *sole*
power to grant an exemption under Article 85(3). This means that if a
national court concludes that an agreement, decision or concerted
practive *is* prohibited by Article 85(1), it must check whether it is or will
be the subject of an exemption by the Commission under Article 85(3).
This means that the national court must first examine whether the
procedural conditions necessary for securing exemption are fulfilled,
notably whether the agreement, decision or concerted practice has been
duly notified in accordance with Article 4(1) of Regulation 17.[16] Where
no such notification has been made, and subject to Article 4(2) of
Regulation 17, exemption under Article 85(3) is ruled out, so that the
national court may decide, pursuant to Article 85(2), that the agreement,
decision or concerted practice is void.[17]

If, however, the agreement, decision or concerted practice has been
duly notified, the national court must then assess the likelihood of an
exemption being granted.[18] For this purpose, it may suspend the
proceedings if it takes the view that an individual exemption is possible,
and may await the Commission's decision. It nevertheless remains free,
according to the rules of national law, to adopt any interim measures it
deems necessary.[19]

In order to decide whether the agreement or conduct falls within
Article 85(1) in the first place, it is also necessary to consider whether the
agreement is subject to either an individual or block exemption. If so, in
the case of a block exemption, the national court must assess whether the
agreement comes within the criteria for exemption and if it does, or if an
individual exemption has already been granted, then the court's duty is
to uphold the validity of the agreement.[20] If, on the other hand, the
agreement is incompatible with the requirements for a block exemption
then the national court must take measures to enforce European competition law. If there is neither a block nor individual exemption in
existence, then the procedure described in the paragraphs above applies
and the national court must assess the likelihood of an Article 85(3)
exemption being granted by the Commission.

### Applications for interlocutory ruling

**3–043**    In *Fyffes Plc* v. *Chiquita Brands International Inc*,[21] the facts were that
the second plaintiff and the first defendant had for many years imported
and sold bananas under various "Fyffes" trade marks. The first defen-

---

[16] *Ibid.*, at para. 28.

[17] *Ibid.*, at para. 28.

[18] *Ibid.*, at para. 29.

[19] *Ibid.*, at para. 30.

[20] See Dalby and MacLean, "New Era of Trust within the European Community" (1993)
137 S.J. 325 at p. 326.

[21] *Fyffes Plc and Another* v. *Chiquita Brands International Inc. and Another* [1993] E.C.C.
193.

dant's bananas were imported from South America and sold in continental Europe where they held several national registrations for "Fyffes"
marks. The bananas of the second plaintiff, which was formally a wholly-
owned subsidiary of the first defendant, were imported from the
Caribbean and sold in the U.K. In 1986, the first plaintiff bought the
second plaintiff from the first defendant, subject to an agreement
regulating the use of the "Fyffes" trade marks outside the U.K. and
Ireland.

The second plaintiff began to import into and sell in continental
Europe under other trade marks. After the period from 1986 to 1989
when it had unrestricted use of the "Fyffes" trade marks outside the
U.K. and Ireland, the second plaintiff attempted to avoid the non-use
provisions in its agreement with the first defendant by complaining to the
E.C. Commission that those provisions were unlawful under Articles 85
and 86 of the EEC Treaty. In two statements of objections, the
Commission stated that it proposed to find an infringement.

In the English High Court, the plaintiffs sought interlocutory injunctions to prevent the defendants (a) from enforcing any purported rights
in "Fyffes" trade marks in continental Europe, (b) from using the
"Fyffes" marks there, and (c) from enforcing the non-use provisions.
The defendants also sought injunctions to restrain the plaintiffs from
selling bananas under the "Fyffes" marks in continental Europe.

The plaintiffs, in applying for injunctive relief, submitted that the
High Court should treat the Commission's statement of objections as
concluding the question whether the non-use provisions infringed Article
85 and the question whether the first defendant, Chiquita's, threatened
use of the trade mark registered in continental Europe or Chiquita's
application for an interlocutory injunction was a breach of Article 86, at
least until the Commission or ECJ reached a contrary conclusion.

However, it was held by Vinelott J. that until a final decision was **3–044**
reached, the task of the Enlish court was to find a just way of regulating
the position between the parties. He pointed out that the Commission
had not made a final decision and that there was to be a full oral hearing
scheduled to last about four days in the following month. The defendant,
Chiquita, had put in further elaborate submissions and even if the
Commission was not persuaded to retract from its statement of objections, it would be open to Chiquita to seek a review in the ECJ. He said
that the (domestic) court:

"... will attach a very great weight to a decision (even a provisional
decision) of the Commission which is charged with the administration and enforcement of those provisions of the Treaty which are
designed to liberalise trade in the European Community. But until a
final decision has been reached, the task of this Court is to find a
just way of regulating the position between the parties."[22]

It was eventually held in the *Fyffes* case that, given that damages may
not be an adequate remedy for either party, the Court must weigh the

---

[22] *Fyffes, op. cit.*, p. 211 at para. 63.

balance of convenience and in the judgment of Vinelott J., where other factors appear to be evenly balanced, it is "a council of prudence to take such measures as may preserve the status quo."[23] He concluded that it would be premature to grant any interlocutory relief until the defendant, Chiquita, had had an opportunity of discussing with the Commission whether, if the Commission maintained its view that the non-use provisions infringed Article 85(1), those provisions were capable of being modified, for instance by being limited to bananas and for a period of less than seventeen years, in such a way as not to infringe Article 85(1).

In his judgment therefore, consideration of the balance of convenience led irresistibly to the conclusion that the plaintiff, Fyffes, were not entitled to an interlocutory injunction at this stage and that the defendant, Chiquita, was entitled to a continuation of the interlocutory injunction granted earlier by Morritt J.[24] It is suggested by Kon and de Souza[25] that the case may be illustrative of a reticence by national courts to enforce Article 85 in the manner envisaged by the Notice, i.e. by relying on preliminary statements of opinion by the Commission. However, it may be argued on the contrary that in the context of interlocutory proceedings, the court was simply applying the usual and well-settled tests regarding the balance of convenience, and that the reluctance of the High Court to grant an injunction in the absence of a final decision by the Commission was therefore justifiable.[26]

## Procedural aspects of co-operation by national courts with the Commission

**3–045**     Section V of the Notice[27] provides for a mechanism for co-operation between the national courts and the Commission. In particular, national courts may ask for information of a procedural nature to enable them to discover whether a certain case is pending before the Commission, whether a case has been the subject of a notification, whether the Commission has officially initiated a procedure or whether it has already taken a position through an official decision or through a comfort letter sent by its services. If necessary, national courts may also ask the Commission to give an opinion as to how much time is likely to be required for granting or refusing individual exemptions for notified agreements or practices, so as to be able to determine the conditions for any decision to suspend proceedings or whether interim measures need to be adopted.[28]

The Commission has indicated that it will endeavour to give priority to cases which are the subject of national proceedings suspended in this way, in particular when the outcome of a civil dispute depends on them.[29] National courts may also consult the Commmission on points of

---

[23] See *American Cyanamid* v. *Ethicon Ltd.* [1975] A.C. 397, *per* Lord Diplock at 408, cited by Vinelott J., *op. cit.*, n. 21, at p. 218, para. 93.

[24] *Op. cit.*, n. 21, p. 220 at paras. 98 and 99.

[25] *Ibid.*, at p. 30.

[26] See further discussion at paras. 9–033 *et seq.* and paras. 10–001 *et seq.* below.

[27] See Notice, *op. cit.*, at n.1.

[28] *Ibid.*, para. 37(2).

[29] *Ibid.*, para. 37(2).

law,[30] although the answers given by the Commission are not binding on national courts which have requested them.[31] There is, however, no formal procedure in U.K. law whereby the national courts may adopt this course of action and it may require statutory amendments.

National courts can also obtain information from the Commission regarding factual data: statistics, market studies and economic analysis.[32] The Commission will endeavour to provide this information as soon as possible, subject to availability and the principles of confidentiality.[33] However, the value of such consultation may be limited by issues of confidentiality and admissibility of evidence in national courts.[34]

In conclusion, the policy envisaged in the Notice is to establish priorities for the Commission in the policing of European competition law. In *Automec* v. *Commission*[35] the Court of First Instance confirmed that the Commission may, where redress is available at the national level, reject a complaint on the grounds of lack of Community interest. The House of Lords Select Committee on the European Communities has launched an inquiry into the enforcement of E.C. competition rules by the Commission, including the Commission's stated wish that more enforcement of competition rules should take place at national level.[36] Under para. 48, a summary of the answers given by the Commission pursuant to this Notice, will be published in its annual Competition Report.

## Application of the Merger Regulation

Finally, under the Merger Regulation[37] the Commission has specific **3–046** powers to regulate concentrations having a Community dimension which create or strengthen a position whereby competition in the Common Market, or in a substantial part of it, would be significantly impaired.[38] Some of these concentrations may be the subject of an application in the national courts, at the request of third parties, claiming an abuse of a dominant position under Article 86. However, it is suggested by Wooldridge,[39] that in respect of concentrations having a Community dimension, national courts would be reluctant to grant injunctive relief where the Commission was already involved. In respect of concentrations which, however, fall below the thresholds in the Regulation, the Commission has expressly reserved its right to take action under Article 89 of the EEC Treaty, and individual ligitants would also be free either

---

[30] *Ibid.*, para. 38.
[31] *Ibid.*, para. 39.
[32] *Ibid.*, para. 40.
[33] Dalby and MacLean, "New Era of Trust within the E.C." (1993) 137, S.J. 325 at p. 326.
[34] See (Spring 1993) *Competition Law Bulletin*, Linklaters and Paines, p. 10.
[35] *Ibid.*
[36] See *Financial Times*, May 1, 1993. See also Report on the Enforcement of E.C. Competition rules, 1993/94, H.L.P. 7/1, December 20, 1993.
[37] Adopted by the Council of Ministers on December 21, 1989, [1989] O.J. L395/1.
[38] Article 2(2) of the Regulations and see further Wooldridge, "The Council Regulation on the Control of Mergers" (1990) 3 *Law for Business* 35 to 37.
[39] Wooldridge, *op. cit.*, n. 38, p. 37.

to complain to the Commission or to pursue ligitation in national courts in these cases, applying Article 86 in the usual way.[40]

## THE CONCEPT OF "SUBSIDIARITY": RELEVANCE TO DOMESTIC LITIGATION

### Origins

3–047    The concept of subsidiarity has been referred to as ". . . shorthand for a cluster of issues about the sharing of powers between different levels of government in Western Europe."[41]

The principle has its origins in Roman Catholic social teaching,[42] and in particular the Papal Encyclical of Pius XI entitled Quadregisimo Anno. According to the teachings of Pope Pius XI, the Pope sought to reaffirm "the unique nature of man as a responsible being and a founder of social groups of ascending order."[43] It was therefore "a grave evil" for higher authorities to usurp powers which could be exercised more appropriately at a lower level. Lasok describes this concept of subsidiarity as setting "its face against the accumulation of power at the higher levels of government."[44]

### Subsidiarity within the E.C. legal order

3–048    The principle of subsidiarity is made part of the E.C. legal order by the Treaty on European Union.[45] For instance, Article A of the Treaty, in paragraph 2, Title I states that:

> "This Treaty marks a new stage in the process of creating an ever closer union among the peoples of Europe, in which decisions are taken as closely as possible to the citizen."

In Article B of the Treaty, Title II there is a more explicit mention of the principle:

> ". . . The objectives of the Union shall be achieved as provided in this Treaty and in accordance with the conditions and the timetable set out therein while respecting the principle of subsidiarity as defined in Article 3(b) of the Treaty establishing the European Community."

---

[40] See Venit, "The 'Merger' Control Regulation: Europe Comes of Age . . . or Caliban's Dinner" (1990) C.M.L.Rev. 7 at p. 10.

[41] Wilkey and Wallace, "Subsidiarity: Approaches to Power-Sharing in the European Community" (1990) RIIA Discussion Paper Number 27, London.

[42] See further, Lasok, "Subsidiarity and the Occupied Field" (September 11, 1992), New L.J. 1228 at p. 1228.

[43] See Lasok, ibid.

[44] Ibid., p. 1228.

[45] Also referred to as the Maastricht Treaty and discussed at para. 1–002 above. For text see [1992] O.J. C191/1, [1992] 1 C.M.L.R. 791. See further, Emiliou, "Subsidiarity: An Effective Barrier against 'the Enterprises of Ambition'?" (1992) 17 E.L.Rev. 383.

The key provision, in Article 3(b)(2) of the Treaty of Rome (as revised by the Treaty on European Union) states that:

". . . In areas which do not fall within its exclusive competence, the Community shall take action, in accordance with the principle of subsidiarity, only if and insofar as the objectives of the proposed action cannot be sufficiently achieved by the Member States and can therefore, by reason of the scale or effects of the proposed action, be better achieved by the Community."

The European Court at the Edinburgh Summit in December 1992 approved an overall approach to the application of the subsidiarity principle and Article 3(b) of the Treaty on European Union.[46] There appears to be general agreement, however, that subsidiarity has not been defined as a *legal* term.[47] It has been suggested by Lasok that subsidiarity, as written into the E.C. Treaty:

". . . does not change the balance of power or the division of functions in the Community since it neither extends nor restricts the Community competence. But Maastricht, moving towards an economic and monetary union, does extend the Community competence. Therefore, given its historical meaning, subsidiarity ought to be understood as a break on the adventurism of the Community institutions and the ambitions of the bureaucracy, but not an obstacle on the road mapped out by the Treaty."[48]

### Subsidiarity versus exclusive E.C. competence

Toth argues persuasively[49] that by virtue of Article 3(b)(2) of the E.C. **3–049** Treaty the principle of subsidiarity *only* applies to those areas which do *not* fall within the *exclusive* competence of the E.C. Irrespective of the principle of subsidiarity, the Community does not, for example, interfere in situations wholly internal to a Member State.[50] However, the difficulty is that there is no agreed list of matters which remain within the competence of Member States.[51] Article 235 of the E.C. Treaty does, however, provide that:

"If action by the Community should prove necessary to attain, in the course of the operation of the Common Market, one of the

---

[46] See [1992] 25 E.C. Bull, p. 46 and Annex 1. Part A at pp. 12 *et seq*. See further, Weatherill and Beaumont, *EEC Law* (1993), "Postscript: The Edinburgh European Council", p. 773.

[47] See, however, Toth, "The Principle of Subsidiarity in the Maastricht Treaty" (1992) C.M.L.Rev. 1079 at pp. 1086 *et seq*. and House of Lords Select Committee on the E.C., Session 1989–90, 27th Report, "Economic and Monetary Union and Political Union", points 23–24; *id.*, Session 1990–91, 17th Report, "Political Views, Law-Making Powers and Procedures", points 52 to 62, 90 to 99, 122.

[48] Lasok, *op. cit.*, n. 42, p. 1230 and see Emiliou, *op. cit.*, n. 45, p. 383.

[49] Toth, *op. cit.*, n. 47.

[50] See, for example, Case 44/84, *Hurd* v. *Jones (HM Inspector of Taxes)*: [1986] E.C.R. 29 at 55, [1986] 2 C.M.L.R. 1 and see further Lasok, *op. cit.*, n. 47, at p. 1230.

[51] See Clarke, "On Maastricht: An Opportunity for the Legal Profession in Europe" (February 1993) Issue 19 *Lawyers in Europe* p. 3.

objectives of the Community and this Treaty has not provided the necessary powers, the Council shall, acting unanimously on a proposal from the Commission and after consulting the European Parliamnt, take the appropriate measures."

This provision may be treated as adopting a wide formulation of the doctrine of implied powers, according to which the existence of a particular objective or function implies the existence of any power reasonably necessary to attain it.[52] However, the fact that Article 235 gives the Community the power to act does not mean that this is a *carte blanche* means of expanding Community powers. There is an express limitation in Article 235 to the operation of the Common Market so that this Article cannot alone provide for the necessary legal authority for unrelated legislative measures. In other words it cannot be used as a substitute for Treaty provisions which might otherwise provide the correct legal basis for implementing legislation.[53] In fact, it is argued by Toth[54] that far from giving effect to subsidiarity, Article 235 in fact *excludes* the application of that principle. However, so long as the Community has not claimed its competence in a particular area, Member States are free to resort to their residual powers. This is known as the doctrine of the "occupied field."[55]

The Court of Justice may be called on in future litigation to clarify the definition of subsidiarity in Article 3(b) of the revised E.C. Treaty.[56] Clarke suggests that one substantive area of law which might be affected by the principle of subsidiarity is the field of consumer protection. For example, in the context of consumer protection, Member States can currently establish stricter national rules than those provided for by the Community providing that they are not protectionist measures in disguise.[57]

Toth explains that once it can be established that a matter falls within non-exclusive Community competence, the next step is still to determine whether it in fact satisfies the test laid down in Article 3(b) of the E.C. Treaty, for the application of the subsidiarity principle.[58] He points out that Article 3(b) lays down not one, but two tests, which may lead to contradictory results.

Under the first test, the Community shall take action only if, and insofar as, the objectives to be achieved by the Community "cannot be sufficiently achieved by the Member States." He describes this as the test of effectiveness.[59] Under the second test, the Community shall take action only if, and insofar as, the objectives of that action can be better

---

[52] Joined Cases 281, 283 & 287/85, *Germany, France & U.K.* v. *Commission*: [1987] E.C.R. 3203, [1988] 1 C.M.L.R. 11.

[53] See further Lasok, *op. cit.*, n. 42, p. 1230 and Case 45/86, *E.C. Commission* v. *E.C. Council, re: Generalised Tariff Preferences*: [1987] E.C.R. 1493, [1988] 2 C.M.L.R. 131.

[54] Toth, *op. cit.*, n. 47, p. 1082.

[55] See further Lasok, *op. cit.*, n. 42, and Joined Cases 3–4, 6/76, *Officier van Justitie* v. *Kramer*: [1976] E.C.R. 1279 at 1310, [1976] 2 C.M.L.R. 440.

[56] See Clarke, *op. cit.*, n. 51, p. 3.

[57] *Ibid.*, p. 4.

[58] Toth, *op. cit.*, n. 47, p. 1097.

[59] *Ibid.*

achieved by the Community "by reason of the scale or effects of the proposed action." He describes this as the test of scale.[60]

The tests may be applied, for example, to the field of environmental protection and Toth gives the example of responsibility for environmental standards on popular beaches and argues that it is possible for the two parts of the test in Article 3(b) to lead to contradictory results. In addition, even if a matter satisfies both tests, it will be dealt with by the "Member States". This does not assist in the attainment of one of the aims of subsidiarity to ensure that "decisions are taken as closely as possible to the citizen."[61] This remains a political statement and the issue of the level at which decisions are ultimately taken, whether at central, regional or local level is a matter in which Community law cannot interfere.[62]

## Use of subsidiarity in domestic litigation

However, all these problems involved in defining subsidiarity mean **3–050** that the use of this principle will no doubt lead to test cases covering the various questions of who should decide disputes, and by what procedure, and whether the principle is in fact applicable in individual cases. The potential use of the principle of subsidiarity in domestic cases is difficult to envisage. However, one example is provided by the House of Lords decision of *R.* v. *London Boroughs Transport Committee, ex parte, Freight Transport Association.*[63] The case has been referred to at paragraph 3–021 above. The appellant, a traffic regulatory authority acting on behalf of the relevant local authorities, imposed a ban on lorry traffic at night in London, in order to reduce noise and pollution. However, licences were granted, by way of exception, for certain goods vehicles. A condition for the grant of such a licence was that the vehicle should be fitted with a device to silence air brakes, as produced by one of three specified manufacturers. The applicants in the original action contended that this condition was unlawful because it was in breach of two Community Directives laying down manufacturing standards for braking devices and sound levels for exhaust systems. They also contended that it was in breach of Article 30 of the EEC Treaty, concerning the free movement of goods.

The leading judgment was given by Lord Templeman, who did not **3–051** expressly refer to the principle of subsidiarity. However, it is suggested that this was in fact at the heart of his argument. Article 130 rule (4) of the EEC Treaty provides that:

> "The Community shall take action relating to the environment to the extent to which the objectives referred to in para. 1 can be attained better at Community level than at the level of the individual Member State. Without prejudice to certain measures of a Com-

---

[60] *Ibid.*
[61] Article A, Treaty on European Union: [1992] O.J. C191/1, [1992] 1 C.M.L.R. 719.
[62] Toth, *op. cit.*, n. 47, p. 1099.
[63] *R.* v. *London Boroughs Transport Committee, ex p. Freight Transport Association and Others* [1992] 1 C.M.L.R. 5.

munity nature, the Member States shall finance and implement the other measures."[64]

Lord Templeman said that:

". . . London's environmental traffic problems cannot be solved, although they can be ameliorated by Council Directives to control every vehicle at all times throughout the Community.

The attainment of the Community object of preserving, protecting and improving the quality of the environment requires action at level of individual Member States. A vehicle which complies with all the weight, size, sound level and other technical requirements and standards of Directives issued by the Council pursuant to Article 100 and is therefore entitled to be used in every Member State throughout the Community is not thereby entitled to be driven on every road, on every day, at every hour throughout the Community. In the interests of the environment, traffic authorities of Santiago de Compostella may ban all or some Community vehicles from medieval streets. The traffic authorities of Greater London may ban all or some Community vehicles from residential streets at night."[65]

It is suggested by Emiliou that in this way, Article 130, rule (4) of the EEC Treaty is interpreted to mean that local authorities are better equipped to attain the objectives of Article 130, rule (1) of the EEC Treaty and should be encouraged to protect the environment against damage in urban areas.[66]

## Role of the ECJ in defining subsidiarity

3–052    Clearly, the issue in the *Freight Transport Association* case was a complex one. It has been persuasively argued by Weatherill[67] that that case should have been referred to the ECJ. Certainly a case which is based substantially on the principle of subsidiarity is likely to have to be referred to the European Court of Justice for determination. It is argued by Toth,[68] that while the Court will be able to decide whether a matter falls within exclusive Community competence and is therefore excluded from the scope of the subsidiarity principle, the Court may be less willing or even unable to examine the propriety of the exercise of the discretionary powers of the Council and Commission, in a situation where the application of the principle of subsidiarity may be in dispute. In any event, the statements about subsidiarity in the preamble and in Title I of the Treaty of European Union are *excluded* from the Court's jurisdiction in the special circumstances mentioned in Article L of the Treaty of European Union.

---

[64] This Atricle has been substantially altered by the Treaty on European Union signed at Maastricht: see further, Toth, *op. cit.*, n. 47, p. 1092.

[65] *Op. cit.*, n. 63, paras. 32 to 33.

[66] Emiliou, *op. cit.*, n. 45, p. 395.

[67] Weatherill, "Regulating the Internal Market: Result Orientation in the House of Lords," (1992) 17 E.L.Rev. 299 to 322.

[68] Toth, *op. cit.*, n. 47, p. 1102.

It is suggested by Emiliou,[69] that in view of the uncertainties which arise in connection with the principle of subsidiarity, the proper role of subsidiarity in the Community legal order should simply be that of "a guiding principle for the political institutions of the Community but not a general principle of law amenable to judicial review by the Court." On the other hand it is possible that the Court may decide to develop the concept of subsidiarity, so that it does in fact join other general principles, such as the principle of proportionality, and may become an additional ground by which the Court of Justice may be able to control the legality of acts of Community institutions and Member States, for the ultimate benefit of individuals. However, it is unlikely to be relevant in the vast majority of domestic cases involving Community law. The determination of the relevance of the principle would generally require a reference for a preliminary ruling under Article 177 to the ECJ.[70]

---

[69] Emiliou, *op. cit.*, n. 45, p. 404.
[70] See further discussion at paras. 3–016 *et seq.* above.

# DIRECT EFFECT OF TREATY PROVISIONS

**4–001** The theoretical basis for determining whether a provision of the Treaty of Rome has direct effect (and can therefore be relied upon by individuals in the U.K. courts under section 3(1) of the European Communities Act 1972) was established by the European Court in Case 26/62, *Van Gend en Loos* v. *Nederlandse Administratie der Belastingen*.[1] The main issue in *Van Gend en Loos* was whether Article 12 of the Treaty of Rome "must be interpreted as producing direct effects and creating individual rights which the national courts must protect." Article 12 states that:

> "Member States shall refrain from introducing between themselves any new customs duties on imports or exports or any charges having equivalent effect, and from increasing those which they already apply in their trade with each other".

Article 12 is addressed to Member States. It does not refer to private individuals. Nevertheless, the Court concluded that it had direct effect. The test it laid down has been modified and refined by later cases. A substantial number of the Treaty provisions and of Community legislation have now also been held to have such effect.[2] The essential requirements of "directly effective" Treaty provisions have been summarised by Collins and are discussed below.[3]

## THE TREATY PROVISION MUST NOT BY ITS NATURE CONCERN ONLY RELATIONS BETWEEN STATES, *INTER SE*

**4–002** The fact that a particular provision only mentions Member States and not individuals has not prevented it from having direct effect.[4] On the

---

[1] Case 26/62, *Van Gend en Loos* v. *Nederlandse Administratie der Belastingen*: [1963] E.C.R. 1, [1963] C.M.L.R. 105. In Case C–128/92, *H.J. Banks and Company Ltd.* v. *British Coal Corporation*: Opinion of Advocate General Van Gerven delivered on October 27, 1993, not yet reported, the Advocate General stated that the criteria for direct effect developed in connection with the law relating to the EEC Treaty must also be applied as such to the ECSC Treaty; see para. 26 of the Opinion.

[2] See Oliver, "Enforcing Community Rights in the English Courts" (1987) M.L.R. 881 at p. 882. See also the helpful summary of directly effective provisions of the EEC Treaty in Collins, *European Community Law in the U.K.* (1990), 4th ed., pp. 122 *et seq.*

[3] Collins, *op. cit.*, p. 48.

[4] See Case 6/64, *Costa* v. *ENEL*: [1964] E.C.R. 585 at p. 595, [1964] C.M.L.R. 425.

other hand, if a provision is by its nature only applicable to inter-State relations, then it cannot confer direct rights.[5]

## THE TREATY PROVISION MUST BE CLEAR AND PRECISE

Various Treaty articles have been held not to have direct effect because **4–003** they lack sufficient clarity and precision. For example, Article 2 of the EEC Treaty (prior to amendments made by the Treaty on European Union), provided:

> "The Community shall have as its task, by establishing a common market and progressively approximating the economic policies of Member States, to promote throughout the Community a harmonious development of economic activities, a continuous and balanced expansion, an increase in stability, an accelerated raising of the standard of living and closer relations between the States belonging to it."

In Case 126/86 *Gimnez Zaera* v. *Instituto Nacional de la Seguridad Social*[6] this Article was held not to have direct effect because of its general terms and the fact that it depends on the progressive approximation of economic policies.

Similarly, Article 5 was held in Case 28/67, *Molkeroi-Zentrale Westfalen* v. *Hamptzollampt Paderborn*[7] not to be directly effective. Article 5 provides that:

> "Member States shall take all appropriate measures, whether general or particular, to ensure fulfilment of the obligations arising out of this Treaty or resulting from action taken by the institutions of the Community. They shall facilitate the achievement of the Community's tasks.
>
> They shall abstain from any measure which could jeopardise the attainment of the objectives of this Treaty."

It lays down a general policy objective without specifying the measures by which these are to be achieved and is therefore too imprecise to be effective without further legislation.

Another example is Article 6(1) of the EEC Treaty which provided:

> "Member States shall, in their co-operation with the institutions of the Community, co-ordinate their respective economic policies to the extent necessary to attain the objectives of this Treaty."

It is suggested by Hartley[8] that this provision is also too vague to have

---

[5] See Collins, *op. cit.*, n. 2, p. 48.
[6] Case 126/86, *Gimnez Zaera* v. *Instituto Nacional de la Seguridad Social*:[1987] E.C.R. 3697, [1989] 1 C.M.L.R. 827.
[7] Case 28/67, *Mölkerei-Zentrale Westfalen* v. *Hamptzollampt Paderborn*:[1968] E.C.R. 143, [1968] C.M.L.R. 187.
[8] Hartley, *The Foundations of European Community Law* (1990), 2nd ed., p. 189.

direct effect. In particular, it would require judges to determine the degree of economic co-ordination necessary to attain Treaty objectives. (Article 6 has since been substantially amended by the Treaty on European Union.)

### Partial direct effect

4–004    However, it is possible for a provision to have *partial* direct effect. For example, Article 119 of the E.C. Treaty requires the application of the principle of equal pay for equal work regardless of the sex of the employee. The Court has held that Article 119 may have direct effect in its application to "direct and overt discrimination" in such matters as discrimination arising from national legislation or collateral labour agreements. However, it is insufficiently precise, on its own, to apply to "indirect and disguised discrimination" which requires further elaboration under Community or national law. Thus, if a provision is only partly suitable for judicial application to individuals it may be only partly directly effective.[9]

Sometimes a provision which is not itself directly effective may, in conjunction with other provisions, become directly effective. For instance Article 7 of the EEC Treaty (prior to amendment by the Treaty on European Union), which provided that "within the scope of application of the Treaty, and without prejudice to any special provisions, discrimination on the ground of nationality is prohibited" is unlikely to have direct effect.[10] However, in conjunction with other Treaty articles or regulations, Article 7 was found to have direct effect.[11]

## THE TREATY PROVISION MUST BE UNCONDITIONAL AND UNQUALIFIED AND NOT SUBJECT TO ANY FURTHER MEASURES ON THE PART OF THE MEMBER STATES OR OF THE COMMUNITY

4–005    The requirement for the measure to be unconditional means that the provision in question may be enforced without requiring something which is within the control of another body, such as a Community institution or Member State. For example, Article 92(1) of the E.C. Treaty is concerned with state aids which distort competition by favouring certain enterprises or products at the expense of others. Under Article 92(1) this is "incompatible with the Common Market." However, Article 92(2) and (3) make this conditional on decisions of the Court and the Commission[12] and Article 92(1) is therefore incapable of having direct effect.

---

[9] See the second *Defrenne* case, Case 43/75, *Defrenne* v. *Sabena*: [1976] E.C.R. 455, [1976] 2 C.M.L.R. 98 and Hartley, *op. cit.*, n. 8, p. 190.

[10] See, *e.g. Jensen* v. *Corporation of the Trinity House of Deptford* [1982] 2 Lloyd's Rep. 14 (C.A.).

[11] See, *e.g.* Case 1/78, *Kenny* v. *National Insurance Company*: [1978] E.C.R. 1489, [1978] 3 C.M.L.R. 651.

[12] See Case 77/72, *Capolongo*: [1973] E.C.R. 611, [1974] 1 C.M.L.R. 230, paras. 4 to 6, where the Court held that in relation to and in operation at the time the Treaty went into effect, Article 92(1) is not directly effective in the absence of a decision under Article 93(2), and Hartley, *op. cit.*, n. 8, p. 191.

However, an obligation which is originally conditional or qualified may, by lapse of time or as a result of some event, become unconditonal or unqualified and directly effective. In Case 18/71, *Eunomia di Porro* v. *Italian Ministry of Education*[13] the Commission brought proceedings against Italy under Article 169 of the EEC Treaty on the basis that Italy had failed its obligations under Article 169 of the Treaty which required the abolition, at the latest by January 1, 1962, of Italian export tax on articles of artistic or historical interest. The Court agreed and held that the combined effect of Articles 9 and 16, which imposed a clear and precise prohibition on export duties (which took effect on January 1, 1962), was not dependent for its implementation on any act by another body such as the State or the Community. They were therefore capable of direct effect.

The provision must not require further measures to be taken. In practice, the Court has modified this rule so that if a provision specifies a time limit for implementation, it can become directly effective if not implemented by the deadline. In the second *Defrenne*[14] case, Article 119 was held to require that Member States bring the principle of equal pay for equal work into operation by a certain deadline, referred to as the end of the first stage. This requirement of further action did not, however, prevent Article 119 from being directly effective thereafter.[15]

This means that in certain circumstances, for example, the expiry of a deadline by which the State must adopt national measures, the relevant Treaty provision may be substituted for existing legislation which should have been repealed or modified in order to achieve the objectives of the Treaty provision in question.[16]

The basic rule is that a provision which does not require any legislative intervention is capable of having direct effect (provided the other conditions are satisfied). Thus, for example, Article 12 was held to be directly effective because the prohibition in it is imposed unconditionally on the Member State.[17]

Similarly in *Costa* v. *ENEL*,[18] the Court held that Article 37(2):

". . . contains an absolute prohibition not an obligation to do something but an obligation to refrain from doing something. This obligation is not accompanied by any reservation which might make its implementation subject to any positive act of national law."

The prohibition in Article 37(2) was therefore held to be capable of producing direct effects.

---

[13] Case 18/71, *Eunomia di Porro* v. *Italian Ministry of Education*: [1971] E.C.R. 811, [1972] C.M.L.R. 4.
[14] *Op. cit.*, n. 9, p. 455.
[15] See further, Hartley, *op. cit.*, n. 8, p. 194.
[16] See Winter, "Direct Applicability and Direct Effect: Two Distinct Concepts in Community Law" (1972) C.M.L.Rev. 425 at p. 434.
[17] See *Van Gend en Loos, op. cit.*, n. 1.
[18] *Op. cit.*, n. 4.

## THE TREATY PROVISION MUST NOT LEAVE ANY SUBSTANTIAL LATITUDE OR DISCRETION TO MEMBER STATES

**4–006**     The requirement for some consultative procedures, for example, before the Commission, is likely to deprive a provision of direct effect.[19]

Similarly, the granting of a certain amount of discretion to Member States can also negative direct effect. In Case 10/71, *Ministère Public of Luxembourg* v. *Hein née Muller*[20] the Court considered whether Article 90(2) had direct effect. The provision applies the competition rules in Articles 85 to 94 to public undertakings if "the application of such rules does not obstruct the performance in law or in fact, of the particular tasks assigned to them." The Court held that:

> "Article 90(2) does not lay down an unconditional rule. Its application involves an appraisal of the requirements, on the one hand, of the particular tasks entrusted to the undertaking concerned and, on the other hand, the protection of the interest of the Community. This appraisal depends on the objective of general economic policy pursued by the states under the supervision of the Commission."

This therefore left a certain discretion to States which meant that the provision could not have direct effect.

However, even if a Treaty provision requires a Member State to take positive action, failure to do so may not necessarily preclude the provision from having direct effect providing that the Member State had no appreciable margin of discretion in executing or implementing the provision in question.[21] In the *Salgoil*[22] case the Court stated that, in principle, a measure of discretion will preclude a provision from conferring enforceable rights on private individuals.

## IT IS IRRELEVANT THAT THE EUROPEAN COMMISSION OR OTHER MEMBER STATES HAVE ALTERNATIVE REMEDIES FOR BREACH OF THE PROVISION IN QUESTION

**4–007**     The availability to other Member States and/or to Community institutions of alternative remedies for breach of a Treaty provision will not have negative direct effect.[23] The Court held in *Van Gend en Loos* that:

---

[19] See *Costa* v. *ENEL, op. cit.*, n. 4, in relation to Articles 93 and 102.

[20] Case 10/71, *Ministère Public of Luxembourg* v. *Hein née Muller*: [1971] E.C.R. 723 at 730.

[21] See Winter, *op. cit.*, n. 16, p. 434. In Case C–128/92, *Bank* v. *British Coal Corporation, op. cit.*, n. 1, the Advocate General Van Gerven emphasised the eminently practical nature of the "direct effect" test by reference to the Court's case law on the direct effect of directives, and took the view that if a provision is sufficiently operational in itself to be applied by a court, it has direct effect (para. 28 of the Opinion). In other words, the clarity, precision, unconditional nature, completeness or perfection of the rule and its lack of dependence on discretionary implementing measures are merely aspects of one characteristics feature, namely, can it be applied by a court to a specific case. See further discussion in relation to provisions of directives at para. 5–008 below.

[22] *Salgoil*: Recueil XIV at 674.

[23] See in particular, *Eunomia di Porro, op. cit.*, n. 13, and Collins, *op. cit.*, n. 2, p. 59.

"A restriction of the guarantees against an infringement of Article 12 by Member States to the procedures under Articles 169 and 170 would remove all direct legal protection of the individual rights of their nationals. . . The vigilance of individuals concerned to protect these rights amounts to an effective supervision in addition to the supervision entrusted by Articles 169 and 170 to the diligence of the Commission and of the Member States."[24]

In addition, the Court suggested in *Ministère Public of Luxembourg*,[25] that even if a Treaty article (*i.e.* Article 90) contemplates enforcement by the Commission, this will also of itself not negative direct effect and individuals can still rely on it in national courts.

## PROSPECTIVE AND RETROSPECTIVE DIRECT EFFECT (TEMPORAL EFFECT)

As a general principle, the Europe Court has held that individual **4–008** rights must be fully and uniformly applied in all Member States from the date of their entry into force[26] and not from the date of a ruling from the European Court that a particular measure is directly effective.[27] In Case 61/79, *Amministrazione delle Finanze dello Stato* v. *Denkavit*[28] the Italian government argued that the ruling of the Court should be influenced by the immense burden that would be placed on it were a retroactive decision to be given in the context of the claims for restitution. This argument was specifically rejected by the Court.[29]

On occasion, however, the Court has varied this principle in exceptional circumstances by holding that the relevant provision has prospective direct effect only. For instance, in Case 43/75, *Defrenne* v. *Sabena*[30] the Court was influenced by the fact that there would be a floodgate of litigation if it declined to limit the temporal effect of its ruling to the date of judgment.[31] It is suggested by Ward that the reason for this decision was the uncertainty in the case as to whether Article 119 of the Treaty of Rome (providing for equal pay for equal work for men and women) was in fact directly effective.[32] Similarly, in Case 24/86, *Blaizot* v. *University of Liège*[33] there was confusion as to whether university education

---

[24] *Van Gend en Loos, op. cit.*, n. 1, p. 13.
[25] *Ibid.*
[26] See Case 106/77, *Amministrazione delle Finanze dello Stato* v. *Simmenthal*: [1978] E.C.R. 629 at 643, [1978] 3 C.M.L.R. 263.
[27] See Case 309/85, *Barra* v. *Belgian State and the City of Liège*: [1988] E.C.R. 355, [1988] 2 C.M.L.R. 409 and see further, Ward, "Government Liability in the United Kingdom for Breach of Individual Rights in European Community Law" (1990) 19 *Anglo-American Law Review* 1 at p. 4.
[28] Case 61/79, *Amministrazione delle Finanze dello Stato* v. *Denkavit*: [1980] E.C.R. 1205, [1981] 3 C.M.L.R. 694.
[29] *Ibid.*, 1220 to 1224.
[30] Case 43/75, *Defrenne* v. *Sabena*: [1976] E.C.R. 455, [1976] 2 C.M.L.R. 98.
[31] *Ibid.*, pp. 480 to 481 and see Ward, *op. cit.*, n. 27, p. 4.
[32] Ward, *op. cit.*, n. 27, p. 4.
[33] Case 24/86, *Blaizot and Others* v. *University of Liège and Others*: [1988] E.C.R. 379, [1989] 1 C.M.L.R. 57.

constituted vocational training for the purposes of Article 128. This Article provides for the establishment of a common vocational training policy. The Court held that it was not possible for students to bring actions to recover illegally levied tuition fees paid before its ruling on direct effect.[34]

The European Court has also determined the temporal effect of individual rights in connection with the reimbursement of illegally levied charges.[35] In Case C–262/88, *Barber* v. *Guardian Royal Exchange Assurance Group*,[36] the Court held that Article 119 applied with direct effect to pensions paid under "contracted-out" pension schemes, *i.e.* schemes which are recognised in the U.K. as substitutable for the earnings-related part of the State pension. However, it limited the application of the direct effect of Article 119 to the date of the judgment, except for workers or those claiming under them who had initiated legal proceedings before that date or raised an equivalent claim under the applicable national law. This was in recognition of the potentially devastating effect on employers of allowing retrospective claims. Unfortunately, the limitations laid down by the Court were themselves capable of five possible interpretations[37] and have given rise to a Protocol to the Treaty on European Union adopted at Maastricht and further references to the Court.[38] In the references in question, the Advocate General Van Gerven took the restrictive view that Article 119 only applied to claims based upon benefits earned after the date of the Court's judgment in *Barber*. This view was subsequently upheld by the Court.[39]

Only the European Court has the power to make a determination limiting the temporal effect of a Community law provision. National courts have no such power.[40]

---

[34] *Ibid.*, pp. 67 to 69.

[35] *e.g.*, Case 199/82, *San Giorgio*: [1983] E.C.R. 3595, [1985] 2 C.M.L.R. 658. See further, paras. 10–022 *et seq.* below.

[36] Case 262/88, *Barber* v. *Guardian Royal Exchange Assurance Group*: [1990] I E.C.R. 1989, [1990] 2 C.M.L.R. 513.

[37] See further, Honeyball and Shaw, "Sex, Law and the Retiring Man" (1991) E.L.Rev. 47 at pp. 56 *et seq.*

[38] See, for example, the Joined Cases C–109/91, *Ten Oever*, C–110/91, *Moroni*, C–152/91, *Neath* and C–200/91, *Coloroll Pension Trustees Ltd.*, Opinion of the Advocate General, April 28, 1993, judgment of October 6, 1993, not yet reported.

[39] See Case C–109/91, *Ten Oever: The Times*, October 12, 1993 and Case C–110/91, *Moroni*: judgment of December 14, 1993, not yet reported. See also Case C–152/91, *Neath* v. *Steeper: The Times*, January 21, 1994 at p. 134.

[40] See *Barra* v. *Belgian State*, *op. cit.*, n. 27.

# DIRECT EFFECT OF DIRECTIVES

Article 189(3) of the EC Treaty provides:                                    **5–001**

> "A directive shall be binding, as to the result to be achieved, upon each Member State to which it is addressed, but shall leave to the national authorities the choice of form and methods."

Unlike regulations, directives are therefore not "directly applicable", and, in principle, require implementation by national law. (Direct applicability is discussed at paragraph 2–002 above). The European Court has recognised an exception to this in situations where the general principles of constitutional or administrative law in the State concerned render the enactment of specific legislation superfluous, providing certain conditions are satisfied. These were referred to in Case 29/84, *Commission v. Germany*[1] and may be summarised as follows:

(a) The relevant principles guarantee full application by national authorities.
(b) The legal position arising from these principles is sufficiently clear and precise.
(c) Where the Directive creates rights for individuals, they are made fully aware of their rights (especially if they are nationals of other Member States).
(d) Where appropriate, such individuals are afforded the possibility of relying on these rights before the national courts.

However, the vast majority of directives require domestic implementation. As regards implementing legislation, certain discretion is necessarily left to the individual Member States. The directive is binding only "as to the result to be achieved" but leaves the "choice of form and methods" to the national authorities.

It is well established by the case law of the ECJ that directives are capable of direct effect.[2] This was confirmed in the Case 41/74, *Van Duyn v. Home Office*.[3] However, the fact that the "choice of forms and methods" of domestic implementation is left to Member States suggests

---

[1] Case 29/84, *Commission v. Germany*: [1985] E.C.R. 1662 at 1673, [1986] 3 C.M.L.R. 579; see also Case 363/85, *Commission v. Italy*: [1978] E.C.R. 1733.
[2] See para. 2–006, n. 22 above.
[3] Case 41/75, *Van Duyn v. Home Office*: [1974] E.C.R. 1337, [1975] 1 C.M.L.R. 1.

that they retain a discretion with regard to implementation. For this reason, Collins argues persuasively[4] that the requirements for the direct effect of provisions in directives are not necessarily identical to those for Treaty provisions (discussed in Chapter 4, above). The requirements for directives are analysed at paragraphs 6–001 *et seq.* below.

## THE CONDITIONS FOR DIRECT EFFECT OF DIRECTIVES

### Non-discretionary provisions

5–002    The conditions for the direct effect of Treaty provisions have already been discussed in Chapter 4. The Court has essentially applied similar criteria for determining whether directives have direct effect.[5] However, although it is possible to apply the requirements for "clear" and "unconditional" provisions to directives, the requirements for "non-discretionary" provisions must be modified.[6]

The case law of the ECJ suggests first, that if the directly effective provisions of the directive in question leaves the Member State with a margin of discretion, the national court still retains a duty to determine whether the national legislation falls *outside* that margin of discretion. Thus in Case 88/79, *Ministère Public* v. *Grunert*[7] a Council directive on foodstuff additives left a large margin of discretion to Member States as to whether or not to authorise certain preservatives or antioxidants in foodstuffs. However, a *total* ban on the preservatives and antioxidants was held to be contrary to the Directive. Consequently its provisions had direct effect and could be relied upon by individuals before national courts.

This principle also extends to the situation where a Member State has a discretion under the directive, but refuses to exercise it or abdicates it.[8] If the provisions of the directive are sufficiently clear and unconditional, they can nevertheless give rise to direct effects. However, if the discretion is exercised properly and there is correct implementation of the Directive in national law, the Directive will not have direct effect.[9] In other words, individuals must rely on the national implementing measures to enforce their Community rights. However, the Directive still remains relevant as an aid to construction.[10] This is discussed in detail in Chapter 6 below.

---

[4] Collins, *European Community Law in the U.K.*, (1990), 4th ed., p. 65.
[5] See, for example, the submission of the Commission in Case 38/77, *Enka*: [1977] E.C.R. 2203 at p. 2207, [1978] 2 C.M.L.R. 212.
[6] See Advocate General Warner in Case 131/79, *R.* v. *Secretary of State for Home Affairs, ex p. Santillo* [1980] E.C.R. 1585 at p. 1610 and Easson, "EEC Directives for the Harmonization of Laws: Some Patterns of Validity, Implementation and Legal Effects" (1981) 1 Yb. Eur. L. 36 to 37.
[7] Case 88/79, *Ministère Public* v. *Grunert*: [1980] E.C.R. 1827.
[8] See Collins, *European Community Law in the U.K.* (1990), p. 57.
[9] See Collins, *op. cit.*, p. 86 and Wyatt and Dashwood, *European Community Law* (1993), 3rd. ed., p. 72.
[10] See Case 32/74, *Haaga*: [1974] E.C.R. 1201, [1975] 1 C.M.L.R. 32; Case 111/75, *Mazzalai*: [1976] E.C.R. 657, [1977] 1 C.M.L.R. 105; Case 270/81, *Felcitas*: [1982] E.C.R. 2771, [1982] 3 C.M.L.R. 447.

## Unconditional and sufficiently precise

The European Court has provided useful guidance on whether the 5–003
provisions of a directive may be regarded as "unconditional" and
"sufficiently precise" so that they may, in the absence of implementing
measures adopted within the prescribed period, be regarded as being
"directly effective" and be capable of being relied upon against any
national provision which is incompatible with them, insofar as the
provisions define rights which individuals are able to assert against the
State.

### Implications of the Francovich judgment

In Case C–6 & 9/90 *Francovich* v. *Italian Republic* and *Bonifaci* v. 5–004
*Italian Republic*[11] the Court examined whether the provisions of Directive
80/987 regarding employees' rights were unconditional and sufficiently
precise. The Directive is intended to guarantee employees a minimum
degree of protection at Community level, in the event of the insolvency
of their employer. (This is without prejudice to more favourable
provisions enforced in the Member States.) It provides, *inter alia*, for
specific guarantees of payment of the outstanding claims of employees
relating to pay. The Court focused on three aspects of the Directive,
namely identifying who is covered by the guarantee established under its
provisions, the nature of that guarantee and, finally, the identity of the
party liable under the guarantee.

The Court noted that as regards the persons to be covered by the
Directive, it was possible for a national court to determine whether the
person concerned is deemed to be an employee under national law and
whether he/she is excluded, in accordance with Article 1(2) and Annex I
of the Directive. It was also possible to determine whether one of the
possible states of insolvency, provided for in Article 2 of the Directive,
was applicable. In other words, there was sufficient guidance in the
Directive itself for a national court to be able to accurately determine
whether the applicant was covered or not.

As regards the nature of the guarantee, the Directive left it to the
Member States to decide the date from which the payment of claims
must be guaranteed. However, the Court took the view that the fact that
the Directive gave Member States some leeway in respect of the methods
for defining the guarantee and limiting the sums involved, did not affect
the precise and unconditional nature of the result prescribed by the
Directive. The Court accepted the argument of the Commission and of
the plaintiffs, that it was possible to calculate at least the *minimum*
guarantee established by the Directive by using as the basis for calculation the date which, if chosen, imposed the least burden on the guarantee
institution.

The Court also said that although the Directive left it to the Member
State to decide the date from which the payment of claims must be

---

[11] Joined Cases 6 & 9/90 *Francovich and Bonifaci and Others* v. *Italian Republic:* [1991] 1
E.C.R. 5357, [1993] 2 C.M.L.R. 66.

guaranteed, it was implicit in the case law of the Court [12] that the fact that the State can choose from a multiplicity of possible methods for achieving the result prescribed by a directive, does not preclude individuals from asserting before national courts rights whose nature can be determined sufficiently precisely on the sole basis of the provisions of the Directive.

5–005    Furthermore, the Court made it clear that a Member State which has failed to fulfil its obligations to transpose a directive, may not obstruct rights which the Directive confers on private individuals by relying on an option in the Directive to limit the sum of the guarantee, which the State could have exercised if it had taken the necessary measures to implement the Directive.[13]

The Court therefore concluded in *Francovich* that the provisions in question were unconditional and sufficiently precise as regards the nature of the guarantee. However, it was also necesssary to identify the party who is liable under the guarantee. The terms of Article 5 of the Directive indicate that the Member State is under an obligation to organise an appropriate, comprehensive, institutional guarantee system. The Court held that those provisions did not identify the party liable under the guarantee and secondly, that the State could not be deemed liable just because it did not adopt transposition measures within the prescribed period. Even though the Directive provided that the guarantee system may be fully financed by public authorities, the Court took the view that this did not mean that the State can be identified as the party liable to pay outstanding claims.

The result was that the provisions of Directive 80/987 could not be interpreted as meaning that persons concerned could assert rights against the State before national courts, if they were adversely affected by the absence of implementing measures adopted within the prescribed period. In other words, the relevant provisions were not sufficiently precise and unconditional so as to give rise to *full* direct effects, which could be enforced in national courts. However, the Court nevertheless went on to establish a liability of the State in respect of damage sustained as a result of its failure to fulfil the obligations incumbent upon it under Community law. In this way, the fact that the provisions of the Directive were not in themselves directly effective, did not ultimately prevent the Court from stating that individuals had a right to compensation for the failure of a State to implement Community law, in certain situations. This is discussed further at paragraphs 8–008 *et seq.* below.

*Extent of unconditionality required to create direct effects*

5–006    The degree of precision and of unconditionality required to confer provisions of a directive with direct effect were also relevant in Case C–60/91, *Portugal* v. *Jose Antonio Batista Morais*.[14] The defendant, a driving

---

[12] The Court cited its judgments in Case 71/85, *FNV*: [1986] E.C.R. 3855, [1987] 3 C.M.L.R. 767 and Case 286/85, *McDermott and Cotter*: [1987] E.C.R. 1453, [1987] 2 C.M.L.R. 607.

[13] The Court referred to its earlier judgment in Case 8/81, *Becker*: [1982] E.C.R. 53, [1982] 1 C.M.L.R. 499.

[14] Case 60/91, *Portugal* v. *José Antonio Batista Morais*: [1992] 2 C.M.L.R. 533.

instructor in Portugal, was fined for giving a driving lesson on a motorway situated with the district of Lourdes, which is adjacent to Lisbon. The grounds for the fine were that the driving school at which he was employed was not authorised to give lessons outstide the distict of Lisbon. Mr Morais appealed to the Tribunal da Relação, (Court of Appeal) Lisbon, contending that the national measures in the Portuguese Decree-Law 6/82 were contrary to Article 6(1) of Council Directive 80/1263[15] on the introduction of a community driving licence. He argued that the national measures were contrary to the Directive because they did not permit driving instruction to be given on a motorway.

One of the questions raised, on a reference pursuant Article 177 to the European Court, was whether paragraph 9 of Annex II to the Driving Licence Directive, in conjunction with Article 6(1) of that Directive, created rights which could be invoked by individuals before the national court.

In the Opinion of the Advocate General Jacobs, the Directive did not impose upon Member States any precise and unconditional obligation to conduct a part of the driving test on the motorway; rather, each Member State enjoyed a discretion to decide, in the light of national circumstances, whether or not it is possible to lay down such a requirement. So far as the location of the driving test is concerned, paragraph 9 of Annex II of the Directive provided that:

"The part of the test described in paragraph 5 may be conducted on a special testing ground, in which case precise criteria should be laid down for measuring objectively the candidate's ability to handle the vehicle. The part of the test described in paragraph 6 shall, wherever possible, be conducted on roads outside built-up areas and on motorways as well as in urban traffic."

The defendant Mr Morais argued that from the second sentence of **5–007** paragraph 9, it is clear that wherever possible, a part of the driving test must be conducted on motorways and on roads outside built-up areas. Accordingly, driving instructors in Lisbon had the right to provide driving instruction on the motorway, and that right can moreover be relied upon before a national court in order to prevent the application of Section 7(1) of the Decree-Law.[16]

The Advocate General took the view that the wording of the Directive gave each Member State a discretion to decide, in the light of national circumstances, whether or not it is possible to lay down such a requirement. He was of the opinion that Portugal had not exceeded the limits of its discretion in refusing to provide for a part of the test to be conducted on a motorway. The Court concurred with this view. The question of the direct effect of paragraph 9 of Annex II to the Directive did not therefore form part of the judgment. However, the Advocate General referred to earlier case law and reiterated that:

---

[15] [1980] O.J. L375/1.
[16] See Opinion of the Advocate General, *op. cit.*, n. 14, p. 541.

". . . The fact that a provision imposing an obligation upon a Member State gives the State a certain power of appraisal, does not in itself preclude that provision from having direct effect, since the exercise of the power may also be subject to judicial control. Thus, for example, Article 48 EEC has direct effect, not withstanding that Article 48(3) subjects the rights implied by the free movement for workers to limitations which may be imposed by the Member States and which are justified on grounds of public policy, public security or public health. Accordingly, the rights guaranteed by Article 48 can be invoked by individuals before the national courts in cases where the Member State cannot, in the circumstances, rely upon those limitations: See Case 41/74, *Van Duyn* v. *Home Office*."[17]

However, in the *Morais* case, for the reasons stated above, Portugal had not exceeded the limits of its discretion and the relevant provisions of the Directive did not give rise to direct effects.

## Effect of exceptions permitted by the directive

**5–008**     Other cases which illustrate the reasoning of the Court with regard to "precise and unconditional" terms of directives, are Joined Cases C–19 and 20/90, *Marina and Nikolaos Karellas* v. *Minister of Industry and the Organisation for the Restructuring of Enterprises*.[18] The decision in this case was given in response to a reference for a preliminary ruling made by the highest Administrative Court of Greece. By Law No. 1386 of August 5, 1983, Greece set up the Organisation for the Restructuring of Enterprises (ORE) the aim of which was, *inter alia*, to facilitate the economic rehabilitation of enterprises facing serious financial difficulties.[19]

The crucial provision of Article 8(8) of the Law (which has since been amended) declared that, by way of exception from the general rules of company law, the ORE had the power to increase the capital of the company but the pre-emption rights of existing shareholders were safeguarded. Such an increase required ministerial approval. The applicants were shareholders of a public company, the administration of which had been undertaken by ORE. They applied for judicial review of the ministerial decision authorising an increase of capital on the ground that it was contrary to the Greek Constitution and the requirements of the Second Company Law Directive, Article 25(1) of which declares that "Any increase in capital must be decided upon by the general meeting."[20]

The Greek court referred this, among other questions, to the Court of Justice. Article 25(1) of the Directive did allow for two exceptions. Article 25(2) states that the statutes or instruments of incorporation or

---

[17] Case 41/74, *Van Duyn*: [1974] E.C.R. 1337, [1975] 1 C.M.L.R. 1, para. 7.

[18] Joined Cases 19–20/90, *Marina and Nikolaos Karellas* v. *Minister of Industry and the Organisation for the Restructuring of Enterprises*: [1991] I E.C.R. 2691, [1993] 2 C.M.L.R. 865.

[19] See summary by Takis Tridimas, in "Current Survey of Company Law" 17 E.L.Rev. 148 at p. 158.

[20] See Tridimas, *op. cit.*, p. 159.

the general meeting may authorise an increase in the subscribed capital up to a maximum amount, in which case an increase may be decided within the limits of that amount by the company body empowered to do so. Such authorisation is limited to a maximum period of five years and may be renewed one or more times by the general meeting, each time for a period not exceeding five years. In addition, Article 41(1) provides that Member States may derogate from certain provisions of the Directive, including that of Article 25, to the extent necessary "to encourage the participation of employees, or other groups of persons defined by national law, in the capital of undertakings."[21]

The Court of Justice conclued that despite the fact that there were exceptions provided for in the Directive, it nevertheless established in clear, precise and unconditional terms the competence of the general meeting to decide upon an increase of capital. Its unconditional character was therefore not affected by the exceptions since they were strictly limited and did not permit Member States to derogate in other ways except for those specifically provided in the Directive. The Court therefore decided that Article 25(1) had direct effect and that Article 8(8) of the Greek law was incompatible with it.

The case therefore supports the earlier reasoning of the Court, that the existence of a limited discretion in favour of the Member State does not automatically mean that the provisions may not, nevertheless, have direct effect so long as they are sufficiently precise and unconditional.[22]

## Time limits for implementation

The direct effect of a directive is also conditional on the date having 5–009 passed by which the Member State should have implemented the directive, before its provisions may be capable of having direct effect. In Case 148/78, *Pubblico Ministero* v. *Ratti*[23] the defendant, Ratti, was an Italian solvent manufacturer selling both solvents and varnishes in Italy. The firm decided to package and label its products so as to comply with two Directives, even though neither had been implemented in Italy. When the firm put its products on the market, it was prosecuted for failure to comply with the provisions of Italian law passed in 1963, which applied to both products but was in some ways more lenient than the Directives and in other ways, stricter. Ratti admitted that he had not

---

[21] Tridimas, *ibid.*, n. 3.

[22] In Case C–128/92, *H.J. Banks and Company Ltd.* v. *British Coal Corporation*: Opinion of the Advocate General Van Gerven delivered on October 27, 1993, not yet reported, concerning the possible direct effect of ECSC Treaty provisions, the Advocate General referred to the "eminently practical nature of the 'direct effect' test" (para. 27 of the Opinion). He took the view that the "clarity, precision, unconditional nature, completeness or perfection of the rule and its lack of dependence on discretionary implementing measures are in that respect merely aspects of one and the same characteristic feature which that rule must exhibit, namely it must be capable of being applied by a court to a specific case, *i.e.* be sufficiently operational in itself to be applied by a court." See further discussion in relation to Treaty provisions at para. 4–006 above.

[23] Case 148/78, *Pubblico Ministero* v. *Ratti*: [1979] E.C.R. 1629, [1980] 1 C.M.L.R. 96.

complied with the Italian law but his defence was that compliance with the Directives was sufficient.

The Italian court hearing the prosecution made a reference to the European Court for a ruling on whether the Directives were directly effective. The ECJ held that a directive only became directly effective when the deadline for implementation had expired. This was the case in relation to only one of the two Directives. As a result, the "Euro-defence" raised by Ratti succeeded in relation to the charges relating to solvents, but not to those concerning varnishes. However, it is of interest that in Case 80/86, *Officer Van Justitie* v. *Kolpinghaus Nijmegen BV*[24] discussed in detail at paragraph 6–006 the Court held that the State cannot rely, in a criminal prosecution, on pre-existing national law to the *detriment* of the individual, even if the date for implementation of the Directive has passed.

One reason for the principle that direct effects only arise after the expiry of the time limit for implementation is to ensure uniformity in the application of directly effective provisions of directives throughout the E.C.[25] In the Joined Cases C–140–141 and 278–279/91, *M Suffritti* v. *Instituto Nazionale della Providenza Sociale (INPS)*,[26] Italian employees sought to rely on Council Directive 80/987 which provided certain protection for salaried workers in the event of the insolvency of their employers. However, the Directive did not have to be implemented by Member States until October 23, 1983. Italy failed to implement the provisions of the Directive in time. When it eventually did so, the relevant Italian Law No. 297/82, which provided for a guarantee fund set up with the INPS for payment of an allowance on the termination of the employment relationship, was limited by Article 2 of that law to the termination of the employment relationship which had occurred *after* the entry into force of the law. The plaintiffs had all left their jobs due to the non-payment of their salaries. Their employers were all subsequently declared to be insolvent, but at dates *before* October 23, 1983. They were therefore unable to rely on the direct effect of the Directive because the relevant acts of insolvency all took place before the Directive had to be implemented by the Italian State.

*Effect of implementation before expiry of time limit*

5–010    This leaves open the question of whether an individual may rely on a directive which has been implemented, *but incorrectly*, *before* the expiry of the time limit. In one view, the Member State has voluntarily implemented the Directive at an earlier time and must correspondingly accept the obligations under it, from the earlier date. On the contrary, it could

---

[24] Case 80/86, *Officer Van Justitie* v. *Kolpinghaus Nijmegen BV*: [1987] E.C.R. 3969, [1989] 2 C.M.L.R. 18.
[25] See de Búrca, "Giving Effect to European Community Directives" (1992) M.L.R. 215 at p. 218.
[26] Joined Cases C–140–141 and 278–279/91, *M. Suffritti and Others* v. *Instituto Nazionale della Providenza Sociale (INPS)*: judgment of December 3, 1992, not yet reported.

be argued that the State should not be prejudiced by the fact that it has implemented the Directive before the relevant deadline, however incorrectly, and also that greater legislative harmony will be achieved between Member States by using a uniform time limit before imposing the obligation to interpret domestic law in conformity with a non-implemented or badly implemented directive.[27]

This point has not yet been determined under Community law. If the reason for using a directive rather than, for example, a regulation was a deliberate policy decision to give Member States flexibility as to the choice of form and methods of implementation then arguably the requirement of purposive construction should not arise until the time limit has expired.[28]

However, the incorrect implementation of a directive before the deadline for implementation has expired may, nevertheless, give rise to issues of interpretation in national law, e.g., the implementing measure may be ruled *ultra vires* by the national courts. For instance, if subordinate legislation is passed under Section 2(2) of the European Communities Act 1972 (as amended), but the relevant provisions misconstrue the Community provision which they are designed to implement and go substantially beyond Community provision, the implementing measure may be ruled *ultra vires* by the English courts.[29] This could also occur if for some reason the Community provision itself is invalid, though a reference under the Article 177 procedure may be necessary to obtain a ruling on the interpretation or validity of the Community provisions.

In a recent judgment of the Court, in Case C–208/90, *Emmott* v. *Minister for Social Welfare*[30] the Court stated that a national limitation period may not begin to run until a directive had been properly incorporated into national law, even if the relevant provisions of the directive have direct effect. This is discussed further at paragraphs 5–011 *et seq.* below.

## Direct effect of a directive and national limitation periods

In general, a cause of action based on Community law arises from the **5–011** moment when a conflict occurs between national law and Community law and concerning rights which have direct effect.[31] However, in cases where individuals make claims against the State in respect of rights arising under Community law, the question of time limits for bringing the action can arise. This causes particular difficulties where the rights which are sought to be enforced are contained in a Community directive

---

[27] de Búrca, *op. cit.*, n. 5, p. 218.
[28] *Ibid.*, p. 219.
[29] Hartley, *The Foundations of European Community Law* (1988, reprinted 1990), p. 241.
[30] Case 208/90, *Emmott* v. *Minister for Social Welfare and Another*: [1991] I E.C.R. 4869, [1991] 3 C.M.L.R. 894.
[31] See Freeman, summary of a lecture "Enforcement of Community Rights in National Courts" by Barling and Hutchings, Autumn 1992, *Lawyers' Europe* 8 at p. 8.

which has either not yet been implemented by a Member State, or has been incorrectly implemented.

## Facts of the Emmott case

**5-012**    An important decision of the European Court of Justice on these questions is Case C–208/90, *Emmott* v. *Minister for Social Welfare*.[32] This case was concerned with the principle of equal treatment for men and women in matters of social security. Mrs Emmott was an Irish national who was married with two dependent children. Article 4(1) of EEC Social Security Directive 79/7 was held by the European Court of Justice in Case 286/85, *McDermott and Cotter* v. *Minister for Social Welfare and Attorney General* (hereinafter referred to as *McDermott and Cotter (No. 1)*),[33] to prohibit all discrimination on grounds of sex in matters of social security and that in the absence of measures implementing Article 4(1) women are entitled to have the same rules applied to them as are applied to men who are in the same situation.

In May 1986, the Irish Government transposed the Social Security Directive in question into Irish law[34] but although Mrs Emmott received a benefit at the rate applicable to a man from that date, she did not receive any increases for dependent children until November 1986. She also did not receive an invalidity pension calculated at the personal rate normally applicable to a man, together with an increase for dependent children, until 1988. She argued that she was entitled to the same amount of benefits as that paid to a married man in an identical situation to hers, and that that entitlement ran from December 23, 1984, the date by which Member States were required to implement Directive 79/7. (The Social Welfare (No. 2) Act 1985 was not made retrospective to December 23, 1984.)

In July 1988, Mrs Emmott sought leave to institute proceedings for judicial review under Irish law, for the purpose of recovering the benefits. The Irish Government took the view that her claim was time barred under Order 84, rule 21(1) of the Rules of the Superior Courts 1986. These provide:

> "An application for leave to apply for judicial review shall be made promptly and in any event within three months from the date when grounds for the application first arose, or six months where relief sought is certiorari unless the court considers that there is good reason for extending the period within which the application shall be made."

## Reliance on expiry of national time limits in Emmott

**5-013**    The Irish High Court referred to the European Court of Justice for a preliminary ruling, the question whether the Member State could rely

---

[32] Case 208/9, *Emmott* v. *Minister for Social Welfare and Another*: [1991] I E.C.R. 4869, [1991] 3 C.M.L.R. 894.

[33] Case 286/85, *McDermott and Cotter* v. *Minister for Social Welfare and Attorney General*: [1987] E.C.R. 1453, [1987] 2 C.M.L.R. 607.

[34] Following enactment of the Social Welfare (No. 2) Act 1985.

upon national procedural rules, in particular rules relating to time limits, in order to restrict or refuse the claim for compensation in respect of alleged discrimination, as in the case of failure to apply to a married woman the rules applicable to men, in the same situation.

It appears from the Opinion of the Advocate General Mischo, that Mrs Emmott was unaware of the existence of the relevant Directive, until she learned through the press about the entry into force of the Irish leglislation implementing it. (Presumably, this was between the period July 16, 1985 (when the Social Welfare (No. 2) Act was passed) and various dates in 1986 when relevant provisions of it entered into force.)

However, she seems only to have realised after March 24, 1987, when the European Court gave judgment in the case of *McDermott and Cotter (No. 1)*, that the Directive had given her a right to equal treatment which she had been entitled to exercise since December 23, 1984. Some days after the delivery of that judgment, she entered into correspondence with the Minister of Social Welfare to obtain the benefit of the provisions of the Directive with effect from December 23, 1984. The Irish Minister replied by letter on June 26, 1987 that so long as the *McDermott and Cotter (No. 1)* case had not been finally settled by the High Court on the question of retroactivity of the relevant benefits to December 23, 1984, no decision could be taken in her case. They let it be understood that her application would be considered as soon as that case was settled.[35]

In January 1988, Mrs Emmott finally instructed solicitors. In July 1988, they obtained leave to bring an action before the High Court, subject to the respondent's rights to plead failure to observe the procedural time limit. This was the question which was finally referred to the European Court of Justice.

The key issues were (1) whether the Irish State was entitled to plead any time limit as against Mrs Emmott and, if so, (2) how long that time limit may be and from what time may it begin to run?

Mrs Emmott argued that to allow the competent Irish authority to rely upon an alleged delay in commencing legal proceedings would be to allow them to obtain a possible benefit from their default, namely failure to transpose the relevant provisions of the Directive with effect from December 23, 1984. She also submitted, as a further reason, that since married men had, between the period December 23, 1984 and November 19, 1986, been treated in a more beneficial manner in respect of dependence than was the case in respect of married women, and that since such treatment was given to married women by the Minister for Social Welfare without any necessity to commence proceedings to obtain it, to impose a precondition on married women, namely the need to commence proceedings without delay to obtain equal treatment, would be to allow the Irish State to treat such married women in a discriminatory way.

---

[35] Judgment was in fact given on June 10, 1988, [1990] 2 C.M.L.R. 94.

## Reasonableness of the time limit in Emmott

5–014    On the question of whether there could be any time limit, the Advocate General took the view that it was possible, as argued by the respondent Irish authorities and the governments of the U.K. and the Netherlands and the European Commission, to apply the Court's established case law relating to the recovery of undue payments. Those cases also concern situations in which a Member State, by act or omission, had committed a breach of Community law. This had not, however, stopped the Court from taking the view that individuals had to comply with national procedural rules, including time limits, if they wished to obtain the benefits of Community law.

The Advocate General cited, in particular, an extract from Case 33/76, *Rewe-Zentralfinanze eG and Rewe-Zentral AG* v. *Landwirtschaftskammer für das Saarland*,[36] where the Court of Justice held that in the absence of harmonising measures, Community rights must be exercised before national courts in accordance with domestic rules of procedure. The *Rewe* case also made it clear that that position would be different only if the conditions and time limits made it impossible in practice to exercise the rights which the national courts are obliged to protect. This is not the case where reasonable periods of limitation for such actions are fixed.

In applying those principles to the *Emmott* case, the Advocate General regarded the three month's limitation period in the Irish Rules of Procedure to be reasonable. He noted, however, that the rule 21(1) required that the application for leave to apply for judicial review shall be made "promptly" and took the view that if that meant that a claim had to be made less than two months after the date on which the the facts on which it is based first became known, then that would be incompatible with the criterion of a "reasonable time limit."

He noted that according to the case law cited, the procedural rules of national law applying to actions at law intended to protect the rights which citizens derived from the direct effect of Community law, did not appears to be less favourable than those relating to similar actions of a domestic nature. However, the Advocate General did not comment on one of the submissions made by the applicant, which was that certain claims based directly on the constitution were not subject to limitation periods. It would appear that the Advocate General also did not comment on whether the constitutional claims were an appropriate basis for comparison with social security claims based on directly effective Community law, since this is a matter left to the national courts.[37]

## Date from which the time limit runs

5–015    The Advocate General did, however, consider whether the conditions and time limits provided for by national law made it impossible in practice to exercise the rights which the Irish courts are obliged to

---

[36] Case 33/76, *Rewe-Zentralfinanze eG and Rewe-Zentral AG* v. *Landwirtschaftskammer für das Saarland*: [1976] E.C.R. 1989, [1977] 1 C.M.L.R. 535.
[37] See Szyszczak, case note on the *Emmott* case, (1992) C.M.L.Rev. 604 at p. 608.

protect. This condition is fundamental, because it is based on the principle of the *"effet utile"* of Community law.[38] The Advocate General considered one matter, on which the European Commission had also laid stress, namely that the Irish government department had indicated that it was not yet able to consider an application and had let Mrs Emmott to understand that a decision would be reached as soon as the court seized of the matter (in *McDermott and Cotter (No. 1)*) had given a ruling. The question therefore was whether that national authority should subsequently be allowed to plead lapse of time once the person concerned finally decides to go to court.[39] The Advocate General said that it is for the national court to rule on the effect of the letter sent by the Irish Minister for Social Welfare to Mrs Emmott dated June 26, 1987 and to consider whether the administration's conduct may have been such as to make it impossible in practice for Mrs Emmott to exercise her rights.

The Advocate General was concerned, in particular, with the second issue, which was that date from which the "reasonable period" could begin to run. He noted with surprise that the government authorities who sought to rely upon the bar constituted by the national time limit, had nowhere in their submissions stated what that date should be. The Advocate General did not consider that the period could reasonably run from the date on which the Directive ought to have been transposed. His conclusions, which were similar to those of the Commission in this respect, were that time could not in all fairness run before the claimant could reasonably have been aware of the direct effect of the provision under which he is claiming, and, if necessary, of its precise scope if this was not clear.

The judgment of the Court in *Emmott* went much further than the Opinion of the Advocate General and is important because it establishes a clear ruling as to the starting point from which time begins to run against a litigant, in cases involving directly effective provisions in a directive. The European Court of Justice reaffirmed the principles in *Rewe*[40] and held that:

> "Community law precludes the competent authorities of a Member State from relying, in proceedings against them by an individual before the national courts in order to protect rights directly conferred upon him by a directive, Article 4(1) of Directive 79/7 on the progressive implementation of the principle of equal treatment for men and women in matters of social security, on national procedural rules relating to time limits for bringing proceedings so long as that Member State had not properly transposed that Directive into its domestic legal system."[41]

---

[38] See, for example, Case 9/70, *Franz Grad* v. *Finanzamt Traunstein*: [1970] E.C.R. 825, [1971] C.M.L.R. 1.

[39] See the *Emmott* judgment at n. 32, p. 393, para. 34.

[40] *Op. cit.*, n. 36.

[41] *Rewe*, judgment *op. cit.*, at n. 36, para. 25.

## Reasoning of the ECJ in Emmott

**5–016** The reasoning of the Court is based, in particular, on the framework of Article 189(3) and the previous case law of the Court. It cited the ruling in Case 14/83, *Von Colson and Kamann* v. *Land Nordrhein-Westfalen*[42] and explained that the discretion on how to implement a directive was governed by the obligation to adopt, within the domestic legal system, all the measures necessary to ensure that the Directive is fully effective.

In general, the Court has placed emphasis on legal certainty in order to enable individuals to be put in a position to assert their rights. This can only happen when the directive has been properly transposed into national law. Accordingly, a Member State in default of its Community law obligations may not rely on limitation periods to bar claims based on the provisions of a directive, and such limitation periods cannot begin to run until the Directive has been properly transposed into national law. In Case C-338/91, *Steenhorst-Neerings* (not yet reported), the opinion of the Advocate General Marco Darman suggests that the principle in *Emmott* is to be broadly construed and is not limited to situations where the Member State is at fault in some way for non-implementation.[43]

In this way, the Court has stressed the need to secure the maximum effect of directives within national legal systems, whilst at the same time adopting the framework provided by Article 189 of the Treaty of Rome.[44] This position is unlikely to alter in the post-Maastricht era. The *Emmott* case provides another spur to compel Member States into speedy compliance with Community law obligations in directives. This does not, however, address the question of the lack of comparability across the various Member States which can produce divergent results when the same Community rights are being exercised within different Member States. This was, to some extent addressed in the second preliminary reference in Case 271/91, *Marshall* v. *Southampton and South West Hampshire Area Health Authority (Teaching) (No. 2)* from the House of Lords,[45] and discussed further at paragraphs 9–025 *et seq.* below, where the Court of Justice provided further guidance on how far national courts may make use of Community law to tackle the inadequacies in national procedural rules and remedies.

## Application of the Emmott judgment in U.K. litigation

**5–017** The reasoning of the European Court of Justice in *Emmott* has subsequently been applied by the High Court in the U.K. case of *Cannon v. Barnsley Metropolitan Borough Council*.[46] The applicant Mrs Cannon, a

---

[42] Case 14/83, *Von Colson and Kamann* v. *Land Nordrhein-Westfalen*: [1984] E.C.R. 1891, [1986] 2 C.M.L.R. 430.

[43] See Duffy, "E.C. Briefing" (June 4, 1993) S.J. 532 at p. 532. In *R.* v. *Minister of Agriculture, Fisheries and Food, ex p. Bostock* [1991] 1 C.M.L.R. 687, leave to apply for judicial review was granted out of time where doubt had been cast on a decision by a subsequent E.C. instrument.

[44] See Szyszczak, *op. cit.*, n. 37, p. 611.

[45] Case 271/91, *Marshall* v. *Southampton and South West Hampshire Area Health Authority (Teaching) (No. 2)*: [1993] 3 C.M.L.R. 293.

[46] Case EAT/406/90, *Cannon* v. *Barnsley*: [1992] 2 C.M.L.R. 795.

head teacher, was made redundant two months before her 60th birthday in 1985. Under the relevant provisions of English law at the time, a deduction was therefore made from her redundancy payment, pursuant to Schedule 4 of the Employment Protection Consolidation Act 1978. However, a man dismissed at the same age as Mrs Cannon would have received the full redundancy payment without any deduction (because deductions would have applied to his 64th year, since the retirement age for men is 65). Mrs Cannon became aware of the EEC directives on sex discrimination in 1990 and brought a case based on alleged sex discrimination in respect of this deduction made by her employers, Barnsley Metropolitan Council, in the Sheffield Industrial Tribunal on February 28, 1990. In the meantime, U.K. domestic law was changed by section 16(2) of the Employment Act 1989 which implemented the relevant EEC directives on sex discrimination as regards redundancy by applying the same criteria to both men and women. It came into force on January 16, 1990 but was not retroactive. The Industrial Tribunal dismissed Mrs Cannon's claim as being out of time. Her appeal to the Employment Appeal Tribunal was allowed.

The EAT held that as far as domestic law was concerned, the deduction had been correctly made. Mr Justice Knox said that the relevant provisions of the 1978 Act clearly discriminated between men and women in that the reductions were operative for women between 59 and 60, whereas they only applied to men between 64 and 65. The discriminative treatment was, however, an infringement of Directive Number 75//117 on equal pay and Directive Number 76/207 on equal treatment. (U.K. domestic law has since been changed by Section 16(2) of the Employment Act 1989, which was made operative on January 16, 1990.)

The Industrial Tribunal had erred in saying that Mrs Cannon's claim was specifically brought under the Sex Discrimination Act 1975 which imposed a three month time limit. Mrs Cannon had made it clear that she was relying on the Directive in advancing her claim.

The EAT held that where there was a right under European law, as opposed to domestic law, the principles applicable to the imposition of time limits had been authoritatively decided in the *Emmott* case. (In *Cannon* the relevant provisions of the EEC directives on sex discrimination were directly effective.) However, the situation here was that there was no relevant provision in national law setting out a particular time limit in respect of claims under European law. Knox J. said that:

"It does not follow from that that any claim under European law could be made at any point in time however remote. That would be a truly intolerable situation. In principle, English law was perfectly capable of evolving, if necessary by analogy to statutory or common law periods which are clearly laid down in terms of months and years, a time limit for the bringing of similar but sufficiently different claims for them not to fall within the strict letter of the statutory or common law limitation period."[47]

---

[47] *Ibid.*, p. 802 at para. 11.

**5–018**    Accordingly, it was not an insuperable task to take from the 1978 Act, the time limits for making claims for redundancy payments. The *Emmott* case had made it clear that the State and its emanations were disabled from relying on any running of time "right down to the day when the failure of the State to comply with its obligations under the relevant directive has been made good."[48]

In the present case, the application had been brought only one month and twelve days after Parliament introduced the requisite legislation. No system of law would have introduced a shorter time limit. The EAT held that the application had not been made out of time and Mrs Cannon's claim for the repayment of the amount deducted should succeed.

However, in *R. v. Secretary of State for Health and General Medical Council, ex parte Goldstein*,[49] Popplewell J. distinguished both the *Emmott* and *Cannon* cases and refused leave to apply for judicial review against the General Medical Council for alleged failure to publish a list of doctors holding specialist qualifications, contrary to the First Medical Directive, E.C. Council Directive 75/362 (on the mutual recognition of medical qualifications). The Directive had been implemented by the Medical Qualifications (EEC) Recognition Order 1977 (as amended). In his reasoning, the principle established in *Emmott* was that time did not begin to run in relation to a directive until it had been implemented in national law, *clearly and with certainty*. Popplewell J. took the view in *Goldstein*, that the fact that the directive had been implemented seventeen years earlier (by an Order of 1977) was sufficient and he went on therefore to apply the normal national procedural rules. The application had not, in his view, been made promptly nor within 3 months as required under R.S.C., Order 53, rule 4. (The Secretary of State expressly declined to take the time limit point against Dr Goldstein and leave for judicial review was in fact granted against the Secretary of State alone.) However, the substantive application was later dismissed by Schiemann J. on March 30, 1993[50] although it is suggested by Sharpston[51] that that decision may well be appealed. It is submitted that the reasoning of Popplewell J. may not be correct. The *Emmott* principle applies wherever there has not been proper implementation of a directive, and time does not therefore begin to run until such implementation has taken place.

*Relevance of Emmott to cases not concerned with directives*

**5–019**    Although the *Emmott* case was concerned with time limitations in relations to directives, the reasoning in it may arguably apply to other directly effective Community law provisions. In general, it may be

---

[48] *Ibid.*, p. 803.
[49] *R. v. Secretary of State for Health and General Medical Council, ex p. Goldstein: The Times*, April 5, 1993 discussed by Sharpston, *Interim and Substantive Relief in Claims Under Community Law* (1993), p. 81.
[50] *Ex p. Goldstein: op. cit.*, n. 39.
[51] *Ibid.*

argued that, for example, a directly effective E.C. Treaty provision confers rights on individuals from the moment that the Treaty (as an international instrument) is given effect in national law. For practical purposes, this would mean the date of entry into force of the European Communities Act 1972 or, where appropriate, the date of entry into force of the European Communities (Amendment) Act 1993. A person relying on a directly effective E.C. Treaty provision would then be subject to normal domestic rules on the point in time when the cause of action arose as well as limitation requirements, under U.K. national law. In fact, the court in *Emmott* emphasised that such procedural matters are generally to be determined by the domestic laws of the Member State. There is, therefore, no suggestion that limitation periods in national law may not apply, *so long as* the conditions imposed on cases brought under Community law are not less favourable than those relating to similar actions of a domestic nature and are not framed so as to render virtually impossible the exercise of rights conferred by Community law.[52] This suggests that normal limitation periods, such as statutory limitation periods, are prima facie acceptable, unless it can be shown that in their application they unreasonably prevent the exercise of Community rights or render these ineffective. In the situation where, for example, a provision of a regulation which required specific implementation had *not* been specifically implemented in national law, an important issue would be whether the individual litigant was aware of his/her rights. However, the practical importance of this possibility is limited because in respect of directly effective Community law (other than directives) the general principle is that *no* domestic implementation is required in the first place.[53]

However, the situation may arise where national law is in fact silent on the issue of the relevant time limits. In *Rankin* v. *British Coal Corporation*,[54] the appellant, Mrs Rankin, was dismissed by reason of redundancy on March 31, 1987 when she was aged 61. At the time, the Employment Protection (Consolidation) Act then in force did not give her a claim for statutory redundancy pay because she was over 60. However, men were so entitled until the age of 65. This difference in treatment was removed by section 16(1) of the Employment Act 1989, with effect from January 16, 1990. However, this legislative amendment was not retrospective.

On May 17, 1990, the European Court issued its decision in *Barber* v. *Guardian Royal Exchange Assurance Group Ltd.*,[55] which made clear that statutory redundancy payments fall within the definition of "pay" in Article 119 of the EEC Treaty. In any event, prior to that decision, Mrs Rankin had brought an application to a Scottish Industrial Tribunal claiming that she was entitled under Article 119 to the redundancy payment she would have received under U.K. law had she been a man.

---

[52] See judgment in *Emmott op. cit.*, n. 32, at para. 16.
[53] See further para. 2–002 above.
[54] *Rankin* v. *British Coal Corporation* [1993] I.R.L.R. 69.
[55] *Barber* v. *Guardian Royal Exchange Assurance Group Ltd.* [1990] I.R.L.R. 240, discussed further at para. 4–008 above.

However, the Industrial Tribunal dismissed her application on the grounds that it was out of time. The Tribunal based its decision on s.101(1) of the Employment Protection (Consolidation) Act, which required an application for a redundancy payment to be made within six months or, if the Industrial Tribunal considers it just and equitable, within one year from the date of dismissal. Mrs Rankin's claim was presented more than one year from the date of her dismissal.

On appeal to the Employment Appeal Tribunal, it was not disputed that Mrs Rankin's right was free-standing, *i.e.* that Article 119 conferred on her an independent right, which was not dependent on amending or modifying the relevant domestic legislation. It was also accepted by both parties that it was only after the decision in *Barber* that it was clearly established that statutory redundancy payments fall under Article 119.

The respondents argued that, *inter alia*, there must be time limits for such claims, particularly as, in the absence of any time limit, women would be placed in a better position than men. The appellant submitted that there were no relevant time limits contained in any other applicable legislation.

5–020    The EAT agreed that there were no time limits for a free-standing claim under Article 119, nor any general time limit, in any statute or regulation, applying to all proceedings brought before an Industrial Tribunal. The time limit under s.101 of the 1978 Act applies to redundancy payments under that Act, and Mrs Rankin's claim was based on Article 119 and not the Act.

The EAT did not attempt to lay down general rules for all claims, but did have regard to whether Mrs Rankin's claim could be regarded as timeous. It took the view that the principle of legal certainty required that there must be some time limit placed upon claims. This was regarded by the Tribunal as a principle which was also one of the principles of Community law to which a national court is required to give effect. In addition, the time limit should be reasonable and should not discriminate as between rights conferred by the Treaty and rights under national law.

The critical question was to decide at what point of time the period for the bringing of claims should be held to begin. The choice appeared to lie between the date of the redundancy, March 31, 1987 or the date upon which it could reasonably be said to be clear that a person affected, such as the appellant, could properly bring a claim. However, Mrs Rankin had in fact brought her claim before the date of the operative decision in *Barber*. The EAT noted that the general policy in legislation, concerned not only with redundancy but with similar statutory claims such as those under the equal pay and racial and sexual discrimination provisions, suggests that a period for bringing claims in the region of three to six months could not properly be stigmatised as unreasonable, given that the starting date for the running of the period is also reasonable.

The EAT eventually took the view that the claim should be brought within a reasonable period after the coming into force of the amending legislation. Since the appellant's claim was brought within three months from the date on which the legislation came into force, the appeal was allowed.

The EAT also noted in passing, that no argument had in fact been run in the *Rankin* case to the effect that an "emanation of the State" (such as the respondents) should not be entitled to rely on a time limit operating prior to the correction of a failure to execute Community law, where that failure was the responsibility of the State, (similar to the doctrine in *Emmott* in relation to directives). However, the EAT considered that it was in any event not necessary for it to express its view on that point.

For practical purposes, it is always preferable for claims based on directly effective E.C. Treaty provisions to be brought at the earliest opportunity. Where appropriate, requests can then be made for an Article 177 reference,[56] to determine the application of the relevant Community law, or for a stay of the proceedings, pending the outcome of other litigation on the same or related points.

# THE RATIONALE FOR DIRECT EFFECT OF DIRECTIVES

## *Political implications*

The Court has concluded that the provisions of directives can have **5–021** direct effect, even though this is not implicit in the wording of Article 189 of the EEC Treaty.[57] This will continue to be the position in the post-Maastricht era. In Case 41/74, *Van Duyn*[58] the Court held for the first time that a directive could confer rights enforceable by individuals in national courts. It is suggested by Hartley[59] that the main reason for this judgment was that without attributing "direct effect" to directives, the only means of enforcing Community law would be under the procedures in Articles 169 to 171 of the Treaty of Rome, whereby the Commission or another Member State can bring an action before the Court. Such actions would be limited in practice to only a few cases per year and mean that large numbers of directives would remain unimplemented. The attribution of direct effect has the additional advantage of shielding the Commission from policical pressure and of transferring the burden of ensuring compliance to the national courts.[60] In other words, by endowing directives with direct effect, the Court promoted the practical implementation of Community law. However, Marcini points out[61] that there was an important constitutional basis for the Court's approach, which was to ensure respect for the Community rule of law,

---

[56] See further discussion at paras. 3–016 *et seq.* above.
[57] Curtin, "The Province of Government: Delimiting the Direct Effect of Directives in the Common Law Context" (1990) 15 E.L.Rev. 195 at p. 196.
[58] Case 41/74, *Van Duyn*: [1974] E.C.R. 1337, [1975] 1 C.M.L.R. 1.
[59] Hartley, *The Foundation of European Community Law* (1988, reprinted in 1990) 2nd ed., p. 204.
[60] See Hartley, *op. cit.*, p. 204.
[61] Marcini, "The Making of a Constitution for Europe" (1989) C.M.L.Rev. 569 at p. 602.

*i.e.* to ensure that the legitimate expectations of Community citizens on whom a Directive may confer rights, are not frustrated either by allowing Member States to rely upon their own malfeasance or the Community's failure to enforce compliance.[62]

### Principle of effectiveness versus estoppel

5–022    At first, the Court based its legal reasoning on two related general principles. First, the status of Community law as an integral part of the Member States' national legal order and secondly on the civil principle that a legal measure must be presumed to have useful effect (*effet utile*).[63] In 1979 in Case 148/78, *Pubblico Ministero* v. *Tullio Ratti*[64] the Court stated that the effectiveness of Community law would be weakened if individuals were prevented from relying on directives which placed a duty on Member States to adopt a certain course of action.[65] However, the Court also relied on estoppel, whereby Member States should not be able to rely on their own failure to implement Community law.[66] Following this reasoning, the State could not be permitted to enforce inconsistent national legislation against a private individual who is seeking to rely on the terms of the Directive. Otherwise the State could rely on its own wrong. Under this approach, the Directive does not directly confer rights on individuals but indirectly does so out of the obligation imposed on Member States. This reasoning has the effect of limiting the consequences of direct effect to relations between the State and a private individual (*i.e.* vertical direct effect). It means that directives cannot create enforceable rights as between private individuals (*i.e.* horizontal direct effect).[67]

The principle of effectiveness, on the other hand, is considerably broader than that of estoppel in that it allows directives to apply to legal disputes involving individuals. Curtin suggests that this judicial restraint was related to the hostility displayed by some national courts to the whole concept of direct effect of directives.[68] There are some legal arguments which have been put forward to justify the view that directives should not be horizontally directly effective.[69] First, that since

---

[62] Marcini, *ibid.*, p. 602.
[63] See, for example, Case 9/70, *Grad* v. *Finanzamt Traunstein*: [1970]. E.C.R. 825, [1971] C.M.L.R. 1; Case 33/70, *Spa SACE* v. *Italian Minister of Finance*: [1970] E.C.R. 1213, [1971] C.M.L.R. 123; Case 41/74, *Van Duyn* v. *Home Office*: [1974] E.C.R. 1337, [1975] 1 C.M.L.R. 1.
[64] Case 148/78, *Pubblico Ministero* v. *Tullio Ratti*: [1979] E.C.R. 1629, [1980] 1 C.M.L.R. 96.
[65] *Ratti, ibid.*, para. 21.
[66] See Curtin, *op. cit.*, n. 57, p. 196.
[67] See further para. 2–010 above and Morris and David, "Directives, Direct Effect and the European Court: The Triumph of Pragmatism — Pt. II" (May 1987) E.B.L.Rev., pp. 116 to 118 and continued on pp. 135 to 136.
[68] Curtin, *op. cit.*, n. 57, p. 197, n. 14: see, for example, judgment by the French *Counseil d'Etat* of December 22, 1978 in *Ministère de l'Intérieur* v. *Cohn Bendit*: (1979) R.T.D.E. 157 to the effect that directives may not even enjoy vertical direct effect and the judgment of the German *Bundesfinanzhof* of July 16, 1981: (1981) EuR 442.
[69] See Wyatt and Dashwood, *European Community Law* (1993), 3rd ed., p. 73 and see generally, Easson, (1979) 4 E.L.Rev. 67 at pp. 70–73.

there is no legal requirement to publish directives, they should only bind the addressee. Secondly, if directives are accorded horizontal direct effect, it would effectively assimilate directives and regulations, contrary to Article 189 of the Treaty. Thirdly, that it would lead to legal uncertainty since individuals would not know whether or not they may rely on national implementing legislation or rely instead on the Directives themselves.

In Case 152/84, *Marshall* v. *Southampton and South West Hampshire* **5–023** *Area Health Authority* (referred to as *Marshall (No. 1)*),[70] the Court followed its line of reasoning based on estoppel, and interpreted Article 189 of the EEC Treaty in a way which supported a conclusion that provisions of a directive which had either not been implemented at all by the Member State in question or had been incorrectly transposed into national law could not create so-called "horizontal direct effect". They could, however, have "vertical direct effect", giving individuals rights against the State.

The European Court stated that:

"With regard to the argument that a directive may not be relied on against an individual, it must be emphasised that according to Article 189 of the EEC Treaty the binding nature of a directive, which constitutes the basis for the possibility of relying on the Directive before a national court, exists only in relation to each Member State to which it is addressed. It follows that a directive may not of itself impose obligations on an individual and that a provision of a directive may not be relied on as such against such a person."[71]

It is suggested by Morris and David[72] that the Court in *Marshall (No. 1)* relied on a literal interpretation of Article 189 to support its conclusion that directives could not create horizontal direct effect. This view is open to the criticism that a literal interpretation of Article 189 would logically result in a denial of *any* form of direct effect to a directive, thus limiting direct effect to regulations only. However, this is clearly not the approach taken by the Court in its earlier decisions. In the subsequent Case 271/89, *Marshall* v. *Southampton and South West Hampshire Area Health Authority (Teaching)*,[73] (referred to as *Marshall (No. 2)*), the Advocate General Gerven in his Opinion suggests that "the coherence of the Court's case law would benefit if the Court were now also to confer horizontal direct effect on sufficiently precise and unconditional provisions of Directives."[74] The Court is not bound by its previous

---

[70] Case 152/84, *Marshall* v. *Southampton and South West Hampshire Area Health Authority*: [1986] E.C.R. 723, [1986] 1 C.M.L.R. 688.

[71] *Ibid.*, para. 48.

[72] Morris and David, *op. cit.*, n. 67, p. 118.

[73] Case 271/91, *Marshall* v. *Southampton and South West Hampshire Area Health Authority (Teaching) (No. 2)*: [1993] 3 C.M.L.R. 293.

[74] *Ibid.*, para. 12 see also the test of Advocate General Van Gerven's lecture, "The Horizontal Direct Effect of Directive Provisions Revisited—The Reality of Catchwords," Institute of European Public Law, Lecture Series, University of Hull, 1993. See further discussion at paras. 9–025 *et seq.* below.

decisions, but in practice it does not often depart from them.[75] However, in the second *HAG* case[76] the Advocate General Jacobs did not follow the doctrine of common origin laid down in the first *HAG* case[77] and urged the Court to do likewise. He said "that the Court shall in an appropriate case expressly overrule an earlier decision is I think an inescapable duty even if the Court has never before expressly done so." The Court's judgment in *HAG II* made it clear that the doctrine of common origin had been overruled.[78]

The question whether the provisions of a directive may have horizontal direct effect is currently pending before the ECJ in a case under Article 177 from an Italian court, Case C–91/92, *Re Paola Faccini Dori*.[79] It concerns the interpretation of Article 5 of Council Directive 85/577[80] under which a consumer has the right to resile from a contract concluded outside the seller's commercial premises, within seven days of its signing. The Italian judge has asked for a ruling on whether Ms Faccini Dori can rely upon Article 5, as against the seller, to terminate a contract for the sale of language courses, even though the directive has not yet been transposed into Italian law. The ECJ has made the unusual request that E.C. Member States and the Commission should comment in writing on the legal issues raised by the case. However, there does not appear to be any support from either the Member States or the Commission for the creation of horizontal direct effect for directives. The Court is therefore unlikely to take such a dynamic course in the short term, since it is unlikely to be politically acceptable to Member States. In the meantime, the only potentially effective way of using Community rights to establish the liability of individuals in the *absence* of direct effect, is to try to persuade a national court to interpret Community law in a purposive manner. This has been referred to as "indirect" direct effect and is discussed in detail in the next chapter.

---

[75] Arnull, "Owning up to Fallibility: Precedent and the Court of Justice" (1993) C.M.L.Rev. 247 at p. 248.

[76] Cassse C–10/89, *CNL-SUCAL* v. *HAG GF*: [1990] I E.C.R. 3711, [1990] 3 C.M.L.R. 571.

[77] Case 192/73, *Van Zuylen* v. *HAG*: [1974] E.C.R. 731, [1974] C.M.L.R. 127.

[78] Arnull, *op. cit.*, p. 261.

[79] Case C–91/92, *Re Paolo Faccini Dori*. This case has been argued before the Court. The Opinion of Advocate General Lenz is to be delivered on a date not yet fixed. The case has been referred to by Advocate General Van Gerven in the text of his lecture, *op. cit.*, n. 74.

[80] [1985] O.J. L372/31.

# "INDIRECT" DIRECT EFFECT: PURPOSIVE INTERPRETATION OF COMMUNITY LAW

## PRINCIPLES LAID DOWN BY THE ECJ

There is a line of cases where, regardless of the existence of direct **6–001** effects, the Court seemed to be urging national courts to interpret national law more dynamically in order to give directives maximum effect.[1] In Case 14/83, *Von Colson and Kamaan* v. *Land Nordrhein Westfalen*[2] and Case 79/83, *Harz* v. *Deutsche Tradex*[3] the Court held that the Equal Treatment Directive[4] which was under consideration in both cases, was *not* directly effective with regard to the question of remedies. Nevertheless, the Court emphasised that Article 5 of the EEC Treaty (which has not been amended by the Treaty on European Union), placed the national judge under as much a duty as the executive or the legislature to ensure that Treaty obligations were observed. The *Von Colson* case[5] concerned the question of availability of adequate compensation for breach by an employer of the Equal Treatment Directive.[6] Although the relevant provisions were not directly effective, national courts were obliged to "interpret their national law in the light of the wording and the purpose of the Directive."[7]

In other words, it was the national court's duty to explore the possibility of interpreting their national legislation in a manner consistent

---

[1] Curtin, "The Province of Government: Delimiting the Direct Effect of Directives in the Common Law Context" (1990) 15 E.L.Rev. 195 at p. 221.

[2] Case 14/83, *Von Colson and Kamaan* v. *Land Nordrhein Westfalen*: [1984] E.C.R. 1891, [1986] 2 C.M.L.R. 430.

[3] Case 79/83, *Harz* v. *Deutsche Tradax*: [1984] E.C.R. 1921, [1986] 2 C.M.L.R. 430.

[4] Directive 76/207 on the implementation of the principle of equal treatment for men and women as regards access to employment, vocational training and promotion and working conditions, [1976] O.J. L39/40.

[5] *Von Colson, op. cit.*, n. 2.

[6] Directive 76/207, *op. cit.*, n. 4.

[7] *Von Colson, op. cit.*, n. 4, para. 26.

with the provisions of a relevant directive.[8] This meant that any variation provided for by the Member State must guarantee real and effective judicial protection of the individual and have a deterrent effect on the employer. Nominal compensation in that case was held to be insufficient.

### Extent of national court's discretion

6-002    However, this duty of national courts is limited by the extent of the discretion which such courts may have in matters of legal interpretation under national law. In particular, it is not clear what the limits of this interpretative obligation may be in the situation where national courts are faced with a domestic provision which uses language clearly contrary to a directive.[9] In his Opinion in Case 271/89, *Marshall* v. *Southampton and South West Hampshire Area Health Authority (Teaching)*,[10] referred to as *Marshall (No. 2)* the Advocate General Van Gerven confirmed that national courts are under an obligation to interpret *ambiguous* national law in such a way that it is in conformity with a relevant directive, even if the relevant provisions of the Directive are *not* directly effective.[11] However, the obligation does not require the national court to interpret national law such as, for example, a specific rule on sanctions, *contra legem*. However, at a later point in his Opinion he suggests that these difficulties could be avoided if the Court were now also to confer *horizontal* direct effect on sufficiently precise and unconditional provisions of directives.[12]

In the *Von Colson* case, the German Court which originally referred the case to Luxembourg, concluded that it could disregard the customary method of interpretation under German law if this was necessary to achieve a solution in accordance with the provisions of the Directive.[13] As Curtin suggests,[14] if such an approach is followed by national courts then the provisions of directives can be applied indirectly to individuals in legal proceedings *inter se* by the interpretation of national legislation so as to conform with the directive. The direct effect as such of the directive is then no longer essential to create rights and obligations for individuals under domestic law. This will be of particular importance if the proceedings were being brought not against the State or an emanation of it,[15] but against a private party, against whom a directive is not horizontally effective.

---

[8] Curtin, *op. cit.*, n. 1, p. 220.

[9] See de Búrca, "Giving Effect to European Community Directives" (1992) M.L.R. 215 at p. 217.

[10] Case 271/89, *Marshall* v. *Southampton and South West Hampshire Area Health Authority (Teaching) (No. 2)*: [1993] 3 C.M.L.R. 293. See also discussion at paras. 9–025 *et seq.* below.

[11] *Op. cit.*, para. 22.

[12] *Op. cit.*, para. 12. See also para. 5–023 above, n. 74.

[13] See Curtin, *op. cit.*, n. 1, judgment of the *Arbeitsgericht* Hamm of September 6, 1984 *Der Betrieb 2700*.

[14] *Op. cit.*, n. 10, p. 221.

[15] See further discussion at Chap. 7 below.

Curtin further argues[16] that it is only if the terms of the relevant Directive cannot be satisfied in this indirect way that the question of direct effect of the provisions of the Directive then arises. For example, a purposive interpretation was adopted by Advocate General Darmon in Case 177/88, *Dekker* v. *Stichting Vormingscentrum Voor Jong Volwassenen*,[17] although the case was not specifically concerned with the effect of the Court's ruling in national law.[18] The Advocate General did refer, however, to the primary duty on national courts to interpret national law in the light of Community law and suggested that the direct effect of directives was simply an "*ultima ratio*". If it is possible to give complete *effet utile* to Article 189(3) of the E.C. Treaty by interpreting national law in the light of Community law, then this technique should be preferred before the question of direct effect is raised. In *Dekker*, the Advocate General had no difficulty in suggesting that ambiguous national law be interpreted in a manner consistent with the Directive in question and hence the whole question of the direct effect of the Directive did not fall to be considered.

It is also suggested by Curtin[19] that in order for the indirect interpreta- **6–003** tive route to be open to national courts, some national legislation must exist which is capable of being interpreted so as to give maximum effect to the Directive or other Community provision. It may therefore be of no assistance where a private individual is attempting to rely on a directive against another individual and there has been no implementing legislation. This is of some practical importance, since a number of Member States have failed to enact directives within the required time limit. The consequence is that there is often no national legislation on which a court can base a reasoning in the light of Community obligations of the Member State.[20]

However, the above proposition may no longer apply in the light of the judgment of the European Court in Joined Cases C–6 & 9/90, *Francovich and Bonifaci* v. *Italian Republic*,[21] where despite the fact that the relevant provisions of the Directive were held *not* to be directly effective and had not been implemented in any way, the Court still found a right to compensation for the individual who had suffered. This right to compensation existed even though, and in fact because of, the failure of the State to enact national laws to give effect to the provisions of the Directive.

---

[16] *Op. cit.*, n. 1, p. 221.
[17] Case 177/88, *Dekker* v. *Stichting Vormingscentrum Voor Jong Volwassenen*: Opinion of November 19, 1989, judgment of November 8, 1990, [1991] I.R.L.R. 27 (Dutch).
[18] See Shaw, "Pregnancy Discrimination in Sex Discrimination" (1991) 16 E.L.Rev. 313 at p. 318.
[19] *Op. cit.*, n. 1, p. 221.
[20] See Morris and David, "Directives, Direct Effect and the European Court: The Triumph of Pragmatism — Pt. II" (1987) E.B.L.Rev. 116 at p. 117.
[21] Joined Cases C–6 & 9/90, *Francovich and Bonifaci*: [1991] I E.C.R. 5357, [1993] 2 C.M.L.R. 66.

## Absence of implementing legislation

6–004    The "indirect" interpretative route, as established in cases such as *Von Colson*,[22] has been reaffirmed by the European Court in Case C–106/89, *Marleasing SA* v. *La Comercial Internacional de Alimentación SA*.[23] The Company Marleasing SA brought an action in the Spanish Courts seeking to annul the defendant Spanish company, La Comercial, on the grounds that the legal basis for establishing that company was void under Spanish law. It argued that it had been created solely for the purposes of putting the assets of a third company beyond the reach of creditors, who included Marleasing. The view that the formation of a company is governed by contractual principles has had wide influence in Spanish law. Under the Spanish Civil Code, contracts may be set aside for lack of legal consideration.

The defendant company successfully argued before the Court of Justice that Article 11 of the First EEC Company Law Directive 68/151 nevertheless applied and that it did not provide for the nullity of a company to be declared on such grounds. By Article 395 of the Act of Accession of Spain and Portugal[24] this Directive was required to be implemented in Spain at the time of Spain's accession.[25] At the time the case was referred to the European Court, no Spanish legislation had been promulgated to give effect to the Directive.

The Court was asked whether the relevant Article of the Directive was directly effective. The Court recalled its earlier case law according to which a directive could not by itself create obligations for an individual and, accordingly, its provisions could not be relied on as such against such a person. The Court then reformulated the question referred by the Spanish judge and considered whether a national judge who is seized of an action in a matter which falls under the provisions of a directive, is bound to interpret national law in the light of the text and the aims of that directive so as to prevent a declaration of nullity, in the given case, of a limited company, for a reason other than those set out in Article 11 of the Directive.[26]

The Court referred to its previous ruling in the *Von Colson* case[27] and held that it followed from the obligation in Article 5 of the EEC Treaty on Member States to take all measures appropriate to ensure the performance of their obligation to achieve the result provided for in directives, that in applying national law, *whether it was a case of provisions prior or subsequent to that directive*, the national court called on to interpret it was required to do so as far as possible in the light of the wording and

---

[22] *Op. cit.*, n. 2.

[23] Case C–106/89, *Marleasing SA* v. *La Comercial Internacional de Alimentación SA*: [1990] I E.C.R. 4135, [1992] 1 C.M.L.R. 305.

[24] [1985] O.J. L302/23.

[25] January 1, 1986.

[26] See para. 7 of the judgment *op. cit.*, n. 23, and discussion by Phillip Mead, "The Obligation to Apply European Law: Is Duke Dead?" (1991) 16 E.L. Rev. 490 at p. 491.

[27] *Op. cit.*, n. 2.

purpose of the Directive in order to achieve the result sought by the Directive, and thus to comply with Article 189(3) of the Treaty. (This ruling by the Court is uneffected by any amendment made at Maastricht by the Treaty on European Union.)

There is therefore no longer any doubt that the duty to interpret domestic law in conformity with a directive is *not* limited to *implementing* legislation.[28] This follows from the Court's observation that even law *pre-dating* the Directive can be interpreted in line with it. Furthermore, it appears that *any* national law, *e.g.* the common law (and not just statutory law) may be interpreted in line with an unimplemented directive. The Court concluded that the grounds for declaring a company null and void in the Directive were exhaustive and had to be strictly construed.[29] This appears to put the obligation of purposive construction in very strong terms. The defendant therefore won the case.

The "indirect interpretative route" was therefore followed in *Marleasing* and the question of whether the Directive had direct effect was avoided. The result was to affect the rights and obligations of individuals *inter se*. It should, however, be noted first, that this was a judgment by a chamber and not the full Court and therefore arguably does not carry the same weight of authority. Secondly, by the time of the Court's judgment in *Marleasing*, the Spanish government had in fact implemented the relevant Directive and this may have had a bearing on the reasoning of the Court. It is a judgment which has been criticised informally by Sir Gordon Slynn[30] and it remains to be seen what impact it has in domestic law. Although *Marleasing* shows that individuals may be able to obtain protection of Community rights which are *not* directly effective, the weakness is that it requires a willingness on the part of national courts to treat the obligations contained in Article 5 of the E.C. Treaty as relevant in a particular case.[31]

## Supremacy of directly effective provisions

When a directive *is* directly effective it can, of course, be relied upon **6–005** despite conflicting domestic law.[32] In the *Verbond* case,[33] the European Court held that the concept of "capital goods" in the Second VAT Directive could be relied on rather than the wider phrase "business assets" which was used in Dutch implementing legislation. In such cases, parliamentary sovereignty gives way to the supremacy of directly effective Community law. (However, the case involved an action against a State authority *i.e.* the Directive was capable of *vertical* direct effect.)

---

[28] See de Búrca, "Giving Effect to European Community Directives" (1992) M.L.R. 215 at p. 223 and Ross, "Beyond *Francovich*" (1993) M.L.R. 55 at p. 56.

[29] *Marleasing*, *op. cit.*, n. 23, para. 12 of the judgment.

[30] Formerly a judge of the European Court, now a Lord of Appeal in the House of Lords.

[31] Ross, *op. cit.*, n. 28, p. 56.

[32] See Case 51/76, *Verbond van Nederlandse Ondernemingen* v. *Inspecteur der Invoerrechten en Accijnzen*: [1977] E.C.R. 113, [1977] 1 C.M.L.R. 413 and discussion at paras. 3–012 *et seq.* above.

[33] *Ibid.*

111

In Case 222/84, *Johnston* v. *Chief Constable of the RUC*[34] the European Court considered the application of the Equal Treatment Directive[35] to a policewoman in Northern Ireland who claimed sex discrimination against her employer, the Royal Ulster Constabulary (RUC), for failure to renew her contract. There had been specific legislation to give effect to the Directive. The Court held that where there was a conflict between the Directive and the implementing legislation, the applicant should rely on the doctrine of direct effect.[36] On the facts the Applicant could succeed in this way, since the RUC fell within the definition of "emanation of the State."[37] However, the Court clearly relied on direct effect rather than the "indirect interpretation" route suggested in the later case of *Marleasing.*[38]

*Expiry of time limit for national implementation*

**6–006**    In Case 80/86, *Officier van Justitie* v. *Kolpinghaus Nijmegen BV*[39] however, the European Court suggested that a court cannot, relying on a directive for which the date for implementation has passed, alter *pre-existing national law* to the *detriment* of an individual.[40] The case concerned a prosecution in the Netherlands for the stocking for sale and delivery of goods which were of "unsound composition". The latter phrase was undefined in Dutch law but the authorities sought to include products which did not conform to Directive 80/777 on the exploitation and marketing of natural mineral waters.[41] However, the Directive had not been implemented in Dutch law but the date for implementation had expired three weeks prior to the commission of the alleged offence. The Court held that a directive could not, independently of implementing legislation, create or aggravate the *criminal* liability of one who breached its provisions, because the duty of the national courts to interpret law in the light of the Directive was limited by the general principles of law and, in particular, the principles of legal certainty and non-retroactivity.

The Court's ruling specified that the national court's duty to interpret provisions of national law in accordance with relevant directives *is unaffected by the question of whether or not the time limit for implementation has expired.* However, this does not necessarily imply that national courts are obliged to construe domestic law in conformity with directives, as soon as they are *adopted.*[42] It may be that in *Kolpinghaus* the Court merely

---

[34] Case 222/84, *Johnston* v. *Chief Constable of the RUC*: [1986] E.C.R. 1651, [1986] 3 C.M.L.R. 240.

[35] Council Directive 76/207 on equal treatment as regards access to employment, vocational training and working conditions, [1976] O.J. L39/40.

[36] *Johnston, op. cit.*, n. 34, pp. 1690–91 in para. 54.

[37] *Mead, op. cit.*, n. 26, p. 494.

[38] *Op. cit.*, n. 23.

[39] Case 80/86, *Officer van Justitie* v. *Kolpinghaus Nijmegen BV*: [1987] E.C.R. 3969, [1989] 2 C.M.L.R. 18.

[40] See Howells, "European Directives: The Emerging Dilemmas" (1991) M.L.R. 456 at p. 460.

[41] [1980] O.J. L229/1.

[42] See further discussion at paras. 5–009 *et seq.* above.

intended to state that the Directive could not be used as an interpretive aid to *impose retroactive criminal* liability either before or after the expiry of the time limit.[43] It does not resolve the question of how national courts are to interpret domestic law after the adoption of a relevant directive but *before* the expiry of the time limit for its implementation. However, on the basis of the general principle established in Case 148/78, *Pubblico Ministero* v. *Ratti*,[44] discussed in detail at paragraph 5–009 above, it may be that in accordance with the proviso that directives are only capable of direct effects *after* the date for their implementation has passed, the duty on national courts to adopt a purposive approach also only applies *after* the expiry of the time limit for implementation.

## PURPOSIVE INTERPRETATION BY ENGLISH COURTS

The House of Lords rejected a purposive approach to the interpreta- **6–007** tion of Community law in *Duke* v. *GEC Reliance Ltd.*[45] in construing section 6(4) of the Sex Discrimination Act 1975 in the light of the relevant E.C. Directive. The case concerned a female employee claiming sex discrimination under the Sex Discrimination Act 1975 and Equal Treatment Directive[46] because her contract of employment permitted her dismissal at the statutory retirement age of 60, when equivalent male employees could continue working until the age of 65. In that case, the Act had been passed *before* the Directive was enacted and Lord Templeman (with whom the other judges concurred) held that:

"Section 2(4) of the European Communities Act does no more than reinforce the binding nature of legally enforceable rights and obligations imposed by Community law. [It] does not . . . enable or constrain a British court to distort the meaning of a British statute in order to enforce against an individual a Community directive which has no direct effect between individuals. Section 2(4) applies and only applies where Community provisions are directly applicable."[47]

The substance of this decision is not affected by the entry into force of the Treaty on European Union and consequent amendments to the 1972 Act made by the European Communities (Amendment) Act 1993.[48]

*Relevance of horizontal direct effect*

It is clear that national courts are required to ignore incompatible **6–008** national law where there is a conflict with *directly effective* Community law, *i.e.* directly effective provisions of Regulations and E.C. Treaty

---

[43] See de Búrca, *op. cit.*, n. 28, p. 218, n. 24.
[44] Case 148/78, *Pubblico Ministero* v. *Ratti*: [1979] E.C.R. 1629, [1980] 1 C.M.L.R. 96.
[45] *Duke* v. *GEC Reliance Ltd.*: [1988] A.C. 618.
[46] Council Directive 76/207: equal treatment as regards access to employment, vocational training and working conditions, [1976] O.J. L39/40.
[47] *Duke*, *op. cit.*, n. 45, p. 680.
[48] See further, Chap. 2, above.

provisions. With regard to directives, however, since they cannot give rise to horizontal direct effects,[49] this principle of supremacy of Community law only applies in actions against the State or an emanation of the State. Thus the European Court in Case 152/87 *Marshall* v. *Southampton and South West Hampshire Area Health Authority (Marshall (No. 1))*[50] accepted that:

> "If this means that employees of private employers are at a disadvantage compared with State employees it is for the State, as its duty is to do, to remedy the position by conferring the same advantages upon other employees."[51]

The conclusion of the House of Lords in *Duke* was that section 2(4) of the European Communities Act 1972 does not require an English court to set aside English law which may be incompatible with Community law in a case concerning two private litigants and involving a directive which is not directly effective. However, it has been argued by Foster[52] that section 2(4) when combined with section 2(1) of the European Communities Act (as amended) can permit a purposive construction of Community law despite the absence of horizontal direct effect. Otherwise, Community law which is not directly effective can, when combined with inaction or dilatory action by a Member State, serve to defeat the Community rights of individuals.[53]

It has also been argued that the reasoning in *Duke*[54] is not consistent with that of the European Court.[55] In *Von Colson*[56] the Court did appear to limit purposive interpretation to the situation where legislation had been enacted specifically to implement a directive. However, there are dicta which suggest that pre-existing legislation is also covered.[57] The subsequent decision in Case 106/89, *Marleasing* v. *La Commercial*[58] now makes it clear that purposive interpretation also applies to pre-existing legislation.[59] This is a logical approach, otherwise the *Von Colson* principle of purposive interpretation could not apply where there was no need for the amendment of existing national legislation to give effect to a directive.[60]

---

[49] See discussion at para. 2–010 above.

[50] Case 52/84, *Marshall (No. 1)*: [1986] E.C.R. 723, [1986] 1 C.M.L.R. 688.

[51] *Marshall (No. 1)*, *ibid.*, p. 735.

[52] (1988) C.M.L.Rev. 629 at p. 637.

[53] *Ibid.*, p. 638.

[54] *Op. cit.*, n. 45.

[55] Szyszczak, "Sovereignty Crisis, Compliance, Confusion, Complacency?" (1990) 15 E.L.Rev. 480 at p. 484 and see further, Foster, (1988) C.M.L.Rev. 629; Arnull (1988) 13 E.L.Rev. 42; Fitzpatrick (1989) 90 J.L.S. 336.

[56] Case 14/38, *Von Colson*: [1984] E.C.R. 1891.

[57] See, for instance, Advocate General Mischo in Case 80/86, *Criminal Proceedings against Kolpinghaus Nijmegen BV*: [1987] E.C.R. 3639; Advocate General Van Gerven in Case C–262/88, *Barber* v. *Guardian Royal Exchange Assurance Group*: [1990] I E.C.R. 1989, [1990] 2 C.M.L.R. 513.

[58] Case 106/89, *Marleasing*: [1990] I E.C.R. 4135.

[59] See further paras. 6–001 *et seq.* above.

[60] Szyszczak, *op. cit.*, n. 55, p. 485.

It is also argued by Collins[61] that it is not necessary to rely on either section 2(1) or section 2(4) of the European Communities Act (as amended) to support the argument that national legislation must comply with Community law. The general principle of statutory interpretation applies and legislation must be construed so as to conform with the U.K.'s international obligations.[62]

## Legislation not intended to implement Community law

Nevertheless, the reasoning adopted by the House of Lords in *Duke*[63] **6–009** was followed in the subsequent case of *Finnegan* v. *Clowney Youth Training Programme Ltd.*[64] which was an appeal to the House of Lords from the Northern Ireland Court of Appeal. The case involved the interpretation of Article 8(4) of the Sex Discrimination (Northern Ireland) Order 1976 (which was a parallel provision to section 6(4) of the Sex Discrimination Act 1975). The Northern Ireland Industrial Tribunal upheld a complaint of sex discrimination by interpreting section 8(4) to comply with the Equal Treatment Directive as interpreted in *Marshall (No. 1)*.[65] The Northern Ireland Order 1976 had been enacted after the Directive was adopted and the European Court had already ruled in Case 222/84, *Johnston* v. *Chief Constable of The RUC*[66] that the Order should be interpreted in the light of that Directive. However, the House of Lords decided that the purposive rule of construction contained in section 2(4) of the European Communities' Act 1972 does not apply to legislation which *was not designed to implement that directive*.[67] It was therefore a different situation from that of the regulations in *Pickstone* v. *Freemans Plc*[68] and *Litster* v. *Forth Dry Dock and Engineering Co. Ltd.*[69] where the legislation had been intended to implement Community law.[70] The Order merely enacted the Sex Discrimination Act 1975 in Northern Ireland and the date of the Order was irrelevant. Since the Directive did not give rise to direct effects in *Finnegan* the House of Lords also ruled that there was no point of Community law involved and no reference to the European Court was required.

The *Finnegan* case may be anomalous decision arising out of its relationship with the *Duke* case and the possible concern of the House of

---

[61] Collins, *European Law in the U.K.* (1990), 4th ed., p. 135.
[62] See further Duffy, "English Law and the European Convention on Human Rights" (1980) 29 I.C.L.Q. 585 to 592 in which he cites *Ahmed* v. *ILEA* [1978] Q.B. 36 and *Williams* v. *Home Office* (May 9, 1980). See also *Jarman* v. *Mid Glamorgan Education Authority*, The Times, February 11, 1985 cited by Foster, *op. cit.*, n. 55, p. 639, n. 36.
[63] *Op. cit.*, n. 45.
[64] *Finnegan* v. *Clowney Youth Training Programme Ltd.* [1990] 2 All E.R. 546.
[65] *Ibid.*
[66] Case 222/84, *Johnston* v. *Chief Constable of the RUC*: [1986] E.C.R. 1651, [1986] 3 C.M.L.R. 240.
[67] See Szyszczak, *op. cit.*, n. 55, p. 485.
[68] *Pickstone* v. *Freemans Plc* [1989] A.C. 66 discussed below at para. 6–010.
[69] *Litster* v. *Forth Dry Dock Engineering Co. Ltd.* [1989] I.R.L.R. 161 and see further below at paras. 6–012 *et seq.*
[70] *Finnegan, op. cit.*, n. 64, judgment of Lord Bridge.

Lords not to construe identical words differently in Northern Ireland from the rest of the U.K.[71] However, it may also suggest a reluctance to give a "pro-European" interpretation.[72] In any event, this decision must now be seen in the light of the subsequent European ruling in *Marleasing*,[73] which suggests that the national court's duty to interpret domestic law in conformity with a directive is not limited to implementing legislation and may also apply even though a directive is not directly effective against other individuals.

## Absence of ambiguity

**6–010**   In *Pickstone* v. *Freemans Plc*[74] the employers employed both men and women as warehouse operatives and as checker/warehouse operatives. The applicants, who were female warehouse operatives, claimed against the employers that they were entitled to equal pay with a male checker/warehouse operative on the basis that they were doing work of equal value within the meaning of section 1(2)(c) of the Equal Pay Act 1970, as amended by the U.K. Equal Pay (Amendment) Regulations 1983.[75]

An Industrial Tribunal dismissed the claim, holding that because the applicants were employed on like work with other male employees in the same establishment within the meaning of section 1(2)(a) of the Act, they were not entitled to rely on the equal value provisions contained in section 1(2)(c) thereof, or upon any rights derived from Article 119 of the EEC Treaty.

The Appeal Tribunal dismissed the applicants' appeal. However, on appeal by the applicants to the Court of Appeal, the appeal was allowed. The Court of Appeal found that the words used in section 1(2)(c) were *not* ambiguous and therefore on the assumed facts, the applicants did not fall within section 1(2)(c). However, the applicants were entitled to pursue equal value claims under Article 119 of the EEC Treaty on the basis that it was directly effective. Purchas L.J. took the view that there were two courses open to the Court:

> "(1) to refer two questions to the European Court asking (a) Does section 1(2)(c) comply with Article 119?, (b) Is Article 119 directly enforceable in the United Kingdom courts in cases where the discrimination arises in cases of unequal pay for work to which an equivalent value is attributed?
>
> (2) to construe section 1(2) of the Act of 1970 so as to conform with the principles of Article 119 by inserting the words necessary to achieve a result that is not inconsistent with Community law as I understand it. This involves an otherwise unjustifiable qualification of what are in fact clear words."

---

[71] See Howells, "European Directives: The Emerging Dilemmas" (1991) M.L.R. 456 at p. 462.

[72] Howells, *ibid.* and see further, Court of Appeal decision in *J. Rothschild Holdings Plc* v. *Commissioners of Inland Revenue* [1989] 2 C.M.L.R. 621, noted (1980) 7 Co.Law 131.

[73] Discussed further at para. 6–004 above.

[74] *Pickstone* v. *Freemans Plc* [1989] A.C. 66.

[75] S.I. 1983 No. 1794.

Purchas L.J. decided that since Article 177 references to the European Court were discretionary, and since he was firmly of the view that Article 119 was directly enforceable, he favoured the second of the two courses.[76]

In the House of Lords, the appeal by the employers was also **6–011** dismissed. However, the House of Lords found in favour of the respondents on the grounds that it was sufficient for them to rely on section 1(2)(c) of the 1970 Act, as amended, by adopting a purposive construction of the relevant provisions. It was therefore unnecessary to consider the ground on which the Court of Appeal found in favour of the respondents, namely that Article 119 was directly enforceable in such a way as to enable their claim to be supported irrespective of the true construction of the 1983 regulations.[77]

Lord Oliver of Aylmerton commented in his judgment:

". . . the intention of parliament has, it is said, to be ascertained from the words which it has used and those words are to be construed according to their plain and ordinary meaning. The fact that a statute is passed to give effect to an international treaty does not, of itself, enable the treaty to be referred to in order to construe the words used other than in their plain and unambiguous sense. Moreover, even in the case of ambiguity, what is said in parliament in the course of the passage of the Bill, cannot ordinarily be referred to assist in construction. I think, however, that it has also to be recognised that a statute which is passed in order to give effect to the United Kingdom's obligations under the EEC Treaty falls into a special category and it does so because, unlike other Treaty obligations, those obligations have, in effect, been incorporated into English law by the European Communities Act 1972. . . . subsection 1(2)(c) of the Equal Pay Act 1970 was inserted into the Act . . . by the Equal Pay (Amendment) Regulations 1983 . . . and it is perfectly plain that the amendments to the Act were inserted for the purpose of completing the compliance by the United Kingdom with its Treaty obligations under Article 119 and the Equal Pay Directive by remedying what was then perceived as the only remaining lacuna, namely that a woman was excluded from making an equal value claim unless she could persuade her employer to initiate a work evaluation study. . . .

Those regulations having been passed with the manifest and express purpose of producing a full compliance with the United Kingdom's obligation, they fall to be construed accordingly and that which I have suggested as falling to be implied into section 1(2)(c) is necessary to achieve that purpose. . . .

In the instant case, the strict and literal construction of the section does indeed involve the conclusion that the Regulations, although

---

[76] *Pickstone, op. cit.,* n. 74, p. 96, para. E.
[77] *Ibid.,* see judgment of Lord Keith of Kinkel at p. 112, para. E.

purporting to give full effect to the United Kingdom's obligations under Article 119, were in fact in breach of those obligations. . . .

That doubt removed, I am satisfied that the words of section 1(2)(c), whilst on the face of them unequivocal, are reasonably capable of bearing a meaning which will not put the United Kingdom in breach of its Treaty obligations. This conclusion is justified, in my judgment, by the manifest purpose of the legislation, by its history, and by the compulsive provision of section 2(4) of the Act of 1972. . . .[78]

(This judgment is in substance unaffected by the amendments made to the 1972 Act by the European Communities (Amendment) Act 1993.)

## Purposive versus literal construction

**6–012**   The House of Lords concluded in *Pickstone* that the U.K. Equal Pay (Amendment) Regulations 1983 had been enacted in order to comply with the Equal Pay Directive and a ruling of the Court in Case 61/81, *E.C. Commission* v. *United Kingdom*.[79] The Regulations had therefore been intended to comply with Community law. The House of Lords did not adopt a literal interpretation of the legislation but treated the issue as one of construction so as to comply with the U.K.'s EEC Treaty obligations.

The circumstances in which the courts are now allowed to look at Hansard and other parliamentary materials, in order to construe statutes and statutory instruments, have been widened following the decision by the House of Lords in *Pepper* v. *Hart*[80] in which the House of Lords held (Lord Mackay of Clashfern, Lord Chancellor dissenting) that subject to any question of parliamentary privilege, the previous rule excluding reference to parliamentary material as an aid to statutory construction should be relaxed so as to permit such reference where (a) legislation was ambiguous or obscure or led to absurdity, (b) the material relied upon consisted of one or more statements by a minister or promoter of the Bill together, if necessary, with such other parliamentary material as was necessary to understand such statements and their effect and (c) the statements relied upon were clear.[81]

A purposive interpretation such as that urged by the European Court in *Von Colson*[82] and applied by English courts in *Pickstone* was extended a year later by the House of Lords in *Litster* v. *Forth Dry Dock and Engineering Co. Ltd.*[83] In that case the House of Lords applied the judgment in the *Von Colson* case[84] and implied words into regulation 5(3)

---

[78] *Ibid.*, at pp. 126 *et seq.*
[79] Case 61/81, *Commission* v. *U.K.*: [1982] E.C.R. 2601, [1982] 3 C.M.L.R. 284.
[80] *Pepper* v. *Hart* [1992] 1 W.L.R. 1032, [1993] 1 All E.R. 42.
[81] See further, Victor Tunkel, "Research after *Pepper* v. *Hart*" (May 12, 1993), Vol. 90/18 *Gazette* 17 to 19.
[82] *Von Colson*: [1984] E.C.R. 1891, [1986] 2 C.M.L.R. 430.
[83] *Litster* v. *Forth Dry Dock and Engineering Co. Ltd.* [1989] I.R.L.R. 161.
[84] *Von Colson, op. cit.*, n. 82.

of the Transfer of Undertakings (Protection of Employment) Regulations 1991 in order to enable the Regulations to conform to the Directive which they were designed to implement. It therefore adopted a purposive construction of English law.[85] The House of Lords took this purposive approach even though the relevant U.K. statute was *not* ambiguous. It was nevertheless interpreted so as to be consistent with Community obligations provided that the statute is "honestly capable" of that meaning.[86]

In *Litster* the twelve appellants were employed by Forth Dry Dock, a company which went into receivership in September 1983. On February 6, 1984, at about 3.30 pm, they were summarily dismissed with immediate effect by the receivers. Later that day, Forth Estuary purchased the business assets of the company from the receivers. Immediately after the transfer, Forth Estuary began to recruit labour but none of the appellants was engaged. They complained that they had been unfairly dismissed by the receivers of Forth Dry Dock. Forth Estuary, the transferees, were joined as parties to the complaints and they argued that the Transfer of Undertakings Regulations did not apply in that the appellants were not employed in the business "immediately before the transfer" within the meaning of regulations 5(3). In the House of Lords, all five Law Lords were unanimous in finding for the dismissed employees.

In *Litster*, it was clear that the Transfer of Undertakings Regulations **6–013** had been designed to give effect to Council Directive 77/187 and in particular to Article 3 thereof by which the Council of Ministers of the E.C. directed that upon the transfer of a business from one employer to another the benefit and burden of a contract of employment between the transferor (the old owner) and a worker in the business should devolve on the transferee (the new owner). The object of the Directive was expressed to be: "to provide for the protection of employees in the event of a change of employer, in particular to ensure that their rights are safeguarded." The obligations in Article 3 of the Directive were implemented, *inter alia*, by Article 5(1) of the Regulations. In the words of Lord Keith of Kinkel:

> "It is plain that if the words in regulation 5(3) of the Regulations of 1981 'a person so employed immediately before the transfer' are read literally, as contended for by the second respondents, Forth Estuary Engineering Limited, the provisions of Regulation 5(1) will be capable of ready evasion through the transferee arranging with the transferor for the latter to dismiss its employees a short time before the transfer becomes operative. . . . In these circumstances, it is the duty of the court to give to regulation 5 a construction which accords with the decisions of the European Court upon the

---

[85] Mead, "The Obligation to Apply European Law: Is Duke Dead?" (1991) 16 E.L.Rev. 490 at p. 496.
[86] Curtin, "The Province of Government: Delimiting the Direct Effect of Directives in the Common Law Context" (1990) 15 E.L.Rev. 195 at p. 223.

corresponding provisions of the Directive to which the regulation was intended by Parliament to give effect. The precedent estabished by *Pickstone* v. *Freemans Plc* indicates that this is to be done by implying the words necessary to achieve that result."[87]

Lord Oliver of Aylmerton said that:

"The approach to the construction of primary and subordinate legislation enacted to give effect to the United Kingdom's obligations under the EEC Treaty have been the subject matter of recent authority in this House. (See *Pickstone* v. *Freemans Plc* [1988] I.R.L.R. 357) and is not in doubt. If the legislation can reasonably be construed so as to conform with those obligations—obligations which are to be ascertained not only from the wording of the relevant directive but from the interpretation placed upon it by the European Court of Justice at Luxembourg—such a purposive construction will be applied even though, perhaps, it may involve some departure from the strict and literal application of the words which the legislature has elected to use."[88]

After a detailed consideration of the relevant case law, Lord Oliver came to the view that:

"If this provision fell to be construed by reference to the ordinary rules of construction applicable to a purely domestic statute and without reference to Treaty obligations, it would, I think, be quite impermissible to regard it as having the same prohibitory effect as that attributed by the European Court to Article 4 of the Directive. But it has always to be borne in mind that the purpose of the Directive and of the Regulations was and is to 'safegaurd' the rights of employees on a transfer and that there is a mandatory obligation to provide remedies which are effective and not merely symbolic to which the Regulations were intended to give effect. . . . *Pickstone* v. *Freemans Plc* [1988] I.R.L.R. 357 has established that the greatest flexibility available to the Court in applying a purposive construction to legislation designed to give effect to the United Kingdom's Treaty obligations to the Community enables the Court, where necessary, to supply by implication words appropriate to comply with those obligations. See particularly the speech of Lord Templeman at pp. 359–364. . . . In effect, this involves reading regulation 5(3) as if there were inserted after the words 'immediately before the transfer' the words 'or would have been so employed if he had not been unfairly dismissed in the circumstances described in regulation 8(1).' For my part, I would make such an implication which is entirely consistent with the general scheme of the Regulations and which is necessary if they are effectively to filfil the purpose for which they were made of giving effect to the provisions of the Directive."[89]

---

[87] *Litster, op. cit.*, n. 83, p. 163 at para. 3 and para. 5.
[88] *Ibid.*, p. 165, para. 21.
[89] *Ibid.*, p. 172, para. 50.

In other words, in *Litster* the *ordinary* rules of construction and analysis of the words "immediately before the transfer" would have excluded the appellants from the benefits of the Acquired Rights Directive. There was no ambiguity in the words used in the U.K. legislation. However, by reference to the purpose of the Directive, it was possible to infer or imply extra words so as to enable the legislation to give effect to the U.K.'s obligations under Community law.

## Inaccurate/inconsistent national implementation

A difficulty does, however, arise where the relevant U.K. legislation is **6–014** not ambiguous, but nevertheless is an inaccurate or inconsistent attempt at giving effect to the provisions of a directive. For example, the EEC Council Directive 77/187 (hereinafter referred to as the Acquired Rights Directive)[90] was given effect in U.K. law by the 1981 Transfer of Undertakings (Protection of Employment) Regulations (hereinafter referred to as TUPE).[91] They came into force in the U.K. partly on February 1, 1982 and wholly on May 1, 1982 (regulation 1(2)). Under Article 1(1) of the Directive:

> "This Directive shall apply to the transfer of an undertaking, business or part of a business to another employer as a result of a legal transfer or merger."

However, under TUPE, regulation 2(1) defines a relevant "undertaking" (to which the Directive is intended to apply), to include any trade or business but to *exclude* "any undertaking or part of an undertaking *which is not in the nature of a commercial venture*" (emphasis added). (This exclusion was subsequently removed by section 33(2) of the Trade Union Reform and Employment Rights Act 1993.)[92] The original TUPE Regulations therefore created a distinction between transfer of commercial and non-commercial undertakings. This affected the nature of the transfer caught by the U.K. government's policy of Compulsory Competitive Tendering (CCT), whereby government authorities, local authorities and other bodies place various public services out to tender (including, for example, hospital and school meals contracts, photocopying services, the running of prisons, prison service stores, hospital cleaning, catering and maintenance contracts as well as professional and technical services such as information technology and accountancy services). It was argued that central and local government contracting-out exercises were not affected by TUPE (prior to its amendment)

---

[90] Council Directive 77/187 on the approximation of the laws of the Member States relating to the safeguarding of employees' rights in the event of transfers of undertakings, business or parts of businesses [1977] O.J. L61/26. The Court of Justice has given 14 judgments regarding this Directive: see further De Groot, "The Council Directive on the Safeguarding of Employee's Rights in the Events of Transfers of Undertakings: An Overview of the Case Law" (1983) C.M.L.Rev. 331 to 350.

[91] S.I. 1981 No. 1794.

[92] This section entered into force on August 30, 1993; S.I. 1993 No. 1908 of July 27, 1993.

because the institutions concerned were not commercial undertakings and/or the relevant activities (prior to the transfer) were in the nature of a public service which was not intended to make a profit.

The express words of TUPE (prior to amendment by the Trade Union Reform and Employment Rights Act 1993) therefore conflicted with the Acquired Rights Directive. However, there was nothing in the Preamble of the Directive, nor in its Section I on "Scope and Definitions" to support the *exclusion* of non-commercial undertakings. It did appear, however, that at the time of drafting of the Directive, the European Commission stated that non-profit making organisations were outside its scope.[93] However, it was unlikely that resort to such *travaux préparatoires*, on its own, would be sufficient to support this construction.[94] The European Commission instituted Article 169 proceedings against the U.K. government on the basis of a failure to implement fully the Acquired Rights Directive.[95]

*Purposive construction and legitimate expectation*

**6–015**  Whether or not the relevant provisions of the Acquired Rights Directive are "directly effective", they were not *horizontally* directly effective against private contractors who were successful in tendering for such public service contracts prior to the TUPE amendment. Nevertheless, it may be argued on the basis of *Von Colson*[96] and *Marleasing*[97] that the U.K. courts were under an obligation to adopt a purposive interpretation of TUPE (prior to its amendment) and to interpret it in such a way as to be consistent with the intention of the Acquired Rights Directive and thereby to apply TUPE to appropriate contracts under the CCT programme. The rights of employees affected by CCT would thereby have been protected under the Directive and/or TUPE.

Such an interpretation would, of course, adversely affect the interests of certain private employers and it is not clear how the "purposive interpretation" required by the ECJ is to be reconciled with the principle, also reiterated by the ECJ, of the protection of legitimate expectations.[98] For example, in Case 212–217/80, *Salumi*[99] the Court stated that the principles of legal certainty and the protection of legitimate expectations were principles "by virtue of which the effect of Community legislation must be clear and predictable for those who are subject to it."[1] The later case of *Kolpinghaus*[2] does not necessarily

---

[93] See, *Harvey on Industrial Relations and Employment Law*, S/2, para. [6].
[94] See D'Sa, "The Acquired Rights Directive: Consequences of Incorrect Implementation in English Law" (1993) 4 E.B.L.Rev. 132 at p. 132.
[95] Case C–382/92: [1992] O.J. C306/9.
[96] *Von Colson*: [1984] E.C.R. 1891, [1986] 2 C.M.L.R. 430.
[97] Case C–106/89, *Marleasing* v. *La Commercial*: [1990] I E.C.R. 135, [1992] 1 C.M.L.R. 305 discussed further at para. 6–004 above.
[98] de Búrca, "Giving Effect to European Community Directives" (1992) M.L.R. 215 at p. 227.
[99] Joined Cases 212–217/80, *Salumi*: [1981] E.C.R. 2735.
[1] *Ibid.*, p. 275.
[2] Case 80/86, *Officier van Justitie* v. *Kolpinghaus Nijmegen BV*: [1987] E.C.R. 3969, [1989] 2 C.M.L.R. 18 discussed at para. 6–006 above.

support the proposition that if non-implementing legislation is construed in conformity with a directive and against an individual it constitutes a breach of the principle of legitimate expectations.[3] The *Kolpinghaus* case can equally be understood on the basis of non-retroactivity of penal litigation which is itself a fundamental right protected by Community law.[4]

On the contrary, the principle of legitimate expectations is itself not an absolute one.[5] In the context of proceedings where one private party wishes to rely on the purposive construction of a directive, the other party may have contrary expectations based on the provisions of a national law.[6] For instance the national law, whilst purporting to implement the Directive, may have created certain expectations. Should be party relying on a clear provision of national law in these circumstances be penalised? On the reasoning in *Marleasing*[7] the answer is affirmative. It is argued by de Búrca[8] that this does not conflict with the principle of legitimate expectations because individuals must now be as much aware of the provisions of E.C. directives as they are of Treaty articles or regulations. In other words the ruling of the ECJ in *Marleasing* implies that the party who is disadvantaged by "indirect" enforcement should *not* be surprised. Nevertheless, the interpretative obligation created by the ECJ remains only a *supplementary* means of ensuring that Directives are given domestic effect. The primary obligation remains on the *State* to transpose directives properly into national law.[9] Some litigation has subsequently been commenced by various trade unions against the U.K. government for its failure to implement the Acquired Rights Directive between 1981 and 1993.[10]

## Purposive construction in the Webb case

An issue involving purposive construction has also been raised by the **6–016** House of Lords case of *Webb* v. *EMO Air Cargo (U.K.) Ltd.*[11] where the employers engaged the applicant to replace a pregnant employee while she was on three months' maternity leave. The applicant was required to start work immediately so as to undertake six months' training before the employee she was replacing went on maternity leave. Two weeks after starting work the applicant discovered that she was herself pregnant and was dismissed when she informed her employers of that fact.

She complained to the Industrial Tribunal on the ground of unlawful sex discrimination contrary to section 1(1)(a) of the Sex Discrimination

---

[3] de Búrca, *op. cit.*, n. 98, p. 229.
[4] de Búrca, *op. cit.*, n. 98, p. 229; Case 63/83, *R.* v. *Kirk*: [1984] E.C.R. 2689, [1984] 3 C.M.L.R. 522.
[5] de Búrca, *op. cit.*, n. 98, p. 229; see, *e.g.* Case 331/88, *FEDESA*: [1990] I E.C.R. 4023, [1991] 1 C.M.L.R. 507.
[6] de Búrca, *op. cit.*, n. 98, p. 230.
[7] *Marleasing*, *op. cit.*, n. 97.
[8] de Búrca, *op. cit.*, n. 98, p. 231.
[9] *Marleasing*, *op. cit.*, n. 97.
[10] See further *Financial Times*, November 30, 1993, p. 10.
[11] *Webb* v. *EMO Air Cargo (U.K.) Ltd.* [1992] 4 All E.R. 929 (H.L.)

Act 1975. The Tribunal dismissed her claim on the ground that the real reason for the dismissal was not her pregnancy but her anticipated inability to carry out the primary task for which she had been employed, namely maternity cover for a pregnant employee. If a man had been recruited for the same purpose he would also have been dismissed if he had told the employer that he would be absent during the pregnant employee's maternity leave.

This decision was upheld by the EAT and the Court of Appeal. The appellant appealed to the House of Lords. She relied on the European Court of Justice ruling that refusal of employment of a woman for any reason related to her pregnancy constituted unlawful direct discrimination on the grounds of sex. She argued that since only a woman could be pregnant, dismissal for any reason related to her pregnancy was discrimination on the grounds of her sex and was direct discrimination, which is contrary to Council Directive 76/207 on the principle of equal treatment for men and women as regards access to employment.[12]

The House of Lords confirmed the view of the Court of Appeal that a dismissal related to pregnancy may, but will not necessarily, always amount to unlawful direct discrimination on the part of the employer. Lord Keith of Kinkel on behalf of the Court was of the opinion that in general, to dismiss a woman because she is pregnant or to refuse to employ a woman of child bearing age because she may become pregnant is unlawful direct discrimination. However, on the facts of *Webb* there was no unlawful direct discrimination because it was the appellant's non-availability during the relevant period which was the critical factor. He regarded it as legitimate to make a comparison between the non-availability of a woman by reason of expected confinement and the non-availability of a man (which may or may not be for medical reasons).

In addition, the House of Lords held that the appellant had not been indirectly discriminated against under section 1(1)(b) of the 1975 Act. It was accepted that the possibility of pregnancy meant that more women than men were likely to be unable to satisfy the condition for employment that the worker should be in such physical condition as to be able to do the job in question. Furthermore, the applicant had suffered detriment because she had been unable to comply with the condition that there should be someone to cover for the absent employee during her maternity leave. However, that condition was a reasonable one and, objectively viewed, outweighed the discriminatory effect of the condition which the employer had imposed.[13] It has been pointed out by Napier[14] that to do otherwise could lead to some absurd results. For instance, the employer who advertises for a person to take the part of "Father Christmas" and who subsequently finds that the person appointed will be unable to work in the weeks immediately before Christmas because of her pregnancy could not be dismissed because of Council Directive 76/207.

---

[12] [1976] O.J. L39/40.
[13] *Webb, op. cit.*, n. 11, p. 936 d to e and p. 941 a to d.
[14] Napier, "A Pause Over Pregnancy" (February 3, 1993) 90/5 *Gazette* 21 at p. 23.

One of the arguments raised in *Webb* was whether, quite apart from questions of interpretation of the Sex Discrimination Act 1975, Miss Webb could rely, in addition, directly on the provisions of Directive 76/207. This provides for equal treatment for men and women, including conditions governing dismissal. However, even if Miss Webb's treatment was incompatible with Directive 76/207, she would not have been able to rely on it directly, because the employer EMO was not "an emanation of the State."[15] However, Miss Webb argued that the Court of Appeal was under an obligation to interpret the Sex Discrimination Act 1975 "in the light of the purpose and the wording of the Directive." In order for Community law to be of benefit to Miss Webb, she therefore needed to persuade the Court of Appeal that her dismissal was contrary to the Directive and that the relevant provisions of the 1975 Act were capable of being interpreted consistently with the Directive's requirements.[16]

This point has now been referred by the House of Lords to the **6–017** European Court. It is argued by Arnull that the Court of Appeal followed the approach of the House of Lords in *Duke*[17] rather than that adopted in *Pickstone*[18] and *Litster*,[19] because the relevant provisions of the 1975 Act had not been adopted to give effect to Directive 76/207. However, this may be inconsistent with the dicta of the European Court in the *Von Colson* case[20] which suggests that the same approach is to be taken to the construction of domestic legislation, irrespective of whether or not it was introduced to give effect to the requirements of Community law. In addition, the three Court of Appeal judges may have failed to approach the domestic litigation in the light of European law as now required by *Marleasing*.[21] They had instead examined domestic law first and then considered whether Community law affected their interpretation of domestic law.[22] In *Marleasing*[23] the Court appears to have confirmed the principles laid down in *Vol Colson*, and has made it clear that national courts must interpret their national law in the light of the wording and the purpose of relevant directives whether the legislation was adopted before or after the Directive in question. Arnull suggests that the duty laid down in the *Von Colson* applies identically to all national legislation which occupies the same field as a directive.[24]

Lord Keith in the House of Lords in *Webb* clearly took note of the requirement for a purposive interpretation of the domestic statute:

---

[15] See Case 152/84, *Marshall* v. *Southampton and South West Hampshire Area Health Authority (Teaching) (Marshall No. 1)*: [1986] E.C.R. 723, [1986] 1 C.M.L.R. 688. See also discussion at paras. 7-001 *et seq.* below.

[16] See further Anthony Arnull "When is pregnancy like an arthritic hip?" (1992) 17 E.L.Rev. 265 at p. 270.

[17] *Duke* v. *GEC Reliance Ltd.* [1988] A.C. 618.

[18] *Pickstone* v. *Freemans plc* [1988] A.C. 66.

[19] *Litster* v. *Forth Dry Dock and Engineering Co. Ltd.* [1989] I.R.L.R. 161.

[20] *Von Colson*: [1984] E.C.R. 1891, [1986] 2 C.M.L.R. 430.

[21] *Marleasing*: [1990] I E.C.R. 135, [1992] 1 C.M.L.R. 305.

[22] See Harrison, "Pregnancy and Discrimination in the Court of Appeal" (April 3, 1992) N.L.J. 462 at p. 463.

[23] *Marleasing*: *op. cit.*, n. 21.

[24] Arnull, *op. cit.*, n. 16, p. 272.

> "Directive 76/207 does not have direct effect upon the relationship between a worker and an employer who is not the State or an emanation of the State, but nevertheless it is for a U.K. court to construe domestic legislation in any field covered by a Community directive so as to accord with the interpretation of the directives laid down by the European Court, if that can be done without distorting the meaning of the domestic legislation: See *Duke* v. *GEC Reliance Limited* [1988] 1 All E.R. 626 at 636, [1988] A.C. 618 at 639–640, *per* Lord Templeman."[25]

However, Lord Keith goes on immediately to affirm that:

> "This is so whether the domestic legislation came after, or, as in this case, preceded the Directive: See Case C106/89, *Marleasing SA* v. *La Commercial Internacional de Alimentación SA* [1990] E.C.R. 4135. . . . As the European Court said, a national court must construe a domestic law to accord with the terms of a directive in the same field only if it is possible to do so. That means that the domestic law must be open to an interpretation consistent with the Directive whether or not it is also open to an interpretation inconsistent with it."

The point which has been referred to the ECJ is whether the dismissal of a woman in the position of Miss Webb is in fact compatible with Directive 76/207, *i.e.* as being based on the appellant's unavailability for the job and not her pregnancy. If not, then the House of Lords will then have to consider whether it can interpret the 1975 Act in such a way as to comply with the requirements of the Directive. If it cannot do this, then the U.K. government may be exposed to an action for liability in damages before the English courts, at the suit of Miss Webb (following the principles in *Francovich*[26] or the possibility of an action by the European Commission against the U.K. government under Article 169.

*Irreconcilable conflict with national law*

6–018    In *R.* v. *British Coal Corporation and The Secretary of State for Trade and Industry, ex parte Alan Vardy*,[27] the Queen's Bench Division of the High Court, on an application for judicial review, also took a purposive approach and applied the dicta in *Litster*.[28] Glidewell J. accepted the principle of statutory construction that where a statute or statutory instrument is expressly enacted for the purpose of complying with a Council directive, the courts of the U.K. are under a duty to give a purposive construction to the statute so as to accord, if possible, with the

---

[25] Webb: *op. cit.*, n. 11, p. 939C.
[26] Joined Cases C–6 & 9/90, *Francovich and Bonifaci*: [1991] I E.C.R. 5357, [1993] 2 C.M.L.R. 66, discussed further at paras. 8–008 *et seq.* and see Arnull, *op. cit.*, n. 16, p. 273 and Napier, "A Pause over Pregnancy" (February 3, 1993) 90/5 *Gazette*, 21 at p. 24.
[27] *R.* v. *British Coal Corporation and The Secretary of State for Trade and Industry, ex p. Alan Vardy and Others* [1993] 1 C.M.L.R. 721.
[28] *Litster, op. cit.*, n. 19.

decisions of the European Court on the Directive.[29] However, it was held that the difference in wording between the relevant Directive[30] and section 188 of the Trade Union Labour Relations (Consolidation) Act 1992 which had been intended to give effect to the Directive, was such that the section could *not* be interpreted as having the same meaning as that intended by Article 2(2) of the Directive, in that the latter required consultation *before* the employer had actually decided to close the plant and create redundancies and when he was merely contemplating that possibility, whereas section 188 of the Act allowed consultation to start *after* the decision had been taken. The difference between the two was so great that it could not be removed by mere interpretation. The Court noted further, that the Directive could only have vertical direct effect but found it unnecessary to consider whether British Coal was an emanation of the State and so susceptible to vertical direct effects because on the facts, British Coal had voluntarily undertaken subsequently to comply with Article 2 of the Directive.[31]

The judgment in *Marleasing* suggests a line of reasoning intended to assist national courts to interpret and apply Community law more widely and to give effect to Community law in relationships between individuals *inter se* and not limit its application to individuals and the State or to State institutions. However, as a matter of law, the President of the European Commission, Mr. Jacques Delors has confirmed in answer to a written question, on behalf of the Commission, that the ruling in *Marleasing*:

". . . cannot be taken to acknowledge that directives have 'horizontal effect' enabling individuals to benefit from the application of the clear, unconditional and sufficiently precise provisions of a directive not incorporated in national law as such *vis-à-vis* another individual. *It follows that these rights may be guaranteed less fully than they would be if the Directive had been incorporated in national law.*"[32]

### Purposive interpretation in Germany: an illustration

A German case concerning the possibility of "purposive interpretation" is of interest. In *Re A.R. Rehabilitation Centre*[33] the Federal Supreme Labour Court considered an appeal in a case of alleged sex discrimination, on the question of whether the plaintiff could claim damages in the amount of six months' pay or, alternatively, damages for an amount set at the Court's discretion. The Federal Supreme Labour Court confirmed the decision of the Land Labour Court to the effect that the plaintiff had been subject to sex discrimination. However, the terms of the Civil Code[34] did not provide for damages other than for the

**6-019**

---

[29] *Ex p. Vardy: op. cit.*, n. 27, see judgment of Glidewell L.J. at p. 751, para. 119.
[30] Article 2 of the Collective Redundancies Directive 75/192, [1975] O.J. L48/29.
[31] *Ex p. Vardy: op. cit.*, n. 27, p. 752, para. 125.
[32] Written Question No. 2804/91 by Mr Alen Donnelly, December 5, 1991, 92/C–209/43 and Answer by Mr Delors (March 31, 1992), [1992] O.J. C209/22 (emphasis added).
[33] Case 8 AZR 351/86, *Re A.R. Rehabilitation Centre*: [1992] 2 C.M.L.R. 21.
[34] Section 611A(2).

employer to make good losses resulting from frustration of expectation. That generally included the costs involved in applying for the position. The national law had been enacted to implement the Equal Treatment Directive.[35] However, the German Federal Supreme Labour Court found that the restriction of the claim to losses resulting from frustration of expectations had been intended by the legislature.[36] The Court referred to the judgment of the the European Court in *Von Colson*[37] to the effect that:

> ". . . if a Member State decides to penalise breaches of the prohibition on discrimination by the award of compensation, its amount must in any event be adequate in relation to the injuries sustained, so as to ensure its effectiveness and deterrent effect; the compensation must therefore be more than a purely nominal amount, such as the reimbursement of only the expenses incurred in connection with the application. It is for the national court to interpret and apply the legislation adopted for implementation of the Directive in accordance with the requirements of Community law in so far as it is given discretion to do so under national law."

In the *Rehabilitation Centre* case, the German court took the view that even when these principles in *Von Colson* are taken into account, section 611A(2) of the Civil Code:

> ". . . cannot be relied upon as the basis for a claim in damages in excess of those available for frustration of expectation. The clear wording of the provision opposes such a cause. An interpretation 'in conformity with the Directive', with the object of deducing a claim for damages exceeding those laid down in the section is not permissible. It is a matter for the national legislature how an E.C. directive binding on the Member States is implemented in its national law. (Article 189(3) EEC.) Even an interpretation of statutes by reference to conformity with the Constitution reaches its limits where it would come in to conflict with the wording and evident intention of the legislature. The position can be no different as regards the interpretation of national law in the light of the wording and purpose of a directive under Article 189(3) EEC."

The headnote of the judgment makes it clear that the court cannot extend unambiguous national law beyond its natural scope in order to comply with the EEC Directive where, in the circumstances, *that Directive does not have direct effect*, even if it was enacted precisely to implement the Directive.

However, although the German court was not prepared to take a purposive interpretation of German legislation, in the absence of horizon-

---

[35] E.C. Council Directive 76/207 of February 9, 1976 on the implementation of the principle of equal treatment for men and women as regards access to employment, vocational training and promotion, and working conditions [1976] O.J. L39/40.

[36] See judgment, *op. cit.*, n. 33, para. 10, p. 25.

[37] *Von Colson, op. cit.*, n. 20.

tal direct effect of the Directive, it was clear that usually, in such cases, the applicant would have had a right to reasonable compensation for "infringement of the individual's general right of personal development under sections 823(1) and 847 of the Civil Code.[38] Unusually, in the present case, there was no breach of rights of personality and the consequence was that the plaintiff was not entitled to adequate compensation. The case was, however, decided before the decision of the European Court in *Marleasing*,[39] and *Marshall (No. 2)*, discussed in detail at paragraphs 9–025 *et seq.*, below.

## Alternatives to the "indirect" direct effect approach

In *Doughty* v. *Rolly Royce Plc*,[40] (discussed at paragraphs 7–011 *et seq.*, **6–020** below), the Court of Appeal does not appear to have attempted an "indirect" approach in order to provide a remedy for the applicant against her employer, but relied instead on a consideration of principles laid down by the European Court in *Foster* v. *British Gas*[41] which adopted the traditional approach of defining what constituted an "emanation of the State".

However, it must be remembered that even in the case of *Von Colson*[42] the European Court said that the duty of national courts to interpret and apply legislation implementing a directive in conformity with Community law *is limited by the extent of discretion that a national court has to do so under national law*. This recognises that in the absence of direct effect, the interpretation of domesitc law and its compatibility with Community law is not a matter over which the European Court has jurisdiction. The only solution for individuals who are left without remedy where a European directive has either not been implemented or has been incorrectly implemented, and where it is not directly effective, is for the Commission to bring proceedings under Article 169 of the E.C. Treaty.[43] Alternatively, it is suggested by Usher[44] that rather than relying on a purposive approach, such as in *Marleasing*, it may be more appropriate that a private remedy should be available against national authorties which have failed to give full internal effect to their Community obligations, rather than imposing such liability on traders or employers by a purposive interpretation of the national legislation, where the underlying Community legislation is not itself directly effective.[45] This possibility has now been recognised by the European Court in

---

[38] *Op. cit.*, n. 33, para. 20.

[39] *Marleasing*: *op. cit.*, n. 21.

[40] *Doughty* v. *Rolls Royce Plc* [1992] 1 C.M.L.R. 1045.

[41] Case 188/89, *Foster* v. *British Gas*: [1990] I E.C.R. 3313, [1990] 2 C.M.L.R. 833.

[42] *Von Colson*: *op. cit.*, n. 20.

[43] See Howells, "European Directives: The Emerging Dilemmas" (1991) M.L.R. 456 at p. 463. For discussion of Article 169 see further para. 1–003 above.

[44] Usher, "The Imposition of Sanctions for Breaches of Community Law" (1992) F.I.D.E. XV Congress, "La sanction des infractions au droit Communautaire" (Associação Portuguesa de Direito Europeu).

[45] *Ibid.* at p. 9.

*Francovich*[46] and discussed further at paragraphs 8–009 *et seq.* However, it would still be necessary to show that the Community rules which had not been implemented were intended to give rise to individual rights. This may be difficult to satisfy, unless the provisions are in fact directly effective.[47]

---

[46] Joined Cases C–6 & 9/90, *Francovich and Bonifaci*: [1991] I E.C.R. 5357, [1993] 2 C.M.L.R. 66.

[47] See further discussion at paras. 8–009 *et seq.* below.

# VERTICAL DIRECT EFFECT OF DIRECTIVES

## THE SCOPE OF THE TERM "STATE"

The principle of "vertical" direct effect means that all directly effective **7–001** provisions of Community law (including those of a directive), are binding on the "State".[1] If litigation is envisaged against a Minister or other government official or a government department, it will clearly involve an action against "the State". However, there are potentially a wide number of public institutions whose relationship with "the State" is not clear as a matter of Community law. In the important Case 152/84, *Marshall v. Southampton and South West Hampshire Area Health Authority (Marshall No. 1)*,[2] the Court did not give any guidelines for deciding when a particular body is to be regarded as synonymous with the "State". It used the words "State authority", "organ of the State" and "emanation of the State" interchangeably with the expression "public authority" without defining the essential characteristics of such bodies.[3]

This may be explained by the fact that the Court of Appeal had stated in the order for an Article 177 reference in *Marshall (No. 1)* that the defendant Health Authority was a public authority.[4] The Court of Appeal in its reference to the ECJ also stated that the Authority was "an emanation of the State".[5] Furthermore, the U.K. had also asserted in its observations that Health Authorities are Crown bodies and their employees, including hospital doctors, nurses and administration staff are Crown servants. It is argued by Curtin[6] that the approach taken by the Court may more aptly be described as "judicial minimalism" in the sense of a preference to decide each case on a narrow and ad hoc basis

---

[1] See also para. 2–009 below.

[2] Case 152/84, *Marshall v. Southampton and South West Hampshire Area Health Authority*: [1986] E.C.R. 7233, [1986] 1 C.M.L.R. 6883, [1986] 2 All E.R. 584.

[3] Curtin, "The Province of Government: Delimiting the Direct Effect of Directives in the Common Law Context" (1990) E.L.Rev. 195 at pp. 197 *et seq.*

[4] *Marshall (No. 1): op. cit.*, n. 2, see judgment of the Court [1986] 2 All E.R. 584 at 600, para. 50.

[5] *Ibid.*, p. 594g.

[6] Curtin, *op. cit.*, n. 3, p. 195.

without giving too much attention to the crucial issue of the relationship between the relevant bodies and the State.[7]

In *Marshall (No. 1)*,[8] the Court stated that it was up to the national court to characterise the party which is said to act in breach of a directive. It did, however, make clear that if an individual is able to rely on the provisions of a directive against the State, he or she may do so regardless of the capacity in which the latter is acting, whether as employer or public authority.[9] In the words of Advocate General Slynn, the "State" must be:

> "taken broadly as including all the organs of the State. In matters of employment . . . this means all the employees of such organs and not just the central civil service."[10]

The Court therefore made it clear that the concept of the State extended to cover "public authorities", without defining the concept further.[11]

In certain fields it may not be necessary to distinguish State bodies from those which are not, in order to determine liability under directly effective provisions of a directive. For example, in relation to public procurement, Directive 71/305[12] on the co-ordination of procedures for the award of public works contracts, expressly applies to State, regional and local authorities (Article 1(b)) and *also* to authorities specified in Annex I of the Directive.[13] This list now includes, *inter alia*, in relation to England and Wales, categories of institutions such as universities and polytechnics, maintained colleges and schools, national museums and galleries, research councils, fire authorities, national health service authorities, police authorities, new town development corporations and urban development corporations. It also covers named bodies: the Central Blood Laboratories Authority, Design Council, Health and Safety Executive, National Research Development Corporation, Public Health Laboratory Services Board, Advisory, Conciliation and Advisory Services (ACAS), Commission for the New Towns, Development Board for Rural Wales, English Industrial Estates Corporation, National Rivers Authority and the Welsh Development Agency.[14]

However, in the vast majority of cases in which the vertical direct effect of Commuity law is relied on it will be necessary to establish that the relevant body is a public authority or "emanation of the State". The fact that the same body may regarded as a public authority for other

---

[7] *Ibid.* at p. 198.

[8] *Marshall (No. 1): op. cit.*, n. 2.

[9] *Ibid.*, p. 600f.

[10] *Ibid.*, p. 594.

[11] Curtin, *op. cit.*, n. 3, p. 197.

[12] [1971] O.J. Spec. Ed. 685, as amended by Directive 89/440, [1989] O.J. L210/10.

[13] That Annex has been substituted by Commission Decision 92/456 of July 31, 1992 concerning the updating of Annex I, [1992] O.J. L257/33 to 41. See further para. 10–028 below.

[14] It also covers the Northern Ireland Housing Executive, Scottish Enterprise, and Scottish Homes.

purposes, *e.g.* under the above Directive on the award of public works contracts, will arguably not be conclusive in relation to other fields. However, it would nevertheless be useful evidence that that body has been treated as synonymous with the State for other purposes, under Community law.

## Foster v. British Gas: the factual background

In May 1989, the House of Lords asked the Court for further guidance **7–002** on the question of which bodies are to be regarded as an "emanation of the State" in Case C–188/89, *Foster* v. *British Gas.*[15] In *Foster*, a number of employees of the British Gas Corporation (hereinafter referred to as BGC) brought a claim for unlawful discrimination based on the practice of BGC to retire women once they reached the State pension age of 60, while male employees could continue to work until they reached the State pension age of 65. The gas industry was subsequently privatised in 1986 under the Gas Act. British Gas plc was established and on August 24, 1986 it succeeded to the rights and liabilities of the BGC. The crucial issue was whether the employer BGC could be brought within the vertical direct effects of Article 5(1) of the Council Directive 76/207 by equating BGC with "the State".

The possibility of intepreting the relevant U.K. law, *i.e.* the Sex Discrimination Act 1975, in such a way as to conform with the relevant provisions of the Council Directive 76/207 was not possible because the House of Lords had decided in *Duke* v. *GEC Reliance Limited*[16] that it is impossible in an action between workers and a *private* employer, to interpret the Sex Discriminaion Act 1975 (as it applied before the amendments introduced by the Sex Discrimination Act 1986) in such a way as to make it consistent with Directive 76/207.

It was common ground between the parties that if Directive 76/207 was applicable, BGC's practice at making men and women retire at different ages would be illegal. The appellants, Mrs Foster and others, argued that the term "State" must be taken broadly as including all the organs of State, including those engaged in commercial and related activities. Since the Court had, in previous cases such as *Marshall (No. 1)* and Case 222/84, *Johnston* v. *RUC*,[17] used the words "State", "organ of the State", "emanation of the State", "State authority", and "public authority" interchangeably, and since BGC was a nationalised industry and public authority, they argued that it was covered by the ruling in *Marshall (No. 1)*.

The Judge Rapporteur, G.F. Mancini noted that as a matter of English law, the BGC was a "public body" and a "public authority" for the purposes of various domestic statutes and in English common law.

---

[15] Case 188/89, *Foster* v. *British Gas*: [1990] I E.C.R. 3313, [1990] 2 C.M.L.R. 833, [1990] 3 All E.R. 897.
[16] *Duke* v. *GEC Reliance Ltd.* [1988] 1 All E.R. 626; see further paras. 6–007 *et seq.* above.
[17] Case 222/84, *Johnston* v. *RUC*: [1986] E.C.R. 1651, [1986] 3 C.M.L.R. 240 and see discussion at para. 6–005 above.

He referred to the situation under the Gas Act 1948 and cited the judgment of the House of Lords in *DPP* v. *Holly; DPP* v. *Manners* [1977] 1 All E.R. 316, [1978] A.C. 43.[18] However, the Judge Rapporteur also noted that the BGC was not regarded as an agent of the Secretary of State and its employees were not in Crown employment for the purposes of United Kingdom employment law.

### Appellant's arguments in Foster

7–003    The appellants argued first, that there was no reason in principle why a directive should not have direct effect against bodies which have been constituted by the State, but which perform duties other than the "classic" duties of the State. In any event, they argued that since the BGC had a State monopoly from 1948, its functions must have become classic duties of the State, since only the State was able to perform them.

They also argued that there were no grounds for limiting the application of the direct effect of directives to public authorities of a "non-commercial" character. Such a test would be contrary to the principle that a Member State must not take advantage of its own failure to comply with Community law. They argued that it would be difficult to apply in certain cases such as, for example, the provision of medical services, which may be of a commercial character even though it is a nationalised service financed by the State.

### The case for the respondent, British Gas Plc

7–004    The respondent, British Gas Plc, on the other hand argued that the judgments of the Court were consistent with the classic idea of the State as comprising the legislature, the executive and the judiciary. The only other organs or "emanations of the State" on which individuals may exercise claims in reliance on a directive were organs which were agents of the State or to whom the State had delegated certain functions. BGC was not to be regarded as either an organ or an agent of the State. They also argued that the fact that a body is subject to a substantial degree of government control, for example in relation to the appointment of administrators, does not lead to it being considered as equivalent to the State for these purposes. In addition, the BGC was a nationalised industry which, according to the decisions of the English courts, was not part of the State in the sense of the Crown.[19]

### U.K. government views

7–005    The U.K. government stated that the BGC was not part of the State since it did not perform the functions of the State directly or as an agent or delegate. It argued, *inter alia*, that "public authorities" did not extend to bodies having an industrial or commercial character. It also argued by

---

[18] Foster, *op. cit.*, n. 15 [1990] 3 All E.R. 897 at p. 900h.
[19] *Ibid.*, p. 903.

analogy from Council Directive 71/305 concerning the co-ordination of procedures for the award of public works contracts, as amended by Council Directive 89/440, that the term "a body governed by public law" is defined as any body "established for the specific purpose of meeting needs in the general interest, *not having an industrial or commercial character*" (emphasis added). It mentioned that the BGC was not included in Annex 1 to that directive as a body governed by public law.

The U.K. argued that the BGC was a body having commercial character. It was not performing any of the central functions of the State, such as legislative, judicial or law and order functions. As a matter of English law, the employees of the BGC were not Crown servants. It is also well established in English law that a nationalised industry is not an organ of the Crown.

The U.K government also pointed out that in its view, the existence of a power of control is not the determining factor of whether a body is part of the State. For reasons of public policy, a wide variety of bodies, such as banks, insurance companies, and independent schools, are regulated, to various degrees and in various ways, by the State, without those bodies thereby becoming part of the State.

## European Commission's view

The European Commission took the view that the Court in *Marshall* **7–006** *(No. 1)* only intended to provide for two categories of employment: the State (or emanations of State), which could not plead as against individuals its own failure to legislate in order to implement a directive, and, on the other hand, private employers who were not the addressees of the Directive and who had no responsibility in relation to national legislation. The Commission therefore rejected the possibility of any third, intermediate category of entities which, while being "public authorities" are not "State authorities".

The Commission argued that a body carrying out a public function on behalf of the State, should be regarded as a "State authority". For example, it pointed out that in *Marshall (No. 1)* the Court showed no hesitation in accepting the view of the national court and treating as a "public authority", a body carrying out functions in the field of public health, which is not necessarily a State function.

However, the Commission pointed out that the criteria of exercising a public function on behalf of the State did not cover commercial companies in which the State owned all or the majority of the shares, or even a blocking minority, although in reality it is likely that the State exercised a great degree of control over them. An approach based on the existence of control would have substantial evidential difficulties. It suggested that the "economic reality" approach, consisting of checking whether the State really could exercise control over the policy of a body, though not a precise legal test, would have the advantage of being in conformity with the Court's approach in other areas. However, it went on to say that any test based on the existence of control will fail to cover a number of public authorities, such as bodies that are constitutionally independent, such as professional societies and universities. (This is considered further at paragraph 7–017 below.)

135

Thus it concluded that no one criterion could be formulated which would cover all situations which could arise. It suggested that the House of Lords should therefore be given a specific answer, dealing solely with the case of the BGC and other bodies of the same type. Its preferred formulation was that of a "body exercising a public function on behalf of the State."

### Opinion of the Advocate General in Foster

**7–007**     The Advocate General Walter Van Gerven agreed that no support could be found in the judgments of the Court for the existence of an intermediate category. He assumed that what the Court must do was to draw a dividing line in Community law which would assist national courts in distinguishing the concept of "the State" from the concept of "individual". However, he placed emphasis on the need to ensure that the concept of "the State" is given full and proper effect in the sense of achieving the goals of the measure in question. He stated that:

> ". . . Depending on the aim of the measure the term "State" may be interpreted broadly (for example, in connection with aid measures governed by Art. 92 (para. 12 above) or in connection with public works contracts (para. 15 above)), or a distinction may be drawn according to the role played by the State (for example, in connection with the transparency of relations between Member States and public undertakings, by distinguishing between the State *qua* authority and *qua* owner (para. 12 above), and in connection with the levying of VAT, by distinguishing between its activities as an authority and its activities as a taxable individual (para. 14 above)."[20]

He pointed out that whenever the concept of "the State" was given a broad interpretation, reference was made to the criterion of actual control, dominating influence and the possibility on the part of the authorities to give binding directions, regardless of the manner in which such control was exercised (by means of ownership, financial participation, dependence for the purposes of management or finance, or through legislative provisions).[21] He said that in each case there was:

> ". . . an assumption that there was a 'core' of authority (broadly defined to include all central, regional and public authorities) which, for the purpose of the measure concerned, imparts a public character by its control and influence to other bodies or transactions, even where these were governed by private laws."[22]

However, he disagreed with the appellants that every undertaking which is actually controlled by the political authorities, such as the BGC at the material time, must be brought under the concept of "the State".

---

[20] *Ibid.*, p. 915e, para. 16.
[21] *Ibid.*, p. 915g.
[22] *Ibid.*, p. 915h.

In his view that was too extreme because such control may having nothing to do with the matter to which the Member State's failure to implement a particular provision of a directive in national law relates. On the other hand, he thought the respondent took too restrictive a view and that the criterion of the State as either comprising the three elements of the State (the legislature, executive and judciary) or including bodies which exercise the authority of those three elements of the State by way of delegation, was too restrictive and was not a suitable basis for a Community framework of assessment.

Similarly, he thought that the distinction made between classical and **7–008** non-classical duties of the State was also of no service, particularly in the light of the *Johnston*[23] judgment. There were also difficulties of determining precisely what constituted the classical functions of the State, and, in particular, of the executive. He pointed out an inconsistency in the U.K. government arguments that public security was included (although that function can be "privatised" to a certain extent by contracting out to approved security services) but not the supply of water, gas and electricity, although in a modern welfare state such supplies are of essential importance for the population and industry.

In conclusion, he took the view that it appeared from previous case law that the concept of the public body must be understood very broadly and that all bodies which pursuant to the constitutional structure of a Member State can exercise any authority over individuals fall within the concept of the "State". In that respect he took the view that it was immaterial how that authority is organised and the various bodies which exercise that authority are related.[24]

He concluded that:

> ". . once the State (in the broad sense) has retained such a power to exercise influence over a person (in this case the BGC) with regard, *inter alia*, to the subject matter of the relevant provision of a directive, from the point of view of individuals it has brought that person within its sphere of authority. For that reason individuals may then rely against that person on the Member State's failure to implement a directive."[25]

On this basis, the Advocate General proposed that individuals could rely on an unconditional and sufficiently precise provision of a directive against a body, in this case a public undertaking:

> ". . . in respect of which the State (understood as anybody endowed with public authority, regardless of its relationship with other public bodies or the nature of the duties entrusted to it) has assumed responsibility which put it in a position decisively to influence the conduct of that person or body in any manner whatsoever (other

---

[23] Case 222/84, *Johnston*: [1986] E.C.R. 1651, [1986] 3 C.M.L.R. 240 referred to above at para. 7–002.

[24] Foster, *op. cit.*, n. 15, p. 917j.

[25] *Ibid.*, p. 918e.

than by means of general legislation) with regard to the matter in respect of which the relevant provision of a directive imposes an obligation which the Member State has failed to implement in national law."[26]

He pointed out that it was for the national courts to apply that criterion in specific cases. However, it seemed to him that binding instructions could have been given to the BGC to comply with the provisions of Directive 76/207, which at the material time had not yet been formally implemented in U.K. law.

### Reasoning of the European Court

7–009    In its judgment, the European Court noted that by virtue of the Gas Act 1972, which governed the BGC at the material time, the BGC was a statutory corporation responsible for developing and maintaining a system of gas supply in Great Britain, and had a monopoly of the supply of gas. The members of the BGC were appointed by the competent Secretary of State. He also had the power to give the BGC directions of a general character in relation to matters affecting the national interest and instructions concerning its management. The BGC was obliged to submit to the Secretary of State periodic reports on the exercise of its functions, its management and its programme. Those reports were then laid before both Houses of Parliament. Under the Gas Act 1972, the BGC also had the right, with the consent of the Secretary of State, to submit proposed legislation to Parliament. The BGC was also required to run a balanced budget over two successive financial years. The Secretary of State could order it to pay certain funds over to him or to allocate funds to specified purposes. The BGC was privatised under the Gas Act 1986. Privatisation resulted in the establishment of British Gas Plc, the respondent in the main proceedings, to which the rights and liabilities of the BGC were transferred with effect from August 24, 1986.

On the question of whether the provisions of the Directive could be relied upon against a body such as the BGC, the Court reiterated the general principle that if a Member State has not adopted the implementing measures required by a directive, within the prescribed period, it may not plead, as against individuals, its own failure to perform the obligations which the Directive entails. Thus, wherever the provisions of a directive appear, as far as their subject matter is concerned, to be unconditional and sufficiently precise, those provisions may, in the absence of implementing measures adopted within the prescribed period, be relied on against any national provision which is incompatible with the Directive or insofar as the provisions define rights which individuals are able to assert against the State.

The Court in its judgment listed different kinds of public authorities which it had already found in earlier cases to be the subject of the vertical direct effects on directives. These were tax authorities,[27] local or

---

[26] *Ibid.*, p. 918g.
[27] Case 8/81, *Becker* v. *Münster-Innenstedt Finanzamt*: [1982] E.C.R. 53, [1982] 1 C.M.L.R. 499; Case 221/88, *ECSC* v. *Acciaierie e Ferriere Busseni SpA* (in. liq): [1990] I E.C.R. 495.

regional authorities[28] constitutionally independent authorities for the maintenance of public order and safety[29] and public authortities providing health services.[30]

The Court tailored its judgment to the factual situation of the BGC. It did not elaborate guide lines for the qualification of an entity for the purposes of direct effect. It found that:

". . . a body, whatever its legal form, which has been made responsible, pursuant to a measure adopted by the State, *for providing a public service under the control of the State* and which has for that purpose special powers beyond those which result from the normal rules applicable in relations between individuals is included in any event among the bodies against which the provisions of a directive capable of having direct effect may be relied on."[31]

The Court referred back to the House of Lords the question of whether the BGC fell within the criteria elaborated and, in particular, whether it was a body which had been responsible, pursuant to a measure adopted by the State, "for providing a public service under the control of the State and which has for that purpose special powers beyond those which result from the normal rules applicable in relations between individuals."[32]

The Court laid some emphasis on whether the public authority has special powers beyond the normal functions of the State to govern relations between the public authority and individuals, as being a determining factor in giving rise to vertical direct effect. The Court also ruled that while the legal form for the public body is irrelevant, the public body must be established pursuant to a measure adopted by the State in order *to provide a public service under the control of the State*. This is an important extra condition which was not included in the Advocate General's Opinion.[33]

The judgment in *Foster* has been criticised by Prechal[34] on the grounds that the criteria above are in themselves vague and leave a large margin of appreciation to national courts, which may jeopardise the uniform application of Community law.

## Judgment of the House of Lords in Foster

In the House of Lords, Lord Templeman, speaking for the Court and **7–010** applying the criteria laid down by the ECJ, held that first BGC was a body which was made responsible pursuant to a measure adopted by the

---

[28] See Case 103/88, *Fratelli Costanzo SpA* v. *Comune Di Milano*: [1989] E.C.R. 1839, [1990] 3 C.M.L.R. 239.

[29] See Case 222/84, *Johnston* v. *RUC*: [1986] E.C.R. 1651, [1986] 3 C.M.L.R. 240.

[30] Marshall (No. 1), *op. cit.*, n. 2.

[31] Foster, *op. cit.*, n. 15, p. 922 at para. 20c (emphasis added).

[32] *Ibid.*, p. 922, para. 22.

[33] See Szyszczak, Case note on *Foster* (1990) C.M.L.Rev. 859 p. 867.

[34] Prechal, "Remedies after Marshall" (1990) C.M.L.Rev. 451 at p. 461.

State for providing a public service. BGC was established as a body corporate. The Secretary of State was authorised to make regulations with regard to the appointment and tenure and vacation of office by members of the Corporation. By virtue of section 2 of the Gas Act 1972 it is provided that:

> "(1) it shall be the duty of the Corporation to develop and maintain an efficient, coordinated and economical system of gas supply to Great Britain, and to satisfy, so far as it is economical to do so, all reasonable demands for gas in Great Britain."[35]

In other words, the supply of gas nationwide amounts to the provision of a public service and the relevant provisions of the Gas Act 1972 constituted the "measures adopted by the State".

In addition, it was further held that BGC performed its public service of providing a gas supply "under the control of the State". Lord Templeman referred to section 4 of the 1972 Act, by which BGC was directed to report to the minister who was authorised to:

> ". . . give to the Corporation such directions as he considers appropriate for securing the management of the activities of the Corporation and their subsidiaries is organised in the most efficient manner; and it shall be the duty of the Corporation to give effect to any such directions."[36]

By section 7, the Secretary of State was authorised to:

> ". . . give to the Corporation directions of a general character as to the exercise and performance by the Corporation of their functions . . . in relation to matters which appear to him to affect the national interest, and the Corporation shall give effect to any such directions."[37]

In addition, section 8 provided that the Corporation was ordered to make an annual report to the Minister, in such form as might be specified in the direction on the exercise and performance by the Corporation of its functions during the year and on its policy and programme.

Under Part II of the 1972 Act, the Secretary of State was given general control over the finances of the Corporation and, in particular, was authorised to direct it to pay over to him so much of its excess revenue as appeared to him surplus to its requirements.

Lord Templeman rejected the submissions by Counsel for the respondent that the Secretary of State did not possess the control contemplated by the ECJ, because BGC had wide powers to act in the performance of its functions and because the Secretary of State did not possess executive control or day to day control over the affairs of BGC. Lord Templeman reiterated the principle laid down by the ECJ, namely

---

[35] *Foster and Others* v. *British Gas Plc* [1991] 2 C.M.L.R. 217 (H.L.) at p. 222, para. 8.
[36] *Ibid.*, p. 223, para. 9.
[37] *Ibid.*, p. 223, para. 9.

that the State must not be allowed to take advantage of its own failure to comply with Community Law. In his judgment, the policy of BGC, which involved discrimination against women in breach of the Equal Treatment Directive, was thought to be in the financial and commercial interest of BGC.[38] He was of the view that the advantages of that policy would accrue indirectly to the State, which provided, through BGC, a supply of gas for all citizens generally and which was entitled to the surplus revenue of BGC. The day to day control exercised by BGC over its activities did not render it independent. "In the final analysis British Gas was under the control of the State and nobody else."[39]

The House of Lords also held that BGC had "special powers beyond those which resulted from the normal rules applicable to relations between individuals", thereby satisfying the third criteria specified by the European Court for defining an "emanation of the State". These special powers were conferred on British Gas by the 1972 Act and included an express power to prevent anyone else from supplying gas in the U.K. That power was a special power which could not have resulted from transactions between individuals.

The appeal was therefore allowed and the proceedings were referred to the Industrial Tribunal to assess the compensation payable to the appellants for the discrimination which had obliged them to retire at the age of 60.

## Doughty v. Rolls Royce Plc: factual background

The test laid down by the ECJ in *Foster* has subsequently been 7–011 considered in the case of *Doreen Sylvia Doughty* v. *Rolls Royce Plc.*[40] Mrs Doughty was an employee of Rolls Royce Plc, a commercial company wholly owned by the Crown. The company manufactured and sold gas turbine engines for aircraft. At a time when all its shares were held by nominees of the Crown, it operated a policy whereby men retired at 65 and women at 60. Mrs Doughty was dismissed by the employer on reaching 60, and complained that she had been unfavourably dismissed and discriminated against on the ground of her sex, contrary to section 6(2)(b) of the Sex Discrimination Act 1975 and the Equal Treatment Directive.[41] Under English law she had no case because at the relevant time, section 6(4) of that Act excluded discrimination arising out of provisions in relation to retirement. Subsequently, the disconformity of the domestic legislation with the international obligations imposed by the Directive were put right by an amendment to section 6(4) in the Sex Discrimination Act 1986, but the effective date was too late to save Mrs Doughty's claim under English law. The Industrial Tribunal therefore considered as a preliminary issue, whether she was entitled to rely

---

[38] *Ibid.*, p. 224, para. 15.
[39] *Ibid.*, p. 225, para. 15.
[40] *Doughty* v. *Rolls Royce Plc* [1992] 1 C.M.L.R. 1045.
[41] European Council Directive 76/207, [1976] O.J. 39/40, [1979] 1 *Commercial Laws of Europe* 34.

directly on Article 5(1) of the Equal Treatment Directive on the basis that the employer was an "emanation of the State" and as such she had a right of action against it.

The Industrial Tribunal found that the State was the sole shareholder and that the employer was an emanation of the State, rather than a corporate body with a distinct legal entity. It therefore held that Mrs Doughty was entitled to rely on the Directive. However, on appeal, the Employment Appeal Tribunal, (EAT) held that the correct question was whether the body concerned was an organ or agent of the State carrying out a State function. Rolls Royce was a commercial company in which the State had an interest, but it was essentially a corporate body distinct from the State. Accordingly, it held that the Industrial Tribunal erred in law and the applicant was not entitled to rely on Article 5(1) of the Directive.[42]

In the reasoning of the EAT, it took the view that there was substantial difference between the mere exercise of influence over a separate and independent legal persona, and the assured control of a servant or agent.[43] In addition, the EAT took the view that it was necessary to consider whether what was being done was, in the broad sense, a function of the State.[44] The employer, Rolls Royce Plc, was held not to be an organ or agent of the State, nor was it carrying out a State function.

### Application of the reasoning in Foster

7–012    At the time of the further appeal to the Court of Appeal, the *Foster* case[45] had been decided by the European Court. The Court of Appeal referred to the decision of the European Court in *Foster* and considered that the question which lay at the root of the appeal was:

> "did the act of the respondent company in denying to the appellant the opportunity to continue in service for a further five years amount to reliance by the United Kingdom upon its own failure to bring English law into conformity with the Equal Treatment Directive?"[46]

Mustill L.J. speaking for the Court of Appeal applied the principles abstracted from various judgments of the European Court, and sought to answer two questions. First, whether the appellant was correct in contending that the sole test, for present purposes, of whether the entity in question fell within the doctrine of *Becker*[47] and *Marshall (No. 1)*[48] was

---

[42] See *Rolls Royce Plc* v. *Doughty* [1987] I.C.R. 932.

[43] *Ibid.*, 943a.

[44] *Ibid.*

[45] *Foster: op. cit.*, n. 15.

[46] *Doreen Sylvia Doughty* v. *Rolls Royce Plc* [1992] 1 C.M.L.R. 1045 at 1048, para. 7 (judgment of Mustill L.J.)

[47] Case 8/81, *Becker*: [1982] E.C.R. 53, [1982] 1 C.M.L.R. 499.

[48] *Op. cit.*, n. 2.

whether it was under the control of the State. Secondly, if that contention was not correct, to what extent did the answer furnished by the Court of Justice in *Foster* constitute an exhaustive statement of the criteria for determining the status of the entity; and if it was not exhaustive, what test should be applied to the present case.[49]

The Court of Appeal held that the sole test was not whether the entity in question was "under the control of the State". Mustill L.J. said that the logic of the Advocate General's approach in *Foster* was also that *de facto* control was what mattered, so that "the doctrine would operate whenever the State could if it had wanted have caused the entity to change its terms of employment, regardless of the size of its shareholding and regardless of whether any attempt had ever been made or even contemplated to bring about such a change."[50]

However, he took the view that the opinion of the Advocate General, whilst not explicitly repudiated by the Court of Justice had, nevertheless, been incorporated into a much wider test in "which the power of control is one of only several cumulative criteria."[51] It was therefore necessary to consider whether all three criteria established by the formula in *Foster* were satisfied in the present case. Mustill L.J. was prepared to assume that the second criteria, namely that whatever "service" Rolls Royce provided was at the material time "under the control of the State". The Court noted the finding of the Tribunal that the character, status and power of Rolls Royce's sole shareholder (the government) significantly influenced the policies of the Board of Directors and the business carried on by the respondent.[52]

However, Mustill L.J. was unable to see, in respect of the other two **7–013** criteria, first, how the respondent company Rolls Royce could be said to have been "made responsible, pursuant to a measure adopted by the State for providing a public service." Rolls Royce Plc was a commercial undertaking of which part of its business traded with the State on terms which were negotiated at arms length. Mustill L.J. noted that this trading connection was of importance to the defence of the realm, an activity peculiar to the State, and was liable to become even more so in times of war.[53] The importance of this was manifested not only by the closeness of the watch kept on the trading relationship but also by the importance attached by officers of State to ensuring that the respondent kept its trading capacity fully in being. Nevertheless, on the evidence before the Industrial Tribunal, Mustill L.J. held that the "services" of the respondent were provided to the State and not to the public for purposes which were of benefit to the State. This may be regarded as a somewhat narrow approach. It is clear that the additional requirement laid down by the ECJ in *Foster* for the entity concerned to provide "a

---

[49] *Doughty* v. *Rolls Royce, op. cit.*, n. 46, p. 1056, para. 19.
[50] *Ibid.*, para. 21.
[51] *Ibid.*, para. 22.
[52] *Ibid.*, p. 1050 at para. 9.
[53] *Ibid.*, p. 1058 at para. 25.

public service" (which went beyond the test laid down by the Advocate General), was of crucial importance and provided the Court of Appeal with the means to construe the concept of "emanation of the State" in a restrictive way.

Finally, Mustill L.J. could not see any evidence that the respondent possessed or claimed to exercise any "special powers" of the type enjoyed by the British Gas Corporation in the *Foster* case.

In conclusion, Mustill L.J. was of the view that the *Foster* test was not intended to provide the answer to every category of case. However in a case:

> ". . . of the same general type as *Foster*, the Court's formulation must always be the starting point, and will usually be the finishing point. If all the factors identified by the Court are present it is likely to require something very unusual to produce the result that an entity is not to be identified with the State. Conversely, although the absence of a factor will not necessarily be fatal, it will need the addition of something else, not contemplated by the formula, before the *Marshall* principle has a prospect of being brought into play."[54]

Leave to appeal to the House of Lords was refused.

### Relevance of the Francovich decision

7–014    The principle that directives do not of themselves impose obligations on individuals and cannot be enforced against them, *i.e.*, they do not have "horizontal" direct effect, is not affected by the *Doughty* case. On the other hand, the Court of Appeal did not hear argument on (and therefore left open the possibility of) an action in damages against the U.K. Government on the basis of State liability to an individual who has suffered loss as a result of the acts of a private party which were incompatible with a directly applicable directive to which the State ought to have, but had not, given effect to by legislation. The effect of the judgment in the *Francovich* case[55] was therefore not considered and left open the possibility of Mrs Doughty bringing a separate action against the U.K. government for compensation for breach of Community law.[56]

### Subsequent U.K. case law

7–015    The principles established in the *Foster*[57] and *Marshall (No. 1)*[58] cases have also been applied in the later case of *R. v. London Boroughs Transport Committee, ex parte Freight Transport Association Limited*.[59] In

---

[54] *Ibid.*, p. 1058 at para. 24.
[55] Joined Cases C–6 & 9/90, *Francovich and Bonifaci and Others* v. *Republic of Italy*: [1991] I E.C.R. 5357, [1993] 2 C.M.L.R. 66.
[56] See further paras. 10–009 *et seq.* below.
[57] *Foster: op. cit.*, n. 15.
[58] *Marshall (No. 1): op. cit.*, n. 2.
[59] *R. v. London Boroughs Transport Committee, ex p. Freight Transport Association Ltd. and others* [1990] 1 C.M.L.R. 229 and discussed at paras. 3–021 *et seq.* and 3–050 *et seq.* above.

that case, the High Court considered, *inter alia*, whether the respondent, the London Boroughs Transport Committee (which acted on behalf of 22 London boroughs, *i.e.* local authorities) should be regarded as an emanation or organ of the State and was therefore subject to the vertical direct effect of various directives concerned with manufacturing standards on permissible sound levels and exhaust systems and on braking devices.[60] The respondent contended that a local authority cannot be so described, arguing that it was an independent corporation, whose employees are not servants of the Crown. Furthermore, it is a body elected by universal franchise, its powers are statutory, and providing it acts within those powers it cannot be interfered with.

However, Lord Justice Watkins did not agree. He took the view that a local authority is a creation of statute by Parliament[61] and that local authorities, such as the respondents, are to be regarded as "the governing authority, being itself derived from the legislature."[62] Accordingly, he had no difficulty in coming to the conclusion that the London Boroughs Transport Committee was subject to the vertical direct effect of the relevant EEC Directive. The decision of the ECJ in Case 103/88, *Fratelli Costanzo SpA* v. *Comune Di Milano*,[63] establishing that local or regional authorities are covered by the principle of vertical direct effect, does not appear to have been referred to in the *Freight Transport* case.

## Potential for future litigation

The above cases illustrate the fact that the designation of an institution **7–016** as an "emanation of the State" can therefore be crucial to the success of private claims. One further example of the potential for its application in future litigation is discussed by Geddes[64] and illustrated by Directive 84/5, "On the Approximation of the Laws of Member States relating to Insurance against Civil Liability in Respect of the Use of Motor Vehicles (as amended)."[65] Article 1(4) of this Directive requires Member States to designate a body to compensate victims in road traffic accidents caused by unidentified or uninsured vehicles. Article 1(4) provides that:

> "Each Member State shall set up or authorise a body with the task of providing compensation at least up to the limits of the insurance obligation for damage to property or personal injuries caused by an unidentified vehicle or a vehicle for which the insurance obligation provided for in paragraph 1 has not been satisfied. . . ."

---

[60] Directive 70/157 and Directive 71/320.

[61] *Ex p. Freight Transport, op. cit.*, n. 59, p. 240, para. 42.

[62] *Ibid.*, p. 242 at para. 44.

[63] Case 103/88, *Fratelli Costanzo SpA* v. *Comune Di Milano*: [1989] E.C.R. 1839, [1990] 3 C.M.L.R. 239.

[64] Geddes, "Difficulties Relating to Directives Affecting the Recoverability of Damages for Personal Injury" (1982) E.L.Rev. 408.

[65] Directive 84/5 of December 30, 1993: [1984] O.J. L8/17. This directive has subsequently been amended by Directive 90/232: [1990] O.J. L129/33. The latter is implemented in the U.K. by the Motor Vehicles (Compulsory Insurance) Regulations 1992: S.I. 1992 No. 3036.

Paragraph 1 of Article 1 provides that:

"The insurance referred to in Article 3(1) of Directive 72/166 shall cover compulsorily both damage to property and personal injuries."

The combined effect of these provisions is that the body designated under Article 1(4) must provide compensation at least to the limits required by national law on compulsory insurance, where the party liable is not insured in accordance with that national law or cannot be identified.

However, a difficulty could arise where a victim cannot recover against the designated body (*i.e.* the Motor Insurers' Bureau (MIB) in the U.K.) because the MIB has not agreed to compensate the victim in full in accordance with Article 1(4) of Directive 84/5. One such possibility is pointed out by Geddes.[66] Under paragraph 4 of the 1972 Agreement between the U.K. government and the MIB in relation to unidentified vehicles,[67] the MIB excludes any liability to make a payment where the victim has died, in respect of damages for loss of expectation of life or for pain and suffering. However, under English law[68] drivers are still required to insure themselves against such liability. Geddes argues[69] that this exception to the MIB's liability is contrary to the terms of the Directive which requires the designated body to provide compensation at least up to the limits of the insurance obligation for damage to property or personal injuries imposed by national law. However, if the MIB is not an "emanation of the State" the victim (or his/her personal representative) will have no claim in damages for such loss as is excluded under paragraph 4 of the 1972 Agreement.

It is argued by Geddes[70] that it is doubtful whether a national MIB may be classified as an "emanation of the State" within the meaning of *Foster*. For instance, it may be difficult to establish that part of the criteria laid down in *Foster*,[71] *i.e.* that the MIB had been established by the State in order "to provide a public service *under the control of the State.*" The arrangements between the MIB and the State may be treated as voluntary, and not necessarily under the control of the State. If this is the case, it would mean that the doctrine of direct effect could not be relied on against the MIB, for breaches of the provisions in the Directive.

However, under the doctrine in *Francovich*,[72] there may nevertheless be a possibility of damages against the State for incorrect implementation of the Directive in these circumstances.[73]

---

[66] Geddes, *op. cit.*, n. 62, pp. 413 *et seq.*

[67] Agreement of November 22, 1972 between the Secretary of State for the Environment and the Motor Insurers' Bureau on Compensation of Victims of Untraced Drivers (to be amended).

[68] Road Traffic Act 1988, s.145(3).

[69] Geddes, *op. cit.*, n. 62, p. 414.

[70] *Ibid.*, p. 411.

[71] *Foster: op. cit.*, n. 15.

[72] See further paras. 8–008 *et seq.* and 9–016 *et seq.* below.

[73] See further Geddes, *op. cit.*, n. 62, p. 414.

# IS THE TEST FUNCTIONAL OR BASED ON STATE CONTROL?

In essence, two types of tests were discussed in *Foster*. The first is a **7–017** functional test according to which any entity carrying out a public function on behalf of the State, or a body entrusted with a public duty, is to be considered part of the State. However, the difficulty with it is that what constitutes a public duty may vary from jurisdiction to jurisdiction and can also alter over time. For example, in the U.K. National Health Service bodies may be considered to be carrying out a public function but this may not be so in other jurisdictions, such as the Netherlands.[74] Even in the case of health matters in the U.K., these did not become "State" functions until as late as 1976. The test may also be classified as a functional one in the sense that it envisages the relevant body performing a particular type of activity, *i.e.* "the provision of a public service which it performs in the public interest."[75]

The alternative approach is based on the existence of control on the part of the entity involved, in relation to the person or entity concerned. Prechal[76] suggests that two forms of control are conceivable. The first is regulation by the State in the sense of subjecting the body concerned to specific directions from the State. Difficulties may arise, however, where the activity in issue is not subject to specific directions from the State, *e.g.* dismissal policies. Another form of control may be described as the "economic reality approach"[77] whereby if the State owns the majority of shares in a commercial company, or even a blocking minority, it could be argued that the State controls the company's policies and should therefore be equated with the State. However, difficulties arise where, for instance, the State only subsidises the body concerned and it is not then clear how far control must go or what kind of control is required to qualify that body as a public authority.

The relevant case law of the European Court on this subject has been extensively analysed by Curtin.[78] She points out that greater importance must be attached to function than to legal form and cites, in support, the European Court's judgment in Case 249/81, *Commission* v. *Ireland*,[79] where it held that the actions of the Irish Goods Council, a State-sponsored body created to encourage Irish industry, were attributable to the Irish government even though its legal form was that of a private company incorporated under the Companies legislation.

---

[74] See Prechal, "Remedies after Marshall" (1990) C.M.L.Rev. 451 at 458.
[75] See dicta of the Advocate General in Joined Cases 266–267/87, *The Queen* v. *The Royal Pharmaceutical Society of Great Britain et al.*: [1989] E.C.R. 1295, [1989] 2 C.M.L.R. 751, judgment of May 18, 1989.
[76] Prechal, *op. cit.*, n. 74.
[77] *Ibid.*, p. 458.
[78] Curtin, "The Province of Government: Delimiting the Direct Effect of Directives in the Common Law Context" (1990) 15 E.L.Rev. 195 to 223.
[79] Case 249/81, *Commission* v. *Ireland*: [1982] E.C.R. 4005 at 4020, [1983] 2 C.M.L.R. 104.

It may be that bodies which essentially carry out economic activities of an industrial or commercial nature may also be covered, if these can be shown to be a sufficient degree of influence exercised by the State over the commercial decisions of the undertakings in question.[80] She argues that the deciding factor in any event is not the amount of participation in the capital, but rather the *actual* influence of the State on commercial decisions.[81] This is a similar test to that advocated by the Industrial Tribunal in *Doughty* v. *Rolls Royce plc.*[82]

In the Opinion of the Advocate General Van Gerven in *Foster*, it is not possible to formulate an exhaustive set of criteria, to be applied uniformly across Community law and also within the different legal systems of the Member States. Factors such as control, regulation, exercise of "classic functions" of the State, and the supply of public services are indicative, but not conclusive, that the entity concerned should be bound in the same way as the government of a Member State, by Community law obligations. It would seem that with regard, for example, to bodies such as NHS Trust Hospitals, professional societies and universities, the test as laid down by the ECJ in *Foster* may be inconclusive. For instance, the provision of educational services by a university may well satisfy the functional test in that it may be argued that education is a "public service". However, the degree of control exercised by the State will vary from one university to another, particularly in relation to those which are "privately" constituted.[83] However, for practical purposes, the test laid down in *Foster* may not in fact be critical, if a national court can be persuaded to adopt a *purposive* interpretation of Community law in any event.[84]

## Adoption of both tests by the European Court

**7–018**   In general, the Court of Justice adopted both tests in its judgment in *Foster*. It has placed two limitations in that the entity involved must firstly be providing "a public service" (*i.e.* a functional test) and that it must be doing so under the control of the State, using special powers. If the public service provided is one of the "classic duties of the State", *e.g.* law and order as in the *Johnston* case, then it is submitted, as argued by Szyszczak,[85] that this would almost certainly bring the entity involved within the definition of "the State". However, the question remains as to how a "public service" is to be defined in Community law. Can it be said, for example, that when a State acquires a total or partial shareholding in a commercial undertaking, it is performing a public service? Under the Court's judgment in *Foster*, it would seem that the under-

---

[80] Curtin, *op. cit.*, n. 78, p. 218.
[81] *Ibid.*
[82] *Doughty* v. *Rolls Royce Plc* [1992] 1 C.M.L.R. 1045, see discussion at paras. 7–011 *et seq.* above.
[83] See also *Turpie* v. *University of Glasgow*, Industrial Tribunal decision, 1986, unreported.
[84] See further Chap. 6 above.
[85] Case note on *Foster* (1990) C.M.L.Rev. 859 at p. 868.

taking in question should itself be providing a public service, rather than the State providing a public service through its public investment in that undertaking.[86]

## Relevance of purposive construction

Neither the Court of Justice nor the Advocate General discuss in *Foster* 7–019 the alternative route of securing the binding obligations of Community law in the private sector, through the use of "indirect" direct effect, *i.e.* purposive construction of Community law.[87] Advocate General Van Gerven specifically stated that he would not discuss the duty of national courts to interpret provisions of national law in accordance with Community law since the House of Lords had not submitted any question in that respect.[88]

Curtin[89] points out that a flexible, interpretive approach is desirable when seeking to delineate between public and private sectors. This is particularly apt when, as in the *Foster* case analogy, workers employed by the same undertaking may find themselves alternatively in the public or the private sector depending on whether the undertaking is privatised or nationalised. If, on the other hand, the interpretation of Community law involves a purposive interpretation, then the need to establish direct effect is avoided and with it, the need to conceptualise the relationship of the undertaking in question with the State for particular purposes.[90]

---

[86] See Szyszczak, *op. cit.*, n. 33, p. 870.
[87] *Ibid.*
[88] *Foster, op. cit.*, n. 15, p. 908c. He did, however, note his own opinion in *Barber* [1990] 2 All E.R. 660 at p. 693, para. 50.
[89] Curtin, *op. cit.*, n. 78.
[90] See further Chap. 6 above.

# GENERAL PRINCIPLES OF COMMUNITY LAW REGARDING REMEDIES

**8–001** One of the primary tasks of the Court of Justice is laid down by Article 164 of the E.C. Treaty as follows:

"The Court of Justice shall ensure that in the interpretation and application of this Treaty, the law is observed."

The Court has ultimate and binding authority as regards the interpretation of Community law.[1] By virtue of Section 3(1) of the European Communities Act 1972 (as amended):

"For the purposes of all legal proceedings any question as to the meaning or effect of any of the Treaties, or as to the validity, meaning or effect of any Community instrument, shall be treated as a question of law (and, if not referred to the European Court, be for determination as such in accordance with the principles laid down by and any relevant decision of the European Court or any court attached thereto)."[2]

Judicial notice is to be taken of the Treaties, the Official Journal of the Communities and any decision of, or expression or opinion by, the European Court, by virtue of Section 3(2) of the 1972 Act (as amended).

However, responsibility for the application and enforcement of Community law is left to national tribunals.[3] The fact that enforcement of Community law must be left to national courts and tribunals has implications for the availability, and uniformity, of remedies in the various Member States in the event of breaches of the Community rights of individuals. The position was summarised by the Advocate General Reischl, in Case 61/79, *Amministrazione delle Finanze dello Stato* v. *Denkavit Italiana Srl*[4] as follows:

---

[1] See Article 177 of the E.C. Treaty and Case 26/72, *Van Gend en Loos*: [1963] E.C.R. 1 at pp. 2 to 13, [1963] C.M.L.R. 105

[2] This latter phrase was added by the European Communities (Amendment) Act 1986 and was included in order to encompass the Court of First Instance, which was established in 1989. By virtue of amendments made by the European Communities (Amendment) Act 1993, the definition of "the Treaties" to which the 1972 Act applies is broadened to include those parts of the Treaty on European Union signed at Maastricht which relates to the European Communities. See further discussion at para. 2–001 above.

[3] *Van Gend en Loos, op. cit.*, n. 1, and see also, Article 192 of the E.C. Treaty regarding the enforcement of decisions of the Council and Commission (*e.g.* fines) against individuals in accordance with national law.

[4] Case 61/79, *Amministrazoine delle Finanze dello Stato* v. *Denkavit Italiana Srl*: [1980] E.C.R. 1205 at p. 1233, [1981] 3 C.M.L.R. 694.

"That the legal position of the individual may thus differ in the various Member States is simply a consequence of the implementation of Community law by the Member States, which is accepted by the Community legal system."

In other words, it may not be possible to achieve total uniformity of Community law because of the diversity of legal systems among the Member States. However, so long as Community law is effectively implemented by national authorities (which includes the national courts), in accordance with the basic principles of Community law, then the legal obligations of Member States are satisfied.[5]

The lack of uniform application of Community law in all Member States has also been acknowledged by the Court in Case 130/79, *Express Dairy Foods* v. *International Board for Agricultural Produce*[6] which concernd an action for the repayment of sums paid by way of monetary compensation, under Community regulations which turned out to be invalid. The Court held:

"In the regrettable absence of Community provisions harmonising procedure and time limits the Court finds that this situation entails dfferences of treatment on a Community scale. It is not for the Court to issue general rules of substance of procedural provisions which only the competent institutions may adopt. The rules to be adopted should involve equal treatment as regards conditions of form and substance in which traders may contest Community charges imposed upon them and claim their recovery in the event of undue payment together with a similar harmonisation of the conditions in which the administrative authorities of a Member State, acting on behalf of the Community, impose the said charges and, where appropriate, recover financial benefits which have been irregularly granted. In the absence of Community rules however, the necessary deference to national laws is nevertheless subject to limits the need for which have been acknowledged in as much as the application of national legislation must be effeced in a non-discriminatory manner having regard to the procedural rules relating to disputes of the same type, but purely national, and in so far as procedural rules cannot have the result as making impossible in practice the exercise of rights conferred by Community law."[7]

Member States are not obliged to adopt a specific course of action, *e.g.* **8–002** to choose sanctions of a particular kind unless the remedies required to be available are expressly provided for and the relevant provisions are directly effective, that is they must be sufficiently clear, unconditional and precise.[8] If remedies are *not* expressly provided for, then Member

---

[5] Green and Barav, "Damages in the National Courts for Breach of Community Law" (1986) 6 Y.E.L. 55 at p. 55.

[6] Case 130/79, *Express Dairy Foods* v. *International Board for Agricultural Produce*: [1980] E.C.R. 1887, [1981] 1 C.M.L.R. 451.

[7] *Ibid.*, p. 1900.

[8] See, for example, Case 14/83, *Von Colson*: [1984] E.C.R. 1891, Advocate General Rozès at p. 1915, [1986] 2 C.M.L.R. 430.

States are free to choose from among existing sanctions available under national law. For instance, if the question of sanctions is not dealt with in the relevant Community measure then "periods of limitation, rights of set off, the extent of rights or reimbursement of improper charges, payment of interest and so on are matters to be regulated by the domestic law of the Member States in whose courts the individual right-holder seeks to proceed."[9]

Apart from the express rules laid down in the E.C. Treaty and in secondary legislation, the Court of Justice has, however, developed certain general principles of law regarding remedies and other, more general, issues. These principles are derived from various sources, notably the legal systems of the Member States themselves. These general principles have been extensively discussed elsewhere.[10] They include principles such as that of proportionality, legal certainty and legitimate expection, the principle of equality and the right to a hearing. Although a distinction may be drawn between such "general principles" and "fundamental rights", the latter have been declared by the Court to constitute an integral part of the general principles of law which the court is bound to uphold.[11]

However, certain of these general principles of Community law specifically concern the issue of remedies.[12] These have been identified and are set out below. One or more of these principles may need to be pleaded as either the main basis for litigation in domestic courts, or in addition to a claim based on some other breach of a substantive rule of Community law.

The principles below apply not only to actions brought by private parties (against the State or another private party) but also to actions brought by public authorities.[13] Furthermore, Community law can be used as either a sword or as a shield, *i.e.* to defend an action, on the basis of the above principles.[14]

## PRINCIPLE OF EFFECTIVENESS

8–003   It is a logical outcome of "directly effective" Community law that Member States are obliged to provide the remedies and procedures

---

[9] *Bourgoin SA* v. *Ministry of Agriculture, Fisheries and Food* [1986] Q.B. 716 at p. 755 *per* Oliver L.J. (dissenting), [1986] 1 C.M.L.R. 267.

[10] See the contribution of Hartley, *The Foundations of European Community Law* (1990) 2nd ed., p. 129 and Wyatt and Dashwood, *European Community Law* (1993), 3rd ed., p. 88. See also the helpful summary in Sharpston, *Interim and Substantive Relief in Claims under Community Law* (1993), pp. 9 to 10.

[11] See Case 4/73, *Nold* v. *Commission*: [1974] E.C.R. 491, [1974] 2 C.M.L.R. 338 and discussion at paras. 3–060 *et seq.* above.

[12] See Ward, "Government Liability in the U.K. for Breach of Individual Rights in European Community Law" (1990) 19 *Anglo-American Law Review* 1 to 35.

[13] See Oliver, "Enforcing Community Rights in the English Courts" (1987) M.L.R. 881 at p. 883.

[14] See Ward, *op. cit.*, n. 12, and D'Sa, "State Liability for Breaches of E.C. Law" (May 13, 1992) 89/18 *Gazette* 27 to 31. For a general discussion of "Euro-defences," see paras. 10–056 *et seq.* below.

whereby the law can be enforced, otherwise such law may be totally ineffective and unenforceable. This "principle of effectiveness" was accepted in *Van Gend en Loos*,[15] where the Court expressly stated that national courts were under a duty to protect the rights created by directly effective provisions. This was reiterated in Case 45/76, *Comet* v. *Produktschap voor Siergewassen*[16] and in Case 33/76, *Rewe-Zentralfinanze* v. *Landwirtschaftskammer für das Saarland*[17] in which the Court stated that:

> "Applying the principle of co-operation laid down in Article 5 of the Treaty, it is the national courts which are entrusted with ensuring the legal protection which citizens derive from the direct effect of the provisions of Community law . . . ."

Another landmark judgment establishing the principle of effectiveness is Case 106/77, *Amministrazione delle Finanze dello Stato* v. *Simmenthal* (referred to as *Simmenthal*).[18] The ECJ considered the validity of a rule of Italian law which reserved to the Italian Constitutional Court the right to set aside national legislation adopted after the entry into force of the EEC Treaty and contrary to Community law. The ECJ found this to be contrary to the principle of direct effect and held that:

> ". . . any provision of a national legal system and any legislative, administrative or judicial practice which might impair the effectiveness of Community law by withholding from the national court having jurisdiction to apply such law the power to do everything necessary at the moment of its application to set aside national legislative provisions which might prevent Community rules from having full force and effect are incompatible with those requirements which are the very essence of Community law."

In other words, directly effective Community law is supreme, and national courts must do everything necessary to give effect to it even if this means setting aside national law, even temporarily (as in the case of interim relief) to ensure complete and effective judicial protection.[19] Member States must design remedies in such a way that it is not impossible in practice to exercise the rights which the national courts have a duty to protect. In Case C–128/92, *Banks and Company Ltd.* v. *British Coal Corporation*, the Advocate General Van Gerven confirmed that, for example, national rules of evidence may not make it practically

---

[15] *Op. cit.*, n. 1. In Case C–128/92, *H.J. Banks and Company Ltd.* v. *British Coal Corporation*: Opinion of Advocate General Van Gerven, delivered on October 27, 1993, not yet reported, the Advocate General confirmed that the right to obtain an effective legal remedy against measures which are contrary to the rules of Community law is a general principle of Community law; see para. 4 of the Opinion of the Advocate General.

[16] Case 45/76, *Produktschap voor Siergewassen*: [1976] E.C.R. 2043, [1977] 1 C.M.L.R. 533.

[17] Case 33/76, *Rewe*: [1976] E.C.R. 1989 at p. 1997, [1977] 1 C.M.L.R. 533.

[18] Case 106/77, *Simmenthal*: [1978] E.C.R. 629, [1978] 3 C.M.L.R. 263.

[19] Toth, case note on Case C–213/89, *R.* v. *Secretary of State for Transport, ex p. Factortame Ltd. and Others (Factortame (No. 2))*: [1990] I E.C.R. 2433, [1990] 3 C.M.L.R. 1, (1990) C.M.L.Rev. 573 at 584 and see discussion at para. 3–014 above and paras. 9–034 *et seq.* below.

impossible or excessively difficult to obtain redress as required by Community law, particularly by means of presumption or rules of evidence which place an unreasonably heavy onus of proof on the individual in question.[20] This principle does not apply to prevent the fixing of a reasonable period of limitation, within which an action must be brought.[21] It may, however, extend to a right to challenge by means of judicial review, decisions, *e.g.* an unjustified failure to grant an import licence, which may have an impact on fundamental principles such as the free movement of goods.[22]

The existence of a judicial remedy against a refusal by a national authority to give the benefit of a Community right (*e.g.* free access to employment) has been held to be essential for the individual's effective protection of that right,[23] and may also extend to a requirement by the competent national authority to notify the reasons on which its refusal is based, either in the decision itself or in a subsequent communication made at the request of the party affected.[24]

### Duty to create new remedies?

8-004    In relation to interim relief, the principle implies that "effective protection" includes ensuring that the inevitable time delay between the time a right comes into existance and the time when it is definitively established by judicial proceedings, does not in itself make it impossible to exercise the right, thereby depriving it of substance.[25] This raises the issue of whether there is any obligation on national courts to create a domestic remedy if it does not already exist. In *Factortame (No. 2)*,[26] the applicants and the European Commission argued, on the basis of the principle of effectiveness, that a national court must have jurisdiction to grant interim protection for directly applicable Community rights. The United Kingdom, on the other hand, relied on dicta in the *Rewe* case[27] that Community law "was not intended to create new remedies in the national courts to ensure the observance of Community law other than those already laid down by national law."[28]

The Court's judgment in *Factortame (No. 2)*[29] was that the "full effectiveness of Community law" would be impaired if "a rule of national

---

[20] *Op. cit.*, n. 15, para. 48 of the Advocate General's Opinion. See also judgment in Case 198/82, *San Giorgio*: [1983] E.C.R. 3595, [1985] 2 C.M.L.R. 658 at para. 14, discussed further at para. 10–022 below. See also Case 45/76, *Comet BV* v. *Produktschap Voor Siegewasen*: [1976] E.C.R. 2043, [1977] 1 C.M.L.R. 533.

[21] See further paras. 5–011 *et seq.* above and also the *Express Dairy Foods* case, *op. cit.*

[22] See Case C–18/88, *Régie des Télégraphes et des Téléphones* v. *SA "GB-Inno-BM"*: [1991] I E.C.R. 5941. See also Case C–97/91, *Oleificio Borelli* v. *E.C. Commission*: judgment of December 3, 1992, not yet reported.

[23] See Case 222/86, *UNECTEF* v. *Haylens*: [1987] E.C.R. 4097, [1989] 1 C.M.L.R. 901.

[24] *UNECTEF, op. cit.*, at paras. 14 and 15 of the judgment.

[25] See Gravells, "Effective Protection of Community Law Rights: Temporary Disapplication of an Act of Parliament" (Summer 1991) *Public Law* 180 at 183.

[26] *Factortame (No. 2): op. cit.*, n. 19.

[27] *Rewe: op. cit.*, n. 17.

[28] See further, Oliver, "Interim Answers: Some Recent Developmets" (1992) C.M.L.Rev. 7 at p. 15.

[29] *Factortame (No. 2): op. cit.*, n. 19.

law could prevent a court seized of a dispute governed by Community law from granting interim relief in order to ensure the effectiveness of the judgment to be given on the existence of the rights claimed under Community law." It therefore concluded that:

"Community law must be interpreted as meaning that a national court which, in a case before it concerning Community law, considers the sole obstacle which precludes it from granting interlocutory relief is a rule of national law must set aside that rule."[30]

It has been argued by Oliver[31] that although it is possible to treat the *Factortame (No. 2)* judgment as simply requiring national courts to set aside national rules, *i.e.* the presumption of validity of an Act of Parliament and the immunity of the Crown from interim relief which constitute obstacles to the grant of interim relief, on a broader view it actually obliges them to create this remedy if it does not exist.[32] In other words, the extension of the right to interim relief to categories of proceedings where it was not available before, can be viewed either as the removal of an obstacle to such relief or the creation of a new remedy.[33] However, the criteria to be applied in deciding whether or not to grant interim relief was held by the ECJ to be matter of national law, as was the question of what specific measures may be ordered.[34] It has been suggested by Gravells[35] that the reliance by the House of Lords primarily on the principle in *American Cyanamid* v. *Ethicon Ltd.*[36] supports the view that the case did not involve the creation of a new remedy but simply the modified application of an existing one (*i.e.* the interlocutory injunction). The view of Advocate General Mischo in Case C–6/90, *Francovich* v. *Italian Republic*[37] was that a necessary implication of Community law, including the *Factortame* case, was that "an appropriate legal remedy must be created if one does not exist."[38]

## Immediate protection

Since enforcement is to be governed by national law, the national **8–005** system must also decide matters such as which court has jurisdiction to hear such actions.[39] National court must provide "direct and immediate protection" for directly effective or applicable measures from their date

---

[30] The House of Lords subsequently granted interim relief in its Order of July 1990 and its Judgment of October 1990: [1990] 3 W.L.R. 818, [1990] 3 C.M.L.R. 375 and see Oliver, *op. cit.*, n. 28, p. 16.

[31] *Ibid.*

[32] *Ibid.* See further, Toth, (1990) C.M.L.Rev. 573 at p. 596.

[33] See Oliver, *op. cit.*, n. 28, p. 17.

[34] See further paras. 9–034 *et seq.* below.

[35] Gravells, *op. cit.*, n. 25, p. 189.

[36] *American Cyanamid* v. *Ethicon Ltd.* [1975] A.C. 396, [1975] 2 W.L.R. 316 and see discussion at paras. 9–035 *et seq.* below.

[37] Joined Cases C–6 & 9/90, *Francovich and Bonifaci* v. *Italian Republic*: [1991] I E.C.R. 5357, [1993] 2 C.M.L.R. 66, discussed in detail at paras. 8–008 *et seq.* above.

[38] See further Ross, "Beyond Francovich" (1993) M.L.R. 55 at p. 56.

[39] See Case 13/68, *Salgoil* v. *Italian Foreign Trade Ministry*: [1968] E.C.R. 453 at p. 463, [1969] C.M.L.R. 181.

of entry into force. However, the Court has sometimes varied this rule in certain circumstances. For example, in Case 43/75, *Defrenne* v. *Sabena*,[40] the Court limited the effect of its ruling to the date of its actual judgment, to take account of the floodgate of litigation which might otherwise have been caused. Further examples are given at paragraph 4–008 above. However, in general, past as well as future conduct is covered. The impact of this requirement in relation to applications for interim relief is considered in relation to the *Factortame* litigation at paragraphs 9–034 *et seq.* below.

### Deterrent effect

8–006     Sanctions must "be such as to guarantee real and effective judicial protection. Moreover they must have a real deterrent effect."[41] For instance, if Member States choose to provide a remedy in damages they must be "adequate in relation to the damage sustained and therefore amount to more than purely nominal compensation."[42] In the U.K. case of *Marshall* v. *Southampton and SW Hants Area Health Authority (No. 2)*[43] an Industrial Tribunal assessed compensation due to the claimant in the U.K., following her enforced discriminatory retirement contrary to Community law. The Tribunal found that the U.K. statutory maximum for such compensation (which was £6,250 at the time of the dismissal and £8,500 at the date of the hearing) was "inadequate" within the meaning intended by the European Court in *Von Colson*.[44] The statutory maximum amount of compensation was found to be inadequate compared with other comparable claims and with national wage levels. The Tribunal found that she should receive £19,405 less £6,250 which she had already received, and it made her an award accordingly. The Tribunal held that, although technically the remedies of declaration and recommendations were available, in practical terms the only remedy which was appropriate was compensation. The Tribunal therefore concluded that the statutory compensation did not constitute a deterrent, except in relation to very small employers[45] and therefore allowed the claimant to enforce her Community right directly and ignored the statutory maximum limit of compensation. The issue of what level of damages is to be considered adequate under Community law in this case was subsequently referred by the Court of Appeal to the ECJ which held that the statutory limit on compensation for sex discrimination was unlawful under Community law and is discussed in detail at paragraphs 9–025 *et seq.* below.

---

[40] Case 43/75, *Defrenne* v. *Sabena*: [1976] E.C.R. 455, [1976] 2 C.M.L.R. 98.
[41] See Case 79/83, *Harz* v. *Deutsche Tradax GmbH*: [1984] E.C.R. 1921, [1986] 2 C.M.L.R. 430 and *Von Colson*: [1984] E.C.R. 1891 at 1908, [1986] 2 C.M.L.R. 430.
[42] See Case 79/83, *Harz* v. *Tradax, op. cit.*, n. 41, p. 1942.
[43] *Marshall (No. 2)* [1988] I.R.L.R. 325.
[44] *Von Colson: op. cit.*, n. 41.
[45] See further, "The Enforcement of EEC Law in the Courts of the Member States: What Does Direct Effect Really Mean?" in *Droit Sans Frontiers* (Hand and McBride ed. 1991) 265 at p. 273.

# PRINCIPLE OF NON-DISCRIMINATION

Non-discrimination is a very broadly applicable and general concept **8–007** of E.C. law. For example, various Treaty articles such as Article 6 of the E.C. Treaty (formerly Article 7 EEC) prohibits discrimination on the grounds of nationality and Article 119 prohibits discrimination on the grounds of sex. These articles have been extensively applied in case law prior to the entry into force of the Treaty on European Union and the principles established by these cases are still valid. In the context of remedies, the principle of non-discrimination means that remedies must not be less favourable than those governing the same[46] or similar[47] rights of action on an internal matter. They must also be available under national rules of procedure or conditions which are not less favourable than those applicable to the enforcement of a similar right of a domestic nature.[48]

However, in the *San Giorgio* case the Court held that:

". . . the requirement of non-discrimination laid down by the Court cannot be construed as justifying legislative measures intended to render any repayment of charges levied contrary to Community law virtually impossible, *even if the same treatment is extended to tax-payers, who have similar claims arising from an infringement of national tax law.*"[49]

In other words it is not sufficient in cases concerning the repayment of sums wrongly levied and paid, to argue that the same procedural disadvantage is also suffered by those claiming such repayments under national law. This was reiterated in Case 54/81, *Fromme* v. *Bundesenstalt für landwirtschaftliche Marktordnung*[50] where the Court stressed that the application of national law must not adversely affect the scope or impair the effectiveness of Community law by making the recovery of sums wrongly paid impossible in practice. The remedy of restitution is discussed in detail at paragraphs 10–022 *et seq.* below.

---

[46] See Case 45/76, *Comet BV* v. *Produktschap Voor Siergewassen*: [1976] E.C.R. 2043, [1977] 1 C.M.L.R. 533.

[47] See Case 199/82, *Amministrazione delle Finanze dello Stato* v. *San Giorgio*: [1983] E.C.R. 3595 at p. 3612, [1985] 2 C.M.L.R. 658.

[48] Case 199/82, *San Giorgio, op. cit.*, n. 47, (emphasis added) and see Oliver, "Interim Measures: Some Recent Developments" (1992) C.M.L.Rev. 7 at p. 14. See also, Case C–128/92, *H.J. Banks and Company Ltd.* v. *British Coal Corporation*: Opinion of Advocate General Van Gerven, delivered on October 27, 1993, not yet reported, at para. 48, and Joined Cases C–92 & 326/92, *Phil Collins* v. *Imtrat Handelsgesellschaft mbH* and *Patricia Im-und Export Verwaltungsgesellschaft mbH* v. *EMI Electrola GmbH*: judgment of October 10, 1993, not yet reported, concerning the application of the principle of non-discrimination in Article 7 of the EEC Treaty to copyright and related rights belonging to persons who are non-nationals of a Member State, which must be capable of being protected, on a completely equal footing with nationals of that Member State, in a situation governed by Community law.

[49] *San Giorgio: op. cit.*, n. 47, p. 3614.

[50] Case 54/81, *Fromme*: [1982] E.C.R. 1449.

## STATE LIABILITY UNDER *FRANCOVICH*

### *Liability for damages before Francovich*

**8–008**  Prior to Joined Cases C–6 & 9/90 *Francovich and Bonifaci* v. *Italian Republic*,[51] judicial authorities on the question of whether there is a right to compensation against the State for breach of Community law were scant in the European Court. In the earlier Case 69/75, *Russo* v. *AIMA*[52] the plaintiff, an Italian producer of durum wheat, brought proceedings in Italy against the defendant, an Italian agency for intervention on the agricultural market (AIMA). The plaintiff claimed that the defendant had unlawfully interfered with the formation of market prices for durum wheat in Italy, contrary to the Community regulations and that as a result, he had to sell his product at a price lower then he would legitimately have expected to under the Community system. He brought an action for damages against AIMA pursuant to the Italian Civil Code. The plaintiff acknowledged that the action for damages was governed by the rules of each Member State.[53] The Court held that individual producers are vested with a right to sell at a price approximating to the target price and in any event not lower than the intervention price. By virtue of Community law therefore, the plaintiff who had been compelled to sell at a price below the target price, was entitled to claim that he had suffered damage. The Court said that:

> "It is for the national court to decide on the basis of the facts of each case whether an individual producer has suffered a damage. If such a damage has been caused through an infringement of Community law, the State is liable to the injured party for the consequences in the context of the provisions of national law on the liability of the State."[54]

This judgment is authority for the proposition that *if national procedural rules permit it*, national courts must award damages to individuals harmed by a breach of a directly effective provision of Community law.[55]

In Case 181/83, *Roussel Laboratories BV* v. *The Netherlands*[56] and Case 197/84, *Steinhauser* v. *City of Biarritz*,[57] which were both referred to the European Court under the Article 177 procedure, the national judges in the Dutch and German courts respectively found that a breach of the EEC Treaty provisions as interpreted by the European Court had been committed by public authorities, and on that ground ordered the defendants in each case to make good the loss suffered as a result of their

---

[51] Cases C–6 & 9/90, *Francovich and Bonifaci and Others* v. *Italian Republic*: [1991] I E.C.R. 5357, [1993] 2 C.M.L.R. 66, [1992] I.R.L.R. 84, discussed further below.

[52] Case 60/75, *Russo* v. *AIMA*: [1976] E.C.R. 45.

[53] *Ibid.*, p. 50.

[54] *Ibid.*, p. 56.

[55] See Nicholas Green and Ami Barav, "Damages in the National Courts for Breach of Community Law" (1986) 6 Y.E.L. 54 at p. 63.

[56] Case 181/82, *Roussel*: [1983] E.C.R. 3849, [1985] 1 C.M.L.R. 834.

[57] Case 197/84, *Steinhauser* v. *City of Biarritz*: [1985] E.C.R. 1820, [1986] 1 C.M.L.R. 53.

unlawful action. [58] Neither of these cases involved any prior judgment of the European Court in proceedings under Articles 169 or 171 of the EEC Treaty. [59]

## Questions raised in Francovich

The *Francovich* case[60] was also referred for a ruling under Article 177, **8–009** from an Italian court. It raised two questions. Firstly, whether the Directive at issue, 80/987 (on the approximation of the laws of the Member States relating to the protection of employees in the event of the insolvency of their employer), gives rise to direct effects which may benefit individuals. Secondly, if this is not the case, whether individuals may nevertheless claim compensation from the State which had failed to transpose the Directive correctly in national law within the prescribed time. It should be noted that by a judgment of February 2, 1989 *Commission* v. *Italy*[61] the Court ruled that Italy had failed to fulfil its obligations under the Treaty by failing to transpose the Directive into national law by the required date (October 23, 1983) and in fact had still not done so by the date of the proceedings in *Francovich*.

The Court stressed that the full effectiveness of Community provisions would be called into question and the protection of the rights conferred by them would be impaired, if private individuals have no means of obtaining compensation when their rights are infringed by breach of Community law for which a Member State is responsible. It took the view that this principle of the State's liability is inherent in the system of the EEC Treaty. (This part of the judgment is not affected by amendments made by the Treaty on European Union.) In particular, the Court cited Article 5 of the Treaty (which was not amended at Maastricht) as the basis of the obligation on Member States to pay compensation in respect of such damage. It stated that one of those obligations is to make reparation for any unlawful consequences resulting from a breach of Community law. It cited in support of this an earlier judgment in Case 6/60, *Humblet*,[62] which relates to the ECSC Treaty Article 86, which corresponds to Article 5 of the Treaty of Rome.

The Court's decision in *Francovich* is in line with its reasoning in *Von Colson*,[63] *Harz*[64] and *Marleasing* v. *La Comercial*.[65] The lack of direct effect has not prevented the Court from providing a remedy to private individuals where there has been a breach of Community law for which a Member State is responsible. [66]

## Conditions for State Liability

The Court went on to set conditions governing the State's liability and **8–010** made it clear that these conditions depended on the nature of the breach

---

[58] See further *Green and Barav, op. cit.*, n. 55.
[59] The Article 169 and 171 procedure is discussed at paras. 1–003 *et seq.* above.
[60] *Francovich: op. cit.*, n. 51.
[61] Case 22/87, *Commission* v. *Italy*: [1989] E.C.R. 145.
[62] Case 6/60, *Humblet*: [1960] E.C.R. 559.
[63] Case 14/83, *Von Colson*: [1984] E.C.R. 1891, [1986] 2 C.M.L.R. 430.
[64] Case 79/83, *Harz*: [1984] E.C.R. 1921, [1986] 2 C.M.L.R. 430.
[65] Case C–106/89, *Marleasing* v. *La Comercial*: [1990] I E.C.R. 4135, [1992] 1 C.M.L.R. 305 discussed further at para. 6–004 above.
[66] See para. 6–003 above.

of Community law. Where, as in *Francovich*, the Member State had failed to fulfil the obligation incumbent upon it under Article 189(3) of the Treaty (which is not amended by the Treaty on European Union), to take all measures necessary to achieve the result prescribed by a directive, the effectiveness of Community law required a right to compensation providing three conditions were met.

The first of these conditions is that the result prescribed by the Directive should confer rights on private individuals. It is submitted that this means that the content of the Directive should indicate that private individuals are the intended beneficiaries of rights. The second condition is that the nature of those rights should be able to be identified from the provisions of the Directive. This comes close to a requirement of "direct effect" for the relevant provisions, but does not require the same degree of precision and unconditionality as for direct effect. The Court decided that in *Francovich* this could be established from Article 3 of the Directive. The Court said that although Article 3 of the Directive left it to the Member State to decide the date from which the payment of claims must be guaranteed, it was implicit in the case law of the Court that the fact that the State can choose from a multiplicity of possible methods for achieving the result prescribed by a directive, does not preclude individuals from asserting, before national courts, rights whose nature can nevertheless be determined sufficiently precisely on the sole basis of the provisions of the Directive.[67]

The Court decided that the fact that certain Articles of the Directive gave Member States some leeway in respect of the method for defining the guarantee and limiting the sums involved, has no effect on the precise and unconditional nature of the prescribed *result*. Furthermore, it is clear from the judgment that the fact that other provisions identifying the guarantor were insufficiently precise to enable the Court to identify the State as the party liable under the guarantee, did not affect the nature of the guarantee itself.

The third condition which must be satisfied to establish the State's liability is that there should be a causal link between the failure of the State to fulfil its obligation and the damage sustained by the persons adversely affected.

These conditions were all satisfied in *Francovich*. The Court specified that it was then for the national court to guarantee, in the context of national law and liability, the right of employees to obtain compensation in respect of damage sustained by them as a result of the failure to transpose the Directive. In other words, the procedural route by which individuals may make claims for compensation against the State is left for determination by the national authorities.

The doctrine of direct effects, though important in the context of *Francovich*, therefore seems to have given way to a more general principle being established by the Court, of State liability to private individuals for breach of Community law. However, it must be remem-

---

[67] The Court cited its judgments in Case 71/85, *FNV*: [1986] E.C.R. 3855, [1987] 3 C.M.L.R. 76 and Case 286/85, *McDermott and Cotter*: [1987] E.C.R. 1453, [1987] 2 C.M.L.R. 607.

bered that the first two conditions laid down in *Francovich* make it clear that concepts similar to that of "direct effect" may still be relevant. The Directive must first *confer rights on individuals* and secondly these rights must be capable of identification and must therefore be sufficiently precise for that purpose. This does not directly resolve the question of whether or not a directive can have horizontal direct effect, *i.e.* create rights and obligations as between private parties. However, *Francovich* does imply that if a person suffers through the acts or omissions of a non-State entity and those acts or omissions are incompatible with the directly effective provisions of a directive, then the injured person, although not able to sue the other private party directly, may nevertheless have an action in damages against the State itself. Thus the individual still achieves some redress for the relevant breach of Community law. The right to damages which may be available to individuals in these circumstances in English law is dicussed further below at paragraphs 9–016 *et seq.*

### Is Francovich limited to non-implementation of directives?

However, the question arises as to whether *Francovich* is also authority **8–011** for the proposition that there is a compulsory right to compensation by way of damages not only for a failure to implement a *directive*, but also for an infringement of other provisions of Community law which are directly applicable or have direct effect, or which confer rights on individuals. It is arguable that the principles in *Francovich* apply equally to E.C. Treaty provisions. For instance, it has been argued that Articles 90(1) and 92 EEC (which are in substance unamended by the Treaty on European Union) are such provisions, even though they do not have direct effect.[68] It is also arguable that the *Francovich* principle might be extended to certain provisions of the Merger Regulation, in particular Article 9 (distinct market) and Article 21. The issue of whether *Francovich* applies, however, to directly effective treaty provisions is the subject of a reference to the European Court by the High Court in Case 48/93, *R.* v. *Secretary of State for Transport, ex parte Factortame Ltd.* (*Factortame No. 3*)[69] and see also the reference to the ECJ in Joined Cases C–46 and 48/93, *Firma Brasserie du Pecheur* (not yet decided) which is reference from a German court in relation to a damages claim from a French brewer, Brasserie du Pêcheur S.A., against the German authorities, arising out of the German Biersteuergesetz (Law on Beer Duty), whose "Reinheitsgebot" (purity requirement) was held by the Court to be contrary to Article 30 in Case 178/84, *Commission* v. *Germany*: [1987] E.C.R. 1227. The Court has been asked to rule on the conditions under which Member States have an obligation to make good damage caused to individuals through non-conformity of their legislation with Community law and on the way in which such an obligation is to be implemented.

---

[68] See Smith, "The Francovich Case: State liability and the Individual's Right to Damages" [1992] 3 E.C.L.R. 179.
[69] Case 48/93, *R.* v. *Secretary of State for Transport, ex p. Factortame Ltd.* (*No. 3*): not yet decided.

In statements to the Court in *Francovich*, however, the German, British, Italian and Dutch governments ruled out, under Community law, compulsory compensation for such infringement. However, it is submitted that the judgment in *Francovich* should, by logical extension, apply to breaches of directly effective Community law, such as relevant Treaty Articles. This follows from the reasoning of the Court which was based in part on Article 5 of the Treaty of Rome (which is not altered by the Treaty on European Union) and which asserts a general obligation on Member States "to take all appropriate measures, whether general or particular, to ensure fulfilment of the obligations arising out of this Treaty . . . .". This implies a right of action in respect of any infringement of Community law and not just of Community directives. In Case C–128/92, *H. J. Banks and Company Ltd.* v. *British Coal Corporation*,[70] the Advocate General Van Gerven was certainly prepared to accept the application of the rules in *Francovich* to breaches of directly effective Treaty provisions and took the view that the existence of direct effect constitutes an *a fortiori* argument that damages may be awarded for a breach of such provisions. In his Opinion in *Francovich*, Advocate General Mischo also stated that the principle of State liability "is capable of being extended to cover *any* failure of Member States to observe Community law . . . whether the failure is in breach of the Treaty, Regulations or Directives, whether they have direct effect or not."[71] Arguably, it could also cover a failure by national courts to apply Community law.[72]

This reasoning is also supported in the three conditions prescribed in *Francovich* for governing a State's liability, already dicussed. The first of these was that the Directive should confer rights on private individuals. This condition would be satisfied where an E.C. Treaty Article had direct effect. (This would cover, for example, breaches of Article 30 and Article 52.) The second condition was that the nature of the rights concerned must be capable of identification from the provisions of the Directive. This could equally apply to directly effective Treaty Articles. Thirdly, it is necessary to establish a causal link between the failure of the State to fulfil its obligation and the damage sustained by the persons adversely affected. It is submitted that a judgment of the Court establishing the failure of a Member State to fulfil its Community obligations would be evidence of a breach of Community law and might also establish a causal connection.[73] However, it is submitted that the causal connection could be established by other means, without the

---

[70] See Case C–128/92, *H.J. Banks and Company Ltd.*v. *British Coal Corporation*: Opinion of Advocate General Van Gerven, delivered October 27, 1993, not yet reported, at para. 40.

[71] *Francovich, op. cit.*, n. 51, para. 46. See further, Preishel, "The Right of Action against the State for Unimplemented E.C. Directives: the *Francovich* Judgment (June 1992) *International Business Lawyer* 294 at p. 294. See also Steiner, "From Direct Effects to *Francovich*: Shifting Means of Enforcement of Community Law" (1993) 18 E.L.Rev. at p. 10.

[72] Ross, "Beyond *Francovich*" (1993) M.L.R. 55 at p. 70.

[73] See also Duffy, "Damages against the State: A New Remedy for Failure to Implement Community Obligations" (1992) 17 E.L.Rev. 136.

162

necessity of an actual court judgment to that effect.[74] This could be confirmed by means of an Article 177 reference. This might be required where there is *some* national law which might be interpreted so as to comply with a State's Community obligations, unlike the situation in *Francovich* where no attempt had been made to introduce implementing legislation.[75]

It is argued by Duffy[76] that the liability of the State could arise in the absence, for example, of a Court of Justice judgment under the procedures of Article 169 of the E.C. Treaty, if there has been a sufficiently serious breach of Community law such that it would be unjust to those affected to deny damages for losses sustained in the interim. Although the causal connection needs to be clearly established on the facts of each case, a requirement that a final Court of Justice ruling is required before State liability can arise may encourage an over-rigid approach. On this basis, Duffy argues that in relation to U.K. State liability against the Spanish fishing companies involved in the *Factortame*[77] litigation, such liability may have arisen before the date of the final ruling of the House of Lords in *Factortame*. He argues that State liability probably arose from the time the legal position was determined in October 1989 in the interim relief judgment given by the European Court,[78] or after the *Aggregate* and *Jaderow* rulings of December 1989.[79]

## Extension of State liability to public authorities

The decision in *Francovich* also implies that if the relevant conditions 8–012 are satisfied, there is a right of action in damages not only against the State but also its emanations. One illustration of this is provided in the context of the Sunday trading cases in which some U.K. stores have alleged in litigation that provisions of the Shops Act 1950 infringe Article 30 of the EEC Treaty, (which is not amended by the Treaty on European Union), since they have an effect equivalent to a quantitative restriction on imports, by preventing sales of imported goods.[80]

In the Sunday trading case of *Kirkless Metropolitan Borough Council* v. *Wickes Building Supplies Ltd.*[81] discussed in detail at paragraphs 9–042 *et seq.* below, Lord Goff was of the opinion that if the European Court eventually decided that section 47 of the Shops Act 1950 was invalid, as being in conflict with Article 30 of the EEC Treaty, the U.K. might well

---

[74] Ross, *op. cit.*, n. 72, p. 58.
[75] *Ibid.*, p. 59.
[76] See Duffy, *op. cit.*, n. 73, p. 136.
[77] Discussed further at paras. 9–034 *et seq.*
[78] Case C–246/89R, *Commission* v. *United Kingdom*: [1989] E.C.R. 3125, [1989] 3 C.M.L.R. 601.
[79] Case C–3/87, *R.* v. *Ministry of Agriculture, Fisheries and Foods, ex p. Aggregate Ltd.*: [1989] E.C.R. 4459, [1990] 1 C.M.L.R. 366; Case C–216/87, *R.* v. *Ministry of Agriculture Fisheries and Foods, ex p. Jaderow Ltd.*: [1989] E.C.R. 4509, [1991] 2 C.M.L.R. 556.
[80] See further, Chalmers, "Free Movement of Goods within the European Community: An Unhealthy Addiction to Scotch Whisky?" (April 1993) 42, Part 2 I.C.L.Q. 269 to 294.
[81] *Kirklees Metropolitan Borough Council* v. *Wickes Building Supplies Ltd.* [1992] 3 W.L.R. 170.

be obliged on the basis of *Francovich* to make good damages caused to individuals by the breach of Article 30, for which it is responsible. The Court of Justice gave a ruling on the former matter in *Torfaen Borough Council* v. *B & Q Plc*[82] but a second reference on the same issues by the House of Lords in Case C–169/91, *Stoke-on-Trent City Council* v. *B & Q Plc*, has subsequently been decided by the European Court.[83] In the event, the ECJ held in *Stoke-on-Trent* that the U.K. legislation was not incompatible with Community law.

However, although Lord Goff recognised in *Kirklees* the possibility of a claim in damages against the U.K. government in respect of Sunday trading laws, he did not agree that there was any principle of Community law requiring the *local authority* in the *Kirklees* case to give an undertaking in damages. This is discussed further at paragraphs 9–043 *et seq.* below. However, one aspect of his reasoning in not requiring the Council to give an undertaking in damages, was that the effect of requiring an undertaking from the Council would be to impose liability in damages on the local authority *instead of on the U.K. government*. In his view, the latter was properly the party liable if the Shops Act turned out to be in breach of Community law.

It is arguable that Lord Goff was mistaken in coming to this view. The decisions of the European Court on the subject of "emanation of the State", discussed in Chap. 7, suggest that the liability of the State can be attributed to an organ such as a local government authority. In other words, the local government authority may be regarded for these purposes as an "emanation of the State". Certainly the approach of the Court in Case C–188/89, *Foster* v. *British Gas*[84] discussed earlier,[85] is a broad one in relation to what constitutes the "State" in the context of vertically directly effective rights in directives.[86]

It is argued by Bebr[87] that the legislator, the administration and possibly the judiciary are all under a duty to comply with Community law. In its case law, the Court has even considered "professional societies as bodies entrusted with the public duty" to be bound by such an obligation.[88] In other words, he argues that unconditional and sufficiently precise provisions of a directive could be relied upon against organisations if they are sufficiently subject to the authority or control of the State. The implication of this is that the right of action in damages established in *Francovich* would therefore apply against public authorities entrusted with public functions.[89]

---

[82] [1990] 1 C.M.L.R. 337.
[83] Case 169/91, *Council of the City of Stoke-on-Trent and Norwich City Council* v. *B & Q Plc*: [1993] 1 C.M.L.R. 426, [1991] 1 Q.B. 405.
[84] Case 188/89, *Foster* v. *British Gas*: [1990] I E.C.R. 3313, [1990] 2 C.M.L.R. 833, [1991] 1 Q.B. 405.
[85] See para. 7–009 above.
[86] See Ross, *op. cit.*, n. 72, p. 70.
[87] Bebr, Case Note on *Francovich*, *op. cit.*, n. 51, [1992] C.M.L.Rev. 557 to 584.
[88] See, for example, Case 271/82, *Auer* v. *Ministère Public*: [1983] E.C.R. 2727, at p. 2745 para. 19, annotation Bazex (1984) R.T.D.E. 20, 516 to 521, and other cases cited by Bebr, *ibid.*, at p. 578, n. 56.
[89] Bebr, *op. cit.*, n. 87, p. 578.

It has been pointed out that this raises substantial and controversial questions for U.K. courts. In particular, it involves the possibility that the actions of national courts may themselves be counted as "acts of the State."[90] For example, if an individual is denied his/her rights by a failure by the House of Lords to refer a case to the European Court, it may be that such a failure could amount to a denial of Community rights and be actionable.[91] However, this would perhaps not be much of a remedy in practice because it would be politically highly controversial and in any even the House of Lords might simply confirm its original decision in a given case.

## The nature of the breach

In *Francovich* the nature and gravity of the breach was clear. Advocate **8–013** General Mischo described it in the following terms:

"Rarely has our court had to give judgment in a case where the loss caused to individuals concerned by a failure to implement a Directive has been as scandalous as here."[92]

In his reasoning, Advocate General Mischo appears to base liability on serious breaches. He regarded incorrect implementation of a directive as constituting a breach of the fundamental rules of Articles 5 and 189(3) of the EEC Treaty,[93] (which are not amended by the Treaty on European Union). The case was, however, concerned with a deliberate or knowing breach of Community law.

However, there may be failures by Member States which may be only partial, for example faulty or inadequate implementation measures. In addition, such failure may range from deliberate to the negligent or innocent.[94] Thus is has been argued by Steiner[95] that not all such failures should give rise to non-contractual liability on the part of the State. She suggests, *inter alia*, that where, as in the case of the non-implementation of a directive, a Community obligation is clear and leaves little or no discretion to the national authorities as to the ends to be achieved, there is no justification for excluding liability for both primary and secondary legislation. However, if a Community obligation is unclear as to its meaning and scope of application, in other words if there is some area of discretion left to Member States, then some fault, in a sense of culpability, may also need to be proved. She suggests that a deliberate or knowing breach of Community law should certainly attract liability. However, public authorities (*i.e.*, legislator or executive) should also be liable for matters of which they should have had "constructive knowledge."[96] For instance, a Member State should not be able to rely

---

[90] See Ross, *op. cit.*, n. 72, p. 70.
[91] *Ibid.*, p. 71. See further discussion at paras. 3–020 *et seq.*
[92] *Francovich, op. cit.*, n. 51, para. 1.
[93] *Ibid.*, para. 76.
[94] See Steiner, "From Direct Effects to *Francovich*: Shifting Means of Enforcement of Community Law" (1993) 18 E.L.Rev. 3 at p. 11.
[95] *Ibid.*
[96] *Ibid.*, p. 18.

on lack of knowledge, actual or constructive, to defend an act or omission which is clearly at odds with the unambiguous and specific purposes of a Community provision.[97] The Commission is, for example, considering infraction proceedings under Article 169 of the E.C. Treaty in respect of the U.K.'s implementation by Part 1 of the Consumer Protection Act 1987, of the Product Liability Directive 85/374. There is arguably a difference between the meaning of the "state of the art" defence available to the manufacturer of a defective product in the wording of the Directive, and that available under the provisions of the Act (which is regarded as being more generous). Another example could include inadequate implementation of a directive where words are added to the relevant provisions of national legislation, which do not appear in the directive and which conflict with it.[98] The effect of Steiner's arguments is to establish a test for liability based on constructive knowledge, rather than on simple negligence.[99]

In the leading U.K. case on State liability in damages decided by the Court of Appeal in *Bourgoin SA* v. *Ministry of Agriculture, Fisheries and Food*[1] and discussed in detail at paragraphs 9–018 *et seq.* below, the Court of Appeal held by a majority of 2:1 (Oliver L.J. dissenting) that the Ministry could not be liable in damages in respect of a breach of Article 30 of the Treaty of Rome, on the grounds of breach of statutory duty. It has been suggested by Professor Sue Arrowsmith[2] that even after *Francovich*, the *Bourgoin* decision is not necessarily wrong on its facts.[3] She points out that the scope in U.K. law for the liability of public authorities for breach of statutory duty has been traditionally limited because it may induce caution in the exercise of government powers and also may result in wide and heavy liability. She also draws attention to the fact that the Community itself is not generally liable for damages for breach of Community law with respect to legislative measures on economic policy unless there has been a breach, of a manifest and grave nature, of a superior rule of law designed for the protection of individuals.[4] This was certainly an argument used by Lord Justice Parker in *Bourgoin*.[5]

8–014　　　She therefore suggests that damages are not required to be made available as a remedy for breach of Community law in every case, but

---

[97] *Ibid.*, p. 19, n. 94: for example, domestic implementation of a directive in the field of social or consumer protection which limits or undermines the specific protective purpose of the legislation.

[98] See, for example, discussion of the domestic implemenation in the U.K. of the Acquired Rights Directive at paras. 6–014 *et seq.* above.

[99] See further, dicussion by Steiner, *op. cit.*, n. 94, on the principles governing the liability of public authorities both in the Member States and in the Community as well as the Council of Europe's recommendations in this area at pp. 13 *et seq.*

[1] *Bourgoin SA* v. *Ministry of Agriculture, Fisheries and Food*: [1986] 1 C.M.L.R. 267, [1986] Q.B. 716.

[2] Arrowsmith, *Civil Liability and Public Authorities* (1992), at p. 253.

[3] Arrowsmith, *op. cit.*, pp. 255 *et seq.*

[4] See, for example, Joined Cases C–104/89 and 37/90, *Mulder and Others* v. *Council and Commission*: [1992] I E.C.R. 3062.

[5] *Op. cit.*, n. 1, and discussed at para. 9–019 below.

only in more limited circumstances.[6] This is a matter which will ultimately need to be determined by the European Court. In addition, the Court may have to introduce devices to preclude, for example, the recovery of damages for indeterminate economic losses as well as to issue guidance in respect of causation and remoteness of damages.[7] Alternatively, she suggests that the Court may develop some more limited concept of "Community rights" which would limit the individual rights which must be protected by the national courts either by reference to the nature of the interest infringed, *e.g.* to create a "right" only for an individual whose interest Community provisions were intended to protect and/or who are affected in a serious or special way; alternatively these more limited rights might depend on the nature of the conduct of the government. For example, there might be held to be a right "not to be prejudiced by a knowing or careless breach of Community law." Alternatively, the "right" to damages might be limited to circumstances where damages would be available against the Community itself for a comparable breach.[8]

However, it has been persuasively argued by Gerhard Bebr,[9] that such additional limitations have specifically *not* been included by the Court in *Francovich*. The Court has, in his view, opted for:

> ". . . a simpler solution. It decided to place the liability of the Member State on an unconditional and well defined right of individuals subject to no further additional requirements."[10]

Accordingly, Bebr contends that in the Court's view it is the breach of a fundamental Community obligation which is decisive and not the gravity of the infringement.[11] It is also argued by Ross,[12] that since there was no mention of any need for the breach by the State to be deliberate, accidental failures to transpose directives accurately would also result in liability. This would be consistent with the principle of "inherent" liability of the State and is also supported by the fact that the Court gave no indication of any defences which might be acceptable to it.[13] However, it may be, on the other hand, that defences were not mentioned in *Francovich*, simply because the breach was of a manifest and grave nature in that case.

## Further implications of Francovich

As a result of *Francovich*, it is clear that claims may arise for damages **8–015** against Member States where the three criteria laid down in *Francovich*

---

[6] Arrowsmith, *op. cit.*, n. 2, p. 256 and see also Duffy, "Damages Against the State: A New Remedy for Failure to Implement Community Obligations" (1992) 17 E.L.Rev. 136.

[7] See further discussion at para. 10–014 below.

[8] See however the contrary view taken by the Court of Appeal in *An Bord Bainne Co-operative* v. *Irish Dairy Board* [1988] 1 C.M.L.R. 605, [1988] 1 F.T.L.R. 145.

[9] Bebr, Case Note on *Francovich* (1992) C.M.L.Rev., 557 to 584.

[10] Bebr, *ibid.*, p. 576.

[11] See Bebr, *op. cit.*, n. 9, p. 577 and Ross, "Beyond Francovich" (1993) M.L.R. 55 at p. 66.

[12] Ross, *op. cit.*, p. 57.

[13] *Ibid.*

have been satisfied. There is, however, a suggestion made by Ross[14] that the implication of *Francovich* is more far-reaching. He suggests that the reference to Article 5 in the *Francovich* judgment may itself form the basis of actions for damages, *i.e.* actions which do not have any specific base elsewhere in the E.C. Treaty. For instance, the infringement by a Member State of human rights, recognised as falling within the framework of Community law, could arguably form the basis of such claims.[15] However, such claims run the serious risk of entering into policy areas which have traditionally been regarded as solely within the ambit of national law, although the three conditions in *Francovich* would have some limiting effect in any event. Nevertheless, Ross argues that in an appropriate case, where the breach of Community law was sufficiently "fundamental" it could trigger an action for damages by an individual on the basis of Article 5 and the relevant principles of *Francovich*

The doctrine that in actions against the State in respect of unimplemented directives, time does not begin to run until the directive is correctly implemented, was established by the Court in Case C–208/90, *Emmott* v. *Minister for Social Walfare and AG*[16] and has been analysed in detail at paragraphs 5–010 *et seq.*, above. It is therefore arguable that in claims for damages against the State based on *Francovich*, national limitation periods may not begin to run until after correct implementation has taken place.

Finally, it is necessary to consider whether the right to claim damages established in *Francovich* invalidates the possibility of an individual litigant resorting instead to the possibility of "indirect" direct effect which may be arguable in a given case, and is discussed in Chapter 6. It has been suggested that where the plaintiff has such a choice, although the exercise of that choice may be influenced by cost considerations, domestic procedures, as well as matters such as the solvency of the defendants, there is no justification in principle for denying a claim against the State just because there may also be the possible right of action against some private party.[17] Ross argues persuasively that the *Francovich* rule was said by the Court to be "inherent" in the Treaty and therefore should not be capable of being displaced by an alternative remedy.[18] However, he points out that in any event, it might be far more risky for a plaintiff to rely on national courts applying correctly the principles of "indirect" direct effect as developed in *Von Colson*[19] and *Marleasing.*[20]

The extent of State liability as developed by the Court in *Francovich* therefore remains uncertain and gives rise to considerable potential for test cases. The Commission has indicated that it will, however, prepare in due course a notice on the interpretation of *Francovich*. This will

---

[14] *Ibid.*, pp. 66 *et seq.*
[15] *Ibid.*, p. 67 and see discussion at paras. 3–004 *et seq.* above.
[16] Case C–208/90, *Emmott*: [1991] I E.C.R. 4269, [1991] 3 C.M.L.R. 894.
[17] See Ross, *op. cit.*, n. 11, p. 59.
[18] *Ibid.*, p. 59.
[19] Case 14/83, *Von Colson*: [1984] E.C.R. 1891, [1986] 2 C.M.L.R. 430.
[20] Case C–106/89, *Marleasing*: [1990] I E.C.R. 4135, [1992] 1 C.M.L.R. 305; see discussion at para. 6–004 above.

involve consultation with the Member States, to take into account the specific features of each legal system.[21]

## LIABILITY OF INDIVIDUALS: OPINION OF THE ADVOCATE GENERAL IN *BANKS*

The question arises as to what value the *Francovich* judgment has as a precedent, in connection with actions brought by an individual (or undertaking) against another individual (or undertaking) for damages in respect of breach by the latter of directly effective Community law. This issue has arisen in Case C–128/92, *H.J. Banks and Company Limited* v. *British Coal Corporation*, (not yet decided by ECJ)[22] in which the Commercial Court, part of the Queen's Bench Division of the High Court, made a reference under Article 41 of the ECSC Treaty and Article 177 of the EEC Treaty, for a preliminary ruling on a number of questions concerning the interpretation of the competition rules of the ECSC and EEC Treaties.

**8–016**

The reference to the ECJ arose in connection with an action for damages brought by H.J. Banks and Company Limited (Banks) against British Coal Corporation (British Coal), in which Banks alleged that certain provisions of the ECSC Treaty and/or the EEC Treaty had been infinged. The Court of Justice was asked, *inter alia*, whether the national court has the power and/or the obligation under Community law to award damages in respect of breaches of various articles of the ECSC and the EEC Treaties for loss sustainted as a result of such breaches. Advocate General Van Gerven took the opportunity, in his Opinion, of setting out a detailed Community law framework for a right to damages for breach of Community competition rules. He pointed out that in *Francovich* the Court had expressly acknowledged that:

> "It is a principle of Community law that *the Member States* are obliged to make good loss and damage caused to individuals by breaches of Community law for which they can be held responsible."[23]

In his view, that principle also applied to actions by individuals (or undertakings) against other individuals (or undertakings). Although British Coal was a statutory corporation wholly owned by the government, whose statutory rights and duties included a monopoly in relation to the extraction of coal, and was undoubtedly an organisation which fell

---

[21] See *Working Document of the Commission on a Strategic Programme on the Internal Market: Communication from the Commission to the Council and the European Parliament* "Reinforcing the Effectiveness of the Internal Market," (1993) COM (93) 256 final, June 2, 1993. See discussion at para. 1–019 above.

[22] Case C–128/92, *Banks* v. *British Coal*: Opinion of the Advocate General Van Gerven delivered on October 27, 1993, not yet reported.

[23] See judgment in Joined Case C–6 & 9/90, *Francovich and Bonifaci*: [1991] I E.C.R. 5357, [1993] 2 C.M.L.R. 66, at para. 37 (emphasis added by the Advocate General).

within the broad concept of the "State" as developed by the Court in its case law concerning the direct effect of directives, he recommended that the Court should not rely on the principle of State liability. He recommended a clarification of the basis under Community law for the bringing of an action for damages by private undertakings, in respect of breach of the Community competition rules.[24]

The Advocate General pointed out that the right of individuals to rely on the directly applicable provisions of a Treaty provision before national courts *is only a minimum guarantee*, and is not sufficient in itself to ensure the full and complete implementation of the Treaty.[25] Accordingly, the direct effects of the Treaty provision are to be seen merely as the starting point for the full implementation of Community law. Thus the national court is required to play its part in the exercise of its jurisdiction so as to ensure that provisions of Community law produce their full effect.[26] He refers to the judgments in *Simmenthal*, *Factortame* and *Francovich* as the most significant milestones leading to this conclusion.

The judgment in *Francovich* is viewed by the Advocate General as a decisive step insofar as it established that the principle whereby a State must be liable for loss and damage caused to individuals, as a result of breaches of Community law for which it can be held responsible, is *inherent* in the system of the Treaty.[27] He preceeded to apply the Community rules developed in *Francovich* to the liability of individuals for breaches of Community law. In his view it followed, *as a matter of principle*, that the rule of State liability derived from the general system of the Treaty and its fundamental principles as laid down in *Francovich*, also serves as a precedent for the establishment of individual liability.[28] He argued that the full effect of Community law would be impaired if an individual or undertaking did not have the possibility of obtaining reparation from the party which can be held responsible for the breach of Community law, all the more so, if a directly effective provision of Community law is infringed.[29] Accordingly, Articles 85 and 86 of the EEC Treaty (which have been acknowledged in the case law of the Court to be directly effective) as well as Articles 4, 65(1) and 66(7) of the ECSC Treaty which, according to the Advocate General, were also directly effective, were said by him to be provisions of Community law which, if breached, gave rise to liability for loss and damage.[30]

## Rationale for individual liability

8–017    The Advocate General set out two reasons for establishing liability in such cases. First, he stated that is was the only effective method whereby the national court can fully safeguard directly effective provisions of Community law which have been infringed, by restoring the rights of the

---

[24] See Opinion of the Advocate General in *Banks, op. cit.*, n. 22, at para. 41.

[25] *Ibid.*, para. 38.

[26] *Ibid.*

[27] *Op. cit.*, para. 39.

[28] *Op. cit.*, para. 42.

[29] *Op. cit.*, para. 43.

[30] *Op. cit.*

injured party through an award of damages. In his view, even a declaration that the legal relationship between the parties is void (under Atricle 85(2) of the EEC Treaty or Article 64(4) of the ECSC Treaty) is not capable of making good the loss and damage already suffered by a third party.[31] The existence of such a rule on reparation served to make the Community rules of competition more operational and he pointed out that the Commission, as guardian of those rules, had specifically acknowledged that it is dependent on the co-operation of the national courts in enforcing these rules.[32] Consequently, he took the view that the national court is under an obligation to award damages for loss sustained by an undertaking as a result of the breach by another undertaking of a directly effective provision of Community competition law.[33]

Secondly, although the High Court in *Banks* had only submitted to the European court, *inter alia*, the question of whether, in principle, there was a judicial obligation to award damages, the Advocate General took the view that the Court should clarify the detailed rules for bringing an action for damages of this kind. This could not, in the Advocate General's Opinion, be left entirely to national courts, since it would entail serious risks for the uniform and effective application of Community law if too many details were left to national law.[34] He emphasized that the uniform application of Community law stated in the *Zuckerfabrik* judgment was a fundamental requirement of the Community legal order.[35]

The Advocate General went on to reiterate certain general principles of Community law relating to remedies, which lay down minimum requirements which national law must fulfil. (These have been discussed at paragraphs 8–003 *et seq.* and 8–007 *et seq.* above.) However, he noted that the case law of the Court has yet to evolve, to any significant extent, the detailed rules governing an action for damages.[36] Nevertheless, he took the view that it was already possible to glean a number of principles from the case law, especially the judgments concerning the non-contractual liability of the Community under Article 215(2) of the EEC Treaty.[37]

## Conditions for individual liability

The Advocate General in *Banks* went on to state that the value of the **8–018** *Francovich* judgment as a precedent in respect of individual liability is not sufficient as regards the *conditions* for liability.[38] He pointed out that the Court in *Francovich* had itself adopted a qualified position in that it had stated that "the conditions under which . . . (State) . . . liability gives rise to a right to reparation depend on the nature of the breach of

---

[31] *Op. cit.*, para. 44.
[32] *Op. cit.*
[33] *Op. cit.*, para. 45.
[34] *Op. cit.*, para. 47.
[35] Judgment in Joined Cases C–143/88 and C–92/89, *Zukerfabrik*: [1991] I E.C.R. 415, [1993] 3 C.M.L.R. 1, at para. 26.
[36] Opinion of the Advocate General in *Banks, op. cit.*, n. 22, para. 49.
[37] *Ibid.*
[38] *Ibid.*

Community law giving rise to the loss and damage"[39] and that the Court had subsequently confined itself to the conditions for liability in the event of non-compliance by a Member State with the obligation imposed upon it by Article 189(3) of the EEC Treaty, to take all the measures necessary to achieve the result prescribed by a directive.[40]

Advocate General Van Gerven took the view that there were general principles which the Court had inferred from the legal systems of the Member States in decisions concerning Article 215(2) of the EEC Treaty, whereby the liability of the Community depends on the fulfilment of three conditions, namely the existence of damage, a causal link between the damage claimed and the conduct alleged against the institution, and the illegality of such conduct.[41] In his view, those conditions for liability applied equally to actions for breaches of directly effective provisions of Community competition law.

### Existence of damage

8–019    First, the party invoking liability must furnish proof that it has suffered damage.[42] This factor was not referred to in *Francovich* as one of the conditions for State liability. However, the Advocate General points out that this was probably because the requirement (namely, non-payment of employees' wages by their insolvent employer) was obvious in that case. However, according to the Advocate General, there must in the first place be the "fact of damage."[43] Merely speculative damage is therefore inadequate. In order to bring an action for a declaration for liability, "imminent damage foreseeable with sufficient certainty even if the damage cannot yet be precisely assessed" is enough.[44] In other words, the loss must be foreseeable, even if it cannot be precisely quantified.

In assessing the extent of the damage, the Advocate General made reference to factors such as loss of earnings,[45] as well as the obligation on the part of the injured party to mitigate the damage. It was also necessary, in any event, to take account of the Community prohibition on unjust enrichment, *e.g.* to take account of the extent to which the damage has been passed on in the selling prices of the complainant undertaking.[46] The actual proof of damage was, in the Advocate General's Opinion, a matter of evidence which the Court had unfettered discretion to assess.[47]

---

[39] Judgment in *Francovich* , *op. cit.*, n. 23, at para. 38.

[40] Opinion of the Advocate General in *Banks, op. cit.*, n. 22, at para. 49. See para. 39 and 40 of the judgment in *Francovich* which set out these conditions, *i.e.* (i) the result prescribed by the directive must entail the grant of rights to individuals; (ii) it must be possible to identify the content of those rights on the basis of the provisions of the directive; and (iii) there must be a causal link between the breach of the State's obligations and the loss and damage suffered by the injured parties. Note the further discussion of these conditions at para. 8–010 above.

[41] Opinion of the Advocate General in *Banks, op. cit.*, n. 22, para. 50.

[42] *Op. cit.*, para. 51.

[43] *Op. cit.*

[44] *Op. cit.*

[45] *Op. cit.*

[46] *Op. cit.*, para. 51 and see also discussion at para. 10–024 below.

[47] *Op. cit.*, para. 42.

## Causal connection between breach and ensuing damage

Both the case law of the ECJ on Article 215(2) of the EEC Treaty as **8–020** well as the *Francovich* judgment required the existence of a causal connection between the breach of Community law and the damage suffered by the injured party. The Advocate General pointed out that the Court had not defined this requirement in more detail. However, he referred to the Court's judgment in *Dumortier Frères*[48] in which the damage (in that case the closure of a factory), even though it was precipitated by the relevant breach of Community law (the absence of refunds), was not a *direct consequence of the unlawful conduct in question*, and hence there was no liability. He therefore concluded that the principles common to the laws of the Member States to which Article 215(2) of the EEC Treaty refers, cannot be relied upon "to deduce an obligation to make good every harmful consequence, *even a remote one*, of unlawful legislation."[49] The Advocate General therefore confirmed that the applicant must furnish proof of *some* causal connection between the wrongful act or omission alleged and the damaged sustained, and indicated that if the harmful consequence is judged to be too remote or too indirect, it will not give rise to liability in damages, under Community law.

## Illegality of the conduct alleged

The Advocate General took the view that such illegality automatically **8–021** arises if an undertaking infringes the directly effective provisions of Community competition laws. This gives rise to an action for damages on the basis of Community law, without there being any need to prove fault. In other words, since the prohibitions are aimed at safeguarding undistorted competition and freedom of competition for undertakings operating in the common market, the crucial factor is the effect of the prohibited practices and not the intention of those who engage in them.[50] The test is therefore an objective one, in relation to breaches of Community competition rules.

## Damages and interest

The Advocate General reviewed the case law of the Court in relation to **8–022** Article 215 of the EEC Treaty and other cases such as *Von Colson* and *Marshall (No. 2)* and confirmed that the principles enshrined in those cases applied in respect of breaches of prohibitions laid down by Community competition law. This meant that reparation for such breaches must be made *good in full*.[51] In relation to the award of interest, he referred to the judgment of the Court in *Marshall (No. 2)* to the effect that apart from the requirement that damage must be made good in full, the Court had also elicited two important principles. First, the fixing by

---

[48] Case C–45/79, *Dumortier Frères*: [1979] E.C.R. 3091 at para. 21.
[49] *Banks, op. cit.*, n. 22, at para. 52, citing judgment in *Dumortier Frères* (emphasis added by the Advocate General).
[50] *Ibid.*, para. 53.
[51] *Ibid.*, para. 54.

law of an upper limit on the amount of compensation could not be regarded as ensuring adequate reparation and secondly, that in relation to interest which should be awarded on the principle amount from the date of the unlawful discrimination (in *Marshall No. 2*) to the date when compensation is paid, the Court had ruled that full compensation for the damage sustained as a result of discriminatory dismissal cannot leave out of account factors such as the effluxion of time, which may in fact reduce its value. The award of interest, in accordance with the applicable national rules, must therefore be regarded as an essential component of compensation for the purposes of restoring real equality of treatment."[52]

### Further implications of *Banks*

8–023    If the Advocate General's Opinion in the *Banks* case is followed by the Court of Justice, it will have major implications for the establishment of Community law principles concerning the remedy of damages, with particular regard to cases concerning breaches of directly effective Community law. It is clear from the reasoning of the Advocate General that the establishment of such a framework wuld remove any doubts which exist at present as to whether on not there is a basis under Community law for bringing an action for damages in respect, in particular, of breach of the Community rules of competition by private undertakings. However, the Advocate General's Opinion on certain issues, such as the nature of the causal connection required between the breach and the ensuing loss or damage, and on remoteness of damages, still require further elaboration. This has been discussed further below at paragraph 10–014.

It remains to be seen whether the Court decides to follow the dynamic approach of the Advocate General. The defendant, British Coal, is a statutory corporation wholly owned by the Government and therefore capable of being considered as an "emanation of the State." It may, as recognised by the Advocate General,[53] therefore not be necessary for the Court to determine the case on the basis of damages for breaches of the competition rules by private undertakings. The Court may therefore decline the opportunity presented by *Banks* to elaborate on these principles, particularly as it will touch on the highly sensitive area of the jurisdiction of national courts. However, such an approach cannot persist indefinitely as the issues are of increasing importance for litigants.

---

[52] *Ibid.*, para. 54, citing judgment in *Marshall (No. 2)* at para. 31.
[53] *Op. cit.*, at para. 41.

# PUBLIC LAW REMEDIES FOR ENFORCING COMMUNITY LAW

## JUDICIAL REVIEW: THE PREROGATIVE ORDERS OF MANDAMUS, PROHIBITION, CERTIORARI

Judicial review is a procedure for the supervisory control of public **9–001** bodies, which are governed by public law principles. A detailed analysis of this procedure is outside the scope of this work.[1] However, various aspects of the procedure and the available remedies which may be relevant to claims based on Community law are analysed further below.

Judicial review is carried out by way of an application to the High Court for any of the prerogative orders of mandamus, (an order requiring a public authority to do some act), prohibition (an order requiring a public authority to refrain from acting in some way) or certiorari (an order quashing a decision made by a public authority in breach of law). In appropriate cases, the court also has power to grant a declaration or an injunction[2] instead of, or in addition to, a prerogative order, where to do so could be just and convenient. Damages may also be claimed, subject to specific rules.[3] All the relevant remedies can therefore be sought under the one procedure.

Mandamus is available at the suit of a person with standing, to enforce duties imposed, for example, by statute, on Ministers of the Crown or other Crown servants. These are nowadays construed as duties owed to the public and not the Crown (to get round the historical rule that mandamus does not lie against the Crown or a Minister of the Crown when acting purely as a servant of the Crown in the performance of a duty owed by the Crown).[4] The remedy of prohibition may also be used to prevent a breach of directly effective Community law.[5] The preroga-

---

[1] See, *e.g.* Lewis, *Judicial Remedies in Public Law* (1992).
[2] Supreme Court Act 1981, s. 31(1) and Ord. 53, r. 12.
[3] *Ibid.*, s. 31(4) and Ord. 53, r. 7 discussed at paras. 9–016 *et seq.*
[4] *R. v. Powell* (1841) 1 Q.B. 352.
[5] See *Halsbury's Laws of England*, Vol. 51 p. 451, para. 3.73.

tive order of certiorari is a judicial remedy which is available under U.K. law to enforce Community law and has been applied, for example, to quash a decision of the National Insurance Commissioner.[6] Certiorari has also been granted to quash a deportation order on the grounds of violation of Community law.[7]

## DECLARATIONS

9-002    In practice, the most common remedy sought in the context of the enforcement of Community law against public authorities is a declaration. This remedy may be used either to challenge the validity of a U.K. government act in the light of Community law or to challenge the validity of Community acts themselves. For example, in the first category, the case of *Van Duyn* v. *Home Office*[8] illustrated how a declaration could be sought by an individual who claims to be entitled to enter and stay in the U.K. A declaration was sought to declare a decision by a Minister, altering the basis of reimbursement to pharmacists for drugs imported from the Community, to be unlawful under Article 30 EEC Treaty.[9] In *R.* v. *Att. Gen., ex parte ICI Plc*,[10] a decision of the Inland Revenue to adopt a particular approach to valuation in the assessment of the taxation of oil sales was held to be in contravention of Community law and was declared void. In *R.* v. *Secretary of State for Employment, ex parte Equal Opportunities Commission*[10a] the House of Lords held that declarations may be sought to establish that certain provisions of the Employment Protection (Consolidation) Act 1978 were incompatible with Article 119 of the E.C. Treaty and Community Directive 75/117 on equal pay[10b] and Directive 76/207 on equal treatment.[10c] This case is discussed further at paragraphs 9-007 *et seq.* Subordinate legislation, or the relevant part of such legislation, which contravenes Community law must also be declared invalid, or not applied in relation to an individual, to the extent of the inconsistency with Community law.[11] Similarly, subordinate legislation which confers a greater right than necessary to implement a Community obligation may be invalid, at least to the extent that it exceeds the Community obligation.[12] However, in relation to directives, these sometimes impose a

---

[6] See Case 41/77, *R.* v. *National Insurance Commissioner, ex p. Warry*: [1977] E.C.R. 2085, [1977] 2 C.M.L.R. 783, [1978] Q.B. 607.

[7] *R.* v. *Secretary of State for the Home Department , ex p. Dannenberg* [1984] Q.B. 766.

[8] Case 41/74, *Van Duyn* v. *Home Office*: [1974] E.C.R. 1337, [1975] 1 C.M.L.R. 1, [1975] Ch. 358, [1975] 3 All E.R. 190.

[9] *R.* v. *Secretary of State for Social Services, ex p. Bomove Medical Supplies Ltd.* [1986] C.M.L.R. 228.

[10] *R.* v. *Att. Gen., ex p. ICI Plc* [1987] 1 C.M.L.R. 72.

[10a] *The Times*, March 4, 1994.

[10b] [1975] O.J. L45/19.

[10c] [1976] O.J. L39/40.

[11] *MacMahon* v. *Department of Education and Science* [1983] Ch. 227.

[12] See MacKay L.C. in *Hayward* v. *Cammell Laird Shipbuilders (No. 2)* [1988] A.C. 894.

*minimum* obligation, in which case the Member State may go further. For example, in Case C–11/92, *R.* v. *Secretary of State for Health, ex parte Gallagher, Imperial Tobacco and Rothmans International Tobacco (U.K.)*[13] the ECJ was asked to rule on the size of health warnings on cigarette packets and other tobacco products. Under the terms of the tobacco products directive, all cigarette packets must carry health warnings which cover at least 4 per cent. of the surface of the packet. Under U.K. rules implementing the directive, health warnings must cover 6 per cent. of the surface of a packet. Cigarettes imported from *other* E.C. States are deemed to comply with U.K. law if their health warnings comply with the requirements adopted by that State, in implementing the directive. The ECJ accepted that this might lead to *less* favourable treatment for U.K. products compared with imports but held that this was in fact the consequence of the directive setting out only *minimum* requirements on the size of the health warnings required. On the other hand, in Case C–222/91, *Ministero delle Finanze & Ministero dell Sanita* v. *Philip Morris Belgium,*[14] the Court held that as far as *other* tobacco products were concerned the same directive set out different conditions than those for cigarettes, and there was no discretion for Member States to impose more stringent requirements for warnings on tobacco products other than cigarettes.[15]

A declaration may be granted to compel public authorities to exercise statutory powers in order to ensure compliance with Community law. In *R.* v. *Minister of Agriculture, Fisheries and Food, ex parte Bell Lines Ltd.*[16] a declaration was granted requiring a Minister to designate certain ports as authorised ports of entry for the import of milk from Ireland, to ensure compliance with Article 30. In *Bell Lines* and *ICI Plc*[17] the court granted declarations, but could have issued mandamus and prohibition respectively.[18] The case is discussed further at paragraph 9–015 below.

Alternatively, proceedings may be started in national courts to challenge Community regulations, by way of judicial review, and to seek a declaration that the regulations are void under Community law and of no effect and that the U.K. government is not entitled to implement them.[19]

---

[13] Case C–11/92, *R.* v. *Secretary of State for Health, ex p. Gallagher, Imperial Tobacco and Rothmans International Tobacco (U.K.): Financial Times* June 29, 1993 p. 12.

[14] Case C–222/91, *Minister delle Finanze and Ministero dell Sanita* v. *Philip Morris Belgium and Others* judgment of June 22, 1993, *Financial Times,* June 29, 1993 p. 12.

[15] The nature of certain of the provisions of the Second Company Law Directive has also given rise to a great deal of controversy: see Opinion of Tesuaro A.B. in the unreported case of *Meilicke.*

[16] *R.* v. *Minister of Agriculture, Fisheries and Food, ex p. Bell Lines Ltd.* [1984] 2 C.M.L.R. 502.

[17] *Op. cit.,* n. 10.

[18] *Lewis, op. cit.,* n. 1, p. 461.

[19] See, for example, *R.* v. *Ministry of Agriculture Fisheries and Food, ex p. FEDESA* [1988] 3 C.M.L.R. 207 and the Joined Cases 103 & 145/77, *Royal Scholten-Honig (Holdings) Limited* v. *Intervention Board for Argicultural Produce*: [1978] E.C.R. 2037, [1979] 1 C.M.L.R. 675, in which E.C. Council Regulations 1862/76, 1110/77, 1111/77, were challenged.

However, only the ECJ may declare Community legislation invalid and the national court is therefore required to refer such issues to the ECJ for a ruling.[20] The action for a declaration is an important alternative route for an action to annual regulations which may otherwise be brought by private individuals under Article 173 of the E.C. Treaty.[21]

## THE DISTINCTION BETWEEN PUBLIC AND PRIVATE LAW RIGHTS AND REMEDIES

**9–003**     Litigants seeking redress against government authorities for breach of their individual rights must proceed by way of an application for judicial review under R.S.C., Order 53, *i.e.* bring a claim under public law unless they can allege the commission of a tort or the existence of some other right in private law such as breach of contract, in which case the action may be commenced by writ.[22] This is also known as the rule in *O'Reilly* v. *Mackman*[23] but is subject to various exceptions, discussed further below.[24]

The distinction between a public law and a private law right is not an easy one. A private law right enables an individual to seek a remedy, *e.g.* a declaration, injunction or damages by way of an action started by writ, for breach of a duty owed specifically to him or her, *e.g.* breach of contract or breach of a statutory duty.[25] This means that the plaintiff must have *locus standi, i.e.* he/she must show some private legal right or legal interest recognised by law, which has been violated by the defendant.[26]

A public law right on the other hand is a right to have the law enforced and administered by a public authority properly and fairly and the duty is owed to the public at large. In general, a private person cannot bring an ordinary civil action (commenced by writ) in order to assert a public law right, even if the relief claimed is only a declaration. Only the Attorney General may being such a claim in the public interest,[27] although the Attorney General has the power to consent to a private citizen pursuing a relator action *e.g.* to restrain interference with a public right.[28] It is generally assumed that relator actions are not affected by the

---

[20] See further paras. 3–016 *et seq.* above and for a discussion on the national court's powers to grant interim relief see paras. 9–040 *et seq.* below.

[21] See para. 1–003 above.

[22] See *Bourgoin SA* v. *Ministry of Agriculture, Fisheries and Food* [1985] 3 All E.R. 385; and *Cato* v. *Minister for Agriculture, Fisheries and Food* [1989] 3 C.M.L.R. 513 (C.A.).

[23] *O'Reilly* v. *Mackman* [1983] A.C. 237.

[24] See further, Lewis, *Judicial Remedies in Public Law* (1993) pp. 67 *et seq.*

[25] See Brearley, "Remedies in Domestic Courts for Breach of E.C. Law" (November 21, 1990) No. 42 *Gazette* 24 at p. 26.

[26] Andrew Geddes, "Locus Standi and EEC Environment Measures" (1992) Vol. 4, No. 1, *Journal of Environmental Law* 29 at p. 29.

[27] See *Gouriet* v. *Union of Post Office Workers* [1978] A.C. 435.

[28] See Geddes, *op. cit.*, p. 30.

rule in *O'Reilly* v. *Mackman*.[29] However, it is likely that as a matter of practive the Attorney General will not authorise relator actions if the individual could have made an application for judicial review in any event.[30] There is no right to damages in English law for an infringement of a public law right.[31]

## Procedural aspects of judicial review

The case law concerning judicial review is developed by the courts and **9–004** the principles applied are flexible. Among the main characteristics of the procedure is the need for leave to proceed (which will be granted only if an arguable case is shown). This helps to filter out unmeritorious or frivolous claims.[32] Evidence is by affidavit only, making full disclosure of relevant facts. Both discovery[33] and cross examination[34] are not automatic but require leave. This enables the court to control the length of proceedings to a greater extent. Hearings are comparatively short and can be relatively inexpensive.[35] Judicial review applications are heard by judges on the Crown Office List, who have specialist experience of public law issues. However, the courts have a more limited role in judicial review proceedings in that it is a supervisory jurisdiction and not concerned with the merits of a decision by a public body.[36]

There is a short time limit for applying for leave for judicial review. The applicant must bring his/her application promptly, and in any event within three months of the date when grounds for review arise.[37] If an application is made out of time, leave will only be granted if the applicant can show good reason for the delay and it is unlikely that delay resulting from use of the wrong choice of procedure will be accepted as a good reason unless in some way the applicant was still not at fault.[38]

## Rule in O'Reilly v. Mackman

It is an abuse of the process of the court to seek a declaration or **9–005** injunction by ordinary action, (whether started by writ or originating summons), in a public law case if the claim is one which should have proceeded by way of judicial review.[39] The court has powers under Order 18, rule 19, or in its inherent jurisdiction, to strike out such a claim. This is the application of the rule in *O'Reilly* v. *Mackman*[40] referred to above, in which the House of Lords held that as a general rule, public

---

[29] *Op. cit.* and see Lewis, *op. cit.*, p. 200.
[30] Lewis, *op. cit.*, p. 87 and p. 200.
[31] See Brearley, *op. cit.*, p. 26.
[32] Supreme Court Act 1981, s. 31(3) and Ord. 53, r. 3(1).
[33] Ord. 53, r. 8.
[34] *Ibid.*
[35] See further Wade, *Administrative Law* (1988), 6th ed.
[36] See further discussion at para. 9–015 below.
[37] Supreme Court Act 1981, s. 31(6) and Ord. 53, r. 4(1).
[38] Lewis, *Judicial Remedies in Public Law* (1992), p. 70.
[39] See Lewis, *ibid.*, p. 69.
[40] *O'Reilly* v. *Mackman* [1983] 2 A.C. 237 (H.L.).

law issues must be litigated by way of judicial review and not by ordinary action. The only option for the claimant it to make an application for judicial review. Furthermore, there is no power to treat an action begun by writ or originating summons as if it had been commenced by way of judicial review.[41]

However, the precise ambit of the rule in *O'Reilly* v. *Mackman* is unclear and is in any event subject to exceptions. If the case is based solely on public law issues, for example, where the only remedy sought is one to quash or set aside the consequences of a decision of a public body, then it can only be brought by judicial review. Likewise, cases which raise only issues of private law, such as the enforcement of a purely contractual right or a tortious claim such as negligence, should also be brought by way of ordinary action and not by judicial review. However, the same set of facts often give rise to issues of both public and private law. For example, the tort of misfeasance in public office, which can give rise to a right to damages is classed as a private law right, but also requires an act by a public body which is *ultra vires* (*i.e.* a public law issue) as well as the requirement of malice or knowledge of the invalid act.[42]

Where claims in private law and public law arise out of the same set of facts, the Court of Appeal has held that an individual may alternatively choose to pursue such claims by ordinary action rather than seeking judicial review. In *An Bord Bainne Co-operative (Irish Dairy Board)* v. *Milk Marketing Board*[43] the plaintiffs were allowed to proceed by ordinary action for damages in tort for breach of Article 86 of the Treaty of Rome, notwithstanding that other issues involved in the case were classed as public law obligations. However, in *Guevara* v. *Hounslow London Borough Council*[44] the High Court held that the proceedings must be by way of judicial review if substantive elements of public law were involved, even if damages are claimed. Furthermore, in a case *not* involving Community law, *Ali* v. *Tower Hamlets London Borough Council*,[45] the Court of Appeal also compelled resort to judicial review rather than allowing the use of private law proceedings.[46] This case is on appeal to the House of Lords.

As suggested by Lewis,[47] if there is any doubt as to the availability of proceeding by way of the ordinary procedure, the wisest course of action is to apply for judicial review first, as soon as possible but in any event within the three month time limit. The court may, in certain circumstances, direct that an action begun by judicial review may continue as if it had begun by writ.[48] In any event, (since longer time limits apply to

---

[41] Lewis, *op. cit.*, p. 69.
[42] Lewis, *op. cit.*, p. 73 and see further para. 9–022 below.
[43] *An Bord Bainne Co-operative (Irish Dairy Board)* v. *Milk Marketing Board* [1984] 2 C.M.L.R. 584.
[44] *Guevara* v. *Hounslow London Borough Council: The Times* April 17, 1987.
[45] *Ali* v. *Tower Hamlets London Borough Council* [1992] 3 All E.R. 512.
[46] See further Gordon, "Judicial Review" (1992) 136, S.J. 1139 at p. 1140.
[47] Lewis, *op. cit.*, n. 38, p. 70. See also discussion at para. 9–016 below.
[48] Ord. 53, r. 9(5).

ordinary actions), the claimant may bring an action under both procedures if for any reason the judicial review proceedings may not be
determined until after the time limit for bringing the ordinary action has
expired.[49]

A prospective plaintiff can experience a drawback in the situation
where the public and private law issues are inextricably linked, if he/she
opts to proceed by way of an ordinary action. For example, in *Davy* v.
*Spelthorne Borough Council*[50] the case was concerned with private law
rights and a claim for damages arising from an agreement between the
parties whereby the plaintiff agreed not to challenge an enforcement
notice and the allegedly negligent advice of the defendant local authority.
The Court of Appeal allowed the claim for damages to proceed on the
basis of private law rights. However, the plaintiff also sought an
injunction to prevent the implementation of the enforcement notice and
an order setting aside the notice. The Court of Appeal held that these
remedies were essentially public law remedies having the same effect as
an order of certiorari or a declaration under Order 53. Those claims were
consequently struck out on the basis that the public authority was
entitled to claim the protection granted by Order 53 when relief of this
nature is sought. (This aspect of the decision was not appealed to the
House of Lords.)[51]

Lewis points out that the practical draw back of the *Davy* case is that
an individual may have to pursue parallel proceedings dealing with issues
arising out of only one set of facts. He suggests that alternatively, the
plaintiff Davy could have applied for judicial review in respect of the
notice and attached to it the claim for damages, thus enabling both issues
to be dealt with together. This does, however, entail the use of a
procedure, namely judicial review, which may not be best designed for
resolving the relevant issues and may be disadvantageous in terms of
procedural restraints which do not apply in the ordinary writ procedure.
An exemption to the rule in *O'Reilly* v. *Mackman*[52] was suggested where
neither party objects to the use of the ordinary writ procedure or
originating summons. This exception has not featured in the case law,
and it is suggested by Lewis that cases which should have proceeded by
judicial review but where ordinary actions have been allowed, may be
explicable on the basis of implied consent by the public body in not
invoking the rule in *O'Reilly* v. *Mackman*[53]

## Discretionary nature of judicial review

It must be remembered that judicial review is discretionary and that **9–006**
the prerogative remedies as well as the remedies of declaration and
injunction are all discretionary remedies. There are a variety of situations

---

[49] Lewis, *op. cit.*, n. 38, p. 70.
[50] *Davy* v. *Spelthorne Borough Council* (1983) 81 L.R.G. 580.
[51] See Lewis, *op. cit.*, n. 38, p. 75.
[52] *Op. cit.*, n. 40, p. 285.
[53] Lewis, *op. cit.*, n. 38, p. 81, n. 48.

in which the courts have exercised judicial discretion to refuse relief. These include the conduct of the applicant, such as delay or waiver, the circumstances of a particular case, such as the fact that a remedy would be of no practical effect or considerations such as the wider public interest in the need for speed and finality in decision-making as well as the impact on innocent third parties. Judicial review may also not be the only available avenue of challenge, for example where statute has created an appellate machinery to deal with appeals against decisions of public bodies or where judicial review is otherwise impliedly excluded. These issues have been analysed in detail by Lewis.[54] In *R.* v. *Epping and Harlow General Commissioners, ex parte Goldstraw*[55] Sir John Donaldson, M.R. stated that:

". . . save in the most exceptional circumstances, that [judicial review] jurisdiction will not be exercised where other remedies were available and have not been used."

This is referred to as the "exhaustion of remedies" rule.[56] However, the relevant issue is the adequacy of the alternative remedy as a means of resolving the complaint. If the alternative remedy would involve undue delay, the balance may be tipped in favour of allowing judicial review.

## Community law principle of effectiveness

**9–007**  In any event, national law cannot make it difficult or impossible in practice to enforce Community law rights. Therefore a provision which, for example, ousted the jurisdiction of the national courts in respect of Community rights would be unenforceable to that extent. Equally statutory provisions which in some way restrict the range of evidence which might be adduced to support a claim based upon a Community right may be unenforceable. In *Johnston* v. *Chief Constable of the Royal Ulster Constabulary*[57] the European Court held that a statutory provision, which provided that a certificate issued by a Minister was conclusive evidence that a particular act was done for reasons of national security, public safety or public order, was contrary to Community law since it excluded any possibility of review by the courts, and so prevented the courts from ensuring an effective judicial remedy was available.

The issues relevant to breaches of Community law which may arise from the distinction between private law actions and proceedings brought by way of judicial review (for enforcement of a public law right) are well illustrated by the case of *R.* v. *Secretary of State for Employment, ex parte Equal Opportunities Commission.*[58] In that case, a woman worker,

---

[54] *Op. cit.*, pp. 283, *et seq.*
[55] *R.* v. *Epping and Harlow General Commissioners, ex p. Goldstraw* [1983] 3 All E.R. 257 at p. 262.
[56] Lewis, *op. cit.*, n. 38, p. 298.
[57] Case 22/84, *Johnston* v. *Chief Constable of the RUC*: [1986] E.C.R. 1651, [1986] 3 C.M.L.R. 240.
[58] *R.* v. *Secretary of State for Employment, ex p. Equal Opportunities Commission and Another* [1993] 1 All E.R. 1022 (C.A.); *The Times*, March 4, 1994 (H.L.).

Mrs Day, had been employed part time by a local authority and made redundant before she had completed five years' employment. She brought a private law claim before the Industrial Tribunal against her employers for redundancy pay, on the grounds of unfair dismissal under the 1978 Employment Protection (Consolidation) Act on the ground that the relevant provisions of the Act were contrary to E.C. law, *e.g.* Article 119 of the Treaty of Rome and EEC Council Directives 71/117 on equal pay and 76/207 on equal treatment. In particular, the Act provides for a five-year threshold for certain part-time workers to qualify for statutory redundancy pay, whereas full-time workers qualify after two years employment. The Equal Opportunities Commission (which has certain statutory responsibilities) simultaneously brought an application, by way of judicial review. This application referred to the same facts but sought to challenge a statement made in writing by the Secretary of State for Employment, reiterating the government's view that the 1978 Act was not in breach of European Community law relating to equal pay and treatment of men and women.

In the application for judicial review, the Equal Opportunities Commission (EOC) and Mrs Day sought first, a declaration that the Secretary of State and the U.K. were in breach of Community law obligations. They also asked for an order of mandamus, requiring the Secretary of State to introduce legislation to amend the 1978 Act so as to comply with E.C. law. (This claim was later dropped.)[59] The remedies sought would therefore have been different in character from those possible under the private law action for unfair dismissal. In particular, they would have had a much broader result and would have affected the position of others in a similar position to Mrs Day.

The Secretary of State contended, by way of preliminary objections, that he had not made any "decision" susceptible to judicial review but had merely expressed his view in correspondence with the EOC that he was not in breach of Community law obligations. He also contended that the Commission had no *locus standi* because it did not have a "sufficient interest" in the outcome of the proceedings as required by R.S.C., Order 53, rule 3(7).[60] The applicants succeeded in the Divisional Court on these procedural points but failed on the substantive issues.[61] On appeal to the Court of Appeal,[62] the Court rejected the application for judicial review on the basis that the Secretary of State's letter could not be regarded as a decision which was subject to challenge by means of judicial review. In the view of Lord Justice Kennedy the letter did not satisfy Lord Diplock's criteria for reviewability in *Council of Civil Service Unions* v. *Minister for the Civil Service.*[63] It did not alter any right or obligations of any person, or deprive anyone of any benefit or advantage. On the contrary it sought to preserve the status quo.

---

[59] See C.A. judgment, *op. cit.*, p. 1027 e to f (*per* Dillon L.J.)
[60] See further at paras. 9–008, 9–009 *et seq.* below.
[61] [1992] 1 All E.R. 545, Q.B. (D.C.).
[62] [1993] 1 All E.R. 1022 (C.A.).
[63] [1985] A.C. 374 at p. 408.

Lord Justice Kennedy said that "it was not the function of judicial review simply to pronounce upon the law in order to clarify it, especially when in the normal course of events an Industrial Tribunal would have to pronounce upon it in order to decide a specific case." The only way that the relevant U.K. legislation could therefore be challenged, was by Mrs Day seeking to enforce directly effective rights in a private law claim, for which the appropriate forum was the Industrial Tribunal. The Court of Appeal pointed out that it was of course open to the Equal Opportunities Commission to support Mrs Day's case there.

However, on appeal to the House of Lords,[63a] the EOC succeeded. Lord Keith said that the real object of the Commission's attack was not the Secretary of State's letter but the statutory provisions themselves. The question was whether judicial review was available for the purpose of securing a declaration that certain U.K. primary legislation was incompatible with Community law. It was argued for the Secretary of State that Order 53, rule 1(2) of the Rules of the Supreme Court, which gave the court power to make declarations in judicial review proceedings, was only applicable where one of the prerogative orders would be available under rule 1(1), and that if there was no decision in respect of which one of those writs might be issued then a declaration could not be made. That was held to be too narrow an interpretation of the court's powers. *R. v. Secretary of State for Transport, ex parte Factortame Ltd.*[63b] was a precedent in favour of the EOC's resort to judicial review. There was also no need for a declaration that the U.K. or the Secretary of State was in breach of obligation under Community law. A declaration that the threshold provisions of the 1978 Act were incompatible with Community law would suffice for the EOC's purposes and was capable of being granted consistently with the *Factortame* precedent.

## Power to compel amendment to national legislation

9–008    The effect of the House of Lords' judgment in the above case is to render inapplicable and ineffective the relevant threshold provisions of the Employment Protection (Consolidation) Act 1978. Statutory amendment is therefore now likely to be necessary. The approach of Lord Justice Kennedy in the Court of Appeal decision has therefore been overruled. Lord Justice Kennedy had expressly endorsed the view of the Divisional Court that:

"... section 2 of the [European Communities] Act alters the traditional relationship between the courts and Parliament in this country in that it obliges the courts to disregard the laws made by Parliament insofar as they can conflict with directly enforceable Community law. Further than that it does not go. Domestic

---

[63a] *The Times*, March 4, 1994.

[63b] *The Times*, May 19, 1989; [1990] 2 A.C. 85; *The Times*, June 20, and October 12, 1990; [1991] 1 A.C. 603 and 645; *The Times*, September 16, 1991; [1992] Q.B. 680 and discussed further at paras. 3–012 and 9–035.

legislation remains a matter for Parliament, not for the courts. How could it be right for us to tell the Secretary of State that he must introduce legislation amending the 1978 Act, when so far as we can see it would be equally open to him as a Member of Parliament to introduce legislation amending or repealing the 1972 Act? If it would be wrong and unconstitutional, as we believe, for the courts to give him an order in these terms, it must equally be wrong for the courts to make a declaration that such was his duty."[64]

The approach taken by the majority in the House of Lords made it unnecessary to grant a declaration in terms that Parliament must amend the law, but the effect was essentially the same. The crucial issue was the decision by the House of Lords to grant *locus standi* to the EOC, by confirming that since it had a duty to work towards the elimination of discrimination and to promote equality of opportunity between men and women generally, it has sufficient interest to bring the proceedings. Lord Jauncey dissented on this issue, and agreed instead with Lord Justice Kennedy in the Court of Appeal that the EOC did not have the capacity to pursue the proceedings. The majority judgment of the House of Lords on *locus standi* is of considerable significance because it is the first in which a pressure group whose own rights have not been affected, has been granted standing in judicial review proceedings. This raises the issue of whether other bodies such as the Commission for Racial Equality, Greenpeace, trades unions, etc., will, in future cases, also be accorded legal standing to bring judicial review proceedings.[65] It also casts considerable doubt on the correctness of the decision of the High Court in the case of *Twyford Parish Council* v. *Secretary of State for the Environment and Secretary of State for Transport*[65a] discussed further at paragraph 9–014 below.

It does, however, affirm the approach taken in Case C–9/91, *R.* v. *Secretary of State for Social Security, ex parte Equal Opportunities Commission*[66] where the Queen's Bench Division of the High Court appears to have accepted that the Equal Opportunities Commission was entitled in principle to bring an action for judicial review seeking various declarations including a declaration that the Secretary of State for Social Security was in breach of certain obligations in a Directive[67] on the progressive implementation of the principle of equal treatment for men and women in matters of social security. The High Court, before ruling on the EOC's application, submitted a preliminary question to the European Court on the interpretation of Article 7(1)(a) of the relevant

---

[64] See *R.* v. *Secretary of State for Employment, ex p. Equal Opportunities Commission* (C.A.), *op. cit.*, n. 58, p. 1043 e to h.
[65] See *The Times*, editorial, March 5, 1994. See further discussion at para. 9–009 *et seq.* below.
[65a] [1991] C.O.D. 210.
[66] Case C–9/91, *R.* v. *Secretary of State for Social Security, ex p. Equal Opportunities Commission*: [1992] 3 C.M.L.R. 233.
[67] Council Directive No. 79/7 of December 1978; [1979] O.J. L6/24.

Directive. The European Court held that, in effect, U.K. law was not necessarily in conflict with Community law in relation to the maintenance of different contribution periods for male and female workers under the pension schemes which were at issue in the case. However, it seems to be implicit in the making of the Article 177 reference, that the EOC was entitled, in principle, to ask for these declarations.

**9–009**   It is noteworthy that in the Scottish case of *National Union of Public Employees* v. *Lord Advocate*,[68] Lord Cameron of Lochbroom in an application for judicial review based on the Transfer of Undertakings (Protection of Employment) Regulations (TUPE),[69] refused the application as incompetent, because the appropriate remedy lay in an application to an industrial tribunal. The petitioners had sought a declarator that the provision of the Regulations which purported to exclude any undertaking which was not in the nature of a commercial venture from the definition of undertakings to which the Regulations applied, was suspended and ineffective because it was contrary to Community law, in particular Council Directive 77/187.[70] Lord Cameron referred to the case of *R.* v. *Secretary of State for Employment, ex parte Equal Opportunities Commission*[71] citing Lord Justice Hirst's comments:

> ". . . Where an individual . . . is seeking to enforce directly effective rights under Article 119, the appropriate forum for their enforcement is unquestionably the Industrial Tribunal. This Tribunal will be obliged under Section 2(1) of (the European Communities Act 1972) to disapply domestic legislation if, and insofar as, it is inconsistent with Community law, thus ensuring that Community law will prevail.
>
> The Industrial Tribunal, rather than the Divisional Court is moreover, in my judgment, the appropriate forum for the determination of the factual issues which arise in relation to the objective justification of any discriminatory law or practice."[72]

Lord Cameron regarded the above expressions of view as being entirely apposite to the case. He pointed out that an industrial court was also bound to apply relevant EEC law to issues before it, including the obligation set down in Case C–106/89, *Marleasing SA* v. *La Comercial Internacional de Alimentación SA*[73] regarding the duty on national courts to secure the result which directives were intended to achieve. (These principles are not affected by amendments made to the EEC Treaty by the Treaty on European Union.) In *R.* v. *Secretary of State for Employment, ex parte EOC*[73a] (discussed further at paragraphs 9–007 *et seq.*,

---

[68] *National Union of Public Employees* v. *Lord Advocate*, Court of Session: *The Times*, May 5, 1993.
[69] S.I. 1981 No. 1794.
[70] [1977] O.J. L61/26. See further discussion of TUPE at para. 6–014 above.
[71] [1993] 1 All E.R. 1022 (C.A.).
[72] *Ibid.*, p. 1050c.
[73] Case 106/89, *Marleasing* v. *La Comercial*: [1990] I E.C.R. 4135, [1992] 1 C.M.L.R. 305. Discussed further at para. 6–004 above.
[73a] *The Times*, March 4, 1994.

above), the application for judicial review brought by the EOC had been amended to bring in as a second applicant, Mrs Day, who had been adversely affected by the relevant provisions of the Employment Protection (Consolidation) Act 1978 which were at issue in the case. However, the House of Lords dismissed her appeal on the basis that her claim was a private law one against her employers and not against the Secretary of State. The latter was not her employer and was not liable to meet her claim, if sound. The determination of her claim was regarded as a private law claim which had been entrusted by statute to the industrial tribunal (where, in fact, Mrs Day had already instituted proceedings). It may be that the reluctance to grant Mrs Day *locus standi* is based on the discretionary nature of judicial review, referred to above at paragraph 9–006, and the availability of the alternative statutory procedures in the Industrial Tribunal. However, by virtue of its decision to grant *locus standi* to the EOC and to award declarations to the effect that the relevant provisions of the 1978 Act are incompatible with Community law, the House of Lords in effect protected Mrs Day's rights under Community law. The issue of *locus standi* is discussed further at paragraph 9–014 below, in the context of directly effective Community law.

In Case C–6/90, *Francovich* v. *Italian Republic*[74] the Court established that the individual who suffers damage as a result of the non-implementation of a directive for which a Member State is responsible is entitled to damages in certain circumstances. However, the judgment did not go further and it remains to be seen whether individuals may invoke the breach of the duty of Community solidarity required by Article 5 or Article 189 in proceedings based upon *Francovich* to seek a remedy in the national courts, compelling a Member State to comply with Community law obligations.

## Locus standi: a two-stage process

The usual procedure for enforcing public law rights by private **9–010** individuals is by way of application for judicial review. The plaintiff must have *locus standi*, *i.e.* "sufficient interest in the matter to which the application relates," Supreme Court Act 1981, section 31(3) and R.S.C., Order 53, rule 3(7).[75]

Under section 31(3) of the Supreme Court Act 1981, the court should not grant leave to apply for judicial review unless the applicant has a sufficient interest. The question of leave involves a two-stage process.[76] At the leave stage, a provisional view is taken by the court as to whether the applicant has a sufficient interest and at the full hearing, the sufficiency of that interest is fully assessed.[77] The parties cannot waive

---

[74] Case C–6/90, *Francovich*: [1991] I E.C.R. 5357, [1993] 2 C.M.L.R. 66, [1992] I.R.L.R. 84 and see further, paras. 8–008 *et seq.* above.
[75] See further, Geddes, "Locus Standi and EEC Environment Measures" (1992) Vol. 4 No. 1 *Journal of Environmental Law* 29 at pp. 32 *et seq.* and para. 9–008 above.
[76] Lewis, *Judicial Remedies in Public Law* (1992), p. 268.
[77] *R.* v. *IRC, ex p. National Federation of Self-Employed and Small Businesses Limited* [1982] A.C. 617.

the question of standing, and therefore cannot confer jurisdiction on the court by agreeing to treat the applicant as having a sufficient interest.[78]

### Scope of the statutory power or duty

9–011    In deciding whether the applicant has standing, the court must first consider the scope of the statutory powers or duties which apply in the case to decide whether the applicant is within the range of persons entitled to challenge the exercise of that power or to insist upon the performance of a duty. The relevant principles were summarised by Schiemann J. in the case R. v. *Secretary of State for the Environment, ex parte Rose Theatre Trust Company*[79] where he summarised the analysis of the House of Lords in the earlier case of R. v. *Inland Revenue Commissioners, ex parte National Federation of Self-employed and Small Business Limited*[80] as supporting the following propositions:

"(1) Once leave has been given to move for judicial review, the court which hears the application ought still to examine whether the applicant has a sufficient interest.

(2) Whether an applicant has a sufficient interest is not purely a matter of discretion in the court.

(3) Not every member of the public can complain of every breach of statutory duty by a person empowered to come to a decision by that statute. To rule otherwise would be to deprive the phrase "a sufficient interest" of all meaning.

(4) However, a direct financial or legal interest is not required.

(5) Where one is examining an alleged failure to perform a duty imposed by statute it is useful to look at the statute and see whether it gives an applicant a right enabling him to have that duty performed.

(6) Merely to assert that one has an interest does not give one an interest.

(7) The fact that some thousands of people join together and assert that they have an interest does not create an interest if the individual did not have an interest.

(8) The fact that those without an interest incorporate themselves and give the company in its memorandum power to pursue a particular object does not give the company an interest."

In the *Rose Theatre Trust Company*, the remains of a historial theatre were discovered in the course of development of a site in central London. Concerned members of the public, which included eminent persons of expertise and distinction in the fields of archaeology, the theatre, literature and other fields as well as local residents, the local Member of Parliament and other persons set up a trust company with the objects of

---

[78] Lewis, *Judicial Remedies in Public Law* (1992), p. 267.

[79] R. v. *Secretary of State for the Environment, ex p. Rose Theatre Trust Company* [1990] 2 W.L.R. 186.

[80] [1982] A.C. 617.

preserving the remains and making them accessible to the public. The company applied to the Secretary of State for the Environment for the theatre to be listed in the Schedule of Monuments made under section 1 of the Ancient Monuments and Archaeological Areas Act 1979. The Secretary of State, whilst accepting that the remains were of national importance, declined to list them. Among his reasons was his view that the site was not under threat, that scheduling might give rise to claims for compensation, the need to balance the desirability of preservation against the need for a city to thrive, and the likelihood of co-operation by the developers.

The company sought judicial review of the Secretary of State decision. It was argued on behalf of the Secretary of State *inter alia* that a member of the public did not obtain a sufficient interest in the decision by making the application to the Secretary of State and receiving a reply thereto. It was *held* that since the members of the applicant company had no *locus standi* as individuals, the company they had created had no standing to apply for judicial reveiw. (It was agreed by Counsel on behalf of the applicant that if the court found that no individual in the campaign had standing, then it was conceded that the agglomeration of individuals could not have a standing which any one individual lacked."[81]

Schiemann J. went on to apply the approach indicated in the above **9–012** propositions and rejected the application on the dual grounds that the applicant had no standing to make it and that in any event it did not have legal merit.

Where the decision-making mechanism is primarily concerned with the taking of a decision in respect of a particular individual, the recipient of the decision will invariably have standing. In other cases, although the decision may be directed at a particular individual, it may also affect a wider section of the public. For example, Lewis[82] gives the example of the grant of planning permission which is of concern not only to the grantee but also to the owners of adjacent land, residents of the area, and others whose rival applications for planning permission for a particular site may have been refused. Finally, there may be general legislative measures which affect all citizens equally, rather than affecting any particular section. Nevertheless, in *R. v. H.M. Treasury, ex parte Smedley*[83] the Court of Appeal held that a decision to approve a supplementary budget for the European Community is of interest to all tax payers and arguably all electors, so that any tax payer may challenge that decision. However, it is clear from the *Rose Theatre* case that direct financial or legal interest is not required although its existence will strengthen the claim for standing. In the case brought by Lord Rees-Mogg, on behalf of the anti-Maastricht campaign in the U.K., challenging by way of judicial review the government's planned ratification of the Maastricht Treaty in its current form on the basis that the government's

---

[81] See judgment of Schiemann J., *op. cit.*, n. 79, p. 201 at para. H.
[82] Lewis, *op. cit.*, n. 78, p. 270.
[83] *R. v. H.M. Treasury, ex p. Smedley* [1985] Q.B. 657.

approach was legally and constitutionally flawed,[84] the Foreign Secretary, Mr Douglas Hurd, did not dispute Lord Rees-Mogg's legal standing in bringing the case "as a concerned citizen," but successfully contested the substance of his claims.

### Entitlement to make representations/objections

**9–013**    Apart from the scope of the statutory power or duty, the court may also consider whether the individual has a statutory or common law entitlement to make representations or objections during the course of the decision-making process. If so, this may also confer standing on the basis of a legitimate expectation of consultation, if that expectation is not fulfilled.[85] The House of Lords recognised in both *O'Reilly* v. *Mackman*[86] and in *Re Findlay*[87] that a legitimate expectation of consultation may become the basis of *locus standi* in judicial review proceedings.[88]

However, it was held in the *Rose Theatre* case, that an individual cannot, however, acquire a standing simply by making representations to a decision-maker if there is no entitlement or expectation to make representations, even if the decision-maker then sends a considered reply. It may be that the House of Lords has left open the possibility of intervention in extreme cases, where the individual would not normally have standing but the seriousness of the breach or abuse of power is so unacceptable as to merit judicial intervention.[89] Where, however, groups act in a representative capacity, taking action either on behalf of their membership or to protect their members' interest, they will normally have sufficient interest to challenge a relevant decision. For example, representative associations of road haulage contractors were allowed to challenge an order requiring the fitting of silencers to lorries.[90] Pressure groups or societies may also succeed in appropriate cases.[91] The House of Lords decision in *R.* v. *Secretary of State for Employment, ex parte EOC: The Times*, March 4, 1994, discussed above at paragraph 9–007 will have major implications for future cases of this kind.

### Relevance of directly effective Community law

**9–014**    It is arguable that a "directly effective" provision of Community law, *i.e.* one designed to protect individuals or their rights (in particular as regards their health and welfare) confers on individuals the relevant *locus*

---

[84] R. v. *Secretary of State for Foreign and Commonwealth Affairs, ex p. Rees-Mogg* [1993] 3 C.M.L.R. 101.

[85] See *Council of Civil Service Unions* v. *Minister for the Civil Service* [1985] A.C. 374 and for a case where legitimate expectation was not made out, see, *e.g. R.* v. *North-West Thames Regional Health Authority and Others, ex p. Daniels (Rhys William): The Times* June 22, 1993, p. 38.

[86] *O'Reilly* v. *Mackman* [1983] A.C. 237.

[87] *Re Findlay* [1985] A.C. 318 at p. 338.

[88] See further, Richard Gordon, "Judicial Review and the Detained Patient" (January 22, 1993) *Solicitors Journal* 43 at p. 44.

[89] See *R.* v. *Inland Revenue Commissioners, ex p. National Federation of Self-Employed and Small Businesses Limited* [1982] A.C. 617.

[90] See *R.* v. *London Boroughs Transport Committee, ex p. Freight Transport Association* [1992] 1 C.M.L.R. 5, discussed at paras. 3–021 and 3–050 above.

[91] See further Lewis, *op. cit.*, n. 78, pp. 275 *et seq.*

*standi* to enable them to seek judicial review in respect of a failure by a public authority to enforce such rights.[92] The Law Commission has published proposals to improve the process of judicial review and has considered, *inter alia*, the question of whether the procedure should be seen as a broader form of "citizen action" open to all.[93]

However, this approach was not followed in *Twyford Parish Council* v. *Secretary of State for the Environment and Secretary of State for Transport.*[94] In that case, two parish councils and three individuals sought judicial review of the Minister's decision to permit the construction of a motorway across Twyford Down near Winchester, on the ground, *inter alia*, that no environmental impact assessment had been carried out, in breach of EEC Directive 85/337 and that members of the public had not been given an opportunity to express an opinion thereon. The judge found against the applicants on the basis that the Directive did not apply to the specific projects in question. He did, however, find that the relevant provisions of the Directive were unconditional and sufficiently precise and had direct effect and that the applicants were amongst those intended to benefit from it.

However, he went on to say that the applicants could not rely on the Directive because they had not "suffered" as a consequence of the State's failure to implement the directive in question. The *Becker* case[95] was cited in support of this proposition, as analysed in the opinion of the Advocate General Sir Gordon Slynn in *Marshall* v. *Southampton and South West Hampshire Area Health Authority (Teaching), (Marshall No. 1).*[96] It is argued by Geddes[97] that this reasoning is incorrect since the *Becker* case was not concerned with *locus standi*, which is a matter for national law. The correct question was whether, bearing in mind the directly effective nature of the provisions, the applicants had "sufficient interest" within the Supreme Court rules to found an action, and not whether they had suffered as a consequence of the State's failure to implement the Directive. This case must be reassessed in the light of the House of Lords decision in *R.* v. *Secretary of State for Employment, ex parte EOC,*[97a] which took a far more liberal approach to the issue of *locus standi* in respect of the EOC and is discussed at paragraphs 9–007 *et seq.* above.

As a matter of Community law, the correct position seems to be that once a provision of Community law is established as sufficiently clear,

---

[92] See Geddes, *op. cit.*, n. 26, p. 37.
[93] See *Administrative Law Judicial Review and Statutory Appeals*, Law Commission consultation paper No. 126, HMSO.
[94] *Twyford Paris Council and Others* v. *Secretary of State for the Environment and Secretary of State for Transport* [1991] C.O.D. 210, judgment of the High Court, Q.B.D. of October 26, 1990, [1992] 1 C.M.L.R. 276 (H.L.).
[95] Case 8/81, *Becker* v. *Finanzamt Munster-Innenstadt*: [1982] E.C.R. 53.
[96] *Marshall (No. 1)*: [1986] E.C.R. 723; see further para. 7–001 above.
[97] *Op. cit.*, n. 26, p. 35. See also, Ward, (1993) Vol. 5 No. 2 *Journal of Environmental Law* 221 at pp. 232 *et seq.*
[97a] *The Times*, March 4, 1994.

precise and unconditional so as to be directly effective, it automatically constitutes standing to sue for individuals seeking to enforce their Community law rights. Therefore, in such a case, the restrictive view of *locus standi* taken in the *Rose Theatre* case[98] would be unsustainable as a matter of Community law and should not therefore be applied in national law where Community rights are in issue.[99] Furthermore, as a result of Case C–6/90, *Francovich* v. *Italian Republic*[1] this right of action may arguably cover not only failure to implement Community directives but also other breaches of Community law.[2]

## JUDICIAL REVIEW AND ADMINISTRATIVE DISCRETION: RELEVANCE TO COMMUNITY LAW

9–015    In the course of judicial review proceedings, the Court is frequently asked to interfere with an administrative discretion, by using its supervisory or review capacity.[3] The governing principles were laid down by the Court of Appeal in *Associated Provincial Picture Houses Limited* v. *Wednesbury Corporation*[4] which is one of the most frequently referred to cases in administrative law.[5] Under the principles laid down in the *Wednesbury* case, the Court only interferes if:

"there is some demonstrable error in the way of misdirection, either in law or in fact; in other words if the Minister takes into account something he ought not to have done or fails to take into account something he should have done or misdirects himself in law and so on; those are matters which may result in this Court quashing a decision."

In addition, the principle referred to as "Wednesbury unreasonableness" applies. This occurs where it can be shown that a Minister has acted in a way in which no Minister properly directing himself could have acted. It must be emphasised, however, that as regards the facts which were taken into consideration, the court may not substitute its view of the weight to be given to the facts for that of the Minister or relevant body.[6]

---

[98] *Rose Theatre*, n. 79, *op. cit.*
[99] Geddes, "E.C. Environmental Law Progress in 1991" (March 27, 1992) *Solicitors Journal* 289 p. 290.
[1] Case C–6/90, *Francovich*: [1991] I E.C.R. 5357, [1993] 2 C.M.L.R. 66.
[2] See *Ross*, "Beyond *Francovich*" (1993) M.L.R. 55 at p. 72 and detailed discussion at paras. 8–008 *et seq.* above.
[3] See Foulkes, *Administrative Law* (1986), ed., p. 208.
[4] *Associated Provincial Picture Houses Ltd.* v. *Wednesbury Corporation* [1948] 1 K.B. 233, [1947] 2 All E.R. 680 (C.A.). See also *Nottinghamshire County Council* v. *Secretary of State for the Environment* [1986] 1 All E.R. 199 (H.L.).
[5] Wade, *Administrative Law* (1988), 6th ed., p. 206.
[6] See, for example, judgment of Forbes J. in *R.* v. *Minister of Agriculture, Fisheries and Food, ex p. Bell Lines Limited and An Bord Bainne Co-operative Limited (the Irish Dairy Board)* [1984] 2 C.M.L.R. 502 at p. 509. See also discussion at para. 9–002.

However, the principle of proportionality is not yet recognised as an independent ground of judicial review.[7] Proportionality is, however, applied by U.K. courts is cases involving Community law.[8] It is argued by Lord Anthony Lester, Q.C. (citing and supporting the views of Sir John Laws)[9] that in cases where the exercise of discretionary powers affects fundamental rights (as distinct from fact finding cases or cases involving economic policy), English courts should go beyond the *Wednesbury* principle by developing proportionality as an independent ground of review.[10] However, the principle of proportionality may arguably apply to a broader category of cases, as a result of Community law. For example, in the case of *R.* v. *Minister of Agriculture, Fisheries and Food, ex parte Bell Lines Limited and An Bord Bainne Co-operative Limited*[11] the facts of which are referred to at paragraph 9–002 above, it was held that inspite of the *Wednesbury* principle of judicial reticence, when faced with the exercise of ministerial discretion, an English court when called on to provide a remedy must be entitled to examine whether, and to what extent, decisions of the administrative authorities are capable of constituting an impermissible restriction on intra-community trade contrary to Article 30 and 36 of the Treaty of Rome. In other words, U.K. national courts are not precluded by the *Wednesbury* principles from examining, in the context of Articles 30–36 of the Treaty of Rome (as amended), "whether and to what extent the detailed measures of control are capable of constituting an impermissible restriction on intra-Community trade."[12]

In the *Bell Lines* case[13] Mr Justice Forbes decided that in applying *Wednesbury* principles, no reasonable Minister, asking himself the question whether the designation of ports in that case was or was not "a disguised restriction on trade between Member States" could fail to come up with any other answer than that the refusal to designate two ports in that case, with the consequent detriment to the trade of Bell Lines and the Irish Dairy Board was in fact "a disguised restriction on trade between Member States."

"In other words, if the Minister had asked himself that question it seems to me that inevitably he would have had to have answered:

---

[7] See *R.* v. *Secretary of State for the Home Department, ex p. Brind* [1991] A.C. 696 (H.L.); [1981] 1 All E.R. 721.

[8] See, *e.g.* cases concerning Sunday trading: *Stoke City Council* v. *B & Q Plc* [1990] 3 C.M.L.R. 31; *Wellingborough Borough Council* v. *Payless D.I.Y. Ltd.* [1990] 1 C.M.L.R. 773; *W.H. Smith Do-It-All Ltd. and Payless D.I.Y. Ltd.* v. *Peterborough City Council* [1990] 2 C.M.L.R. 577 and also, *e.g. Thomas* v. *Chief Adjudication Officer and Secretary of State for Social Security* [1991] 2 W.L.R. 886 (C.A.); *R.* v. *Secretary of State for Employment, ex p. EOC* [1991] I.R.L.R. 493 (D.C.).

[9] Lester, "The European Legal Dimension to the English Judicial Review: Principles and Remedies" (October 1992) Vol. 18 No. 4 *Commonwealth Law Bulletin* 1397 at p. 1398.

[10] Lester, *ibid.*

[11] *Bell Lines Ltd. op. cit.*, n. 6.

[12] See *United Foods and Van Den Abeele* v. *Belgium*: [1981] E.C.R. 995, [1982] 1 C.M.L.R. 275 and also the Sunday trading cases, *op. cit.*, n. 8 above.

[13] *Bell Lines Ltd. op. cit.*, n. 6.

yes it is a disguised restriction on trade and therefore it does not fall within Article 36 and I should not so operate my power of designation of these ports as to deprive the Irish Dairy Board and Bell Lines of the opportunity of continuing to trade as they have done for many years through those particular ports."[14]

Mr Justice Forbes took the view that in those circumstances, either on the basis of the rule in *Wednesbury* or on the above basis, the application by Bell Lines Limited and An Bord Bainne Co-operative Limited (the Irish Dairy Board) for judicial review in the form of declarations and orders of mandamus should be granted.

Thus, the approach of the court in a judicial review application involving a point of Community law may differ from cases in which only domestic law is involved.[15] This may necessitate a greater use of cross-examination and discovery since the court may have to investigate the facts to a greater extent than in the usual judicial review instances.[16]

# THE CLAIM FOR DAMAGES AGAINST THE STATE OR "EMANATION OF THE STATE"

9–016    Since the amendments to the Rules of the Supreme Court in 1977, it is possible to claim damages in judicial review proceedings[17] provided first that they arise from any matter to which the application relates. Secondly, that they could have been awarded in an action (begun by writ) by the applicant at the same time as his application for judicial review. In other words, the applicant must show that the elements of an existing private law right are also made out.[18]

However, damages cannot be claimed in judicial review proceedings unless one ot the prerogative remedies could also have been sought.[19] If one of the prerogative orders is not appropriate then the matter is ineligible for judicial review, but the court has the power to treat the application as if had been begun by writ. It may thus transfer the proceedings from public to private law proceedings, but not vice versa.[20]

In order for a litigant to obtain damages against the State or a public authority for a breach of Community law, he or she needs to establish the

---

[14] *Bell Lines* case, *ibid.*, p. 513.
[15] See further, *R. v. Secretary of State for Social Services, ex p. Schering Chemicals Ltd.* [1987] C.M.L.R. 277 and *R. v. Ministry of Agriculture, Fisheries and Food, ex p. Roberts* [1991] 1 C.M.L.R. 555.
[16] See Forbes J. in *Bell Lines Ltd., op. cit.*, n. 6, p. 511.
[17] Ord. 53, r. 4.
[18] See Supreme Court Act 1981 s. 31(4)(a)(b) which gives statutory force to the provisions of Order 53, *Secretary of State for the Home Office, ex p. Ruddock and Others* [1987] 1 W.L.R. 1482 and Ward, "Government Liability in the U.K. for Breach of Individual Rights in European Community Law" (1990) 19 *Anglo-American Law Review* 1 at p. 27.
[19] See *Davy v. Spelthorne BC* [1984] A.C. 262 at 277 to 78 and Wade, *op. cit.*, n. 5, p. 672.
[20] See *O'Reilly v. Mackman* [1983] 2 A.C. 237 at 284 discussed at para. 9–003 above.

existence of a private legal interest or right recognised by a law, which has been violated by the defendant State or its emanation. These include, for example, a breach of contract, or a tort, or a claim based on statute such as unfair dismissal, or a right to compensation under public procurement legislation. The use of a cause of action in common law may have drawbacks.[21] For instance, to bring proceedings at common law, in tort, it is necessary to show that the defendant owes the plaintiff a duty of care and that some damage has been caused as a result of a breach of that duty. In certain cases, these may be difficult to show unless a proprietary interest has been affected. The most common cause of action in tort is for breach of statutory duty. This is discussed in detail at paragraph 9–017 below.

## Breach of Statutory Duty

Various duties are placed on Member States by the E.C. and their **9–017** public authorities by virtue of the E.C. Treaty and subordinate Community legislation. In the U.K. these duties are given legal effect by the European Communities Act 1972 (as amended). The breach of a directly effective provision of Community law by a Member State therefore gives rise to a cause of action under Community law, which is given effect in U.K. law by the operation of sections 2(1) and 3(1) of the European Communities Act 1972 (as amended). It is therefore unnecessary to establish, as such, a separate cause of action under national law.[22] This principle is supported by Lord Diplock in *Garden Cottage Foods Limited v. Milk Marketing Board*[23] in relation to Article 86 of the EEC Treaty (and which is not amended by the Treaty on European Union) which, in Lord Diplock's words, had been held by the Court of Justice:[24]

> "To produce direct effects in relations between individuals and to create direct rights in respect of the individuals concerned which the national court must protect. This decision of European Court of Justice as to the effect of Article 86 is one which section 3(1) of the European Communities Act 1972 requires your Lordships to follow. The rights which the Article confers upon citizens in the United Kingdom accordingly fall within section 2(1) of the Act. They are without further enactment to be given legal effect in the United Kingdom and enforced accordingly.
>
> A breach of the duty imposed by Article 86 not to abuse a dominant position in the common market or in a substantial part of it, *can thus*

---

[21] For a discussion in the context of water law see Jackson, " 'Joe Public' and Dried Up Rivers: Courses of Action Open to the Public to Counter the Problem of Low Flows" (September 1992) Vol. 3 Issue 5 *Water Law* pp. 153 to 155.

[22] See Evelyn Ellis, "The Enforcement of EEC Law in the Courts of the Member States: What Does Direct Effect Really Mean?" in *Droit Sans Frontiers* (Hand and McBride ed. 1991), 265 at p. 270.

[23] *Garden Cottage Foods Ltd.* v. *Milk Marketing Board* [1984] A.C. 130.

[24] In Case 127/73, *Belgische Radio en Televisie* v. *SV SABAM*: [1974] E.C.R. 238, [1974] 2 C.M.L.R. 238.

*be categorised in English law as a breach of statutory duty* that is imposed not only for the purpose of promoting the general economic prosperity of the common market but also for the benefit of private individuals to whom loss or damage is caused by a breach of that duty." (emphasis added)

The above principles are not affected by amendments made to the 1972 Act by the European Communities (Amendments) Act 1993. However, it is suggested by Ross[25] that it is "unnecessary and mis-guided" for English courts to try to find an appropriate English description, *i.e.* breach of statutory duty in order to found a cause of action. In other words, there is no necessity "to find a domestic method or classification for acknowledging Community law rights and remedies."[26] Nevertheless, as a matter of practice, it would be prudent in pleadings involving applications for damages and/or injunctions based on Community rights, to plead both a direct claim, based on a breach of a Treaty provision for example, as well as alternative claims in the pleadings, based on "domestic"classifications such as breach of statutory duty.

### Breach of Article 30 to the E.C. Treaty: the Bourgoin decision

9–018    In the leading U.K. decision of the Court of Appeal in the case of *Bourgoin SA* v. *Ministry of Agriculture, Fisheries and Food*[27] the Court did *not*, however, accept that a breach of Article 30 of the Treaty by a Minister could constitute a tort or breach of statutory duty and therefore could give rise to a claim for damages against the State. This Court of Appeal decision is now of doubtful authority following the decision of the ECJ in *Francovich*.[28]

The facts were that in August 1981, the U.K. Ministry of Agriculture, Fisheries and Food (MAFF) imposed a restriction on the import of turkeys from France for animal health reasons. This prevented French turkey producers from exporting to the U.K. at Christmas. They sued MAFF. In a parallel action brought by the Commission against the U.K. under Article 169 of the Treaty, the European Court held in July 1982 that the measures taken by MAFF constituted a quantitative restriction on trade contrary to Article 30 of the Treaty of Rome and was not justified on animal health grounds under Article 36. The real intention was to protect the U.K. market from foreign competition.[29]

After the court's ruling, MAFF amended the system but not until November 1982. This allowed the import of French turkeys to resume but affected the Christmas turkey trade for 1982 as well. The plaintiffs then sued MAFF for about 19 million pounds sterling in lost sales and

---

[25] Ross, "Beyond *Francovich*" (1993) M.L.R. 55 at p. 69.
[26] Ross, *ibid.*, p. 69.
[27] *Bourgoin* [1985] 3 All E.R. 385.
[28] See further discussion below and at paras. 8–013 *et seq.* above.
[29] See Case 40/82, *Commission* v. *U.K.*: [1982] E.C.R. 2793, [1982] 3 C.M.L.R. 497.

the court had to determine a prelininary issue as to whether MAFF could be liable in damages at all.

Argument centred on whether a breach of Article 30 amounted to a breach of statutory duty. Although the *Garden Cottage* case[30] was considered both at first instance and in the Court of Appeal, unlike the *Garden Cottage* case, the *Bourgoin* case involved an action against the government (rather than a private party). It therefore raised an additional problem, namely whether the remedy under national law was to be restricted to the realm of "public law" in which case only judicial review was appropriate, or whether a "private law" claim was also available , in which case damages could be claimed. Article 30 has been held by the Court of Justice to have direct effect and thus to create rights which the national courts must protect.[31]

Although the precise scope of the tort of breach of statutory duty in U.K. law is not defined, it is generally accepted that certain conditions must be satisfied. The plaintiff must prove: (i) that the relevant statute imposes a clear and precise duty owed to the plaintiff rather than to society at large,[32] (ii) that the damage suffered is of a kind which the statute was intended to prevent; (iii) that the defendant infringed his statutory obligations; and (iv) that the infringement caused the defendant's loss.[33] However the courts may take the view that this cause of action is not available where, for example, the statute itself provides adequate remedies (whether by way of criminal penalty of ministerial default powers).[34]

The defendant Ministry in *Bourgoin* pleaded that the relevant para- **9–019** graph of the Statement of Claim disclosed no cause of action and the question was therefore tried as a preliminary issue. At first instance, the plaintiffs succeeded in their argument that Article 30 grounded an action in damages for breach of statutory duty. However, the Court of Appeal held by a majority of 2:1 (Oliver, L.J. dissenting) that it could not, although they did find unanimously that MAFF could be liable in tort on another ground, namely "misfeasance in public office."

Parker L.J. noted in *Bourgoin*[35] that Community law itself does not render its own institutions liable for damages for a breach of the Treaty. The European Court has held that Community institutions are not liable in damages for adopting a legislative act which is unlawful under Article 215. The Community does not incur liability on account of a legislative measure which involves choice of economic policy unless a "sufficiently serious breach of a superior rule of law for the protection of the individual has occurred."[36] Importance has been attached to this

---

[30] *Op. cit.*, n. 23.

[31] See Case 74/76, *Iannelli and Volpi* v. *Meroni*: [1977] E.C.R. 557, [1977] 2 C.M.L.R. 688.

[32] See *Thornton* v. *Kirklees MBC* [1979] Q.B. 626 (C.A.).

[33] See Nicholas Green and Ami Barav, "Damages in the National Courts for Breach of Community Law" (1986) Y.E.L. 55 at pp. 98 *et seq.*

[34] See, *e.g. Southwark London Borough Council* v. *Williams* [1971] Ch. 734, [1971] 2 All E.R. 175 (C.A.).

[35] *Bourgoin: op. cit.*, n. 27, p. 627.

[36] See Joined Cases 83 & 94/76, *HNL*: [1978] E.C.R. 1209, [1978] 3 C.M.L.R. 566 and Case 101/78, *Granaria*: [1979] E.C.R. 623, [1979] 3 C.M.L.R. 1240.

principle by Professor Sue Arrowsmith,[37] who takes a restrictive view of the scope of the decision in *Francovich*.

Parker L.J. argued by analogy that Member States should not be hindered in taking legislative action, by the prospect of actions for damages if their judgment should ultimately be held to be wrong. He held that the right conferred on individuals by Article 30 lay in the public law field and not in private law. Consequently, the only remedy for breach of Article 30 by a Member State was by way of judicial review. He rejected arguments that the direct effect of Article 30 of the Treaty[38] together with secton 2(1) of the European Communities Act necessarily obliged the imposition of a tort (breach of statutory duty).

Oliver L.J. (dissenting) reached the opposite conclusion. He concluded that a breach of Article 30 gave individuals a private law right. He cited in support of this the case of *Simmenthal*[39] where the European Court held that a breach of Article 30 could result in a right to restitution of monies illegally paid to a public authority. He could see no difference between a claim for damages and a claim for restitution for breach of Article 30.

### Correctness of Bourgoin in the light of the Francovich decision

9–020    The *Bourgoin* case was eventually settled out of court and there is therefore no clear authority in the U.K. for suggesting that damages would be available to an injured party for an infringement of Article 30. However, the correctness of the *Bourgoin* decision is very much in doubt[40] as a result of the European Court's decision in Case C–6/90, *Francovich* v. *Italian Republic*[41] discussed in detail at paragraphs 8–008 *et seq.* above.

It is significant that the Advocate General in *Francovich* took the view that there was "no crucial difference between proceedings for repayment and proceedings for calims for damages, because in both cases it is a question of correcting a wrong caused by an infringement of Community law."[42]

This reasoning by Advocate General Mischo supports that of Oliver L.J. (dissenting) in *Bourgoin*[43] that there is no difference between a claim for damages and a claim for restitution for a breach of Article 30. The fact that Article 30 is addressed to Member States and not to individuals did not, per Oliver L.J. alter the private nature of the right as it remained a right personal to each individual which the U.K. had a duty to protect.[44] He therefore held that a breach of Article 30 did amount to a

---

[37] Arrowsmith, *Civil Liability and Public Authorities* (1992), p. 253 and see discussion at paras. 8–013 *et seq.* above.
[38] As confirmed in the European Court desicion of *Volpi, op. cit.*, n. 31.
[39] Case 106/77, *Simmenthal*: [1978] E.C.R. 629, [1978] 3 C.M.L.R. 263.
[40] See, for example, dicta of Lord Goff in *Kirklees* v. *Wickes* [1992] 3 All E.R. 717 (H.L.) discussed further at para. 9–042 below.
[41] Case C–6/90, *Francovich*: [1991] I E.C.R. 5357, [1993] 2 C.M.L.R. 66.
[42] *Francovich: ibid.*, p. 16, para. 41.
[43] *Ibid.*
[44] See Brearley, "Remedies in Domestic Courts for Breach of E.C. Laws" (November 21, 1990) No. 42 *Gazette* 24 at p. 26.

breach of statutory duty which in private law gave an individual the right to claim damages. This statutory duty arises by virtue of Article 30 and section 2(1) of the European Communities Act 1972 (as amended).

*Francovich* establishes the existence of a right to compensation which must be provided in national law for relevant breaches of Community law. This is to be regarded as a specific remedy which must be made available for a certain kind of State default in which the directly effective nature of relevant Community provision is not essential. The conditions which must be satisfied in order to establish the State's liability have been discussed at paragraph 8–010 above. However, it is argued by Ross[45] that *Francovich* only *adds* a specific Community law remedy to the existing duty on Member States (and by extension, national courts) to apply, (and, where necessary to create) adequate national remedies.[46]

It is persuasively argued by a number of writers[47] that *Bourgoin* is no longer correct law in the light of the ruling in *Francovich*. In particular, the judgment in *Francovich* emphasises that rights under Community law are *sui generis* and are derived from the new legal order created by the Treaty (as amended by the Treaty on European Union). Therefore, their effective protection includes, in appropriate circumstances, a right to compensation from a defaulting Member State.[48] The reasoning in *Bourgoin*, on the other hand, was very much based on the pre-*Francovich* philosophy of looking at "analogous" rights under national law and the fact that there is no right to damages for breach of those national rights, under national law. In particular, the view that national rights were adequately safeguarded by the availability of judicial review and also that it is sufficient for a directly effective right under Community law to receive the same, but no greater, protection than that afforded to national law rights, are all issues which Sharpston argues[49] are no longer correct law, following *Francovich*.

The English courts will have the opportunity of reconsidering the position regarding damages against the government, following the reference by the Queen's Bench Division of the High Court in Case C–48/93, *R. v. Secretary of State for Transport, ex parte Factortame Ltd., (Factortame (No. 3)),*[50] in which the plaintiff Spanish fishermen, having established in earlier proceedings in *Factortame (No. 1)*[51] that a U.K. statute infringed directly effective Treaty provisions, now seek to recover damages for their ensuing loss.

---

[45] Ross, *op. cit.*, n. 25, p. 61.

[46] Ross, *ibid.*, p. 72.

[47] See, for example, Sharpston, *Interim and Substantive Relief in Claims under Community Law* (1993), p. 69 and Ross, *op. cit.*, n. 25, pp. 60 *et seq.*

[48] Sharpston, *ibid.*, p. 69.

[49] *Ibid.*

[50] Case C–48/93, *R. v. Secretary of State for Transport, ex p. Factortame Ltd. (Factortame No. 3)*: not yet reported.

[51] *R. v. Secretary of State for Transport, ex p. Factortame Ltd. (No. 1)* [1990] 2 A.C. 85, discussed at para. 3–013 above.

*Claim for damages against the State as a right sui generis*

**9–021**   It is suggested by Ross[52] that there remains much to be done in consolidating "a scheme of Community law remedies to complement the solid base of existing *sui generis* rights." He suggests that a claim for damages brought by way of judicial review against the State and based in English law on a breach of statutory duty may simply be started by the issue of a writ for damages. He argues that such an action should not be struck out by a court as an abuse of process because, for instance, it has not been started as an application for judicial review. In other words, the public/private distinction and/or the common law/equity distinctions made by English law should not become an obstacle for the effective enjoyment of Community law rights, which are required to be protected in English law by virtue of Article 5 of the E.C. Treaty.[53] One practical advantage of proceeding by way of a writ, is that is avoids the short time limits in which judicial review is available, as well as providing more extensive rights to discovery.[54] It has also been suggested by Usher[55] that failure by a State to apply any binding Community obligations should be classified as a new tort in English law of "breach of a Community obligation." However, in *Bourgoin*[56] the Court of Appeal decided that the formulation of an "innominate tort" as a cause of action is obsolete and it is more likely that the established cause of action is that for breach of statutory duty.

Part of the importance of *Francovich* is that it gives rise to an individual right to damages against the State even though the relevant provisions of Community law may not be directly effective. The circumstances in which the three conditions laid down in *Francovich*[57] apply remain to be tested in future litigation. One possibility, which has been put forward by Ross[58] is in respect of unlawful State aids. Under the E.C. Treaty, the grant of any aid by a Member State or through State resources "in any form whatsoever" which distorts competition within the E.C. and which is not regarded as "compatible" (under Article 92(2) or (3)) is unlawful.[59] According to the provisions of the Treaty, there is an obligation on Member States to notify the granting of aid. It is suggested by Ross[60] that a business competitor who is disadvantaged by the payment of an unlawful State aid to a competitor which had not been notified, may be able to seek redress against the State in a national court and claim damages, on the basis of *Francovich*. The difficulty is, that an

---

[52] Ross, "Beyond *Francovich*" (1993) M.L.R. 55 at p. 69.
[53] Ross, *ibid.*, p. 69.
[54] *Ibid.*
[55] Usher, "The Imposition of Sanctions for Breaches of Community Law", F.I.D.E. XV Congress, "La sanction des infractions au droit Communautaire", (Associação Portuguesa de Direito Europeu) September 1992.
[56] *Op. cit.*, n. 27.
[57] See detailed discussion at para. 8-010 above.
[58] *Op. cit.*, n. 52, pp. 64 *et seq.*
[59] See generally Schina, *State Aids under the EEC Treaty* (1987).
[60] *Op. cit.*, n. 52, p. 65.

aid is not rendered "incompatible with the Treaty and unlawful merely because of its non-notification."[61] This principle emerges from Case 301/87, *France* v. *Commission*,[62] also referred to as *Boussac*. Nevertheless, the Court has stated that individuals still have rights which may be protected in such a case.[63] Ross argues that it may be possible to obtain damages against the State for non-notification of a State aid without undermining the fact that the relevant Treaty provisions may not be directly effective, *i.e.* without affecting the position that the actual review concerning the compatibility of aids with the Common Market can only be undertaken by the Commission at Community level. There is authority that damages may be available in English law for breach of the notification required by Article 93(3) in the judgment of Woolf J. in *R.* v. *Attorney General, ex parte ICI.*[64]

Other instances when a *Francovich*-type liability may arise have also been suggested by Helena Smith,[65] for example in relation to unlawful intervention by a Member State under Article 9(8) and 21(3) of the Merger Regulation.[66] The *Francovich* judgment therefore opens up a potentially dynamic new option for obtaining compensation from the State, for parties who would have benefited if Community law (notably in the form of directives) had been correctly implemented.

## Misfeasance in public office

In *Bourgoin*[67] the Court of Appeal suggested that an alternative cause of **9–022** action for which damages are available against the State for a breach of Community law, is the tort of "misfeasance in public office." This should be regarded as an "additional" cause of action to either a *sui generis* right to damages for breach of Community law or a breach of a statutory duty imposed by Community law.[68] Misfeasance in public office is established by showing that the relevant government official was aware that he or she was acting in breach of Treaty obligations and that the action could, and subsequently did, injure the plaintiff. Malice or an intention to harm the plaintiff is not an essential ingredient of this tort.[69]

---

[61] Ross, *op. cit.*, n. 52.
[62] Case C–301/87, *France* v. *Commission*: [1990] I E.C.R 307.
[63] See, for example, Case C–354/90, *Fédération Nationale du Commerce Extérieur des Produits Alimentaires* v. *France*: judgment of November 21, 1991 and see also Case C–294/90, *British Aerospace Plc and Rover Group Holdings Plc* v. *Commission*: [1991] I E.C.R. 493, [1992] 1 C.M.L.R. 853.
[64] *R.* v. *Attorney General, ex p. ICI* [1985] 1 C.M.L.R. 588 at 608.
[65] Smith, "The *Francovich* Case: State Liability and the Individual's Right to Damages" (1992) 3 E.C.L.R. 129.
[66] Council Regulation 4064/89, [1990] O.J. L257 and see discussion at para. 8–011 above.
[67] *Bourgoin*: *op. cit.*, n. 27.
[68] See Ellis, "The Enforcement of EEC Law in the Courts of the Member States: What Does Direct Effect Really Mean?" in *Droit Sans Frontiers* (Hand and McBride ed., 1991), 265 at p. 270.
[69] See Brealey, "Remedies in Domestic Courts for Breach of E.C. Law" (November 21, 1990) 42 *Gazette* 24 at p. 27 and Oliver, "Enforcing Community Rights in the English Courts" (1987) M.L.R. 881 at p. 901.

However, if malice or an intention to damage the plaintiff can in fact be shown this will establish misfeasance in public office.[70]

In *Bourgoin* the Court of Appeal unanimously approved Mann J., at first instance where he concluded that the tort could be established either by showing malice toward the plaintiff or knowledge that a measure was *ultra vires*. It is arguable that misfeasance in public office may also be established by showing the commission of a recognised tort such as trespass, false imprisonment or negligence.[71] In *Bourgoin* the Minister conceded for the purposes of the preliminary issue that he knew his actions breached Article 30 and that the revocation of licences would damage the business of the French turkey procedures.[72]

As far as the question of establishing "knowledge of the breach" is concerned, it is argued by Ward[73] that this should include situations where either the European Commission has given strongly-worded advice to that effect, or where the acts in question have been held to violate Community law in an action in the European Court brought by a Member State (under Article 170 of the E.C. Treaty) or the Commission (under Article 169 of the E.C. Treaty).

However, in *Racz* v. *Home Office*,[74] it was held by Mr Justice Ebsworth that the Home Office could not be vicariously liable for an employee's misfeasance in public office because the tort involved the deliberate abuse of power which carried the employee outside the scope of his employment. In the present case, the plaintiff's claim arose through an alleged incident while he was a prisoner on remand. (No issue was raised that an action would lie against the individual prison officer or officers, but they had not been sued.) Misfeasance in public office was therefore held not to be a cause of action against the Home Office in a claim for vicarious liability and damages for such a tort. The case of *R.* v. *Deputy Governor of Parkhurst Prison, ex parte Hague*[75] was referred to. Although *Racz* did not involve a point of Community law, it could severly limit the effectiveness of this possible cause of action against the State for damages.

The precise nature of the tort of misfeasance in public office remains unclear and neither is it clear whether it applies in U.K. law to all Treaty articles which are addressed to Member States or just to Article 30. If it is applicable at all, there seems to be no reason why it should not have a more general effect. In any event, the *Francovich* case suggests that liability is not based on the state of mind of those responsible but in terms of Community obligations under Article 5 of the E.C. Treaty, to make good the illegal consequences of a breach of Community law.[76]

---

[70] See *Jones* v. *Swansea City Council*, (H.L.) [1990] 3 All E.R. 737, judgment of Lord Lawry at p. 741.

[71] See Wade, *Administrative Law* (1988), 6th ed. p. 782.

[72] See *Bourgoin, op. cit.*, n. 27, p. 587.

[73] Ward, "Government Liability in the U.K. for Breach of Individual Rights in European Community Law" (1990) Vol. 19 *Anglo-American Law Review* 1 at p. 34.

[74] *Racz* v. *Home Office: T.L.R.* November 25, 1992.

[75] [1991] 3 W.L.R. 340.

[76] See J.A. Usher, "The Imposition of Sanctions for Breaches of Community Law", F.I.D.E. XV Congress, *op. cit.*, n. 55, and discussion at paras. 8–009 *et seq.* above.

It is pointed out by Oliver[77] that in the *Bourgoin* case the Court of Appeal did not consider whether, irrespective of any tort of misfeasance, the principle of effectiveness of Community law requires damages to be available for any delay by the authorities in implementing a judgment of the Court. As already mentioned above, the date of the European Court's judgment in June 1982 was not given effect to in the U.K. until November 1982, which was too late for the import of turkeys for the 1982 Christmas season as well.

## Breach of a duty of care (negligence)

Reliance on negligence as a cause of action was expressly rejected in **9–023** *Bourgoin*. However, in *Cato* v. *Minister of Agriculture, Fisheries and Food*[78] an action was brought for negligent misstatement and it was established that a duty of care was owed, but there was found to be no breach. However, it is suggested by Lewis[79] that it would be difficult for an individual to succeed on this (negligence) ground in the light of the current approach to analogous situations in domestic law. For example, in *Rowling* v. *Takaro Properties Ltd.*[80] a decision of the Privy Council on appeal from the Attorney General of New Zealand, the question arose as to whether the Minister owed a duty of care to te appellant company in construing relevant legislation correctly, when considering and deciding on the company's application for consent to issue shares to a foreign investor. Lord Keith of Kinkel stated *per curiam* that whether a duty of care should be imposed is a pragmatic question but various factors indicated against it including: (a) the availability of judicial review to correct an error of law, which means that the only effect of a negligent decision will be delay; (b) the fact that an error of law or misconstruction of a statute will only rarely amount to negligence; (c) the danger of inducing overcaution in civil servants and consequent delay; and (d) the difficulty of identifying a particular case in which the minister is under a duty to seek legal advice.[81]

Oliver[82] suggests, however, that the courts could recognise a form of negligence action for breach of Article 30 when the authorities act unreasonably or in bad faith. Such a remedy would involve arguing that a duty of care was owed to importers. It would be equivalent to an action for breach of statutory duty, without strict liability. There is some support for this argument in the Opinion of the Advocate General in *Francovich*, where he suggests[83] that the failure to transpose a directive constitutes an infringement of Articles 5 and 189 of the Treaty and that this is "an unlawful act, *equivalent to negligence*" (emphasis added), which

---

[77] Oliver, "Enforcing Community Rights in the English Courts" (1987) M.L.R. 881 at 885.
[78] *Cato* v. *Minister of Agriculture, Fisheries and Food* [1989] 3 C.M.L.R. 513.
[79] Lewis, *Judicial Remedies in Public Law* (1993), p. 468.
[80] *Rowling* v. *Takaro Properties Ltd.* [1988] A.C. 475, [1988] 1 All E.R. 163.
[81] *Ibid.*, [1993] 1 All E.R. 163 at pp. 172 *et seq.*
[82] Oliver, "Enforcing Community Rights in the English Courts" (1987) M.L.R. 881.
[83] *Francovich: op. cit.*, n. 41, see para. 68.

has to be rectified by the State when it has caused damage to an individual.

In *Lonrho Plc* v. *Tebbit and Another*[84] Lonrho brought an action in negligence against Mr Tebbit as the former Secretary of State and the DTI, claiming that the Minister owed a duty of care in private law as a result of exercising his public law powers. Lonrho claimed that because of the Minister's dilatoriness and breach of duty it had lost the opportunity to make a rival takeover bid for House of Fraser and that it should be compensated in damages. Lonrho succeeded in the Court of Appeal in resisting an application by the defendants to have the claim struck out as an abuse of process, and the issues fall to be determined on the full facts, at a trial. The nature of any private law duty will have to be defined at that time. However, this action may have been discontinued. The Court of Appeal confirmed that the plaintiff could assert in an action started by writ, a private law right arising out of a background in public law as in *Roy* v. *Kingston and Chelsea and Westminster FPC*.[85] In Case 4/78, *Re an Absence in Germany*[86] it was suggested by the then National Insurance Commissioner that an action for damages would lie against the Department of Employment for breach of duty, and possibly in negligence, by its local officers in giving incorrect advice about a Community regulation concerning social security for migrant workers.

Other existing torts, described as "economic torts" such as conspiracy, intimidation, inducing breach of contract, interfering with trade or business and interference with statutory duties (including duties improved by Community law) may also be pleaded in actions for damages against the State. However, they provide no significant advantage over the tort of misfeasance in actions against public bodies.[87]

## THE LEVEL OF DAMAGES AGAINST "THE STATE"

9–024    Member States are obliged to provide remedies and procedures whereby "directly effective" Community law can be enforced in the national legal system. Otherwise, Community law could be totally ineffective and unenforceable. General principles of Community law relating to remedies have been discussed in Chapter 8, above.

### Issues raised in the Marshall litigation

9–025    The question arises as to what level of damages should be available for a breach of Community law. In Case 152/84, *Marshall (No. 1)*[88] the applicant Miss Marshall was held by the European Court of Justice in

---

[84] [1992] 4 All E.R. 280.
[85] [1992] 2 W.L.R. 239.
[86] Decision C.U. 4/78, *Re an Absence in Germany*: [1978] 2 C.M.L.R. 603.
[87] See further, Lewis, *op. cit.*, n. 79, p. 468. For discussion of issues such as causation and remoteness of damage in private law actions see further para. 10–014 below.
[88] Case 152/84, *Marshall (No. 1)*: [1986] E.C.R. 723, [1986] 1 C.M.L.R. 688.

February 1986 to have been the victim of unlawful sex discrimination, following her enforced discriminatory retirement, contrary to Community law. Upon receiving the European Court's decision, the Court of Appeal (having allowed her appeal) remitted her application back to the Industrial Tribunal, to consider the question of remedy. At the relevant time, the U.K. statutory maximum for compensation in such cases was £6,250. The Industrial Tribunal[89] awarded Miss Marshall £19,405 compensation, less £6,250 she had already received from the employers. The Tribunal applied the ruling of the ECJ in Case 14/83, *Von Colson*[90] where the ECJ held that damages must be "adequate in relation to the damage sustained and therefore amount to more than purely nominal compensation."

The Tribunal held that the statutory limit on compensation (set by section 65(2) of the Sex Discrimination Act) did not provide an "adequate remedy" as required by Article 6 of the EEC Equal Treatment Directive,[91] and as interpreted by the European Court in *Von Colson*. Article 6 of the Directive provides that:

"Member States shall introduce into their national legal system such measures as are necessary to enable all persons who consider themselves wronged by failure to apply to them the principle of equal treatment within the meaning of Article 3(1)(5) to pursue their claims by judicial process after possible recourse to other competent authorities."

The Tribunal accordingly held that the U.K. government was in breach of Article 6 of the Equal Treatment Directive, which requires all Member States to introduce into their national legal systems "such measures as are necessary to enable all persons who consider themselves wronged . . . to pursue their claims by judicial process." It was held that the judicial process must include an adequate remedy and therefore Miss Marshall, as an employee of the State, was entitled to rely upon Article 6 in a complaint before the Industrial Tribunal. Consequently, the Tribunal ignored the statutory limit on compensation under the Sex Discrimination Act.

The Tribunal also took the view that it was empowered (by section 35a of the Supreme Court Act 1981) to include in the award £7,710 representing interest at the rate of 10 per cent. per annum on the total of Miss Marshall's losses from the date of dismissal in 1980 to the date of its decision. The employers paid, without appealing, the balance of the capital sum awarded but they did appeal against the award of interest of £7,710 and the Employment Appeal Tribunal[92] allowed the appeal and the award was reduced accordingly. The EAT held that Miss Marshall was not entitled to rely upon Article 6 of the Equal Treatment Directive.

---

[89] *Marshall (No. 2)* [1988] I.R.L.R. 325 (Industrial Tribunal), [1988] 3 C.M.L.R. 389.
[90] Case 14/83, *Von Colson*: [1984] E.C.R. 1891.
[91] Council Directive 76/207 on equal treatment: [1975] O.J. L45/19.
[92] *Marshall (No. 2)* [1989] I.R.L.R. 459 (EAT).

It took the view that EEC law established that where a State has provided access to the courts, the remedies are for the State, subject only to the principle of *de minimis*, and that Article 6 has no direct effect. Article 6 did not, in any event, specify any particular remedy for the relevant kind of discrimination which occurred.

Miss Marshall appealed against that decision to the Court of Appeal.[93] The primary issue in the Court of Appeal concerned the power of the Industrial Tribunal to award interest in the special circumstances of the case. However, it also raised the issue of the validity of the limit of section 65(2) of the Act because if that section is valid, as against Miss Marshall, it was a complete answer to her claim to interest. She could only have the maximum of £6,250 and no more. The Court of Appeal therefore gave the respondent employers leave to rely on sub-section 65(2), although that point had not been taken in the respondent's notice of appeal.

### Absence of ambiguity: no duty to adopt purposive construction

9–026    The Court of Appeal held that section 65(2) provided a statutory limit for compensation and was clear and unambiguous. It was therefore necessary to consider whether Article 6 of the EEC Equal Treatment Directive nevertheless overrode the limit on compensation in section 65(2) of the Act. The Court of Appeal considered European Court judgments in *Von Colson*,[94] and *Johnston* v. *Chief Constable of the Royal Ulster Constabulary*.[95] It accepted the decision in *Johnston* in which the European Court made a distinction in relation to Article 6 and direct effect. The Court ruled that Article 6 did have direct effect, *i.e.*, was unconditional and sufficiently precise in respect of the requirement for access to the court for a ruling, but was *not* sufficiently precise and unconditional in respect of what sanctions or remedy had to be provided once proper access to the appropriate court is available.[96] Article 6 was therefore not directly effective and so the only other possibility was to consider whether there was any ambiguity in the national legislation. The Court of Appeal considered whether it would construe the word "damages" in section 65(1)(b) to include interest on the primary sum awarded. In the words of Dillon, L.J.:

> "All that can be awarded under section 65(1)(b) is 'compensation of an amount corresponding to any damages' which could have been awarded on a claim under section 66. But though interest, when included in a sum for which judgment is given, is part of compensation, it is not part of the damages; as a matter of accepted terminology, the damages are the sum on which interest, if awarded is calculated.

---

[93] *Marshall (No. 2)* [1990] I.R.L.R. 481 (C.A.), [1990] 3 C.M.L.R. 425.
[94] *Op. cit.*, n. 90.
[95] [1986] I.R.L.R. 263.
[96] See judgment of Lord Justice Butler-Sloss, *op. cit.*, n. 93, p. 486, paras. 47 *et seq.* and Du-Feu and Williams, "The EEC Influence in Sex Discrimination Law" (1991) New L.J. 1220 at p. 1221.

There is no ambiguity, in my judgment, in section 65(1)(b), and it is not possible for us by mere construction to extend the word 'damages' to include interest on the primary sum awarded."[97]

## Arguments based on estoppel

The Court of Appeal also considered whether it was possible for the **9–027** national court, by an application of the estoppel principle which was used by the European Court in Miss Marshall's case, to override section 6(4) of the Act by treating section 65(1)(b) as a broad power to award compensation to a claimant, disregarding the limitation to damages actually stated in the section.

Lord Justice Butler-Sloss adopted the reasoning of Lord Templeman in *Duke* v. *GEC Reliance Systems Limited*[98] and adopted Lord Templeman's words as applying equally to section 65(2):

". . . But the construction of a British Act of Parliament is a matter of judgment to be determined by British courts and to be derived from the language of the legislation considered in the light of the circumstances prevailing at the date of enactment . . . section 2(4) of the European Communities Act 1972 does not in my opinion enable or constrain a British court to distort the meaning of a British statute in order to enforce against an individual a Community Directive which has no direct effect between individuals."

She therefore concluded that even though it was arguable that the limit of allowable compensation under the Act is inadequate and consequently that the U.K. may not have sufficiently complied with Article 6, since that Article was not directly effective, neither the limit on compensation imposed by section 65(2) nor the absence of power in an Industrial Tribunal to award interest in a sex discrimination case could be treated as overruled by the Directive itself.

However, Lord Justice Dillon, dissenting, took the view that the principle of estoppel used by the European Court in Miss Marshall's case to override section 6(4) of the Sex Discrimination Act, and which was reaffirmed in *Foster* v. *British Gas Plc*,[99] could be applied so as to treat section 65(1)(b) as a broad power to award compensation to a claimant, thereby disregarding the limitation actually stated in the section which is not in conformity with Article 6 of the Directive. He said that:

"As the shortfall in the compensation under the Act is due to the national State's failure to perform its obligations under the Directive, the respondents cannot rely on the shortfall as mandatory as against Miss Marshall. The wording of section 5(1)(b) may be unambiguous as it stands, but so is the wording of section 6(4). The estoppel principle is not founded on ambiguity in the national statute."[1]

---

[97] *Marshall (No. 2): op. cit.*, n. 93, p. 484 (C.A.).
[98] [1988] I.R.L.R. 118 at p. 122, para. 29.
[99] *Foster* v. *British Gas Plc* [1990] I.R.L.R. 353.
[1] *Marshall (No. 2): op. cit.*, n. 93, p. 485 (C.A.).

In view of Lord Justice Dillon, the U.K. has an obligation under Article 6 to ensure that compensation is adequate in relation to the damage sustained. As the employers were to be treated as representatives of the State, they could not plead that the machinery for compensation was inadequate because of the State's own failure to perform the obligations required by Article 6.

### Reference of Marshall (No. 2) to the European Court

9–028    The case was referred to the European Court which confirmed in its judgment (discussed further below at paragraphs 9–030 et seq.) that financial compensation for discrimination had to be adequate in that it had to enable the loss and damage sustained as a result of a discriminatory dismissal to be made good in full, including the award of interest.[2] This has important implications since awards with interest could produce substantial sums even if, under U.K. law, the interest on Tribunal awards is limited to run only from the date of the Tribunal's decision on the award.[3] Before the decision in *Marshall (No. 2)* it was arguable that an alternative option would have been for Miss Marshall to bring an action in damages against the *State* for failue to implement Article 6 on the basis of the ECJ's ruling in Case C–6/90, *Francovich* v. *Italian Republic*.[4] However, it was still not clear from *Francovich* what the national courts should do where, as in *Marshall (No. 2)*, there *is* a remedy in national law but its effectiveness is limited or inadequate.[5] The decision in *Marshall (No. 2)* makes the use of this option unnecessary.

The difficulty in *Marshall* was that the overall amount of damages is clearly and unambiguously fixed by statute and if the statute is to be interpreted in accordance with the Directive, the statutory limitation would have to be overriden and a subordinate provision read in its place to the effect that compensation must be adequate to remedy the relevant discrimination.[6] It was unclear whether the European Court's decision in Case C–106/89, *Marleasing* v. *La Comercial*[7] required national courts to go this far (if a relevant provision of a directive is *not* directly effective) and the clarification of the ECJ was therefore required. This is particularly so in view of the traditional view of British courts that their role is limited to the enforcement of parliamentary will.[8] The clarification

---

[2] Case 271/91, *Marshall (No. 2)*: [1993] 3 C.M.L.R. 293 (not yet reported in the E.C.R.).

[3] Du-Feu and Williams, *op. cit.*, n. 96, p. 1228. See also, Moore, " Compensation for Discrimination" (1993) 18 E.L.Rev. 533 at p. 540, and further at para. 9–031 below, the discussion of the Court's ruling on the award of interest and the Sex Discrimination and Equal Pay (Remedies) Regulations 1993 (S.I. 1993 No. 2798), Reg. 10.

[4] de Búrca, "Giving Effect to European Community Directives" (1992) M.L.R. 215 at p. 238 and see further paras. 8–008 *et seq.* above.

[5] *The Times*, December 1, 1992, p. 33.

[6] de Búrca, *op. cit.*, p. 235. See generally, Moore, *op. cit.*, n. 3; Wooldridge and D'Sa, "Damages for Breaches of Community Directives: the Decision in Marshall (No. 2)" (1993) 4 E.B.L.Rev. 255 to 258.

[7] Case 106/89, *Marleasing*: [1990] I E.C.R. 135, [1992] 1 C.M.L.R. 305 discussed at para. 6–004 above.

[8] de Búrca, *op. cit.*, n. 4, p. 238.

of these issues, in the Court's judgment in *Marshall (No. 2)*, may necessitate a reassessment of the developing constitutional role of U.K. courts in the context of E.C. law in order to comply with the obligations of E.C. membership.[9]

## *Opinion of Advocate General Van Gerven in Marshall (No. 2)*

In his opinion in *Marshall (No. 2)*,[10] Advocate General Van Gerven **9–029** rejected the arguments of the U.K. and Irish governments that the court should restrict itself to ruling on the question of simply the interest payable on the maximum compensation award. He took the view that the court should also consider the much wider point of a general compensation limit.

In his opinion Article 6 of the Directive *was* directly effective as against a public body of a Member State in relation to a failure to embody an adequate system of sanctions, contrary to the purpose of the Equal Treatment Directive[11] and Article 6 thereof. He did not regard the imposition of an upper limit in national legislation to be automatically considered a failure to implement Article 6 of the Directive. However, such an upper limit was incompatible, in his view, with Article 6 if it had the result that the compensation (taking account of all its components, including "compensatory interest"), was not adequate in relation to the damage sustained. These components included loss of physical assets (*damnum emergens*), loss of income (*lucrum cessans*), moral damage (injury to feelings) and damage due to effluxion of time. Each component must be taken into account by national courts in assessing whether the compensation is adequate to the damage.[12]

He defined "compensatory interest" as a component of the total compensation for the unlawful conduct which depended on the extent to which the court takes account of damage *up until* the date of its judgment. "Legal interest," on the other hand, begins to run as from the date of the judgment in which the first court determined the amount of compensation (insofar as that judgment is subsequently definitively confirmed).[13] In his view, "legal interest" was also part of the judicial protection required by the requirement of Article 6 of the Equal Treatment Directive.

In conclusion, the Advocate General suggested that the principle of adequacy of compensation was a directly effective concept of Community law and therefore binding on national courts. However, in order to reach this conclusion he accepted that on the face of it, the court's previous ruling in *Johnston* appeared to deny direct effect to Article 6.[14] However,

---

[9] de Búrca, *ibid.*, p. 240. See also discussion at para. 9–008 above.
[10] Case C–271/91, *M H Marshall* v. *Southampton and South-West Hampshire Area Health Authority*: [1993] 3 C.M.L.R. 293 (not yet reported in E.C.R.).
[11] Equal Treatment Directive, *op. cit.*, n. 91.
[12] Opinion of A.G. Gerven, *Marshall (No. 2)*, *op. cit.*, n. 10, para. 18.
[13] *Ibid.*, para. 23.
[14] *Ibid.*, para. 6.

he took the view that the Court's subsequent case law on direct effect had defined the relevant principle sufficiently precisely to justify the opposite conclusion. He concluded that this would "further the development of Community law, since it would then no longer depend on national interpretation rules whether the national court was empowered to interpret its national law in conformity with Community law."[15]

### Judgment ot the European Court in Marshall (No. 2): upper statutory limit unlawful

**9–030**   The final judgment of the Court in *Marshall (No. 2)* effectively confirmed the views of the Advocate General by making clear that Article 6 was directly effective in relation to the requirement to impose adequate sanctions against the State or public authorities. The decision therefore represents an evolution of the jurisprudence of the Court since the *Johnston* case. It makes clear that Article 6 puts Member States under a duty to take the necessary measures to enable all persons wronged by discrimination to prove their claims by judicial process. This obligation implied that the measures in question should be sufficiently effective to achieve the objective of the Equal Treatment Directive and should be capable of being effectively relied on by the persons concerned before national courts. In relation to Article 5(1) of the Directive, a situation of equality could not be restored without either reinstating the victim of discrimination or, alternatively, granting financial compensation for the loss and damage sustained. Where financial compensation was the recourse adopted to achieve the above objective, it had to be adequate in that it had to enable the loss and damage actually sustained as a result of the discriminatory dismissal to be made good in full in accordance with the applicable national rules. This reasoning also meant that the fixing of an upper statutory limit as compensation of the kind at issue could not, by definition, constitute proper implementation of Article 6 since it limited the amount of compensation *a priori* to a level which was not necessarily consistent with the requirement of ensuring adequate reparation for the loss and damage sustained as a result of discriminatory dismissal.

### Compensatory and legal interest

**9–031**   The ECJ was also asked by the House of Lords whether Article 6 required that compensation should include an award of interest on the principal amount, from the date of discrimination to the date when compensation was paid. The Court's reply was that full compensation for the loss and damage:

> "cannot leave out of account factors, such as the effluxion of time, which might in fact reduce its value. The award of interest, in accordance with the applicable national rules, was therefore to be

---

[15] *Ibid.*, para. 11.

regarded as an essential component of compensation for the purposes of restoring real equality of treatment." (Paragraph 31 of the judgment.)

In his Opinion the Advocate General Van Gerven had made it clear that adequate compensation included the payment of both "compensatory interest," *i.e.*, interest accruing up until the time of the Tribunal's decision, as well as "legal interest," which runs from the date of the judgment until payment of the award. Although the judgment of the Court does not distinguish between the two kinds of interest referred to above, it is arguably intended to include both, as part of the compensation to be awarded. This is particularly so as in *Marshall* the sum in despute of £7,710 related to the former category, *i.e.*, to interest accruing between the date of the unlawful discrimination and the date of the Industrial Tribunal's decision of June 21, 1988. The Court certainly regarded the award of interest to be essential for the purposes of "restoring real equality of treatment" and this arguably applies to "compensatory interest." It may be, however, that the issue of the determination of the award of interest is to be regarded as a matter of fact and therefore a matter to be determined by the national court.

Following the judgment of the ECJ in *Marshall (No. 2)*, the Sex Discrimination Equal Pay (Remedies) Regulations 1993[15a] were enacted, and come into force on November 22, 1993. Regulation 2 repeals s. 65(2) of the Sex Discrimination Act 1975, which provided that an award of compensation under Part II of the Act could not exceed a specified sum. The remaining provisions of the regulations relate to cases where an industrial tribunal makes "an award under the sex discrimination legislation", *i.e.* either an award under the Equal Pay Act 1970 of arrears of remuneration or damages, or an award under the Sex Discrimination Act 1975, s. 65(1)(b) for payment of compensation. Regulation 3 provides for the award to include a sum by way of interest, which accrues from day-to-day at specified rates. Regulations 5 to 7 include rules for the calculation of that interest. Under Regulation 7(1), subject to sub-paragraphs 2 and 3 of that regulation, in the case of any sum for injury to feelings, interest shall be for the period beginning on the date of the contravention or act of discrimination complained of and ending on the "day of calculation", *i.e.* the day on which the amount of interest is calculated by the tribunal (which is presumably likely to be the date of the award). In the case of all other sums of damages or compensation in the award (other than any sum referred to in Regulation 6), and all arrears of remuneration, interest shall be for the period beginning on the "mid-point date" and ending on the day of calculation. The "mid-point date" means the date halfway through the period beginning on the date of the contravention or act of discrimination complained of and ending on the day on which interest is calculated. It is doubtful whether this latter provision constitutes a restoration of real equality of treatment

---

[15a] S.I. 1993 No. 2798.

envisaged by the Court since it does not provide for compensatory interest to run from the date of the actual discrimination/contravention complained of. The tribunal does, however, have the power under Regulation 7(3) to depart from the calculation rules where it is of the opinion that there are exceptional circumstances which have the effect that serious injustice would be done, if the rules were applied.

In addition, Regulation 10 alters the effect of the Industrial Tribunal's (Interest) Order 1990[15b] so that an award of interest under the sex discrimination legislation will begin to accrue from the day after the day on which the decision of the tribunal is sent to the parties (and not, as before, from a date 42 days later). However, no interest will be payable under the order in respect of the period after the award if the full amount of the award is paid to the complainant within 14 days of the sending out of the decision (Regulation 10(b)).

### Further implications of Marshall (No. 2)

9–032    The Court's judgment makes it clear that a person injured as a result of discriminatory dismissal may rely on Article 6 of the Directive, as against an authority of the State acting in its capacity as an employer, in order to set aside a provision of national law which sets a statutory upper limit on the amount of compensation recoverable by way of reparation. Although the *Marshall (No. 2)* case is concerned with the adequacy of compensation against the State for breach of the Equal Treatment Directive, its implications may be more far-reaching in relation to the level of compensation which may be payable by the State for breaches of *other* directly effective Community law. The decision suggests a progressive development in the jurisprudence of the Court in favour of adequate compensation for breaches by the State of Community law in situations when the relevant provisions were intended for the benefit of individuals. It appears therefore to support the reasoning employed in the Court's previous ruling in *Francovich* (discussed in detail at paragraphs 8–008 *et seq.*, above. In this connection, the outcome of the reference to the ECJ in *Factortame (No. 3)* (discussed at paragraph 8–011, above) in which damages have been claimed against the U.K. government for breach of directly effective Treaty provisions, will be of particular interest. In the interim, the decision in *Marshall (No. 2)* will have the effect of making non-implementation of Community rules relating to sex discrimination very costly for the government, particularly since the Court has not attempted to limit the effect of its decision to the date of its judgment, as for example in the *Barber* case (discussed at paragraph 4–008, above).

## INTERIM RELIEF AGAINST "THE STATE"

### Claims based on invalidity of national law

9–033    Under section 37 of the Supreme Court Act 1981, the High Court has the power, in actions begun by writ, to grant injunctions (whether

---

[15b] S.I. 1990 No. 479.

interlocutory or final). Under section 31 of the Act, the remedy of an injunction is also available where the application is made by way of judicial review. See discussion at paragraph 9–001, above. Interim relief by way of an injunction is also available in judicial review proceedings. This is confirmed by R.S.C., Order 53, rule 1(10)(b) and also by the Court of Appeal decision in *R.* v. *Kensington and Chelsea Royal London Borough Council, ex parte Hammell.*[16] However, the general principle in *O'Reilly* v. *Mackman* discussed at paragraphs 9–003 *et seq.* applies. This means that an injunction is only available in judicial review proceedings if the matter is a public law one.

## Interim injunctions against the Crown: the Factortame litigation

As a matter of English law, interim injunctions were not, at the time **9–034** *Factortame (No. 1)* was decided, available against the Crown.[17] In *Factortame (No. 1)*[18] the House of Lords initially *held, inter alia,* that the power to grant an injunction against the Crown under section 31 of the Supreme Court Act 1981 only applies to final, and not interlocutory, injunctions. This view was radically altered by the judgment of the European Court following an Article 177 reference for a preliminary ruling on this question. The European Court *held* that:[19]

"It was for the national courts in application of the principle of co-operation laid down in Article 5 of the Treaty, to ensure the legal protection which persons derived from the direct effect of provisions of Community law. Therefore, any provisions or practice of a national legal system which could impair the effectiveness of Community law by withholding from the national court the power to set aside national provisions that prevented Community law from having full effect, was incompatible with Community law."

Accordingly, the rule of national law which precluded the granting of interim relief had to be set aside. The House of Lords gave effect to the European Court's ruling in 1990 by suspending the registration system for shipping vessels under the Merchant Shipping Act 1988.[20]

As a result, U.K. courts now have jurisdiction to grant interim relief against the Crown where Community rights are involved. This is of commercial significance since referrals to the European Court may not be heard for two years or more. The implications were well illustrated in *Factortame* in that the litigants would have been faced with the revocation of their licences for commercial fishing and the consequent loss of their livelihood for a considerable period of time. In fact, if it were not

---

[16] [1989] 2 W.L.R. 90.
[17] *R.* v. *Secretary of State for Transport, ex p. Factortame Ltd. (No. 1)* [1990] 2 A.C. 85. This view was reversed by the House of Lords in *Re M: The Independant,* July 28, 1993.
[18] *Factortame (No. 1), op. cit.*
[19] C–213/89, *R.* v. *Secretary of State for Transport, ex p. Factortame Limited and Others (No. 2):* [1990] I E.C.R. 2433, [1990] 3 C.M.L.R. 1.
[20] *Factortame (No. 2), op. cit.*

for the separate action instituted by the Commission against the U.K. under Article 169 of the EEC Treaty, (which is not amended by the Treaty on European Union), which resulted in interim relief being granted to the Spanish fishermen by the European Court, they would have had no remedy until the main case, brought in the U.K., was finally decided in 1991.

*Conditions for the grant of interim policy: Community law perspective*

9-035    However, in the reference from the House of Lords, the Court did not itself elaborate on the situations when it is appropriate for interim relief to be ordered by the national court. It assumed in its judgment that the preconditions for granting interim relief *as defined by national law* were present. The Advocate General rejected in particular the possibility of an injunction to compel the government or Parliament to enact primary legislation or to adopt a specific measure.[21]

This issue was, however, referred to by the European Commission in it submission in *Factortame*.[22] The Commission submitted that certain matters are to be weighed up by the national courts. First, it considered that the apparent strength of the applicant's case was relevant. However, the Commission took the view that it was not for Community law to determine the criteria for assessing the strength of that case. It pointed out that there were three alternatives. Either the applicant should show a serious issue to be tried (on the authority of the *American Cyanamid Company* v. *Ethicon Limited*),[23] or simply make out a prima facie case, (as required under Article 83(2) of the European Court's Rules of Procedure) or make out a strong prima facie case (on the authority of previous English cases of *De Falco* and *Silvesteri* v. *Crawley Borough Council*[24] and *R.* v. *Kensington and Chelsea Royal London Borough Council, ex parte Hammel*.[25])

Secondly, the Commission referred to the balance of convenience, which includes consideration of urgency, the risk of irreparable damage and the public interest. It suggested that where, as in *Factortame*, the applicant is deprived of his right to carry on his economic activity until the outcome of the main proceedings, great weight must be given to that factor. This was all the more so where, as in *Factortame*, he is likely to go bankrupt as a result.

In conclusion, the Commission suggested that the factors which national courts should give consideration to be summarised as follows:

"In deciding whether to grant interim relief national courts must weigh up the interests involved in each case, without considering

---

[21] See further, Toth, on Case C–213/89, *Factortame* (1990) C.M.L.Rev. 573 at p. 585.
[22] Case C–213/89, *Factortame (No. 2)*, *op. cit.*, n. 19, paras. 72 to 77.
[23] *American Cyanamid* v. *Ethicon* [1975] A.C. 396, [1975] All E.R. 504.
[24] [1990] 1 All E.R. 913 (C.A.).
[25] [1989] 1 All E.R. 1202 (C.A.).

any particular circumstance or set of circumstances as constituting generally an absolute bar to such relief. Moreover, the criteria to be applied by national courts may not be less favourable to the individual than those applying to similar cases relating to national law alone."[26]

The Advocate General Tesauro took the view that it is for the national court to determine whether the preconditions for interim protection are met and that, in the absence of Community harmonisation, those preconditions must be those provided for by the national legal system, with the one proviso that they are not such as to make it impossible in practice "to exercise rights which the national courts have a duty to protect."

For instance, provisions of both national law and Community law are generally presumed to be valid until and unless they are declared invalid in judicial proceedings. However, national law and/or procedure must not have the effect of creating an *irrefutable* presumption that a provision of national law is valid.[27] If such a presumpton were to deny the very possibility of interim relief, this would have the effect of giving greater protection to putative national law rights rather than putative Community rights and would conflict with the general principle of Community law that national law and/or procedure must not afford greater protection to national law rights than to Community rights.[28] On the other hand, this is not to suggest that national courts must always give priority to putative Community law rights but simply that the courts must have jurisdiction to do so if the legal and factual circumstances require it.[29] In the absence of Community rules, it is for national courts to determine whether the preconditions for interim relief are satisfied.

## Conditions for the grant of interim ruling: English law principles

Following the judgment of the European Court in *Factortame (No. 2)*, **9–036** the House of Lords considered whether, on the facts, interim relief should in fact be granted, and the principles of U.K. law which applied. The object of an interlocutory injunction is essentially to preserve the status quo until trial of matters in dispute and it can be granted *ex parte* in an emergency. It is usually negative in form, restraining the defendant from doing some act. It is usual for an undertaking in damages to be given by the plaintiff if he/she eventually loses the case.[30]

The House of Lords held that in determining whether an interlocutory injunction should be granted in the *Factortame* case, the Court should exercise its discretion according to the balance of convenience where it was doubtful whether an adequate remedy in damages to either side

---

[26] *Factortame (No. 2), op. cit.,* n. 19, para. 78.
[27] See Gravells, "Effective Protection of Community Law Rights: Temporary Disapplication of an Act of Parliament" (Summer 1991) *Public Law* 180 at p. 183.
[28] See discussion at para. 8–007 above.
[29] See Gravelles, *op. cit.,* n. 27, p. 183.
[30] See further, *Halsbury Laws of England* (1991) 4th ed., Vol. 20 at para. 804.

would be available. In doing so, the Court should take into account, in particular, the importance of upholding the law of the land in the public interest, bearing in mind the need for stability in society and the duty placed on certain authorities to enforce the law in the public interest. However, the Court should not restrain an apparently authentic law unless it was satisfied, having regard to all the circumstances, that the challenge to its validity was prima facie so firmly based as to justify such an exceptional course being taken. The reasoning applies to cases where, for example, a public authority seeks an interim injunction to restrain some person from acting contrary to the law and that person claims that no such injunction should be granted on the ground that the relevant law is, for some reason, invalid. Alternatively, it applies where an individual litigant seeks an interim injunction to restrain the action of the authority on the same ground.

The leading judgment was given by Lord Goff (with which the House concurred). Lord Goff referred to the guidelines laid down by Lord Diplock in the *American Cyanamid* case,[31] which are to be read in conjunction with section 37 of the Supreme Court Act 1981, under which the Court has power to grant an injunction in all cases in which it appears to it to be just or convenient so to do, and has power to do so on such terms and conditions as it thinks fit. He pointed out that one of the prime purposes of the guidelines established in the *Cyanamid* case was to remove "a fetter" which appeared to have been imposed in certain previous cases, namely, that a party seeking an interlocutory injunction had to establish a prima facie case for substantive relief. It is now clear that it is enough if he/she can show that there is a serious issue to be tried. If he can establish that, then he has, so to speak, crossed the threshold, and the Court can then address itself to the question of whether it is just or convenient to grant an injunction.[32]

However, in a later part of his judgment[33] Lord Goff made reference to the need to assess the measure of the strength of the defendant's attack on what might appear to be an authentic law. He was of the opinion that in such cases as *Factortame* the discretion conferred on the Court cannot be fettered by a rule. He went on to state:

"... I respectfully doubt whether there is any rule that, in cases such as these, a party challenging the validity of the law must (to resist an application for an interim injunction against him, or to obtain an interim injunction restraining the enforcement of the law) show a strong prima facie case that the law is invalid. ... Even so, the Court should not restrain a public authority by interim injunction from enforcing an apparently authentic law unless it is satisfied, having regard to all the circumstances, that the challenge to the validity of the law is, prima facie, so firmly based as to justify so exceptional a course being taken."

---

[31] *American Cyanamid: op. cit.*, n. 23.
[32] *American Cyanamid: ibid.*, p. 118 at paras. d to f.
[33] *American Cyanamid: ibid.*, p. 120 at para. c.

It therefore appears that although Lord Goff did not require the applicant to show a strong prima facie case, it is clear that the strength of the applicant's case was a most material factor in deciding whether or not to grant an injunction.

Returning to the principles in *American Cyanamid*, Lord Goff did not **9–037** consider that in cases such as *Factortame* it was necessary to apply the first stage of Lord Diplock's analysis in *Cyanamid*, namely, consideration of the relevance of the availability of an adequate remedy in damages, either to the plaintiff seeking the injunction or to the defendant, in the event that an injunction is granted against him. Lord Goff took the view that in the present cases damages would not be an adequate remedy, and, in any event, as the law then stood[34] damages were not available against the State in respect of loss suffered as a result of the enforcement of domestic legislation which is incompatible with Community law.[35] Furthermore, an undertaking in damages was not, in his view, an appropriate means of protecting the public interest. In cases such as *Factortame*, Lord Goff noted that it was preferable to go directly to the second stage, namely consideraton of the balance of convenience. He stated that:

> "In this context, particular stress should be placed on the import-ance of upholding the law of the land, in the public interest, bearing in mind the need for stability in our society, and the duty placed on certain authorities to enforce the law in the public interest. This is of itself an important factor to be weighed in the balance when assessing the balance of convenience. So if a public authority seeks to enforce what is on its face the laws of the land, and the person against whom such action is taking challenges the validity of that law, matters of considerable weight have to be put into the balance to outweigh the desirability of enforcing, in the public interest, what is on its face the law, and so to justify the refusal of an interim injunction in favour of the authority, or to render it just or convenient to restrain the authority for the time being from enforcing the law."[36]

In other words where the defendant attacks the validity of what appears to be an authentic law, the measure of the strength of this attack must inevitably call for some consideration in assessing the balance of convenience.

Lord Jauncey of Tullichettle also referred to the *American Cyanamid* case. He referred to the classic statement of Lord Diplock in that case:[37]

> ". . . The use of such expressions as 'a probability', 'a prima facie case', or 'a strong prima facie case' in the context of the exercise of a

---

[34] See *Bourgoin SA* v. *Ministry of Agriculture, Fisheries and Food* [1985] 3 All E.R. 385, discussed further at para. 9–018 above.
[35] See Gravells, *op. cit.*, n. 27, p. 186.
[36] *Factortame (No. 2): op. cit.*, n. 19, p. 119 para. j.
[37] *American Cyanamid: op. cit.*, n. 23, [1977] 1 All E.R. 504 at 510.

discretionary power to grant an interlocutory injunction leads to confusion as to the object sought to be achieved by this form of temporary relief. The court no doubt must be satisfied that the claim is not frivolous or vexatious; in other words, that there is a serious issue to be tried. It is no part of the court's function at this stage of the litigation to try to resolve conflicts of evidence on affidavits as to facts on which the claims of either party may ultimately depend nor to decide difficult questions of law which call for detailed argument and mature consideration. These are matters to be dealt with at the trial."

9–038    However, Lord Jauncey demurred to any suggestion that in no circumstances will it be appropriate to decide questions of law. If the only question of issue between the parties is one of law, it may be possible in many cases, in his view, to decide this at the stage of a contested application of an interim injunction. He was of the view that while the test of "a serious question to be tried" is appropriate to proceedings between private parties, where no presumption favours the position of one party as against the other, it does not follow that the same considerations apply when primary legislation and the public interests are involved.[38]

He went on to suggest that anyone, whether a plaintiff of a defendant, who seeks to challenge the validity of the provisions of an Act of Parliament must at least show a strong prima facie case of incompatibility with Community law. In his view therefore, the presumption in favour of the legislation being challenged made the *American Cyanamid* test of a serious question to be tried inappropriate in a case such as *Factortame*. He did, however, agree that Lord Diplock's approach in *Cyanamid* to the balance of convenience was also applicable in the *Factortame* case.

Lord Bridge of Harwich in his judgment[39] placed some emphasis on the fact that in *Factortame*, if the applicants were to succeed after a refusal of interim relief, the irreparable damage they would have suffered would be very great. On the other hand, he pointed out that if they failed after a grant of interim relief, there would have been a substantial detriment to the public interest resulting from the diversion of a very significant part of the British quota of controlled stocks of fish, from those who sought in law to enjoy it, to others having no right to it. However, it is clear that the likelihood that the Merchant Shipping Act 1988 would be found to violate Community law, led the House of Lords to find that the balance of convenience rested with the applicant. Lord Jauncey, for example, referred to the observations of the President of the European Court in the case brought by the Commission against the U.K. for a declaration that the nationality requirements of section 14 of the Merchant Shipping Act 1988 constituted a failure by the U.K. of its Treaty obligations,[40] and took the view that the applicant had a strong

---

[38] *Factortame (No. 2): op. cit.*, n. 19, p. 123 at para. h.
[39] *Ibid.*, pp. 107 *et seq.*
[40] See Case 246/89 R, *E.C. Commission* v. *U.K.*: [1989] 3 C.M.L.R. 601.

chance of successfully arguing before the European Court that international law does not justify derogation from the prohibition of discrimination on grounds of nationality contained in Articles 52 and 221 of the Treaty of Rome. In those circumstances, he found the balance of convenience to be in favour of granting the applicants the interim relief they sought.

Another consideration which weighed heavily with the House of Lords was the lack of a remedy in damages following the Court's Appeal judgment in *Bourgoin*.[41] It is pointed out by Sharpston[42] that *Factortame* was unusual in that there was already directly relevant jurisprudence from the ECJ leading to the conclusion that the substantive point of Community law at issue would eventually be resolved in favour of the plaintiffs seeking the injunction. In subsequent cases, much will therefore depend on the strength of the case which can be argued as to the *substantive* Community law which applies and whether it has in fact been breached, so as to warrant the grant of interim relief. This approach is taken in *R*. v. *Secretary of State for the National Heritage, ex parte Continental Television BV and Others* when the Court of Appeal held that an important factor which should have been (and was) considered by the trial court in exercising its discretion to injunct or not, was the prospect of success or failure resulting from the European Court's eventual ruling.[43] In *R*. v. *H.M. Treasury, ex parte British Telecommunications Plc: The Times*, December 2, 1993, judicial review proceedings were brought by British Telecommunications Plc (BT) to quash certain provisions of Schedule 2 of the Utilities Supply and Works Contracts Regulations 1992 (S.I. 1992 No. 3279). The Court of Appeal agreed with the view of the Divisional Court, that it was strongly arguable that BT was entitled to be relieved of certain obligations in Directive 90/531 concerning public purchasing by utilities, by virtue of Article 8(1) and that the U.K. regulations had therefore failed correctly to give effect to the directive.

However, it did not judge that the case (wich had been referred to the ECJ on that issue), was bound to succeed, though it could well do so. It held that the court could not and should not try to be more specific than that, since by making a reference to the ECJ it had declared its inability to resolve the question at issue. The right, assuming there was one, to require the U.K. Regulations to be brought in line with the directive, did not urgently call for interim protection. Unlike *Factortame (No. 2)*, (discussed above at paragraphs 9–036 *et seq.*), there was no question of disapplying primary legislation. In that case, by the time interim relief was granted it was fairly clear what the answer to the underlying problem of Community law was going to be. That was not the position in the *BT* case. BT had to accept that where Community law was uncertain, it was asking for a very unusual order, *i.e.* that the Treasury lay an instrument

---

[41] *Bourgoin: op. cit.*, n. 34.
[42] Sharpston, *Interim and Substantive Relief in Claims under Community Law* (1993), p. 41.
[43] *R*. v. *Secretary of State for the National Heritage, ex p. Continental Television BV and Others* [1993] 3 C.M.L.R. 387.

before Parliament to amend the regulations, in a sense contrary to what the Treasury had contended to be the true sense of the directive. The Court of Appeal would not make such an order, save in the most compelling circumstances, which were found not to exist in that case.

In assessing the balance of convenience, the test was that enunciated by Lord Diplock in *American Cyanamid* (discussed above at paragraphs 9–036 *et seq.*). Where, pending a reference to the ECJ, an applicant sought an interim injunction which would have the effect of disapplying national legislation, the Court of Appeal held that is could not adopt a formulaic approach, *i.e.* apply a rule of thumb in a mechanistic way, to its assessment of the balance of convenience. It would attribute varying degrees of weight to all relevant matters which the particular circumstances of the case dictated.

The approach taken in the *BT* case is likely to make it extremely difficult for prospective plaintiffs to assess, in advance, the likelihood of success in applications for interim injunctions, in any other than the most compelling cases brought against the State to set aside national legislation. It does remain to be seen, however, how willing (or otherwise) national courts will be to accept the arguments of the applicant rather than the State, where interim relief is claimed.[44] In *ex parte Continental Television BV* (discussed above) it was held that when the prospect of success or failure in the European Court was evenly balanced, it was a proper exercise of discretion by the trial court to give decisive weight to the public interest in upholding, in the interim, the decision of the Minister which had given rise to the litigation.[45]

## Relevance of alternative proceedings under Article 169/170 E.C. Treaty

9–039    In *Factortame (No. 2)*,[46] the Court of Appeal suggested that the Commission should institute proceedings against the U.K. and request interim measures to be prescribed by the European Court under Article 186 of the EEC Treaty pending the Court's final judgment.[47] It is suggested by Barav[48] that this reliance is misconceived. In particular, the possibility of proceedings under Articles 169 to 171 of the E.C. Treaty (as amended by the Treaty on European Union) are not regarded by the European Court as in any way adversely affecting or prejudicing the rights of private individuals before national courts. For instance, in *Van Gend en Loos*[49] the European Court held that:

"(t)he fact that these Articles of the Treaty (*i.e.* 169 and 170 EEC) . . . enable the Commission and the Member States to bring before

---

[44] Sharpston, *op. cit.*, n. 42, p. 43.
[45] *Ex. p. Continental Television BV*, *op. cit.*, n. 43, judgment of Glidewell L.J., at p. 318, para. 20.
[46] *Factortame (No. 2)* [1989] 2 C.M.L.R. 353 (Q.B.D. and C.A.).
[47] *Ibid.*, [1989] 2 C.M.L.R. *per* Lord Donaldson M.R. p. 398 and *per* Bingham L.J., p. 408.
[48] Barav, (1989) C.M.L.Rev. 369 at 380.
[49] Case 26/62, *Van Gend en Loos*: [1963] E.C.R. 1, [1963] C.M.L.R. 105.

the Court a State which has not fulfilled its obligation does not mean that individuals cannot plead these obligations, should the occasion arise, before a national court, any more than the fact that the Treaty places at the disposal of the Commission ways of ensuring that obligations imposed upon those subject to the Treaty are observed, precludes the possibility, in actions between individuals before a national court, of pleading infringements of the obligations. A restriction of the guarantees against an infringement of Article 12 by Member States to the procedures under Articles 169 and 170 would remove all direct legal protection of the individual rights of their nationals. There is the risk that recourse to the procedure under these Articles would be ineffective if it were to occur after the implementation of the national decision taken contrary to the provisions of the Treaty. The vigilance of individuals concerned to protect their rights amounts to an effective supervision in addition to the supervision entrusted by Articles 169 and 170 to the diligence of the Commission and of the Member States."[50]

Furthermore, in Case 28/67, *Mölkerei-Zentrale*[51] the Court said:

"Every time a rule of Community law confers rights on individuals, those rights, without prejudice to the methods of recourse made available by the Treaty, may be safeguarded by proceedings brought before the competent national courts. Such actions are different from the exercise of the powers conferred on the Community authorities under the Treaty, in particular by Articles 94 and 97, together with Articles 155 and 169. In fact, proceedings by an individual are intended to protect individual rights in a specific case, whilst intervention by the Community authorities has as its object the general and uniform observance of Community law. It thus appears that the guarantees given to individuals under the Treaty to safeguard their individual rights and the powers granted to the Community institutions with regard to the observance by the States of their obligations have different objects, aims and effects and a parallel may not be drawn between them."[52]

It is accordingly argued by Barav[53] that the possibility of proceedings under Article 169 of the E.C. Treaty with potential interim measures being prescribed by the European Court under Article 186 does not defeat in any way the national court's jurisdicton to grant interim relief. Nor is the availability of a Community right or remedy dependent upon a prior judgment by the European Court to that effect.[54]

## Claims based on invalidity of Community Law

The *Factortame* litigation concerned the invalidity of *national* legisla- **9–040** tion which conflicted with Community law. However, circumstances may

---

[50] *Ibid.*, at p. 13.
[51] Case 28/67, *Mölkerei-Zentrale*: [1968] E.C.R. 143, [1968] C.M.L.R. 187.
[52] *Ibid.*, p. 153.
[53] Barav, *op. cit.*, n. 48, p. 381.
[54] *Ibid.*, p. 382.

arise where the national law in question has been enacted to give effect to Community legislation and where the applicant claims that the latter is invalid, for example, as incompatible with the Treaty of Rome and/or fundamental principles of Community law. The applicant may request interim relief from a national court in those circumstances.

In Case 314/85, *Firma Foto-Frost* v. *HZA Lu Beck-Ost*[55] the Court of Justice held that national courts do not have the power to declare acts of the Community institutions invalid. As part of its reasoning, the Court point out that:

". . . Divergences between courts in the Member States as to the validity of Community acts would be liable to place in jeopardy the very unity of the Community legal order and detract from the fundamental requirement of legal certainty."[56]

However, the Court went on to indicate that:

"19, it should be added that the rule that national courts may not themselves declare Community acts invalid may have to be qualified in certain circumstances in the case of proceedings relating to an application for interim measures."[57]

This means that in relation to an application for interlocutory relief, the European Court left open the possibility of a derogation from the rule that only the Court itself can declare secondary legislation by the Community institutions invalid. The issue left open by the *Foto-Frost* case was subsequently decided in Joined Cases C–143/88 & 92/89, *Zuckerfabrik Süderdithmarschen* v. *HZA Itzehoe* and *Zuckerfabrik Soest GmbH* v. *HZA Paderborn*.[58]

The case concerned the issue of whether a Council Regulation 1914/87 of July 2, 1987, which required two sugar factories, Suderdithmarschen and Soest to pay a special levy, was invalid. The sugar factories requested an interim order suspending the payments until a Court decision on the validity of the Regulation could be taken. The customs authorities in Germany did not accept any suspension of the obligation to pay. The financial courts, the Finanzgericht Hamburg and the Finanzgericht Dusseldorf which handled the cases at first instance, both granted the interim relief sought but referred to the European Court the question of whether Article 189(2) of the Treaty of Rome precludes the power of the national courts to suspend the operation of national measures applying a Community regulation. They also requested a preliminary ruling on the validity of the regulation in question.

---

[55] Case 314/85, *Foto-Frost*: [1987] E.C.R. 4199, [1988] 3 C.M.L.R. 57.
[56] *Foto-Frost, ibid.*, para. 15 of the judgment.
[57] *Ibid.*, para. 19 of the judgment.
[58] Joined Cases C–143/88 & 92/89, *Zuckerfabrik Süderdithmarschen* v. *HZA Itzehoe* and *Zuckerfabrik Soest GmbH* v. *HZA Paderborn*: [1991] I E.C.R. 415, [1993] 3 C.M.L.R. 1.

## Condition for suspension of measures based on Community legislation

The Court held that Article 189 of the Treaty of Rome did not **9–041** preclude the power of national courts to suspend the operation of an administrative measure based on a Community regulation.[59] (This ruling is not affected by subsequent amandments made by the Treaty on European Union). However, a suspension may only be granted by a national court when certain conditions are fulfilled:

(a) the national court must have *serious doubts* as to the validity of the Community regulation on which the contested administrative measure is based.

(b) the national court may only grant a suspension and that suspension is only valid until the European Court has delivered a ruling on the question of validity. Consequently, the national court must refer the matter to the Court of Justice if it has not already done so.

(c) there must be an urgent need for the interim measures to be adopted in order to avoid serious irreparable damage to the party seeking them. Purely financial damage cannot be regarded in principle as irreparable.

(d) the national court must take into account the interest of the Community, and must first examine whether the Community measure in question would be deprived of all effectiveness if not immediately implemented.

(e) if suspension of enforcement is liable to involve a financial risk for the Community, the national court must also be in a position to require the applicant to provide adequate guarantees, such as the deposit of money or other securities.[60]

However, the Court ruled that there were in fact no reasons for declaring the Council Regulation 1914/87 invalid. It was clear from the judgment that the procedures and conditions for the grant of an interim order were to be governed by national procedural law. However, it is noted by Sharpston[61] that the approach of the Court in *Zuckerfabrik* was nevertheless to set stricter conditions within which national courts may grant interim relief, where the invalidity of Community legislation is at issue, as contrasted with the Court's judgment in the *Factortame* cases where the Court did not specify the conditions applicable for the grant of interim relief by national courts.[62] However, since the conditions specified by the Court in the *Zuckerfabrik* cases are, in themselves, fairly self-evident and likely to be taken into account in any event in applications for interim relief based purely on national law, it may be

---

[59] See further Schermers, "Case Note on the *Zuckerfabrik* cases" (1992) C.M.L.Rev. 133 at p. 134 and Case C–465/93: [1994] O.J. C76/5.
[60] See discussion at paras. 9–042 *et seq.* below.
[61] Sharpston, *op. cit.*, n. 42, p. 51.
[62] *Ibid.*

that there will not in fact be any serious divergence in the way that the rules are applied in relation to either allegedly invalid national legislation, or invalid Community measures. It is argued by Schermers[63] that the *Zuckerfabrik* cases were a landmark in that they demonstrated the Courts's concern to put the protection of the individual in the foreground and therefore to grant national courts the power not to apply Community law if such application would be unreasonably detrimental to the rights of individuals, providing certain conditions are fulfilled.[64]

## CROSS-UNDERTAKINGS IN DAMAGES FROM "THE STATE"

**9–042**    Under U.K. law, in considering whether it is appropriate to grant interlocutory relief, the principles laid down by the House of Lords in the *American Cyanamid* case[65] will apply. The court considers first whether there is a serious question to be tried. The court then considers whether damages are available and, if so, whether they constitute an adequate remedy for one side or the other. If not, the court goes on to consider whether the balance of convenience lies in favour of granting or refusing the relief sought, bearing in mind that the purpose of an interim injunction is to maintain the status quo until the trial of the action.[66]

If damages would adequately compensate the plaintiff if he or she should succeed at trial of the main action, the injunction will not be granted. If there is doubt as to the adequacy of damages, all relevant factors have to be considered with the view to maintaining the status quo.

It is usual for the plaintiff to give an undertaking in damages, as a prerequisite of the grant of an interlocutory injunction. However, it is a matter for the court's discretion as to whether or not such an undertaking should be given.

In *F Hoffmann La Roche and Company AG* v. *Secretary of State for Trade and Industry*[67] it was held that where the applicant seeks an undertaking in damages from the Crown in the event that individual rights have been breached, and where the Crown is engaged in law enforcement duties, the court has a discretion whether or not to require the Crown to give an undertaking in damages as a prerequsite of the grant of an interlocutory injunction. (On the other hand, in *Factortame (No. 2)*[68] it was decided that an undertaking to pay damages by the

---

[63] Schermers, *op. cit.*, n. 59, p. 137.
[64] *Ibid.*, p. 138.
[65] *American Cyanamid* v. *Ethicon Ltd.* [1975] A.C. 396, [1975] 1 All E.R. 504, discussed at para. 9–036 above.
[66] See Foulkes, *Administrative Law* (1986), 6th ed., pp. 326 *et seq.*
[67] [1974] 2 All E.R. 1128.
[68] *R.* v. *Secretary of State for Transport, ex p. Factortame Ltd. and Others (No. 2)* [1991] 1 All E.R. 70, discussed further at para. 9–034 above.

*applicant* Spanish fishermen was inappropriate because it would be impossible to identify and damage sustained by individuals in the British fishing industry as a result of the continued operation of the applicant's vessels.)

In the Sunday trading case *Kirklees Metropolitan Borough Council* v. *Wickes Building Supplies Limited*,[69] also referred to as the *Wickes* case, the appellant local authority sought an interlocutory injunction pursuant to section 222 of the Local Government Act 1972 restraining the respondent, a do-it-yourself retailer, until trial, from trading on Sundays contrary to section 47 of the Shops Act 1950. Although section 47 makes Sunday trading a *criminal* offence punishable by a fine, some local authorities regarded this sanction as ineffective and therefore began civil proceedings for an injunction. The local authority declined to give a cross-undertaking in damages and at first instance, the Judge Mervyn Davies granted the injunction without requiring the authority to do so, on the ground that since the local authority was seeking to enforce the law in its area under its statutory powers, it was entitled to the same exemption from giving a cross-undertaking in damages, as the Crown had when seeking an interlocutory injunction.

As a result of Mervyn Davies J.'s decision not to require an undertaking in damages, many other local councils sought and obtained inter—locutory injunctions on the same terms, restraining Sunday trading by retail stores. By the time that the *Wickes* case had reached the Court of Appeal, about one hundred injunctions had been granted by judges of the Chancery Division following the approach of Mervyn Davies J.[70]

This approach was, however, rejected in the Court of Appeal on the ground that the judge ought to have required the local authority to give a cross-undertaking in damages before granting the injunction, because the special privilege afforded to the Crown not to give such an undertaking did not extend to local authorities. Secondly, a cross-undertaking in damages was required to protect the Community law rights of the repondent if it was found eventually by the European Court that section 47 of the 1950 Act had been rendered ineffective by Article 30 by the EEC Treaty. (The latter point was finally decided against the Sunday traders in that the U.K. legislation was found by the ECJ not to be incompatible with Community law in the Joined Cases C–306/88, C–304/90 and C–169/91, *Rochdale Borough Council* v. *Anders, Reading Borough Council* v. *Payless DIY* and *Stoke-on-Trent and Norwich City Councils* v. *B & Q*.)[71]

---

[69] *Kirklees* v. *Wickes* [1992] 3 All E.R. 717 (H.L.).

[70] See, for example, *Rochdale Borough Council* v. *Anders* [1988] 3 All E.R. 490.

[71] Cases 306/88, 304/90 and 169/91, *Rochdale Borough Council* v. *Anders, Reading Borough Council* v. *Payless D.I.Y. and Others, Stoke-on-Trent and Norwich City Council* v. *B & Q* judgment of December 16, 1992; [1993] 1 C.M.L.R. 426, [1993] 1 All E.R. 481. See further the landmark judgment in Joined Cases C–267–268/91, *Keck and Another*: judgment of November 24, 1993; *The Times*, November 25, 1993, in which all 13 judges expressly reversed previous rulings of the Court and decided that national laws

However, on appeal to the House of Lords the local authority succeeded in its argument not to give a cross-undertaking in damages as a precondition to the grant of the injunction. The House of Lords took the view that the *Hoffmann La Roche* case has not been correctly applied. In the view of Lord Goff (with which Lord Keith of Kinkel and Lord Ackner concurred), the principle in that case related not to the Crown as such, but to the Crown when performing a particular function, namely law enforcement actions.[72] In those circumstances, Lord Goff was of the view that the same principle should apply, in similar circumstances, to other public authorities when exercising the function of law enforcer in the public interest. To do otherwise would result in a situation whereby a local authority, acting under a statutory duty, would be required to give an undertaking in damages, whereas the Crown would not.

*Possibility of a Community law right to an undertaking in damages*

**9–043**    The House of Lords in *Wickes* also considered whether the respondent had any Community law right which required the granting of an undertaking in damages from the Council if an interlocutory injunction was to be granted. The Court of Appeal had held that such a right existed on the basis that it is the duty of the national court to ensure the legal protection which persons derive from the direct effect of a provision of Community law; secondly Article 30 was such a provision; thirdly if the respondent, Wickes was right that section 47 of the 1950 Act was incompatible with Article 30 of the Treaty of Rome, it had a current right to open its stores for Sunday trading, and it was the duty of the national court to protect that right; fourthly in the absence of an undertaking in damages, Wickes would have been restrained from opening on Sundays, without any right to compensation; and fifthly that there was no need for that purpose to assess the strength of Wickes' challenge to section 47 on the basis of Article 30, it being enough that the challenge was not without foundation.[73]

In *Wickes*, the plaintiff Council argued that the question of whether an undertaking in damages from the plaintiff should be required as a condition of the grant of an injunction is a question to be resolved by national law, being a question of procedure, which, on established principles of Community law is left to national law. The authority cited for this proposition was that of the European Court in *Factortame (No.*

---

restricting or prohibiting certain selling arrangements which apply to products from other Member States were not such as to hinder directly or indirectly, actual or potential trade between Member States within the meaning of the *Dassonville* judgment (Case 8/74: [1974] E.C.R. 837, [1974] 2 C.M.L.R. 436), provided that those laws applied to all affected traders operating within the national territory and provided they affected in the same manner, in law and in fact, the marketing of domestic products and of those from other Member States. Such rules therefore fall outside the scope of Article 30. See further text at para. 10–059 below.

[72] *Kirklees* v. *Wickes* [1992] 3 All E.R. 717 (H.L.) see judgment at p. 728, para. 3.

[73] See judgment in *Wickes* at p. 729, para. d.

2)[74] where the European Court in its judgment did not answer the second question posed for its consideration by the House of Lords, namely the criteria to be applied by the national court in deciding whether or not to grant interim protection of the rights claimed.

Lord Goff took the view that the matter was not necessarily to be regarded as one of procedure for the national law, where the imposition of the term under consideration is directed towards preserving rights which may arise under the Community law. Lord Goff, in reaching this view, took into account the dicta of the European Court in *Zuckerfabrik Süderdithmarschen AG* v. *Hauptzollamt Itzehoe* and *Zuckerfabrik Soest GmbH* v. *HZA Paderborn*[75] where the Court laid down conditions for the grant of a stay of execution of a national administrative act based on a Community regulation, because of doubts on the part of the national court as to the validity of the regulation.[76]

However, Lord Goff decided that as a result of the decision of the European Court in *Francovich*[77] the effect of requiring an undertaking would be to impose an obligation on the Council to idemnify *Wickes* against the damage suffered by it, in the event of section 47 being held to be invalid as inconsistent with Article 30, irrespective of whether in such circumstances Wickes had a right to damages. However, Lord Goff did recognise that although such a right to damages had been rejected in the leading case of *Bourgoin*[78] there was now doubt as to whether that case had been correctly decided.

His second reason for not requiring an undertaking in damages from the Council was if, following *Francovich's* case, there was held to be a right to damages in such circumstances, the effect of requiring an undertaking from the Council would be to impose liability and damages on the Council instead of on the United Kingdom. In his view, the latter was properly the party so liable since it was the government which would have failed to ensure that section 47 was amended or repealed as necessary.[79] For these reasons, Lord Goff was of the opinion that Wickes's argument that the Council should be required to give an undertaking in damages had no justification in Community law.

He went on to consider whether, following ordinary principles of English law, the grant of the injunction was the correct exercise of the Court's discretion in accordance with the principles stated by the House of Lords in the *Factortame (No. 2)* case. He was of the view that there were sound reasons why the discretion could not be said to have been

---

[74] *Factortame (No. 2), op. cit.*, n. 68.
[75] Joined Cases C–143/88 & 92/89, *Zuckerfabrik*: [1991] I E.C.R. 415, [1993] 3 C.M.L.R. 1 discussed at paras. 9-042 *et seq.* above.
[76] *Ibid.* see paras. 22 to 23 of the judgment of the Court.
[77] Joined Cases C–6 & 9/90, *Francovich and Bonifaci* v. *Italian Republic*: [1991] I E.C.R. 1, [1993] 2 C.M.L.R. 66; discussed at paras. 8–008 and 9–020 above.
[78] *Bourgoin SA* v. *Ministry of Agriculture, Fisheries and Food* [1985] 3 All E.R. 385, discussed further at para. 9-018 above.
[79] See judgment in *Wickes*, n. 72, at p. 735, para. d and discussion on this point at para. 8–012 above.

wrongly exercised, notably because, in practical terms, proceedings by way of injunction were the only means open to the Council to perform its duties to enforce the provisions of Section 47. The effect of requiring an undertaking in damages from the Council would be to cause the collapse of the law enforcement process in this area of law; further that the enforcement of the law was not merely desirable as such in the public interest, but that small retailers would well suffer if large retailers such as Wickes were able to continue to trade with impunity during a significant period, in contravention of what might well prove to be perfectly valid law.

9–044     However, although the exercise of the discretion may have been valid, it is arguable that Lord Goff was mistaken in coming to the view that the liability in damages, if any, was solely that of the United Kingdom government and that to impose liability in damages on the Council was inconsistent with that liability. This is because the reasoning of previous case law of the European Court on the subject of "emanations of the State" which have been discussed in detail above[80] suggest that the liability of the State can be attributed to an organ such as local government authority, which may be regarded, for these purposes, as an "emanation of the State".

However, the House of Lords declined, as requested by Wickes, to make a reference to European Court on the issue of whether Community law required an undertaking in damages from the local council. It is therefore necessary to await any guidance which may be forthcoming from the European Court as a result of references in other cases.

It is of interest to note, however, that in the European Court judgment in *Zuckerfabrik*,[81] which referred to by Lord Goff in *Wickes*, one of the conditions which was the European Court set as a condition for granting a suspension (stay of execution) of a national administrative measure which was based upon a Community regulation, was whether such a stay of execution was likely to lead to a financial risk *for the Community*. In that situation, the national court must be in a position to require *the applicant* to provide sufficient guarantees such as payment of a deposit.[82] Although the case was concerned with the situation where the national law involved was based upon a Community regulation, it is interest that the Court did consider the equivalent of an undertaking in damages by the applicant as a precondition of the granting of the stay of execution. However, in *Zuckerfabrik*, a primary condition for such a stay of execution by a national court was that the circumstances of fact and law relied upon by the applicants must lead the national court to the conviction that there were serious doubts as to the validity of the Community regulation upon which the disputed administrative act is based. This condition goes further than that of considering whether there is a "serious issue to be tried" as required under the principles in the

---

[80] See paras. 7–001 *et seq.* above.
[81] *Zuckerfabrik: op. cit.*, n. 58, discussed at paras. 9–040 *et seq.* above.
[82] *Ibid.*, p. 161.

*American Cyanamid* case.[83] However, the determination of whether the Community regulation is in fact invalid, as a matter of Community law, remains exclusively for the Court of Justice to determine.

---

[83] *Op. cit.*, n. 65, see further Jacques Algazy, "The Crown, Interim Relief and EEC Law" (1991) New L.J. 1303 to 1304.

# PRIVATE LAW REMEDIES FOR ENFORCING COMMUNITY LAW

## INJUNCTIONS

**10–001**     A private legal person such as an individual or company can obtain an injunction against another private person to restrain the latter from infringing a directly effective provision of Community law.[1] The grant of an injunction or interim injunction to prevent a breach of Community law is subject to the normal domestic rules.[2]

In *Garden Cottage Ltd.* v. *Milk Marketing Board*,[3] the defendant Milk Marketing Board, which was the major producer of bulk butter in England, decided to rationalise its sales policy. It limited the sale of butter to four distributors. The plaintiffs, who were previously distributors for the butter, applied for an injunction to restrain the Milk Marketing Board from withholding supplies, on the basis that its refusal to sell constituted an abuse of a dominant position contrary to Article 86. The House of Lords was unanimous in stating that the English courts had jurisdiction to grant the plaintiff an injunction to prevent the defendant breaching Article 86 of the Treaty of Rome.

Lord Diplock, speaking for the majority in the House of Lords (Lord Wilberforce dissenting) noted that Articles 85(1) and 86 of the Treaty of Rome had been acknowledged by the European Court to have direct effects in relations between individuals and which therefore national courts were under an obligation to safeguard.[4] (These Articles have not been amended by the Treaty on European Union and the principles discussed in the case law referred to below are therefore still valid.)

---

[1] See *Budget* v. *British Sugar Corporation* (1979) February 16 (unreported, but noted in [1979] E.L.Rev. 417); *Engineering and Chemical Supplies (Epsom and Gloucester) Limited* v. *AKZO Chemie U.K. Limited* (1979) December 6 (unreported, but noted in E.C. Commission Decision 83/462; [1983] 3 C.M.L.R. 694 (*ECS/AKZO*)).

[2] See further, *Halsbury's Laws of England* (1991), 4th ed., Vol. 51, para. 3.74.

[3] *Garden Cottage Foods* v. *Milk Marketing Board* [1984] 1 A.C. 130, [1983] 2 All E.R. 770.

[4] See Case 127/73, *Belgische Radio en Televisie and Société Belge des auteurs, compositeurs et editeurs V.SV SABAM and N V Fonior*: [1974] E.C.R. 51, [1974] 2 C.M.L.R. 238.

He concluded that:

> "A breach of the duty imposed by Article 86 not to abuse a dominant position in the common market or in a substantial part of it, can thus be categorised in English law as a breach of statutory duty that is imposed not only for the purpose of promoting the general economic prosperity of the Common Market but also for the benefit of private individuals to whom loss or damage is caused by breach of that duty."

Although the House of Lords did not give a *final* decision that a breach of Article 86 of the Treaty of Rome can form the basis of a cause of action in English law, it was subsequently accepted by Mr Justice Neill in *An Bord Bainne Co-operative Limited (The Irish Dairy Board)* v. *The Milk Marketing Board*[5] that the speeches nevertheless provide "compelling support for the proposition that contraventions of EEC regulations which have "direct effects" create direct rights in private law which the national courts must protect."[6] The principle established by the House of Lords in this case would appear to apply not only to a statutory body, such as the Milk Marketing Board, but to any trading organisation.[7]

## Condition for the grant of injunctions: English law principles

The principles applied in the *Garden Cottage* case to determine **10–002** whether or not to grant an injunction were those ennunciated in *American Cyanamid Company* v. *Ethicon Ltd.*[8] The House agreed that in *Garden Cottage* there was a serious issue to be tried in the case. However, the majority of the House of Lords concurred with the view of Lord Diplock that an infringement of Article 86 of the EEC Treaty would give rise in English law to a remedy in damages at the suit of an individual citizen who suffered pecuniary loss by reason of the infringement. (The Court of Appeal had been uncertain whether damages would be recoverable by the plaintiffs in the event of their success.) Lord Diplock concluded that since damages would also be an adequate remedy for the plaintiffs and the trial judge had been entitled to conclude that damages would be an adequate remedy, the Court of Appeal was wrong to interfere with the exercise of the judge's discretion and to grant an injunction. The appeal was accordingly allowed and the injunction was discharged.

It is of importance that Lord Diplock also concluded that it was, in his view, unarguable that a contravention of Article 86 could only give rise to a remedy by way of injunction to prevent *future* loss being caused, but

---

[5] *An Bord Bainne Co-operative Ltd. (The Irish Dairy Board)* v. *The Milk Marketing Board* [1984] 2 C.M.L.R. 584.
[6] *Ibid.*, para. 24.
[7] See *Halsbury's Laws of England, op. cit.*, n. 2, p. 456. See further discussion at para. 10–012 below.
[8] *American Cyanamid Company* v. *Ethicon Ltd.* [1975] A.C. 296, 1 All E.R. 504 and discussed further at para. 9–036 above.

no remedy in damages to compensate for loss *already* caused by that contravention.[9] He suggests that this proposition, advanced by the Court of Appeal (but disclaimed by both parties to the action) was based on the misunderstanding by the Court of Appeal of an *obiter dictum* of Roskill L.J. in the earlier case of *Valour International Limited* v. *Application des Gas SA*[10]

Lord Wilberforce in his dissenting judgment, however, took the contrary view. He pointed out that:

"All that section 2 (of the European Communities Act 1972) says (relevantly) is that rights arising under the Treaty are to be available in law in the United Kingdom, but this does not suggest any transformation or enlargement in their character. Indeed the section calls them "enforceable community rights" not rights arising under United Kingdom law. All that the relevant cases (Case 33/76, *Rewe-Zentralfinanze G* v. *Landwirtschaftskammer für das Saarland* [1976] 3 E.C.R. 1989, Case 826/79, *Amministrazione delle Finanze dello Stato* v. *Mireco* [1980] 3 E.C.R. 2559) tell us that it is for international laws to designate the appropriate courts having jurisdiction, and to establish the procedural conditions. Does this enable national laws to define the remedy? There is of course nothing illogical or even unusual in a situation in which a person's rights extend to an injunction but not to damages—many such exist in English law."

He concluded that it was not appropriate in interlocutory proceedings for the courts to decide difficult questions of law which call for detailed argument and mature consideration. For this reason, *inter alia*, he would have granted the injunction. He also highlighted the fact that even if the right to damages does exist, the primary remedy against a prohibited act is an injunction against the continuance of it.[11] He also took the view that damages would not provide adequate compensation because in the case in question the effect of not granting the injunction would lead to "irreparable damage.[12] It is submitted that there are also other disadvantages such as the difficulty in obtaining exemplary damages and the question of causation and of remoteness of damage. Furthermore, different rules on the availability or likelihood of obtaining damages might encourage "forum shopping" in the various Member States. These practical difficulties in obtaining damages are discussed further at paragraphs 10–009 *et seq.* below.

10–003    On the practical question of whether it was in fact possible to draft an injunction suitable for interim relief in the *Garden Cottage* case (rather than one suitable for perpetual relief), Lord Wilberforce was of the view that the Commercial Court would have been capable of drafting an injunction which would have prevented the Milk Marketing Board, until

---

[9] *Garden Cottage, op. cit.*, n. 3, p. 145d.
[10] [1978] 3 C.M.L.R. 87.
[11] *Garden Cottage Foods* [1984] 2 All E.R. 770 at p. 784.
[12] *Ibid.*, p. 784.

judgment or further order, from excluding the plaintiff company from purchases of bulk butter and from treating the company less favourably as to quantity, price and conditions of sale than other customers.

In the subsequent case of *Cutsforth* v. *Mansfield Inns Ltd.*[13] it was established that an interlocutory injunction may be granted to restrain a party from breaching Article 85(1) of the Treaty of Rome. In that case, the plaintiffs had for many years supplied coin-operated amusement machines to the tenants of some 57 public houses, under agreements with these tenants. These public houses were taken over by Mansfield Inns in 1985 and shortly after, the defendants made a list of suppliers from whom the tenants could purchase the amusement machines. The plaintiffs were excluded from this list and they sought and obtained an injunction restraining the defendants from limiting the freedom of the tenants to place orders with them. The injunction was granted on the basis that it was seriously arguable that the covenant inserted into the tenancy agreements, which excluded the plaintiffs name, had the object or effect of distorting competition and had the potential to affect trade between Member States, contrary to Article 85(1) of the EEC Treaty. English courts will therefore grant injunctions restraining possible breaches of E.C. competition law under Article 85.

In *Cutsforth* the court applied the principles of the *American Cyanamid* case in the normal way. However, on the issue of whether damages could provide an adequate remedy to the plaintiffs, the view of the Judge Sir Neil Lawson was that:

". . . damages would not be an adequate remedy for the plaintiffs because the denial of interim relief would virtually put an end to a business which has operated with a degree of success over a period of 15 years or more. . . . It would be within the ability of the plaintiffs to pay (they are not, I observe, a limited liability company who could go into liquidation and leave its creditors to sing for their money) damages adequately to compensate the defendants for their loss of 50 per cent of machine takings pending trial, or for any other loss they may incur as a result of the court's order. There are other factors. The plaintiffs have referred their complaint to the European Commission, but the mills there grind very slowly indeed. On the other hand, the defendants in my judgment have behaved in a high-handed manner. I do not consider that there are other factors that weigh more heavily against the defendants than against the plaintiffs."

In conclusion, the injunction was granted.[14]

The invocation of Community law may be of considerable signficance where such invocation provides a remedy where none is available under national law. In *Holleran and Evans* v. *Daniel Thwaites Plc*[15] the English

---

[13] *Cutsforth* v. *Mansfield Inns Ltd.* [1986] 1 W.L.R. 558.

[14] For a case in which interim relief was refused see *Argyll Group Plc.* v. *The Distillers Co. Ltd.* [1986] 1 C.M.L.R. 764.

[15] *Holleran and Evans* v. *Daniel Thwaites Plc* [1989] 2 C.M.L.R. 917.

High Court granted an interim injunction restraining the brewery from enforcing or giving effect to a notice to quit, and from recovering possession of the premises pursuant to the notice to quit. The action by the defendant brewery was valid under English law relating to contract and/or property but was held to be contrary to Community law in that the new agreement (which the plaintiffs refused to sign) infringed Article 85(1) of the Treaty of Rome, and that the balance of convenience lay in favour of granting the injunction.

*Conditions for the grant of injunctions: Irish law case study*

**10–004**     In the Irish case of *Patrick Dunlea* v. *Nissan Ireland Limited*,[16] the Irish High Court considered facts involving an alleged infringement of Article 86 of the Treaty of Rome. The case was brought by the plaintiff to restrain the defendant, its servants or agents, from terminating or taking any or any further steps in purported termination of a franchise agreement between the plaintiff and the defendant made on or about July 8, 1980, pending the trial of the action.

The Irish Court proceeded to apply a test very similar to the principles of English law as ennunciated in the *American Cyanamid* case.[17] These are first, whether there is a serious issue to be tried. Secondly, whether damages are available and, if so, whether they constitute an adequate remedy for one side or the other. If so, the injunction will not be granted. If not, the court goes on to consider whether the balance of convenience lies in favour of granting or refusing the injunction. These principles are discussed further at paragraphs 9–033 *et seq.* above. The Irish Court took these three factors into account in deciding whether the plaintiff was entitled to the relief sought. First, he had to establish that there were serious questions to be tried regarding whether the purported termination of the franchise agreement by the defendant was lawful, having regard to the provisions of Article 86 of the EEC Treaty.

The Court concluded that there were serious issues to be tried and went on to consider whether damages would be an adequate remedy. It noted that the loss of a major franchise for the sale of new vehicles might be regarded by customers or potential customers of the plaintiff as something of a stigma which would cast doubt on his status in the motor trade. Even if ultimately the plaintiff succeeded in this action, and the Nissan franchise was restored to him by the defendant, there was a real risk that he might never recover the volume of new vehicle sales that he previously enjoyed and it would be impossible to quantify that potential loss. This stigma might also inhibit the plaintiff from obtaining an alternative franchise from some other distributor of comparable vehicles. The plaintiff might also require a period of years to build up the new business to the level of the franchise prior to its termination. For all these reasons damages were regarded as not being an adequate remedy.

---

[16] [1992] E.C.C. 169.
[17] *American Cyanamid, op. cit.*, n. 8.

The Irish Court went on to consider the balance of convenience and noted that if the defendant was ultimately successful in the action, loss (if any) which it may have suffered due to the continuance of the franchise agreement at the date of ultimate judgment was readily quantifiable and would be recoverable on the plaintiff's undertaking as to damages. In all the circumstances, the injunction was therefore granted.

### Seriously arguable case under Community law required:

However, the party seeking to rely on a European Community law **10–005** point must of course show that the point is seriously arguable. In *Leyland Daf Limited* v. *Automotive Products Plc*[18] the plaintiff sought a mandatory injunction compelling Automotive Products Plc to supply it with necessary parts for the continuation of its production line. Leyland Daf had ordered products to the value of £6 million from Automotive Products but the former company had subsequently become insolvent and administrative receivers were appointed. Automotive Products continued to supply parts to the insolvent company but claimed in respect of unpaid debts regarding pre-receivership supplies, the benefit of a retention of title clause over some these supplies. They had also threatened to stop supplying Leyland Daf if the receivers refused to pay the pre-receivership debts.

If that threat were carried out, it would have taken some six to eight months testing of new suppliers (due to stringent product liability rules) before a new supplier could be appointed. That would have affected the production line at Leyland Daf which could not have been kept moving. There was effectively therefore, no alternative source of supply for Leyland Daf other than Automotive Products.

In this context, the receivers had applied to the High Court seeking a mandatory injunction. The common law position regarding the granting of such relief was not in dispute, namely that a party could not be forced to trade with another, even if a long term contract was in existence. However, it was argued on behalf of the plaintiffs that this position was in conflict with Article 86 of the Treaty of Rome, which prohibits the abuse of a dominant position within the Common Market or in a substantial part of it and which is directly effective and so forms part of English law.

The Vice-Chancellor considered the concept of "abuse" under Article 86 and examined the relevant case law of the ECJ. He held that "abuse" involved the use by dominant undertakings of methods different from normal commercial operations and that to exert ordinary commercial pressure to obtain payment was not an abuse. He held that the obligation to pay for goods supplied was a normal feature of a commercial competitive market and Article 86 could not have been intended to stop a supplier exerting ordinary commercial pressure to obtain payment simply because the supplier was in a dominant position. On that basis, the Vice-

---

[18] *Leyland Daf Limited* v. *Automotive Products Plc, The Times*, April 6, 1993, p. 37.

Chancellor held that Leyland Daf did not have a seriously arguable case and refused to grant interlocutory relief.

## Injunctions for breach of a directive

**10–006**     In principle, English law does, therefore, provide for the grant of an injunction in private law actions. However, the decided cases referred to above relating to Article 85 and 86 are all based on the direct effect of Treaty of Rome provisions. (They are not affected by amendments made by the Treaty on European Union.) However, where an injunction is sought against another individual for breach of a provision of a *directive*, it will arguably *not* be possible to apply for an injunction, since directives do not create "horizontal" direct effect.[19] In such cases the plaintiff may have to persuade the court to consider the "indirect" direct effect of a directive, *i.e.*, a purposive interpretation of the relevant directive may have to be relied on.[20]

## Injunctions for breach of a regulation: Irish law case study

**10–007**     The Irish case of *Emerald Meats Limited* v. *Minister for Agriculture*[21] concerned the application of a directly effective Community regulation. The plaintiff obtained judgment in 1991 against the Minister for Irish £385,000 in damages for improperly refusing to allow it access to "GATT quota" imports of frozen beef, to which it was entitled under a proper application of Regulation 4024/89. The only argument, at first instance, advanced on the Minister's behalf as to why the Department of Agriculture should not compensate the plaintiff for the loss it suffered, was that the Regulation had merely conferred rights on the plaintiff to obtain a share in the quota and no claim to damages lay for a declaration of such a right. The trial judge concluded that the Regulation did more than confer rights on traders who can show that they imported in accordance with its terms. It also conferred duties on national authorities to carry out its terms. The High Court therefore held that the plaintiff was entitled to damages for breach by the Department of the duties it owed to the plaintiff under the Regulation.

The Minister appealed against that judgment and obtained a stay in respect of the payment of the damages, pending determination of the appeal. In the meantime, the plaintiff had fallen badly into debt and applied for the stay to be removed. It was likely that the appeal would be referred (under the Article 177 procedure) to the European Court in which case there would be further delay. Mr Justice McCarthy in the Irish Supreme Court noted that if the plaintiff company had to await a full hearing of the appeal, it would be likely by then to have ceased business, even if it ultimately succeeded in full.[22]

---

[19] See further discussion at para. 2–010 above.
[20] See further Chap. 6 above.
[21] *Emerald Meats Limited* v. *Minister for Agriculture and Others* [1993] 1 C.M.L.R. 471.
[22] *Emerald Meats Limited, op. cit.*, p. 473 at para. 4.

Mr Justice McCarthy noted that the overriding consideration was to maintain a balance, so that justice would not be denied to either party. On the other hand, Mr Justice Egan noted that the plaintiff had admitted to being in substantial debt and there was therefore a risk that in the event of the appeal by the Minister being successful, any sum paid to the plaintiffs might not be recoverable. He went on to state that:

> "There is no perfect method of balance in these conflicting interests and the only solution I can see to assist in dealing with the problem is an assessment of the likely result of the appeal."[23]

Egan J. and McCarthy J. were heavily persuaded by the views of the trial judge, Mr Justice Costello. In particular, that responsibility in part for the plaintiff's situation was the behaviour of the Department in failing to apply the Regulation 4024/89 correctly in the first place. The stay was therefore removed.

### Other grounds for injunctions

Finally, it should be noted that sometimes, subordinate legislation 10–008 implementing Community law may specifically provide for the grant of injunctions. In addition, under R.S.C., Order 15, rule 16 the court may also make binding declarations of right. This extends to declarations of the rights of individuals under Community law in the private law field.[24]

## ACTIONS FOR DAMAGES

Provisions of Community law which are directly effective (*e.g.* Articles 10–009 85 and 86 of the E.C. Treaty) give rise to rights and obligations on the part of individuals which national courts have a duty to safeguard.[25] These rights and obligations may therefore be enforced in national courts.[26] Thus, for example, in a contract between two parties, a term which infringes Article 86 will be both void and unenforceable in domestic law.[27] Thus, for example, a customer tied by an exclusive purchasing commitment which infringes Article 86 could breach that contractual term by purchasing supplies elsewhere in the knowledge that a national court would not enforce that provision.[28] However, the Court of Justice has held that the automatic nullity provided for in Article 85(2) applies only to contractual provisions which are incompatible with Article 85(1). The remaining provisions may therefore still be valid if it is

---

[23] *Ibid.*, p. 475 at para. 11.
[24] *See Worringham* v. *Lloyds Bank (No. 2)* [1982] 1 W.L.R. 841. For a discussion of the grant of declarations in the public law field, see para. 9–002 above.
[25] See discussion at paras. 2–003 *et seq.* above.
[26] See Case 127/73, *BRT* v. *SABAM*: [1974] E.C.R. 51, [1974] 2 C.M.L.R. 238.
[27] See further Whish, *Competition Law* (1989), pp. 269 to 270.
[28] *Ibid.*, p. 314.

possible to sever the offending clause from the rest of the contract.[29] However, the Court left the mechanism for accomplishing severance to each Member State. The English Court of Appeal in determining this issue has held that where certain provisions of a contract are void under Article 85(2) of the EEC Treaty, the remainder of the contract will stand or fall according to national law relating to contracts, *e.g.* for lack of consideration or fundamental change in its character.[30]

### Damage for breach of E.C. competition rules: the Garden Cottage case

**10–010**    The leading judgment on the availability of damages for breach of E.C. competition rules is that of the House of Lords in the *Garden Cottage Foods* case[31] where it was accepted by the majority that third parties who have suffered harm as a result of an infringement of either Article 85 or 86, are entitled, in principle, to bring an action as a matter of domestic law for both an injunction and for damages. However, Lord Wilberforce dissented and saw nothing illogical in a situation where an individual's rights extended to an injunction but not to damages. There is as yet no reported case in the field of competition law, in which a U.K. court has awarded damages; both reported cases were settled out of court.[32] The position in other Member States on the availability of damages appears to be similar. Although some national courts have recognised the availability of damages for breaches of competition law, there appear to be no reported decisions of such an award.[33]

### Damages for breach of E.C. competition rules: the Banks case

**10–011**    The *Garden Cottage* case was decided long before the decision of the ECJ in *Francovich*, which has been analysed in detail at paragraphs 8–008 *et seq.* and 9–020 *et seq.* above. However, *Francovich* was limited to the issue of *State* liability and in relation to the non-implementation of directives. Support for further principles of Community law establishing the liability of an *individual* (or undertaking) for damage resulting from a breach of directly effective Community law, may now be found in Case C–128/92, *H.J. Banks and Company Limited* v. *British Coal Corporation*

---

[29] *See Case 56/65, La Technique Minière* v. *Maschinenbau Ulm GmbH*: [1966] E.C.R. 235, [1966] C.M.L.R. 357; Case 319/82, *Société de Vente de Cimento ét Béton de l'Est* v. *Kerpen and Kerpen GmbH*: [1983] E.C.R. 4173, [1985] 1 C.M.L.R. 511.

[30] *Chemidus Wavin Ltd.* v. *Société pour la Transformation et l'Exploitation des Resines Industrielles SA* [1983] 3 C.M.L.R. 514, *per* Buckley, Orr and Goff L.JJ. at [18] and [29].

[31] Discussed at para. 10–001 above.

[32] *See Whish, op. cit.*, n. 27, p. 271, n. 2.

[33] See Hoskins, "*Garden Cottage* Revisited: The Availability of Damages in the National Courts for Breaches of the EEC Competition Rules" [1992] 6 E.C.L.R. 257 at p. 258, n. 6; see for example *BMW* October 23, 1979, [1980] E.C.C. 213 (Germany); *Union de Remorquage et de Sauvetage* v. *Schelde Sleepvaartbedrijf* [1986] C.M.L.R. 251 (Belgium); *Cadbury Ireland* v. *Kerry Co-operative Creameries* July 17, 1981, [1981] *Dublin University Law Journal* (Ireland).

(also discussed at paragraphs 8–016 *et seq.* above), in which judgment is awaited.

The Advocate General Van Gerven in *Banks* took the view that the general framework established by the Court in the *Francovich* judgment for determining State liability, also applies where an individual infringes a provision of Community law to which he is subject, thereby causing loss and damage to another individual. This is particularly so in relation to directly effective Community law, such as the competition law provisions of the EEC Treaty (as amended) and the ECSC Treaty. The Advocate General stated (at paragraph 44 of his Opinion) that the only effective method whereby the national court can, in those circumstances, fully safeguard the directly effective provisions of Community law which have been infringed, is by restoring the rights of the injured party by the award of damages. Even a declaration that the legal relationship between the parties is void (as in Article 85(2) of the EEC Treaty (as amended) or Article 65(4) of the ECSC Treaty), is not capable of making good the loss and damage already suffered by a third party. The Advocate General took the view (at paragraph 44) that such a Community rule on reparation would serve to make the Community rules of competition more "operational" in the sense of greater efficiency. He noted that they are already dependent on the co-operation of national courts for their enforcement. He concluded that the national court is under an obligation to award damages for loss sustained by an undertaking as a result of the breach by another undertaking of a directly effective provision of Community competition law (paragraph 45).[34]

It is argued by Sharpston[35] that although the House of Lords in *Garden Cottage Foods* did not fully consider the damages point, it is unlikely that a lower court would hold that damages are not, in principle, available to a private party for a breach of Article 86 by another private party. However, there still remains the difficulty of proving the essential elements of Article 86, *i.e.* dominant position in the relevant market, abuse of that dominant position and damage flowing from that abuse.

## Definition of "undertaking"

In *Irish Aerospace (Belgium) NV* v. *European Organisation for the Safety* **10–012** *of Air Navigation,*[36] the case concerned the detention at Luton Airport of an aeroplane owned by the plaintiffs, Irish Aerospace (Belgium) Limited for alleged non-payment of charges for air navigation services. The dicta of Hirst J. in the Q.B.D. of the Commercial Court appears to confirm that damages are available for breach of Article 86 but the case against the defendant was dismissed on the ground that the latter, although a regulatory body performing the function of a public authority, with the

---

[34] Note the similar view expressed by Weatherill and Beaumont, *EEC Law* (1993), p. 706.
[35] Sharpston, *Interim and Substantive Relief in Claims under Community Law* (1993), p. 74.
[36] Judgment of June 10, 1991, not reported but cited in *XXI Report on Competition Policy 1991*, Commission of the European Communities Brussels/Luxembourg (1992), Annex V at p. 446.

power to impose charges, was not thereby a commercial organisation engaged in economic or commercial activities covered by Article 86.

Article 86 prohibits the abuse by one or more "undertakings" of a dominant position within the Common Market or in a substantial part of it. It has the same meaning as in Article 85.[37] However, the term "undertaking" is not defined in the E.C. Treaty. According to the Commission:

> "The functional concept of 'undertaking' in Article 85(1) covers any activity directed at trade in goods and services, irrespective of the legal form of the undertaking and regardless of whether or not it is intended to earn profits."[38]

It is generally interpreted broadly to cover any entity engaged in economic or commercial activity and may even include state-controlled trade organisations from Eastern Europe.[39] However, the emphasis appears to be on entities which are *themselves* engaged in the activity of trade, rather than regulatory bodies. Thus, although it is clear that state-owned corporations may be undertakings, there has been doubt, for example, whether local authorities and analogous bodies qualify as undertakings.[40] In Case 30/87, *Bodson* v. *Pompes Funèbres de Régions Libérées S.A.*[41] the Court held that Article 85 did not apply to licensing arrangements between French municipalities acting in their capacity as public undertakings entrusted with the provision of a public service.

Nevertheless, the definition of the term "undertaking" as it arose in the *Irish Aerospace* case is an issue which should arguably be referred to the ECJ for a preliminary ruling. However, the Commission did not comment on the substance of the decision when referring to it in its XXI Report on Competition Policy, 1991.[42]

In the later Case C–364/92, *SAT* v. *Eurocontrol*[42a] the German airline SAT relied on an alleged abuse of a dominant position as a defence to claims by Eurocontrol for payment of air traffic control fees. Advocate General Tesauro took the view that an international body such as Eurocontrol, responsible for managing air navigation control on behalf of certain States and for the collection of route fees as a mere agent of the contracting States, does not constitute an "undertaking" within the

---

[37] See Whish, *Competition Law* (1989), 2nd ed., p. 276. The concept of "undertaking" in general is a matter of Community law, so that its content cannot depend on definitions existing in the various Member States; see Opinion of Advocate General Van Gerven in Case C–7/90, *The State* v. *Paul Vandevenne and Others*: [1991] I E.C.R. 4371, [1993] 3 C.M.L.R. 608 at para. 5.

[38] *Film purchases by German T.V. Stations* [1989] O.J. L284/36 at (41). See also Case 32/65, *Italy* v. *Council and Commission*: [1966] E.C.R. 389, [1969] C.M.L.R. 39.

[39] *See Aluminium Imports from Eastern Europe* [1985] O.J. L92/1 at p. 37.

[40] Whish, *op. cit.*, n. 37, p. 215.

[41] Case 30/87, *Corrine*, judgment of May 4, 1988 [1988] E.C.R. 2479, [1989] 4 C.M.L.R. 984.

[42] XXI *Report on Competition Policy, 1991* (1992) European Commission, Brussels/Luxembourg.

[42a] Judgment of the ECJ, January 18, 1994, not yet reported.

meaning of Articles 86 and 90 of the E.C. Treaty. The ECJ confirmed in its judgment that Eurocontrol was not caught by the definition of "undertaking" within the meaning of E.C. competition rules. Regulatory bodies of this kind are therefore likely to be outside the scope of these rules.

## Breaches of other E.C. Treaty articles

The question of damages against the *State* for other breaches, *e.g.*, of **10–013** Article 30 relating to the free movement of goods has been discussed at paragraphs 9–016 *et seq.* In general, it seems to have been decided that Articles 30 to 36 do not apply to the conduct of *private* parties in the sense that it would not prevent a "buy British" policy of a retailer or a decision by individuals to boycott products from another Member State.[43] However, these Articles may nevertheless have *some* effect on private parties such as in the field of intellectual property rights, where the Court has placed some limits on the extent to which a private party may rely on such rights to prevent the importation of goods from another Member State or the sale of goods so imported.[44]

## Rules on causation and level of damages

It is observed by Whish[45] that the rules on causation and remoteness of **10–014** damages as they apply to actions under Articles 85 and 86, the quantification of damages and the availability of exemplary damages are all issues on which Community law does not at present offer sufficient guidance. He recommends that the Council of Ministers adopt a Directive under Article 87(1) of the Treaty on these issues, in order to ensure uniform application of Articles 85 and 86 in the various Community national courts. In the cases to date, applications for interim relief have often ended the litigation, without the need for consideration of the question of damages. For example, an interim order to refrain from predatory pricing may be sufficient to dissuade a defendant from further attempts to undercut the plaintiff's prices. Or alternatively, in a case of refusal to supply, an interim order against the dominant firm not to cut off supplies may be sufficient from the plaintiff's point of view.[46] On the other hand, heavy losses may well be sustanied in such cases in the interval between the breach of a Community obligation and the award of an injunction to restrain further or continuing breaches.

In the *Banks* case referred to above, the Advocate General Van Gerven acknowledged (at paragraph 47 of his Opinion), the serious risks posed to the uniform and effective application of Community law, if too many details relating to an action for damages were left to national law. He

---

[43] See Kapteyn and Verloren, *Introduction to the Law of the EEC* (1989), 2nd ed., p. 380.
[44] See, *e.g.* Case 15/74, *Centrafarm BV et al.* v. *Sterling Drug Inc.*: [1974] E.C.R. 1147, [1974] 2 C.M.L.R. 480 and Case 187/80, *Merck & Co. Inc.* v. *Stephar BV et al.*: [1981] E.C.R. 2063, [1981] 3 C.M.L.R. 463.
[45] Whish, *op. cit.*, n. 37, pp. 271 to 272.
[46] *Ibid.*, at p. 315.

reinforced the importance of the requirement, as a matter of Community law, of a causal connection between the breach of Community law and the damage suffered by the injured party (paragraph 53). However, although he recognised that some harmful consequences would be too remote to constitute a sufficient causal connection as a matter of law, he did not elaborate further on how causation should be defined as a matter of Community law. He did, however, imply that if a plaintiff can show *direct* causal connection between the breach and the ensuing damage, that will certainly suffice.

On the question of damages, however, the view of the Advocate General in *Banks*, following earlier case law of the Court particularly in *Von Colson* and *Marshall (No. 2)* (which are analysed at paragraphs 9–025 *et seq.* above), was that reparation for breach of Community competition law must be made *in full*, and would, in appropriate cases, include the award of interest (paragraph 54). He also stipulated that the party invoking liability must furnish proof of damage and was of the view that the Court has an unfettered discretion in assessing all the evidence of such damage which may be submitted to it (paragraph 51). He indicated that in order to bring an action for a declaration of liability for damages, "imminent damage foreseeable with sufficient certainty even if the damage cannot yet be precisely assessed", is enough (paragraph 51). He also confirmed principles regarding the mitigation of loss, which he said is a general principle common to the legal systems of all Member States, as well as making reference to the Community rule prohibiting unjust enrichment (discussed further below at paragraph 10–025). However, it remains to be seen whether the Court will follow the dynamic approach of the Advocate General or find it unnecessary to determine the question of damages insofar as it relates to actions for damages by private undertakings.

### Breach of statutory duty: possible cause of action

**10–015**   Although it is uncertain to what extent a breach of Article 85 of the E.C. Treaty (which prohibits anti-competition agreements and practices) gives rise to a cause of action in English law by third parties who may suffer loss as a result,[47] the reasoning of the Advocate General in the *Bank* case, discussed above, does suggest that as a matter of Community law, national courts are required to provide a remedy in such cases. The tort of breach of statutory duty is one possible vehicle for the development of a remedy, particularly for damages, in such cases. The various possible causes of action in cases involving breaches of Community law by the State are discussed at paragraphs 9–017 *et seq.* above. In *Garden Cottage Foods* (discussed at paragraph 10–001 above) Lord Diplock made reference to "a cause of action in English law of the nature of a cause of action for breach of statutory duty". It has been persuasively argued by Hoskins[48] that if a cause of action based on breach of statutory duty were

---

[47] Lewis, *Judicial Remedies in Public Law* (1992), p. 466.
[48] Hoskins, "*Garden Cottage* Revisited: The Availability of Damages in the National Courts for Breaches of the EEC Competition Rules" [1992] 6 E.C.L.R. 257 at p. 260.

in fact to be adopted, it would give rise to a number of difficulties in relation to the basis for the award of damages. In particular, the test of causation in respect of a breach of statutory duty is essentially a factual test, *i.e.*, the claimant must show that on a balance of probability, the breach of duty caused or materially contributed to his loss.[49] Hoskins argues that this approach to causation is unsuited to the issue of recovery of competition damages because it can give rise to liability for an indeterminate amount, for an indeterminate time, to an indeterminate class.[50] For instance, if a cartel of manufacturers breached European competition rules and thereby affected the operation of a certain product market, it may be difficult to establish who would be entitled to damages for economic loss, *i.e.*, other manufacturers who did not participate in the cartel, distributors, or even ultimate consumers? Hoskins therefore argues that the indeterminate liability is potentially enormous and might prove ruinous to an otherwise efficient company who had committed a breach of the competition rules.

Furthermore, the difficulties of proof would require extensive analysis of the market affected to ascertain whether the losses were suffered by a particular plaintiff, as a direct result of the anti-competitive behaviour or were perhaps due to other factors such as the recession, a decline in productivity or some other failure on the part of the plaintiff to react to general market conditions. The further down the chain of factual causation one went, the more difficult the problems of proof would become.[51]

## Tort of unlawful interference with trade/business: an alternative cause of action

Hoskins questions whether, as a matter of public policy, the English **10–016** courts should be burdened with such time-consuming exercises in relation to all potential plaintiffs. He suggests that a more helpful cause of action may be found in the economic tort of unlawful interference with trade or business. This tort was discussed by the Court of Appeal and the House of Lords in the case of *Lonrho plc* v. *Fayed*.[52] Its ambit was held by the House of Lords to be unclear. It includes the need to show that the injured party has suffered damage and causation must also be proved. It is also necessary to show that the unlawful act was in some sense directed against the plaintiff or intended to harm the plaintiff. However, the House of Lords held that in order to establish the tort of wrongful interference with trade or business it was *not* necessary to prove either a predominant purpose to injure the plaintiff or the existence of a complete tort between the tortfeasor and the third party against whom the wrong was committed. Hoskins suggests that this tort may therefore

[49] See *Bonnington Casting Limited* v. *Wardlaw* [1956] A.C. 613, cited by Hoskins, *op. cit.*, n. 48. See also discussion at paras. 9–017 *et seq.*
[50] Hoskins, *op. cit.*, p. 260.
[51] *Ibid.*
[52] *Lonrho plc* v. *Fayed* [1989] 2 All E.R. 65.

be advantageous as a cause of action because the limit of damages for this tort depends on a test of legal, rather than factual, causation. However, he accepts that it is not clear whether such an approach would constitute an acceptable means of giving effect to Articles 85 and 86.[53]

*Future development of rules concerning damages*

**10–017**  The alternative would be for the European Court itself to offer some form of guidance as to the limits of a claim for competition damages. This is all the more necessary since in any event the quantum of damages in competition cases may well vary between Member States which will in turn encourage some forum shopping by litigants.[54]

It remains to be seen whether the Commission's Notice "on co-operation with national courts and the Commission in applying Articles 85 and 86 of the EEC Treaty",[55] will encourage more domestic litigation on these points and possibly, through the awaited judgment in the Banks case discussed above and other appropriate references to the ECJ, to the further development of general principles of Community law in respect of actions for damages where non-State entities are involved.

## STATUTORY REMEDIES (INCLUDING REMEDIES IN THE INDUSTRIAL TRIBUNAL)

**10–018**  A vast range of statutes provides for statutory remedies. These include, for example, areas as diverse as the sale of goods, health and safety at work, product liability, consumer credit, occupiers' liability and employment law. It is not possible, in this work, to analyse the entire range of possible statutory remedies. However, some general observations may be made.

The relevant statute may confer original jurisdiction on a tribunal to determine questions of law, or alternatively may provide an appellate machinery for challenging the validity of the decisions of public bodies.[56] Such tribunals will usually have jurisdiction to decide whether or not E.C. law is relevant, even where the Community law rights may be classified as "public law rights".[57] For example, in *R.* v. *Secretary of State for the Home Department, ex parte Malhi*,[58] it was accepted that the immigration law appellate authorities had jurisdiction to consider EEC issues.

*Statutory remedies in employment law*

**10–019**  In the field of employment law, specific statutory remedies exist in relation to both equal pay and to sex discrimination (relating to access to employment and terms and conditions of employment other than pay).

---

[53] Hoskins, *op. cit.*, n. 48, p. 263.
[54] *Ibid.*, p. 264.
[55] [1993] O.J. C39/05 discussed further at paras. 3–032 *et seq.* above.
[56] See Lewis, *Judicial Remedies in Public Law* (1992), p. 88.
[57] Lewis, *op. cit.*, p. 89.
[58] *R.* v. *Secretary of State for the Home Department, ex p. Malhi* [1990] 2 W.L.R. 933.

For example, under section 65(1) of the Sex Discrimination Act 1975, three statutory remedies are provided: a declaration of rights, damages or a recommendation that certain action be taken. These remedies are available in relation to complaints of discrimination rendered unlawful by Part II of the 1975 Act.[59] In addition, complaints of discrimination outside the employment field[60] which are rendered unlawful under Part III of the Act may give rise to a claim in tort (in England and Wales), in the county court where the usual remedies are available. There appears not be any statutory limit on compensation for such cases.

### Relationship between national and E.C. law in the Industrial Tribunal

Industrial Tribunals must apply both national law and Community law **10–020** in dealing with cases brought before them on these issues.[61] However, the precise relationship between statutory remedies in the field of employment and rights derived from Community law has not been clearly resolved. A case which illustrates some of the difficulties is *W.B. Livingstone* v. *Hepworth Refractories Plc*.[62] This was a decision of the Employment Appeal Tribunal from a decision of the Industrial Tribunal, Sheffield. The appellant Mr Livingstone started employment with the respondents, Hepworth Refractories in 1951. He ceased active work on February 7, 1990 prior to his 65th birthday. His company pension was reduced proportionately to the prematureness of his retirement age. On April 9, 1990, a Conciliation Officer from ACAS drew up a COT3 form which was signed by both sides. The form excluded, in particular, its application to "benefits due to the applicant under the rules of the company's pension scheme." On May 17, 1990, the European Court of Justice give its judgment in Case C–262/88, *Barber* v. *Guardian Royal Exchange Assurance Group*.[63] Shortly afterwards the appellant sued his employers alleging sex discrimination in the operation of the pension fund. His pension was discounted, whereas that of a woman of the same age would not have been. The Industrial Tribunal dismissed the action for want of jurisdiction because of the agreement waiving all claims. (The agreement had been made in exchange for payment to the appellant of about £20,400 by the employers.)

The appeal was brought on the basis of a claim under both the Sex Discrimination Act 1975 and/or Community law. The Employment Appeal Tribunal found that the COT3 agreement did not apply, *inter alia*, to claims under the 1975 Sex Discrimination Act and that therefore the Tribunal was entitled to hear his claim under the Act.

In addition, the EAT accepted that Mr Livingstone also had a freestanding right to rely on Community law. However, there were no

---

[59] See Lewis, *op. cit.*, p. 471.
[60] *e.g.* education, and the provision of goods, facilities, services and premises.
[61] See further Lewis, *op. cit.*, n. 56, p. 469 *et seq.*
[62] *W.B. Livingstone* v. *Hepworth Refractories Plc* [1992] 3 C.M.L.R. 601.
[63] Case 262/88, *Barber*: [1990] I E.C.R. 1889, [1990] 2 C.M.L.R. 513 discussed at para. 4–008 above.

procedural rules for the consideration of such a claim. The Tribunal stated that the question of procedures to deal with direct Community claims:

> "has for some time been perplexing those practising within these industrial jurisdictions . . . the issue therefore is: what are the procedural rules to be brought to bear on procedings in an industrial tribunal in which direct Community claims are made? They are of course often linked with claims under domestic law."[64]

They accepted the submission of counsel for the appellant, that the Tribunal could find assistance from the case of C–208/90, *Emmott* v. *Minister for Social Welfare.*[65] In particular, the EAT held that where no domestic provisions had been enacted, national courts should adopt procedures which are not less favourable than those of similar provisions of domestic law provided that they are not so unreasonable as to render "virtually impossible the exercise of rights conferred by Community law."[66] The EAT therefore accepted that the proper approach was to apply the procedures of the Sex Discrimination Act to cover direct claims of sex discrimination under Community law. EAT held that these procedures:

> ". . . would cover not only time limits but also that code which is intended to protect employees against bad bargains. In taking this view we cannot ourselves think that there is any detriment to any one side or the other. Both know where they stand under domestic law and it seems to us that the procedural provisions of domestic law comply with those conditions indicated by the European Court of Justice in *Emmott*."[67]

The EAT also held by a majority that the words "benefits due to the applicant under the rules of the Company's Pension Scheme" were to be understood as meaning "under the rules of the Company's Pension Scheme as legally applicable" and therefore even on the facts of the agreement itself, there was no bar to the appellant bringing his claim. (This was strictly speaking unnecessary since the judgment was based on other grounds, but was included in the event that the EAT were in error on the interpretation of the law.)

### Claims based solely on Community law

10–021    Another difficulty in relation to statutory remedies is that the relevant statute (*e.g.* the Sex Discrimination Act 1975) does not state whether the remedies specified in it are available in respect of a claim based solely on Community law. However, it is clear from Case C–271/91, *M.H.*

---

[64] *Livingstone, op. cit.*, p. 606 at para. 15.
[65] Case 208/90, *Emmott*: [1991] I E.C.R. 4869, [1991] 3 C.M.L.R. 894; discussed in detail at para. 5–011 above.
[66] *Livingstone, op. cit.*, n. 62, p. 608 at para. 19.
[67] *Ibid.*, p. 608 at para. 20.

*Marshall* v. *Southampton and South West Hampshire Area Health Authority* (*Marshall No. 2*),[68] that the Court of Appeal proceeded on the basis that the statutory remedies for discrimination were available where the claimant was relying not on domestic law, but on a directly effective provision of Directive 76/207 on sex discrimination. In other words, Community law rights were treated as being analogous to national law rights. However, the complication in the *Marshall (No. 2)* case was as to whether the statutory limit which could be awarded as compensation for unlawful discrimination was adequate to protect Community law rights since the damages available are limited by statutory instrument. The Court's decision was that the statutory ceiling was unlawful and has led to statutory amendments. This has been discussed further at paragraphs 9–025 *et seq.* above.

In addition, claims under the Sex Discrimination Act 1975 must be brought within three months of the date on which the act complained of is done. It is not clear whether the limitation period applies to rights based on Community law alone,[69] but in any event the limitation period must be viewed subject to the principle laid down in *Emmott*, *i.e.* that in relation to directly effective provisions of directives, time does not begin to run until these have been correctly implemented by a Member State.[70]

# RESTITUTION

In Case 199/82, *Amministrazione delle Finanze* v. *San Giorgio*[71] the **10–022** European Court held that an individual has a right to recover charges that are levied contrary to a directly effective provision of Community law. This therefore requires national courts to provide a restitutionary remedy.[72] The kinds of charges which are prohibited under Community law include, for example, the levying of customs duties or charges having equivalent effect.[73] Member States are also prohibited from charging national of the E.C. countries fees for services which are higher than the fees they charge their own nationals, providing the services in question fall within the scope of the Treaty.[74]

By virtue of section 3 of the European Communities Act 1972 (as amended), questions of Community law are regarded as questions of law.

---

[68] *Case 271/91, Marshall (No. 2)*: Opinion of Van Gerven A.G. delivered on January 26, 1993, judgment of August 2, 1993: [1993] 3 C.M.L.R. 293, not yet reported in E.C.R. See further discussion at paras. 9-025 *et seq.* above.

[69] Lewis, *op. cit.*, n. 56, p. 472 and see further paras. 5–011 *et seq.* above. See also *Rankin* v. *British Coal Corporation* [1993] I.R.L.R. 69 discussed at para. 5–019 above.

[70] See discussion at paras. 5–011 *et seq.* above.

[71] Case 199/82, *Amministrazione delle Finanze* v. *San Giorgio*: [1983] E.C.R. 3595, [1985] 2 C.M.L.R. 658.

[72] Lewis, *Judicial Remedies in Public Law* (1992), p. 423.

[73] See, *e.g.* Article 12, Treaty of Rome (as amended).

[74] See Case 24/86, *Blaizot* v. *University of Liège*: [1988] E.C.R. 379, [1989] 1 C.M.L.R. 57, concerning discriminatory fees for higher education.

Under English law, money voluntarily paid under a mistake of law cannot, as a general rule, be recovered.[75] However, in relation to public authorities, this principle does not apply and there is a general restitutionary right to recover sums paid where a government body demands a payment that it has no legal power to demand and that payment is made, *e.g.* the Inland Revenue Commissioners.[76]

In *Woolwich Equitable Building Society*, Lord Goff point out that one of the reasons why he supported such a general restitutionary right of recovery was the decision in the *San Giogio* case,[77] where the ECJ established that a person who pays charges levied by a Member State contrary to the rules of Community law is entitled to repayment of the charge, such right being regarded as a consequence of, and an adjunct to, the rights conferred on individuals by the Community provisions prohibiting the relevant charges. The Court in *San Giorgio* did, however, accept that Community law did not prevent a national legal system from disallowing repayment of charges, where to do so would entail unjust enrichment of the recipient, in particular where the charges had been incorporated into the price of goods and so passed on to the purchaser. (This is discussed further below.)

Lord Goff commented that:

> ". . . at a time when Community law is becoming increasingly important, it would be strange if the right of the citizen to recover overpaid charges were to be more restricted under domestic law than it is under Community law."

He went on to hold (Lord Keith of Kinkel and Lord Jauncey of Tullichettle dissenting), that money paid by a citizen to a public authority in the form of taxes or other levies made pursuant to an *ultra vires* demand by the authority is prima facie recoverable by the citizen as of right. The decision of the House of Lords in *Woolwich Building Society* therefore reversed the decision by the Court of Appeal in that case whereby the latter had held that there were two exceptions to the principle that there was a general restitutionary right to recover sums paid in response to an unlawful demand for tax or any like demand for which there was no basis in law, *i.e.*, where the payment had been made voluntarily to close a transaction, or had been made under a mistake of law. It is therefore clear that payments made, for example, even under mistake of law, will not preclude the prima facie right of recovery. The illegality of a charge is also a defence to enforcement proceedings to recover that charge.[78]

In Northern Ireland, the High Court has held that an individual could recover charges under a statutory scheme, where these were unlawful as

---

[75] See generally, Goff and Jones, *The Law of Restitution* (1986), 3rd ed., pp. 117 to 136.

[76] See *Woolwich Equitable Building Society* v. *I.R.C.* [1992] 3 W.L.R. 366 (H.L.).

[77] *Op. cit.*, n. 71.

[78] See Case 222/82, *Apple and Pear Development Council* v. *Lewis (KG)*: [1983] E.C.R. 4083, [1984] 3 C.M.L.R. 733.

being contrary to Community law.[79] In Case 181/84, *R. v. Intervention Board of Agricultural Produce, ex parte D E and F Man (Sugar) Limited*[80] the applicant was granted a declaration of entitlement to the repayment of money levied under an invalid Community regulation.

Sometimes, there is a statutory procedure for the repayment of money unlawfully levied. This can be used to repay money levied contrary to Community law.[81]

## Repayment of unlawful State aid

It should be noted that under the Treaty provisions concerning State **10–023** aids, subsidies paid by national authorities in violation of Article 92 may be the subject of an order by the Commission to national authorities, to recover such subsidies from the recipient. For example, in the *Toyota Motor Corporation* Decision,[82] the Commission concluded that the sale of land to Toyota by Derbyshire County Council at an undervalued price constituted an unlawful state aid and the Commission requested the U.K. government to ensure that Toyota refunded the aid immediately. The ECJ has also instructed national courts to declare prematurely implemented aids as illegal.[83] In *Department of Trade* v. *British Aerospace*[84] the Commission ordered the U.K. to recover unlawful State aids paid to British Aerospace. The proceedings in the U.K. courts were adjourned, pending an action to annul the Commission decision under Article 173(2), in the European Court in Case C–212/90, *British Aerospace plc. and Rover Group Holdings plc.* v. *Commission of the European Communities*,[85] where the Court held that if a State does not comply with a Commission decision finding an aid incompatible with the Common Market, or does not observe the conditions on which the Commission approved the aid, the Commission may refer the matter to the Court directly under Article 93(2) of the EEC Treaty. (Article 93 has not been amended by the Treaty on European Union.) If the Commission thinks that new aid has been paid, which has not been examined under the procedure leading to a Commission Decision, the Commission is obliged to institute the special procedure under Article 93(2) of the E.C. Treaty and to give notice to the parties to submit their comments. It may also be possible for an action based on the principles of *Francovich*[86] to be brought to compensate individuals who suffer damage from aids not notified to the Commission.

---

[79] See *Cunningham* v. *Milk Marketing Board for Northern Ireland* [1988] 3 C.M.L.R. 815.
[80] Case 181/84, *R.* v. *Intervention Board for Agricultural Produce, ex p. D E and F Man (Sugar) Limited*: [1985] E.C.R. 2889, [1985] 3 C.M.L.R. 759.
[81] See, for example, *Commissioners of Customs and Excise* v. *Fine Arts Developments Plc* [1989] A.C. 914.
[82] Commission Decision 92/11, 1992.
[83] See Case 354/90, *Fédération Nationale du Commerce Extérieur des Produits Alimentaires* v. *France*: judgment of November 21, 1991.
[84] [1991] 1 C.M.L.R. 165.
[85] Case C–294/90 *British Aerospace Plc and Rover Group Holdings Plc* v. *European Commission*: [1992] I E.C.R. 493, [1992] 1 C.M.L.R. 853.
[86] See further discussion at paras. 9–017 *et seq.* above.

## Application of national procedural rules

**10–024**    However, national procedural conditions which may lawfully be taken into account, in deciding whether taxes levied contrary to Community law should be repaid, include time limitations[87]; unjust enrichment resulting from the taxes having been passed on to third parties[88]; damage to the trade of taxpayers resulting from the imposition of the unlawful tax[89]; and any benefits accruing to a person paying unlawful taxes by virtue of the payment.[90] In addition, the question of whether interest is payable on payments made in contravention of Community law was held to be a matter of national law in Case 6/60, *Humblet*.[91] However, there are a number of subsequent decisions of the Court in which the payment of interest was considered, and the decision in *Marshall (No. 2)* to award interest is an important new development of the relevant principles.[92]

## Unjust enrichment

**10–025**    There has been considerable controversy in connection with the Court's case law on unjust enrichment, *i.e.*, the passing on of charges imposed contrary to Community law. In the *Just* case[93] the question which arose was whether a tax or charge unlawfully levied by the Danish administration could be recovered by a trader who had passed on this charge to his clients in increased prices. Under Danish law, the trader could not recover such charges, on the basis of the principle of unjust enrichment. The Court held that the Danish law rule could also be applied to the recovery of taxes imposed by the Danish authorities *contrary* to Community law. This ruling was reaffirmed on several occasions[94] and has been widely criticised.[95] The main criticism is that it appears to enable Member States to flout Community law with impunity and also, to some extent to benefit from its own wrong doing. From the point of view of the individual, it may be difficult to establish whether a charge has indeed been passed on, since prices may be determined by factors other than the charge itself.

However, the ruling in *Just* must now be seen in the light of the *San Giorgio* case where the State measures were specifically designed to

---

[87]  See Case 33/76, *Rewe*: [1976] E.C.R. 1989, [1977] 1 C.M.L.R. 533; Case 45/76, *Comet*: [1976] E.C.R. 2043, [1977] 1 C.M.L.R. 533; Case C–208/90, *Emmott*: [1991] I E.C.R. 269, [1991] 3 C.M.L.R. 894, discussed at paras. 5–011 *et seq.* above.

[88]  See Case 199/82, *San Giorgio*, *op. cit.*, n. 71.

[89]  Case 68/79, *Just*: [1980] E.C.R. 501, [1981] 2 C.M.L.R. 714.

[90]  Case 177/78, *Pigs and Bacon Commission* v. *McCarren*: [1979] E.C.R. 2161, [1979] 3 C.M.L.R. 389.

[91]  Case 6/60, *Humblet*: [1960] E.C.R. 559.

[92]  See further paras. 9–025 *et seq.* above.

[93]  *Just, op. cit.*

[94]  See, for example, Case 61/79, *Amministrazione delle Finanze* v. *Denkavit Italiana*: [1980] E.C.R. 1205, [1981] 3 C.M.L.R. 694, and Case C–128/92, *H.J. Banks & Company Ltd.* v. *British Coal Corporation*: Opinion of Advocate General Van Gerven, delivered on October 27, 1993, para. 48, not yet reported.

[95]  See further, Oliver, "Enforcing Community Rights in the English Courts" (1987) M.L.R. 881 at pp. 889 *et seq.*

deprive litigants of a remedy and were in fact hightly successful in achieving that aim and were declared unlawful by the Court.[96] The Court of Justice confirmed that national courts might legitimately take into account the fact that unduly levied charges had been incorporated in the price of goods and subsequently passed on to the purchaser. However, the national rule in that case, which was a presumption to the effect that the duties or taxes had in fact been passed on, in the absence of documentary proof to the contrary, had the effect of making it "virtually impossible or excessively difficult" to secure the repayment of charges levied contrary to Community law and was incompatible with it. The Court said that this was particularly so in the case of presumptions or rules of evidence which placed upon the taxpayer the burden of establishing that the charges had not been passed on to third parties, coupled with special limitations concerning the form of evidence to be adduced, such as the exclusion of any kind of evidence other than documentary evidence. The Court emphasised that national rules rendering recovery virtually impossible could not be justified even if they were applied in a similar way to the recovery of taxes paid unduly under national law.[97]

## REMEDIES IN THE FIELD OF PUBLIC PROCUREMENT

One of the main priorities of the internal market is the opening up of **10–026** public procurement to Community-wide competition. Public purchasing (including purchasing by public administrations, public and semi-public enterprises) represent 15 per cent. of the Community's gross domestic product. Public sector contracts for works, supplies and services are estimated to be worth some £420 billion annually.[98] Traditionally, governments have favoured the award of such contracts to domestic suppliers of goods and services, especially in periods of economic recession or as a remedy for structural unemployment. This is a practice which is clearly not compatible with fundamental principles of an Internal European Market.[99]

There is extensive E.C. legislation on public procurement.[1] In general terms, the regime requires contracts awarded by public authorities and those awarded by the utilities industries over certain cost thresholds, to be advertised in the Official Journal of the E.C. and to be awarded in accordance with uniform rules in all Member States. These rules are complex. This work focuses only on the rules relating to remedies.

---

[96] See further, Oliver, *op. cit.*, p. 891.
[97] See discussion at Chap. 8 above.
[98] See Bedford, "New Horizons" (February 24, 1993) 90/8 *Gazette* 19 at p. 19.
[99] See background Report, "Public Procurement: Opening Public Services Contracts" (April 6, 1992), European Commission Office, London, ISE C/D8/92.
[1] See Trepte, *Public Procurement in the E.C.* (1993); Weiss, *Public Procurement in European Community Law* (1993).

However, in summary, the E.C. procurement regime provides for, *inter alia*, different forms of tendering procedures. The regime covers time limits, technical standards and, in particular, provides for non-discriminatory, open and transparent procedures for selecting and awarding contracts. Contracts above the requisite threshold are governed by the E.C. regime and must be advertised in a standard from in the Official Journal. Tenders must subsequently be chosen in accordance with the objective criteria set out in the tender notice.

The main areas covered by E.C. legislation concern the opening up of procurement markets for public supplies,[2] and public works.[3] These have been extended, in relation to works and supplies, by the "Utilities" Directive[4] to the formerly "excluded sectors" of energy, water, transport and telecommunications. Article 29 of the Utilities Directive includes a controversial provision, that any tender made for the award of a supply contract may be rejected by the contracting entity where the porportion of the products originating in third countries exceeds 50 per cent. of the total value of the products constituting the tender if those third countries do not provide "comparable and effective access for Community undertakings" (Article 29(1)).[5] The EEC and the USA have subsequently concluded a Memorandum of Understanding in which they have agreed to make certain reciprocal commitments to open their respective procurement markets in respect of contracts for goods, works and other services.[6] In addition, a "Public Services" Directive has been adopted.[7] The proposal for an additional "Service Utilities" Directive relating to the provision of services to Utilities reached a common position on June 18, 1992 and was adopted on June 14, 1993.[8] It enters into force on July

---

2 Directive 77/62 of December 21, 1976 [1977] O.J. L13/1, last amended by Directive 88/295 [1988] O.J. L127. Now consolidated in Council Directive 93/36 of June 14, 1993 co-ordinating procedures for the award of public supply contracts [1993] O.J. L199/1, hereinafter referred to as the Public Supplies Directive.

3 Directive 71/304 of July 26, 1971 [1971] O.J. Spec. Ed. 678, last amended by Directive 89/440 [1989] O.J. L210. Now consolidated in Council Directive 93/37 of June 14, 1993 covering the procedures for the award of public works contracts [1993] O.J. L199/54, hereinafter referred to as the Public Works Directive.

4 Directive 90/531 of September 17, 1990 [1990] O.J. L297/10. Now consolidated (and amended to include the "Services Utilities" Directive) in Council Directive 93/38 of June 14, 1993 co-ordinating the procurement procedure of entities operating in the water, energy, transport and telecommunications sections [1993] O.J. L199/84, hereinafter referred to as the Utilities Directive.

5 See further Trepte, "The Application of Procurement Procedures in the Hitherto Excluded Sectors: War-torn but Triumphant?" (Winter 1990) *Utilities Law Review* 158 at p. 165.

6 Memorandum of Understanding between the USA and the EEC on government procurement: [1993] O.J. L125/1, May 20, 1993. See generally, Trepte "Partial Solution to the E.C./U.S. Trade Dispute" (1993) P.P.L.R. issue 4.

7 Directive 92/50 of June 18, 1992 [1992] O.J. L209/1. Council Directive on the co-ordination of procedures for the award of public service contracts, hereinafter referred to as the Public Services Directive.

8 Directive 93/88, of June 14, 1993, [1993] O.J. L199/84. Council Directive co-ordinating the procurement procedures of entities operating in the water, energy, transport and telecommunications sectors. Hereinafter referred to as the Services Utilities Directive. See further, *op. cit.*, n. 4.

1, 1994 except in Spain (January 1, 1997) and Portugal and Greece (January 1, 1998). The definition of "services contracts" in both the Services and the Utilities Directive (as amended by the Services Utilities Directive) is designed to supplement the existing regime and, with certain exceptions, to extend them to cover contracts not caught by the rules relating to works and supplies.

Despite this extensive legislation by the E.C. in the field of public procurement, national reports confirm the Commission's own conclusion that legal remedies for the enforcement of individual rights in this area vary widely between Member States.[9]

## Remedies Directive

In order to develop judicial protection and legal remedies in the field **10–027** of public procurement, the Community had adopted two Directives. The first is the "Remedies" Directive.[10] This is intended to ensure the correct application of E.C. rules for the award of public supply, public works and public services contracts. A further directive, the "Remedies Utilities" Directive[11] concerns the application of E.C. rules for public supply and public works contracts in the formerly "excluded sectors" of energy, water, transport and telecommunications and is discussed at paragraph 10–032 below.

### Ambit of the Remedies Directive

The "Remedies" Directive is concerned with national remedies falling **10–028** within the scope of the Public Works, Public Supplies, and Public Services Directives.[12] However, the U.K. implementing regulations, the Public Supply Contracts Regulations[13] and Public Works Contract Regulations[14] (discussed further below) only extend to implementation of the Remedies Directive and of the Public Works and Public Supply Directives. They do not extend expressly to cover the Public Services Directive (which has been given effect to separately in domestic law by

---

[9] See Hancher, "The Madrid FIDE Congress: Application in the Member States of the Directives on Public Procurement" (Winter 1990) *Utilities Law Review* 179 at p. 181.

[10] Directive 89/665 of December 21, 1989 [1989] O.J. L395/33. Council Directive on the co-ordination of laws, regulations and administrative provisions relating to the application of review procedures to the award of public supply and public works contracts. Also known as the "Compliance" Directive. Hereinafter referred to as the Remedies Directive. This Directive has been amended by the Public Services Directive, *op. cit.*, n. 7.

[11] Directive 92/13 of February 25, 1992 [1992] O.J. L76/14. Council Directive co-ordinating the laws, regulations and administrative provisions relating to the application of Community rules on the procurement procedures of entities operating in the water, energy, transport and telecommunications sectors, hereinafter referred to as the Remedies Utilities Directive.

[12] See Article 1(1) of the Remedies Directive, *op. cit.*, as amended by Article 41 of the Public Services Directive, *op. cit.*

[13] Public Supply Contracts Regulations 1991, S.I. 1991 No. 2679.

[14] Public Works Contracts Regulations 1991, S.I. 1991 No. 2680.

the Public Services Contracts Regulations 1993, which came into force on January 13, 1994[14a] and which implements both the Public Services Directive and the Remedies Directive. It should, however, have been in force in the U.K. by July 1, 1993. In that interim period, the U.K. courts would, it is submitted, be required to adopt a purposive approach to construction of the Regulations and would be required to construe them so as to cover the Public Services Directive as well (at least as from July 1, 1993). (See discussion at paragraph 5–009 above.)

The Remedies Directive applies to decisions by contracting authorities which "have infringed Community law in the field of public procurement or national rules implementing that law."[15] However, the Remedies Directive does *not* apply to any breaches of Community law which occur in the course of award procedures but which are not within the scope of the Directives, *e.g.* because they are below the relevant threshold values. In these situations, remedies would only be available under general Community law, rather than under the Remedies Directive. Thus, for example, an aggrieved party could bring an action in national law based either in private or public law, or complain to the European Commission with a view to the latter bringing infraction proceedings under Article 169 of the E.C. Treaty.

The "contracting authorities" covered by the Remedies Directive are those defined in the Public Supplies Directive (Article 1(b)), as amended, and the Public Works Directive (Article 1(b)), as amended. The Public Services Directive also applies to "contracting authorities" within the meaning of the Public Works Directive. The U.K. implementing regulations (Public Works Contracts Regulations 1991, regulation 3(1), the Public Supply Contracts Regulations 1991, regulation 3(1) and the Public Services Contracts Regulations, Reg. 3(1)) provide a list of entities which are defined as contracting authorities. The Public Services Contracts Regulations 1993 amend, in Regulation 33, relevant provisions of the Public Supply Contracts Regulations 1991 to endeavour to ensure that not more than one set of Regulations applies to any one contract.

### Role of the European Commission

**10–029**   It is important to bear in mind that among the principles on which the public procurement rules are based are those aimed at the establishment of the internal market as an area without internal frontiers in which the free movement of goods, persons, services and capital is ensured. Cases have therefore been brought by the Commission against Member States for violations, for example, of Article 30 of the EEC Treaty. (Article 30 has not been amended by the Treaty on European Union.) In Case 45/87, *Commission* v. *Ireland*,[16] also known as the *Dundalk Pipeline* case, the

---

[14a] S.I. 1993 No. 3228.

[15] See further, Arrowsmith, "Enforcing the Public Procurement Rules: Legal Remedies in the Court of Justice and the National Courts" in *Remedies for Enforcing the Public Procurement Rules* 1993 (Arrowsmith ed.), Vol. IV 1 at p. 53.

[16] Case 45/87, *Commission* v. *Ireland*: [1988] E.C.R. 4929, [1989] 1 C.M.L.R. 225.

Dundalk UDC in Ireland invited tenders by the "open procedure" and published the tender in the E.C. Official Journal, for the construction of a water main to improve the drinking water supply to Dundalk. The tender specifications included the following provision:

"Asbestos cement pressure pipe shall be certified as complying with Irish Standard Specification 188: 1975 in accordance with the Irish Standard Mark Licensing Scheme of the Institute of the Industrial Research Standard."

The Commission brought proceedings against Ireland for a breach of Article 30 and the Court held that although E.C. Directive 71/305 (on Public Works) was inapplicable to the tender proceedings because the water sector was an excluded sector, nevertheless a breach of Article 30 had been established in that:

"The fact that a public works contract related to the provision of services cannot remove a clause in an invitation to tender restricting the material that may be used from the scope of the proviso prohibition set out in Article 30."[17] . . . "by incorporating in the notice in question the words "or equivalent" after the reference to the Irish Standard . . . the Irish authorities could have verified compliance with the technical conditions from the outset without restricting the contract only to tenderers proposing to utilise Irish materials."[18]

In Case 21/88, *Dupont de Nemours Italiana SPA*,[19] the ECJ was asked for a preliminary ruling by an Italian Court. A company was in dispute with Carrara District Health Authority concerning the conditions governing the award of contracts for the supply of radiological films and liquid. Under a 1986 Italian law on "special aids for southern Italy", the Health Authority was required to obtain at least 30 per cent. of its supplies from undertakings established in southern Italy. In applying Article 30, the ECJ confirmed that the rules on state aids:

". . . may in no case be used to frustrate the rules of the Treaty on the free movement of goods . . . the fact that a national measure might be regarded as aid within the meaning of Article 92 is . . . not a sufficient reason to exempt it from the prohibition contained in Article 30."[20]

The ECJ has recently rules that the public procurement contract for the construction of a bridge across the Grand Belt in Denmark breached E.C. law. In Case C–243/89, *Commission* v. *Denmark*[21] concerning the

---

[17] Para. 17 of the judgment, *ibid.*
[18] Para. 22 of the judgment, *ibid.*
[19] Case 21/88, *Du Pont de Nemours Italiana SPA*: [1990] I E.C.R. 889, [1991] 3 C.M.L.R. 25.
[20] Para. 20 of the judgment, *ibid.*
[21] Case 243/89, *Commission* v. *Denmark*: judgment June 22, 1993; *Financial Times*, June 29, 1993 at p. 12.

Public Works Directive, the ECJ found that the contract was flawed in two respects. First, by insisting that construction companies were to use as high a percentage of Danish materials as possible, the state-owned company in charge of the project was found to be in breach of EEC law (Article 30, 48 and 59). The removal of this clause at the last stage of the operation, prior to signature of the contract was not, the Court found, sufficient to validate the breach. Secondly, the ECJ found that the successful tender had not been made in conformity with the tender offer conditions. The ECJ held that it was irrelevant that the Public Works Directive on public procurement did not specifically mention the right to equal treatment for tenderers, as that obligation was at the very heart of the Directive. It was intended to ensure an objective comparison between the various tenders. The principle of equality therefore precluded that tender from consideration since it was in breach of Community law.

### Alternative means of redress

10–030   If the Commission cannot be persuaded to take action under Article 169 E.C., an aggrieved individual may also still have a possibility of redress in national law either on the basis of direct effect of the relevant provisions and/or on the basis of the principles estabished in *Francovich*. This has been discussed in detail at paragraphs 8–016 *et seq.* above and further at paragraph 10–037 below. It is likely, for example, that the procurement rules specify rights for the benefit of individuals and are therefore brought within the *Francovich* doctrine. A further issue which would arise is whether contracting bodies covered by the Procurement Directives are to be considered as synonymous with "the State" for the purposes of establishing State liability, as in *Francovich*.[22]

It is noted by Arrowsmith[23] that the distinction between award procedures which are subject to the directives and those which are not is unfortunate and may cause confusion. In the U.K. the implementing regulations for the Remedies Directive, *i.e.* the Public Supply Contracts Regulations,[24] the Public Works Contracts Regulations,[25] and the Public Services Contracts Regulations 1993[25a] discussed further below, expressly refer to procedures falling within the Remedies Directive. It is also pointed out by Arrowsmith[26] that the Remedies Directive only applies to the conduct of "contracting authorities". Thus, if a government department acts in a legislative capacity (and not as a contracting authority) by, for example, enacting a regulation which puts into effect an unlawful procurement preference policy, its actions will not be covered by the Directive because the department is not acting as a "contracting authority," but in another capacity. The Directive would not allow, in those

---

[22] See also discussion at Chap. 7 above.
[23] Arrowsmith, *op. cit.*, n.15, at p. 53.
[24] S.I. 1991 No. 2679.
[25] S.I. 1991 No. 2680.
[25a] S.I. 1993 No. 3228.
[26] Arrowsmith, *op. cit.*, n. 15, p. 14.

situations, for remedies such as an award of damages to be available against that government department but there may nevertheless be other causes of action available in domestic law, such as a breach of statutory duty for non-compliance with Community law. This has been discussed at paragraphs 9–016 *et seq.* above.

## Forms of relief under the Remedies Directive

Article 2 of the Remedies Directive sets out specific forms of relief **10–031** which Member States are required to make available via the designated "review body", which can include non-judicial tribunals. The option has not been taken up in the U.K. where jurisdiction is vested, in England and Wales and Northern Ireland, in the High Court.[27] The specific measures which Member States are required to make available are set out in Article 2(1) of the Directive:

"(a) take, at the earliest opportunity and by way of interlocutory procedures, interim measures with the aim of correcting the alleged infringement or preventing further damage to the interest concerned, including measures to suspend or to ensure the suspension of the procedure for the award of a public contract or the implementation of any decision taken by the contracting authority;

(b) either set aside or ensure the setting aside of decisions taken unlawfully, including the removal of discriminatory technical, economic or financial specifications in the invitation to tender, the contract documents or in any other document relating to the contract award procedure;

(c) award damages to persons harmed by an infringement."

By Article 2(4):

"The Member States may provide that when considering whether to order interim measures the body responsible may take into account the probable consequences of the measures for all interests likely to be harmed, as well as the public interest, and may decide not to grant such measures where their negative consequences could exceed their benefit. A decision not to grant interim measures shall not prejudice any other claim of the person seeking these measures."

The criteria for the award of interim relief is therefore left, in general, to national courts but is subject to the general Community obligation to provide an *effective* remedy.[28] Neither the Remedies Directive nor the U.K. implementing regulations provide, for example, for special rules governing the discovery of documents. In judicial review proceedings it

---

[27] See Regulation 26(3) Public Contracts Regulations, Regulation 31(4) of the Public Works Contracts Regulations and Regulation 32(3) of the Public Services Contracts Regulations. In Scotland, proceedings are brought before the Court of Session.

[28] See Arrowsmith, *op. cit.*, n. 15, p. 62 and discussion at paras. 8–003 *et seq.* above.

is usual, for example, to try questions of fact by reference solely to the sworn affidavit evidence. The principle of effectiveness may arguably require States to make provision for reasonable access to administrative documents relating to a procurement, to allow complainants to prove their case but it remains to be seen whether the judiciary will adopt this kind of approach to proceedings instituted under the Regulations.[29] The availability of a particular form of relief should also not be unduly difficult or impossible to obtain.[30]

In relation to damages, the Directive contains the important innovation of requiring the review body to be able to award damages. However, the Directive is silent on principles for calculating those damages and the matter is therefore left to Member States. (This is discussed further below at paragraphs 10–042 *et seq.* However, as with the interim relief, it is again subject to the limitation that this remedy must be effective and must not be unduly difficult or impossible to obtain. It is of interest that although no rules have been included for the calculation of damages under the Remedies Directive, in the Remedies Utilities Directive (discussed below at paragraphs 10–032 *et seq.*) there is an option in Article 2(1)(c) (which has not been taken up by the U.K., but is applied in Denmark) for dissuasive payments to be made available on the basis of limited damages, such as recovery of bid costs, to all those who can show reasonable chance of success in the award procedure.[31]

The Remedies Directive provides expressly in Article 2(6) that national law may determine whether a contract may be set aside or suspended *after* it has been concluded. Member States may also provide that after the conclusion of a contract, the powers of the review body be limited to the award of damages to any party harmed by an infringement. The U.K. has accordingly taken up this option.[32] This simplifies the position and is advantageous for long-term administrative and commercial planning.[33]

## Remedies Utilities Directive

### Scope of the Directive

10–032    The Remedies Utilities Directive follows a similar approach to that of the Remedies Directive but there are some material differences. The remedies provided for in the utilities sector are regarded as more flexible, to take into account the fact that the contracting entities are often private undertakings.[34] The Remedies Utilities Directive applies to contracts

---

[29] See Weatherill, "Enforcing the Public Procurement Rules in the U.K." in Arrowsmith (ed.), *op. cit.*, 271 at p. 282.

[30] See further discussion at paras. 8–003 *et seq.* above.

[31] See Article 2(7) of the Remedies Utilities Directive.

[32] See Reg. 26(6) of the Public Supply Contracts Regulations and Reg. 31(7) of the Public Works Contracts Regulations.

[33] Weatherill, *op. cit.*, p. 283.

[34] See Trepte, "Remedies in the Utilities Sector: The European Dimension and Application in the U.K., paper presented at a Conference on Implementing and Enforcing the E.C. Procurement Directives, University of Birmingham, April 22 to 23, 1993.

which fall within the scope of the Utilities Directive, and this specifically includes compliance with Article 3(2)(a) of the Utilities Directive which extends public procurement rules to entities subject to the alternative regime for the exploration for and extraction of oil, gas, coal and other solid fuels.[35] Contract awards made on the basis of this alternative regime are therefore also subject to the Remedies Utilities Directive. In the U.K., the Utilities Directive and the Remedies Utilities Directive have been implemented by the Utilities Supply and Works Contracts Regulations 1992 which are discussed at paragraphs 10–050 et seq. below.

The scope of the Remedies Utilities Directive is similar to that of the Remedies Directive in that it extends to decisions which "have infringed Community law in the field of procurement or national rules implementing that rule."[36] It extends to "contracting authorities" covered by the Utilities Directive (Article 2). The Directive also retains in Annexes I–X, an illustrative list of entities in each Member State which are considered to fulfill the relevant criteria. However, Member States are also required to keep such lists under review and there are procedures for any amendments to these lists to be notified to the Commission so that they are as exhaustive as possible.[37]

## Forms of relief under the Remedies Utilities Directive

In the Remedies Utilities Directive, two alternative systems of **10–033** remedies are provided for. The first system is that which exists under the Remedies Directive and concerns the powers to award interim relief, for setting aside and for damages. The second system refers in addition to the possibility of an order "for the payment of a particular sum," sometimes referred to as a dissuasive payment. This second system provides for the power to take, at the earliest opportunity, if possible by way of interlocutory procedure or, if necessary, by a final procedure on the substance, measures other than interim measures or setting aside, with the aim of correcting any identified infringement and preventing injury to the interests concerned. In particular, the Directive provides in Article 2(1)(c) for the power to make an order for the payment of a particular sum in cases where the infringement has not been corrected or prevented. The level of the sum to be paid must be high enough to dissuade the contracting entity from committing or persisting in an infringement.[38]

The option of this system of dissuasive payments may be extended by Member States either to all contracting entities or for categories of entities. If Member States exercise this choice in relation to categories of

---

[35] Article 1(1)(b) of the Remedies Utilities Directive, op. cit., n. 11.
[36] Article 1(1) of the Remedies Utilities Directive, op. cit., and see discussion at paras. 10–027 et seq. above.
[37] See further Armin Trepte, "The Application of Procurement Procedures in the Hitherto Excluded Sectors: War-torn but Triumphant?" (Winter 1990) Utilities Law Review 158 at pp. 158 et seq. See also paras. 10–050 et seq. below.
[38] Article 2(5).

entities, these must be defined on the basis of objective criteria.[39] Although the term "objective criteria" is not defined in the Remedies Utilities Directive, it is likely to include matters such as the nature of the contracting entities in terms of the sector they cover, their size or legal status.

It is left to the discretion of Member States to set the level of the dissuasive payment either generally or in each individual case. In the original proposal presented by the Commission[40] the dissuasive payment had been intended to cover bid costs or costs of participating in the procedure, incurred by the plaintiff. These costs were deemed to be 1 per cent. of the value of the contract, unless it could be proved that the actual costs were greater. However, since damages are required, in any event, to be available,[41] a dissuasive payment may not adversely affect any further claim for damages.

However, the U.K. has opted for the first system, *i.e.* the award of interim relief, setting aside and damages. In addition, the U.K. has taken advantage of the option in Article 2(6) of the Remedies Utilities Directive to provide that once the contract has been concluded, the *only* remedy available shall be damages.[42]

The Remedies Utilities Directive, like the Remedies Directive, merely requires that damages be available. It is silent on the question of the quantum of damages. However, the Remedies Utilities Directive differs in one respect, and that is in relation to the burden of proof, where a claim is made for damages representing the costs of preparing a bid or of participating in an award procedure, in that Article 2(7) provides:

> "Where a claim is made for damages representing the costs of preparing a bid or of participating in an award procedure, the person making the claim shall be required only to prove an infringement of Community law in the field of procurement or national rules implementing that law and that he would have had a real chance of winning the contract and that, as a consequence of that infringement, that chance was adversely affected."

There is no equivalent provision in the Remedies Directive and it is suggested by Armin Trepte[43] that there is no logical reason for this difference between the public sector and the utilities sector.

*Attestation*

10–034    The Remedies Utilities Directive also provides for a system of "attestation." Article 3 specifies that this is an option for the contracting entity itself, rather than the Member State. Under Article 4, contracting entities may have their contract award procedures and practices, which

---

[39] Article 2(1)(c).
[40] COM(90)297 final—Syn 292.
[41] See Article 2(1)(d).
[42] See also discussion at paras. 10–027 *et seq.* above.
[43] Trepte, *op. cit.*, n. 34 above, at p. 6.

fall within the scope of the Utilities Directive, examined periodically with a view to obtaining an attestation that, at that time, those procedures and practices were in conformity with Community law concerning the awards of contract and the national rules implementing the law. The relevant additional procedural requirements are set out in the Directive (Articles 4 to 7). The use of the attestation system will, however, be of little value to a contracting entity if, having undergone attestation they are subsequently found to have committed an infringement. However, the 1993 U.K. implementing regulations do not provide for an attestation procedure. This is discussed further at paragraph 10–055 below.

### Role of the European Commission

Both the Remedies Directive and Remedies Utilities Directive (in **10–035** Article 3 and Article 8 respectively) make provision for the specific application of the Commission's general power of supervision under Article 169 of the Treaty of Rome (which is not amended by the Treaty on European Union), referred to as "the corrective mechanism." This gives the Commission power to intervene at any time before the conclusion of a contract where it considers that there has been a clear and manifest infringement of Community provisions in the field of public procurement during the contract award procedure, falling within the scope of the relevant Directive. The procedures to be followed are set out in the Directive. It provides an additional safeguard in the event either of a tenderer being unable to bring proceedings in the relevant national review body or the inability of national review bodies to provide the necessary remedies.

### Conciliation

Finally, the Directive also provides for "Conciliation" as an additional **10–036** procedure for non-litigious dispute settlement.[44] This procedure is expressly without prejudice to the rights of the European Commission (under Article 169) and of Member States (under Article 170) or of the rights of the Commission to make use of the "corrective mechanism" or of the rights of the persons requesting the conciliation procedure, of the contracting entity or of any other person. The commencement of the conciliation procedure therefore does not preclude the use of litigious remedies, in the event that conciliation fails. Furthermore, the fact that the conciliation procedure has been set in motion does not preclude others from seeking remedial action where that is appropriate.[45]

## Domestic implementation of the Remedies Directive

In the U.K., legislation to implement the Public Supplies Directive (as **10–037** amended),[46] the Public Works Directive (as amended)[47] and the Remedies

---

[44] Chapter 4 of the Directive, *op. cit.*, n. 11. For a more detailed discussion see Gormley, "The New System of Remedies in Procurement by the Utilities" (1992) 1 P.P.L.R. 259 at pp. 266 *et seq.*

[45] Trepte, *op. cit.*, n. 34, p. 9.

[46] Now consolidated in Council Directive 93/36, *op. cit.*, n. 2.

[47] Now consolidated in Council Directive 93/37, *op. cit.*, n. 3.

Directive was enacted on December 21, 1991 in the form of the Public Supply Contracts Regulations[48] and the Public Works Contracts Regulations.[49] The Public Services Directive, including amendments to the Remedies Directive, was enacted in the U.K. on January 13, 1994 by the Public Services Contracts Regulations 1993.[49a] These regulations were made by the Treasury under powers conferred in section 2(2) of the European Communities Act 1972, and were preceded by extensive consultation with interested parties. Prior to 1991 the Public Procurement Directives were implemented by circulars issued by central government which lacked formal legal status and reduced the practical transparency of U.K. rules and procedures.

The Utilities Directive and the Remedies Utilities Directive were also implemented in the U.K. by the Treasury under the same powers and after a similar process of consultation by the Utilities Supply Works Contracts Regulations which came into force on July 13, 1993.[50] These are discussed further at paragraphs 10–050 et seq.

The final stages in the opening up of public procurement to intra-Community competition will be completed when the U.K. implements the Service Utilities Directive.[51]

## Scope of the domestic Regulations

10–038    It is submitted by Weatherill[52] that the U.K. implementation of the public sector procurement directives displays no glaring deviation from the Community measures. Both the Public Supply Contracts Regulations 1991, the Public Works Contracts Regulations 1991 and the Public Services Contracts Regulations 1993 provide for a statutory duty owed, in respect of Public Supply Contracts, by contracting authorities to suppliers, in respect of the Public Works Contracts on contracting authorities to contractors and, in respect of Public Services Contracts on contracting authorities, to service providers.[53] Regulation 31(1) of the Public Works Contract Regulation adds that in the case of a public works concession contract (public works contracts under which the consideration given by the contracting authority consists of or includes the grant of a right to exploit the works or works to be carried out under the

---

[48] S.I. 1991 No. 2679.
[49] S.I. 1991 No. 2680.
[49a] S.I. 1993 No. 3228.
[50] S.I. 1992 No. 3279.
[51] Op. cit., n. 8.
[52] Weatherill, op. cit., n. 29, p. 276.
[53] Reg. 26(1) Public Supply Contracts Regulations, Reg. 31(1) Public Works Contracts Regulations and Reg. 32(1), Public Services Contracts Regulations. It has been suggested by Nuala O'Loan that the fact that the Public Services Contracts Regulations follow the scheme of the Public Supply Contracts Regulations and the Public Works Contracts Regulations is to be welcomed, but that there will, nevertheless, be difficulties of interpretation, particularly in the context of the aggregation rules and the rules pertaining to the selection of service providers: see O'Loan, (1993) 3 P.P.L.R. CS60 at CS67.

contract),[54] obligations imposed on a concessionaire (*i.e.* a person who has entered into a public works concession contract with a contracting authority (regulation 2(1)) to respect stipulated procedural requirements, also comprises a statutory duty owed to contractors, *e.g.* suppliers or sub-contractors. A breach of this duty is actionable by a supplier (or contractor) who in consequence of the breach suffers, or risks suffering, loss or damage. The contracting authorities covered are listed in regulation 3(1) of each set of Regulations.

The term "supplier", "contractor" and "service provider" is specifically defined.[55] A contractor (or supplier) is a person who sought or who seeks or would have wished to be the person to whom the relevant contract is awarded, and who is a national of and established in a Member State. Regulation 31(2) of the Public Works Contract Regulations makes the appropriate addition with regard to concessionaires. A service provider is a person who sought or who seeks or would have wished to be the person to whom a services contract is awarded, or to participate in a design contest, and who is a national of and established in a Member State. A design contest means a competition particularly in the fields of planning, architecture, civil engineering and data processing and is defined in Regulation 2(1) and Regulation 24 of the Public Services Contracts Regulations.

Under regulation 2 of each of the three sets of Regulations, which deals with interpretation issues, "national of a Member State" means in relation to a person who is not an individual "a person formed in accordance with the laws of a Member State and which has its registered office, central administration or principal place of business in a Member State." This definition is drawn from Article 58 of the Treaty of Rome (which is not amended by the Treaty on European Union) and has the effect, for example, of excluding nationals of GATT contracting States.[56]

Under both sets of the 1991 Regulations, and of the 1993 Regulations, the complainant can seek the remedies available providing certain conditions are satisfied.[57] First, a breach of the duty owed must be demonstrated. Secondly, the complainant must notify the contracting entity of the alleged infringement and of the intention to seek review. Thirdly, the complaints must be brought "promptly" and in any event within 3 months from the date when grounds from bringing the proceedings first arose.[58] The formulation of the time limits mirrors the requirements for judicial review proceedings and is intended to facilitiate administrative certainty.[59]

---

[54] See Reg. 25 and interpretation section in Reg. 2(1).
[55] 1991 Public Works Regulations, Regs. 4 and 31(1); 1991 Public Supply Contracts Regulations, Regs. 4 and 31(1); 1993 Public Services Contracts Regulations, Regs. 4 and 32(1).
[56] See further Weatherill, *op. cit.*, n. 29, p. 280.
[57] 1991 Public Works Regulations, Reg. 31(5)(a) and (b); 1991 Public Supply Contracts Regulations, Reg. 26(4)(a) and (b); 1993 Public Services Contracts Regulations, Reg. 32(4)(a) and (b).
[58] 1991 Public Works Regulations, Reg. 31(5)(b); 1991 Public Supply Contracts Regulations, Reg. 26(4)(b); 1993 Public Services Contracts Regulations, Reg. 32(4)(b).
[59] Weatherill, *op. cit.*, n. 29, p. 278.

### Remedies under the domestic Regulations

**10–039**  As to the remedies available, the Court may, under Regulation 31(6) of the Public Works Contracts Regulations:

"(a) by interim order suspend the procedure leading to the award of the contract in relation to the award of which the breach of the duty owed pursuant to paragraphs (1) above is alleged, or suspend the implementation of any decision or action taken by the contracting authority or concessionaire, as the case may be, in the course of following such a procedure; and

(b) if satisfied that a decision or action taken by a contracting authority was in breach of the duty owed pursuant to paragraphs (1) above:—

(i) order the setting aside of that decision or action or order the contracting authority to amend any document, or

(ii) award damages to a contractor who has suffered loss or damage as a consequence of the breach, or

(iii) do both of those things."

By virtue of regulation 31(8) statutory power is given to grant an injunction or interdict against the Crown, thus giving effect to the judgment in the *Factortame* case.[60]

Under the Public Supply Contracts Regulations, and the Public Services Contracts Regulations the powers of the Court are phrased in an identical way under Regulation 26(5) and Regulation 32(5) respectively. Sub-paragraph (7) of both Regulations also makes clear that the Court has power to grant an injunction or interdict against the Crown.

The Court has been given power under both sets of 1991 Regulations and under the 1993 Regulations, to grant appropriate interim and final relief and to award damages, except that where the contract in respect of which there has been an infringement has already been entered into, the Court's powers under the various Regulations is restricted to awarding damages.[61] In the case of public works contracts, the obligation on a concessionaire in respect of sub-contracting works under a public works concession contract is likewise enforceable.[62] This means that a wider range of remedies is available in the pre-contract situation, including the suspension of the awards procedure, or the implementation of a decision taken by the contracting authority.

### Principles relating to grant of interim relief

**10–040**  The Regulations do not provide any guidance on the principles to be applied in deciding whether to order interim measures. The principles elaborated in Article 2(4) of Directive 89/665 (discussed above) provide

---

[60] Discussed further at paras. 9–034 *et seq.* above.
[61] Public Works Regulation 31(7), Public Supply Regulation 26(6) and Public Services Regulation 32(6).
[62] Reg. 31.

for the balance of convenience to be taken into account. It appears that in deciding whether or not to order interim measures, the High Court will apply the usual principles of English law, notably those applied in *American Cyanamid* v. *Ethicon*,[63] which have already been discussed in detail.[64] The intention of the Remedies Directive is clearly to provide quick and effective remedies at an interlocutory stage. However, a key consideration under English law in deciding whether or not to grant interim relief is the availability of a remedy in damages. It is therefore necessary to await the outcome of future litigation in order to gauge the likelihood of the U.K. court granting interim relief. It is suggested by Weatherill[65] that if the availability of damages as a remedy under the Regulations proves genuine and effective, interim orders will be comparatively rarely awarded.

## Setting aside of a decision and amendment of documents

In addition, the remedies of setting aside a decision and of the **10–041** amendment of documents is provided for. There may not be much of a practical difference between the setting aside of a decision and an injunction to prevent the award procedure from continuing.[66] The amendment of documents may, for example, refer to notices given prior to the award procedure and require the removal of discriminatory technical standards.[67]

## Principles governing the award of damages

Both the Remedies Directives and the U.K. Regulations of 1991 are **10–042** silent on the question of what the supplier or contractor has to prove in order to be awarded damages. Apart from the need to show an infringement of Community law in the field of public procurement or national rules implementing that law, it is therefore uncertain whether he/she also has to prove, for example, that he/she would have had a real chance of winning the contract and/or that the infringement has adversely affected his/her chance of winning. The basis of calculation of the damages will depend on whether the action is brought for breach of statutory duty or for breach of contract. If contract damages are available, *i.e.*, the aggrieved party is seeking damages in order to put himself in the position he would have been in if the contract had been correctly performed, then the aggrieved party will be able to claim not only actual loss caused by the unlawful tendering exercise but also the expected loss of anticipated future profits. However, there may be difficulties in estimating loss in a competitive situation[68] and also in proving that the tender would have been successful in any event.

---

[63] *American Cyanamid* v. *Ethicon* [1975] A.C. 396.
[64] See paras. 9–036 and 10–001 above.
[65] Weatherill, *op. cit.*, n. 29, p. 285.
[66] See Mark Lane, "Compliance and Enforcement", paper presented at a Conference on "The Impact of the E.C. Procurement Regime", IBC Legal Studies and Services Ltd., Friday May 22, 1992 1 to 16 p. 6.
[67] Lane, *op. cit.*, p. 6.
[68] See *Chaplin* v. *Hicks* [1991] 2 K.B. 786.

## Damages for breach of statutory duty

**10–043**    However, if damages are to be calculated on the basis of a breach of statutory duty, the tortious standard will apply and compensation is recoverable for loss which was, on the balance of probabilities, caused by that breach.[69] This would usually cover the costs of preparing the tender but would not include damages for loss of profit because if the breach had not occurred the supplier/contractor would have had only a chance, but no more, of winning the contract. Therefore on the balance of probabilities (in most cases) the supplier will have suffered no loss caused by the breach in relation to lost profits. The tortious standard may therefore avoid the need for an assessment of the likelihood of winning a contract as a result of the tendering exercise, or the level of subsequent profit on the contract had it been awarded.[70] It is suggested by Weatherill[71] that although the law of tort does not require the supplier/contractor to prove conclusively that he/she would have won the contract had the breach not occurred, it does require the supplier/contractor to demonstrate that *on the balance* of probabilities the breach caused it to lose the contract. Weatherill argues that in most cases this burden will not be discharged which empties the remedy of damages under the Regulations of much of its impact.[72]

In evidence given to the Select Committee of the House of Lords on the European Communities, the view was taken that, on the whole, any inclusion of damages for "foregone profits or lost opportunities" could lead to speculative and wasteful litigation.[73] The Committee proposed that damages should be recoverable only for tender costs and legal costs. (This would not preclude other heads of damages from being taken into account in other jurisdictions where they may be traditionally available.) The Committee considered that in general, the precedent set in the Local Government Act 1988 (discussed below) was an appropriate precedent for a system whose purpose was to enforce the observance of Community rules on public procurement rather than to guarantee profits to tenderers.[74] It is submitted, as argued by Weatherill,[75] that the Regulations, when read together with the relevant Directives should be interpreted in such a way as to deter defaults. Therefore, the national courts should display a willingness to award damages for loss of the chance of a profit caused by the breach, which is quantifiable at least by reference to the wasted bidding costs.[76]

---

[69] See *Hotson* v. *East Berkshire AHA* [1987] A.C. 750.
[70] See Bennett and Cirell, "Problems with European Public Procurement" (December 18, 1991) No. 46 *Gazette* 19 at p. 20.
[71] Weatherill, *op. cit.*, n. 29, p. 289.
[72] *Ibid.*, p. 290.
[73] See 12th report of Select Committee of House of Lords on the European Communities, "Compliance with Public Procurement Directives", Session 1987–88 (H.L. 72), para. 74, p. 20.
[74] *Ibid.*
[75] Weatherill, *op. cit.*, p. 294.
[76] See further discussion at para. 10–014 above.

## Availability of judicial review

It is also arguable that an additional cause of action will be (in addition **10–044**
to that provided by the Regulations) in public law by way of judicial
review, since there is nothing in the regulations to suggest that judicial
review is not available.[77] However, there does not appear to be any
advantage in opting for judicial review since on the issue of time limits,
for example, the procedural rules are identical.

## Alternative remedy under the Local Government Act 1988

There is also the possibility of a statutory remedy under the Local **10–045**
Government Act 1988, whereby public authorities are required to ensure
that their award of contracts takes no account of "non-commercial
matters".[78] No account should therefore be taken, for example, of the
terms and conditions of employment of the tenderer's workforce, the
conduct of the contractors and industrial disputes, the country of origin
of supplies to the contractors or political, industrial or sectarian affilia-
tions with contractors.[79] The duty imposed on local authorities under
section 17 does not create a criminal offence, but failure to comply with
it would be actionable by any person who suffers loss or damage in
consequence of the authorities' wrongful action. However, compensation
in such cases is limited to damages "in respect of expenditure reasonably
incurred . . . for the purpose of submitting a tender."[80]

## Other causes of action

There may, in addition, be a possibility of basing liability for unlawful **10–046**
acts in the course of public procurement on a private law claim, *e.g.* for
the tort of misfeasance in public office,[81] as well as other torts such as
negligent mis-statement, misrepresentation, or other "economic torts"
such as conspiracy and interference with trade by unlawful means.[82]
However, it is doubtful whether the prospects of recovery, and in
particular the resolution of the problem of causation, discussed above, is
any easier in respect of these alternative claims. However, it is pointed
out by Weatherill,[83] that if other causes of action are available, it may be
possible to argue that other provisions in domestic law are more
advantageous than those in the Regulations and should therefore be
transplanted into them. For example, under the Local Government Act
1988, claims may be instituted by organisations representing contractors,
though this is not permissible under the Regulations. Weatherill argues
that it may be possible to invoke the Community principle of "non-

---

[77] Bennett and Cirell, *op. cit.*, n. 70.
[78] See section 17(1).
[79] Section 17(5).
[80] Section 19(8).
[81] Discussed further at para. 9–022 above.
[82] See further Weatherill, *op. cit.*, n. 29, pp. 302 *et seq.*
[83] *Ibid.*, p. 303.

discrimination"[84] to enable a widening of the remedies which may be available. However, it remains unclear how advantageous such general principles of Community law will be in the future in relation to remedies for breach of the public procurement rules.

### Breach of Article 30, E.C. Treaty

**10–047** Finally, since the scope of the Regulations encompasses "any enforceable Community obligation in respect of a . . . contract",[85] it follows that, for example, breaches of Article 30 of the E.C. Treaty may also be enforced through these Regulations. The advantage would be that damages would accordingly be available, whereas had the action been brought by way of judicial review, the Court of Appeal decision in *Bourgoin* v. *MAFF*[86] may stand in the way of a claim for damages. This has been discussed in detail at paragraphs 9–018 *et seq.* above. The Remedies Directive and its domestic implementing regulations are therefore a significant advance in the provision of remedies such as damages within the domestic legal system, at least in the field of public procurement.

### Practical effectiveness of the Regulations in the U.K.

**10–048** There have not as yet been any reported U.K. court decisions in respect of these new Regulations covering the domestic implementation of the public procurement rules of the E.C. It has been doubted whether legal action of a traditional sort can, in fact, play an important role in securing compliance with these rules, however effective in theory the remedies may be, because of the reluctance of contractors to institute proceedings and to "bite the hand that feeds them." Another difficulty is whether unsuccessful contractors or suppliers will always have sufficient knowledge of breaches in the first place. Nevertheless it is suggested by Bedford[87] that it would be a mistake for authorities to blacklist suppliers or contractors who invoke the regulations and to reject their subsequent tenders out of hand, because tenders can only be rejected for the reasons prescribed in the E.C. rules and the courts would act accordingly if there was a suspicion that these rules were being deliberately breached in this way.

### Application of remedies in other E.C. States

**10–049** In the first case to be brought before a national court under the terms of the recent E.C. legislation on public procurement, the Irish Department of Education has agreed to an out of court settlement. It had been

---

[84] Discussed further at para. 8–007 above.
[85] See Reg. 26(1) of the Public Supply Contracts Regulations, Reg. 31(7) of the Public Works Contracts Regulations and Reg. 32(1) of the Public Services Contracts Regulations.
[86] *Bourgoin* v. *MAFF* [1986] Q.B. 716.
[87] Bedford, "New Horizons" (February 24, 1993) 90/8 *Gazette* 19 to 20.

alleged that the Department had not given adequate publicity to contracts worth Irish £1.5 million for computers, software and other equipment for use in Irish secondary schools. (Under the E.C. legislation, public procurement contracts must be advertised in the E.C. Official Journal.) The Department has since re-advertised the requirements in a revised form.[88]

In Denmark, the review body which has been established under the public procurement regime is that of an Appeal Board for Public Procurement. So far it has only made a decision on one complaint although it has received several more complaints which have either been settled or are still pending before the Board.[89] The decision of the Board, pronounced in August 1992, concerned the procurement of a ferry. A municipality offering a ferry service within its area had purchased a new ferry without inviting tenders in accordance with Community procurement rules. The Danish shipyard which had tendered for the contract but did not get it complained to the Board that the rules in the Public Supply Directive had not been followed. The Board found for the defendant because the Public Supply Directive at the time in question did not apply to public supplies contracts awarded to carriers by sea.

## Domestic implementation of the Remedies Utilities Directive

The Utilities Directive and the Remedies Utilities Directive are given **10–050** effect in the U.K. by the Utilities Supply and Works Contracts Regulations 1992 (the Utilities Regulations).[90] These were made by the Treasury on December 23, 1992, under powers conferred by section 2(2) of the European Communities Act 1972. The Regulations came into effect on January 13, 1993. (This was slightly late, since the date by which the implementing measures should have come into force under both Directives was January 1, 1993). They do not cover the Services Utilities Directive 93/38 discussed above at paragraph 10–026 which comes into force on July 1, 1994 in all Member States except Spain (January 1, 1997) and Portugal and Greece (January 1, 1998) and may require separate domestic implementing Regulations.

### Scope of the Utilities Regulations

The Utilities Regulations follow the format adopted in the Public **10–051** Works Contracts Regulations (the Works Regulations)[91] and the Public Supply Contracts Regulations (the Supply Regulations).[92] Part VII of the Utilities Regulations deals with remedies. The identification of entities

---

[88] See the *Week in Europe*, May 27, 1993, Commission of the European Communities, London WE/21/93.

[89] See Kirsten Hee Larsen, "The First Decision of the Danish Appeal Board for Public Procurement" (1993) 2 P.P.L.R. at CS63.

[90] Utilities Supply and Works Contracts Regulations 1992 (the Utilities Regulations): S.I. 1992 No. 3279.

[91] Public Works Contract Regulations 1991, *op. cit.*, n. 14.

[92] Public Supply Contracts Regulations 1991, *op. cit.*, n. 13.

and activities to be regulated in the U.K. proved to be a difficult exercise.[93] The Treasury has tried to produce as comprehensive a list of regulated entities as possible in Schedule 1 which provides for regulated utilities and activities. Undertakings are defined according to the nature of activity (as provided for in Article 2 of the Utilities Directive) by name, and sometimes also by reference to the holding of a licence under relevant legislation. In several cases there is also a "catch-all" definition of "any other relevant person" not otherwise specified, which will ensure the application of the Regulations where appropriate.

The relevant utilities are only regulated in respect of their procurement in connection with specified activities. Thus, for example, O'Loan gives the example of a bus company which provides a service to the public in the field of transport by bus (which is a regulated activity), and which also runs a coach holiday tour business (which is not regulated, although is subject to the normal rules of competition in that sector). This bus company will therefore be regulated in its procurement in respect of the bus service, but not in relation to the coach holiday tours.[94] It is therefore possible that litigation may arise in which a plaintiff might argue, for example, that a utility is disguising its regulated procurement as unregulated procurement so as to avoid the application of the Regulation.[95] The person for whom the benefit of the Utilities Regulations is available is identical to that followed under the Works and Supply Regulations, *i.e.* "a person who sought, or who seeks or who would have wished to be the person to whom a contract is awarded and who is a national of and established in a Member State." (Regulation 4(1).) This reflects the requirements in both the Remedies Utilities Directive and the Utilities Directive.

Regulation 30 provides for review of the actions of a utility in fulfilling "its obligations to comply with the provisions of these regulations . . . and with any enforceable Community obligation in respect of a Supply or a Works Contract. . . ." The system of challenge is identical to that established under the Works and Supply Regulations (discussed above). In other words, proceedings may only be brought by an aggrieved supplier or contractor in the High Court in England and Wales or in Northern Ireland,[96] provided that the utility is informed beforehand that proceedings are to be brought and provided also that such proceedings are brought promptly and in any event within 3 months.

*Forms of relief available under the Utilities Regulations*

**10–052**    The relief available, *i.e.* the suspension of the contract award procedure, suspension of the implementation of a decision or action, the setting aside of a decision or action, amendment of documentation, and

---

[93] See Nuala O'Loan, "Implementation of Directive 90/531 and 92/13: Utilities Supply Works Contracts Regulations of the U.K." (1993) 2 P.P.L.R. CS55–61 at C56.
[94] *Ibid.*, CS56.
[95] *Ibid.*, CS57.
[96] Or in the Court of Session in Scotland.

the possible award of damages follow the same pattern as for the Works and Supply Regulations discussed above. Once the contract has been concluded, the only remedy available is in damages.

## Measure of damages

Under regulation 30(1) the measure of damages will be the cost in **10–053** preparing the tender and participating in the award procedure, plus damages for any other loss or damage suffered as a consequence of the breaches by the utility under regulation 30(1). There is no provision for a dissuasive payment. Unlike the Public Works Regulations and Public Supply Regulations however, the Utilities Supply and Works Regulations (in accordance with Article 2(7) of the Remedies Utilities Directive, discussed above) require in relation to claims for damages representing the costs of preparing a bid or of participating in an award procedure, that the Court is satisfied that the supplier or contractor "would have had a real chance of being awarded a contract if that chance had not been adversely affected by a breach of the duty owed to him by the utility. . ." (regulation 30(7).)

## Alternative avenues of redress

Regulation 31 also provides for conciliation procedures (as required in **10–054** Articles 10 and 11 of the Remedies Utilities Directive). However, a supplier or contractor has the right under Article 9(2) of the Remedies Utilities Directive to make an application direct to the Commission if it chooses to do so. The main advantage of such a course of action is the fact that it avoids the cost of litigation. It may also be advantageous to rely on the wide investigative powers of the Commission in respect of discovery of documents. The merits and demerits of each alternative has been discussed in relation to competition law cases at paragraphs 3–034 *et seq.*, above and the same general concerns will apply in relation to public procurement.

## Attestation

There is no provision in the Utilities Regulations for a system of **10–055** attestation, as provided in Chapter 2 of the Remedies Utilities Directive. The obligation to provide such a system is expressly stated in Article 3 of the Directive but the U.K. has decided that provisions for attestation are unnecessary at the present time. This position will be reconsidered if the need to do so arise.[97]

The Utilities Regulations broadly implement the Utilities Directive and the Remedies Utilities Directive in most respects, with the exception of the absence of any system of attestation. It is suggested by O'Loan that this omission will not cause any difficulty in the U.K. because of the lack of enthusiasm by utilities themselves for such a system. However, it

---

[97] See O'Loan, *op. cit.*, CS60.

still remains to be seen whether in fact significant savings and the opening up of markets will result from the new Regulations.

## "EURO-LAW" DEFENCES

**10–056**    Community law rights may be used as either a sword or a shield in domestic proceedings. It may be pleaded as a defence in a variety of situations, including actions brought by private individuals and based on directly effective Community rights. An example of the latter, is the case of *Chiron Corporation* v. *Organon Teknika Limited*.[98] This was an interlocutory decision of the English High Court, Chancery Division (Patent Court). The plaintiffs, C, discovered and patented the genome of the hepatitis C virus and immunoassay kits for detecting the anti-bodies. It entered into a joint venture arrangement with O to produce and market the kits and also licensed A in America to produce them, with no restriction on A selling in Britain, which it did with success. M manufactured and sold the kits in Britain (and also exported them to other Member States) but without obtaining a licence from C. C thereupon sued M (and others) for patent infringement. M defended on the grounds that C was abusing its dominant position contrary to Article 6 of the Treaty of Rome, by refusing to license the patent and by charging excessive prices for licences and for its kit.

### Requirement for a viable Euro-Defence

**10–057**    An interlocutory application was made by the plaintiffs to strike out those Euro-defences. Aldous J., made it clear that he intended to scrutinise the Euro-defence with care to see whether counsel for the defendants had been able to demonstrate that there was a viable defence.[99] He conducted a detailed examination into the various elements under Article 86 and concluded that the relevant product market was the immunoassay kits and that there were sufficient grounds for allowing the question of dominant position to go forward to trial. However, it was held that there was no abuse of dominant position in the refusal to license as such and that although the charging of allegedly excessive prices for the kits on the British market might amount to an abuse, and that there was a sufficient nexus between the abuse and the exercise of the patent rights to justify a Euro-defence, there was nevertheless no link between C's abusive prices in Britain and M's export to other Member countries. Consequently there was no effect on inter-State trade and although the dominant position and the abuse were both pleadable, the plea failed on the inter-State trade requirement and was struck out.

The judgment in this case also illustrates why the plaintiff's application to strike out the Euro-defence was so important. Aldous J. commented that:

---

[98] *Chiron Corporation* v. *Organon Teknika Limited* [1992] 3 C.M.L.R. 813 (Ch.D.).
[99] *Ibid.*, p. 817 at para. 12.

". . . If the allegations are allowed to remain in [M's] defence, the plaintiff must give discovery and call witnesses, which could include marketing personnel and an expert. Such witnesses will be cross-examined, thereby prolonging a heavy trial which could be attended by five sets of solicitors and counsel of which only one set is concerned with the Euro-Defence."

In *Curust Financial Services Ltd.* v. *Loewe-Lack-Werk Otto Loewe GmbH & Co. KG*, the Irish Supreme Court held that where the defendant to a breach of contract action had raised a prima facie defence that the contract was prohibited by Article 85 of the EEC Treaty, the onus of establishing an exemption or avoidance of that prohibition rested with the plaintiff.[1]

A Euro-defence was also raised in the case of *Waterlow Directories Limited* v. *Reed Information Services Limited*[2] a decision of Mr Justice Aldous in the English High Court, Chancery Division (Patents Court). The plaintiff was the publisher of the Solicitors' and Barristers' Directory and claimed to be the owner of the copyright in it. The defendant published Butterworth's Law Directory. The plaintiff applied for an interlocutory injunction prohibiting the defendant from continuing until trial with its arrangements to publish its lawyers' directory, some of the information for which was compiled with the use of the plaintiff's very well-known directory. To succeed in the action, the plaintiff had to show that copyright subsisted in its directory, that it owned that copyright and that the defendant had infringed that copyright by copying a substantial part of the plaintiff's directory without its consent.

At the hearing for the interlocutory injunction, the defendant did not contest subsistence or ownership of copyright, but did deny infringement. The defendant accepted that there was a serious issue to be tried on infringement. Mr Justice Aldous therefore proceeded on the basis that copyright did subsist in the plaintiff's directory and that the plaintiff was the owner, and went on to determine where the balance of convenience lay.[3]

Counsel for the defendant raised, *inter alia*, a Euro-defence, the **10–058** substance of which was that the assertion by the plaintiff of its copyright was contrary to Articles 85 and 86 of the Treaty of Rome and that therefore an injunction at trial would not be granted. (It was also submitted that no injunction at trial would be granted as that would derogate from the grant of rights by the plaintiff, made by publishing its directory.)

Aldous J. dealt with the Euro-defence in the following way:

"The defendant also relies upon Articles 85 and 86 EEC. Those Articles only apply insofar as agreements or the like and abuses

---

[1] *Curust Financial Services Ltd.* v. *Loewe-Lack-Werk Otto Loewe GmbH & Co. KG* [1993] 2 C.M.L.R. 808 (Irish Supreme Court).
[2] *Waterlow Directories Limited* v. *Reed Information Services Limited* [1993] E.C.C. 174 (Ch.D.).
[3] See further discussion on balance of convenience at paras. 9–035 *et seq.* above.

affect trade between Member States. There is no evidence of how anything that the plaintiff has done or is doing which could affect trade between Member States. I conclude that this defence is fanciful."[4]

In the litigation broadly concerned with Sunday trading, the defence raised by some defendants seeking to rely on Article 30 of the EEC Treaty was regarded in some cases as merely a device to persuade the court to refer the point to the ECJ and thereby obtain a two-year delay during which trading could continue on Sunday.[5]

Actions to enforce intellectual property rights may sometime be met with the defence that stuatutory provisions creating such rights contravene Articles 30 to 36 of the Treaty of Rome (as amended). For instance, in an action for royalties, the defence of anti-competitive practices was raised,[6] as well as in an action for an injunction to enforce a market-sharing agreement.[7] Defences to an action for statutory debt based on Treaty provisions have also been raised but were unsuccessful.[8] In *Imperial Chemical Industries Limited* v. *Berk Pharmaceuticals Limited*[9] in an action for an injunction against passing off, the Vice Chancellor, Sir Robert Megarry struck out a defence which claimed that the plaintiff company occupied a dominant position in a substantial part of the Common Market and was abusing that dominant position by charging excessively high prices for certain pills, thereby reducing the competitiveness of the defendant which could only be restored by the latter adopting the same getup as the plaintiff. He decided that:

". . . I think that English Courts must be ready to scrutinise a Euro-defence with care, notwithstanding any apparent complexity, and should not adopt the attitude, whether overt or covert, that because it is a Euro-defence it must at least be arguable. If at the end of the examination counsel has been unable to demonstrate that there is a viable defence then the defence, like any other hopeless defence, should be struck out."[10]

The courts will not generally grant the plaintiff an injunction if they have formed the clear view that the Euro-law defence of incompatibility

---

[4] *Waterlow Directories Limited, op. cit.*, p. 182 at para. 23. (Articles 85 and 86 have not been amended by the Treaty on European Union.)

[5] See further discussion at para. 3–030 above and Diamond, "Dishonourable Defences: The Use of Injunctions and the EEC Treaty—Case Study of the Shops Act 1950" (1991) M.L.R. 72 to 87.

[6] *Dymond* v. *Britton (GB) and Sons (Holdings) Limited* [1976] 1 C.M.L.R. 133, [1976] F.S.R. 330.

[7] *Sirdar* v. *les Fils de Louis Mulliez* [1975] 1 C.M.L.R. 378, [1975] F.S.R. 309.

[8] See, for example, *Potato Marketing Board* v. *Drysdale* [1986] 3 C.M.L.R. 333 and *Potato Marketing Board* v. *Robertson* [1983] 1 C.M.L.R. 93.

[9] *Imperial Chemical Industries Limited* v. *Berk Pharmaceuticals Limited* [1981] 2 C.M.L.R. 91 (Ch.D.).

[10] *Imperial Chemical Industries Limited, op. cit.*, p. 98, para. 12, judgment of Sir Robert Megarry.

of English law with Community law is made out.[11] However, in general there is a presumption of compatibility with Community law, but this a rebuttable presumption.[12]

## Euro-defences in criminal law

The use of Euro-defences in criminal law is outside the scope of this **10–059** work. However, some general points may be of interest. Legislation which creates criminal offences contrary to Community law is invalid.[13] Subordinate legislation and statutes enacted before 1972 which violate Community law are also impliedly repealed to that extent.[14] If enacted after 1972 the usual rules of construction apply. Defences based on Community law are matters of law and not issues of fact for the jury.[15]

In Case 148/78, *Pubblico Ministero* v. *Ratti*,[16] the defendant was prosecuted under national law and successfully raised a Euro-defence in respect of one of the charges against him on the ground of his compliance with the directly effective provisions of a directive which were more lenient.[17] In Case 80/86, *Officier van Justitie* v. *Kolpinghaus Nijmegen BV*[18] the Court held that the State could not rely in a criminal prosecution on a directive whose implementation date had passed, independently of implementing legislation, to create or aggravate the criminal liability of someone who breached its provisions, because the duty on national courts to interpret national law in the light of a directive was limited by general principles of law, in particular the principles of legal certainty and non-retroactivity.[19]

Finally, a Community law defence may be invoked in respect of an instrument governed by public law in the course of criminal proceedings. For example, the accused may raise as a defence the invalidity of the subordinate legislation or bye law that he/she is alleged to have violated.[20] Another illustration is provided by the prosecutions commenced by local authorities in the Sunday trading cases referred to above.[21] Such defences may, however, be largely concerned with the practical tactics of litigation and have been regarded as specious in some cases.[22]

---

[11] See *Polydor and RSO Records Inc.* v. *Harlequin Record Shop and Simon's Records* [1980] 2 C.M.L.R. 413 (C.A.).

[12] See *Factortame (No. 1)* [1990] 2 A.C. 85 and *Factortame (No. 2)* [1991] 1 A.C. 603 discussed at paras. 9–034 *et seq.* above and Lewis, *Judicial Remedies in Public Law* (1992), p. 222.

[13] See Case 269/80, *R.* v. *Tymen*: [1981] E.C.R. 3079, [1982] 2 C.M.L.R. 111 and *Henn & Derby* v. *DPP* [1980] 2 W.L.R. 597.

[14] See, *e.g.* Case 63/83, *R.* v. *Kirk*: [1984] E.C.R. 2689, [1984] 3 C.M.L.R. 522, [1985] 3 All E.R. 453.

[15] *R.* v. *Goldstein* [1983] 1 C.M.L.R. 252, [1983] 1 W.L.R. 151, H.L.

[16] Case 148/78, *Pubblico Ministero* v. *Ratti*: [1979] E.C.R. 1629, [1980] 1 C.M.L.R. 96.

[17] See further discussion at para. 5–009 above.

[18] Case 80/86, *Officier van Justitie* v. *Kolpinghaus Nijmegen BV*: [1987] E.C.R. 3969, [1989] 2 C.M.L.R. 548.

[19] See further discussion at para. 6–006 above.

[20] *e.g. R.* v. *Reading Crown Court, ex p. Hutchinson; R.* v. *Devizes Justices, ex p. Leigh* [1988] Q.B. 384.

[21] See further discussion at para. 3–029 above and Diamond, *op. cit.*, n. 5.

[22] See further, Diamond, *op. cit.*, p. 82.

The future potential of its use as a defence in connection with Article 30 of the E.C. Treaty has now been considerably restricted by the landmark ruling of the ECJ in Joined Cases C–267–268/91, *Keck and Mithouard*,[23] in which the Court replied to a request from a French court for a preliminary ruling under Article 177 of the EEC Treaty. The case concerned criminal proceedings brought against Mr Keck and Mr Mithouard for violation of a French law generally prohibiting "resale at a loss". The defendants claimed in their defence that the French law was incompatible with Article 30. The Court held that in view of the increasing tendency of traders to invoke Article 30 of the Treaty as a means of challenging any rules whose effect was to limit their commercial freedom, even where such rules were not aimed at products from another Member State, necessitated a re-examination and clarification of the Court's earlier case law on the matter. The 13 judges unanimously decided, expressly reversing earlier case law, that national laws restricting or prohibiting certain selling arrangements which apply to products from other Member States, were not such as to hinder directly or indirectly, actual or potential trade between Member States within the meaning of the *Dassonville* judgment[24] and that provided those laws applied to all affected traders operating within the national territory and provided they affected in the same manner, in law and in fact, the marketing of domestic products, such national laws fall outside the scope of Article 30.

This case will no doubt lead to extensive analysis by text writers and reflects the uncertainties of the Court's jurisprudence relating to national rules imposing an equal burden on domestic producers and importers. It would now seem that most price fixing and licensing arrangements will in the future be treated by the Court as being outside the ambit of Article 30.[25]

---

[23] Joined Cases C–267–268/91, *Kech and Mithouard*: judgment of November 24, 1993: *The Times*, November 25, 1993. See also discussion at paras. 9–042 *et seq.* above.

[24] Case 8/74, *Dassonville*: [1974] E.C.R. 837, [1974] 2 C.M.L.R. 436.

[25] General literature on Article 30 is extensive; see, in particular, Weatherill and Beaumont, *EEC Law* (1993), pp. 479 to 480; Chalmers, "Free Movement of Goods with the E.C.: An Unhealthy Addiction to Scotch Whisky?" (1993) 42 I.C.L.Q. 269 to 294.

# APPENDIX

## Single Market Compliance Unit Cases

The list below has been supplied by the SMCU. It demonstrates the variety of cases in which the Unit may be of assistance:

The quickest result the Unit achieved was in 1992 when Spanish authorities were persuaded to accept photocopied (and not original) documentation for an exporter of office equipment, allowing his goods to move freely. (This took about five days.)

The Commission has started infraction proceedings against Italy for failing to implement a directive which restricts the use of dangerous substances in some paints. This will put Italian paint manufacturers on the same footing as U.K. ones, which was what the U.K. paint industry asked the SMCU to do.

As a result of SMCU efforts, Spain is now reviewing British standards on gas fires, rather than insisting on Spanish testing, which benefits a U.K. manufacturer of gas fires. "Homologación"—homologation or conformity with Spanish national standards—procedures have caused considerable problems to a wide range of U.K. traders. Goods from steel bars to satellite dishes, gas barbecues to facsimiles, have been delayed in entering the Spanish market because of delays in test dates, inappropriate and expensive tests and lack of information from some Spanish testing houses. A formal U.K. government complaint to the Spanish authorities, through the Embassy in Madrid, ministerial meetings and correspondence, and finally a complaint to the Commission, has resulted in better access for some U.K. exporters.

A U.K. company was refused a licence to fly in order to carry out contracted work in the Republic of Ireland several times. The Irish authorities refused on the grounds that similar Irish companies could carry out the work! The SMCU took up this obvious breach of the Treaty of Rome with the Republic's authorities through the U.K. Embassy in Dublin, and the U.K. company can now get its licence and work in the Republic of Ireland.

French restrictions requiring the translation of labels on goods were applied to books (in English), explaining how to play the U.K.-manufactured "Dungeons and Dragons" computer game, even though the books were published independently and not by the game manufacturer (TSR). This could have exposed the manufacturer to court cases in

France; the SMCU pursued the case with the Commission, which supported the U.K. view and the company is now able to sell its games without hindrance in France.

The SMCU took up with the European Commission the issue of whether an Italian tax on importers and exporters was a new form of taxation which breached Article 12 of the Treaty of Rome, by increasing the tax burden on exports to Italy. A subsequent judgment from the ECJ supported the U.K. view and the Italian tax was changed.

The Danish dropped their 2·5 per cent VAT-related levy (labour market contribution) on imported goods. The levy affected a range of U.K. industries and exporters in shipbuilding, clothing, polymers and metals. The SMCU persuaded the Commission that the levy breached the sixth VAT directive. Infraction proceedings were started, Denmark recognised imminent defeat, dropped the levy and instead increased the overall rate of VAT, which bites evenly on all trade. (The process took over three years.)

British carpet manufacturers noted that public purchasing notifications of tender were sparse or non-existent from all other Member States, although the U.K. notified a number of contracts under the requirements of the Public Supplies Directive. The SMCU raised this with the Commission, supplying evidence from TED (Tenders Electronic Daily Database). The Commission has investigated this and has now issued a request for explanation to each Member State for this uneven advertising.

# INDEX

Abortion, Community law,
  supremacy of, and 3–002,
  3–008
Acquired Rights Directive 6–014
*Acquis communautaire* 1–002
*Acte clair* doctrine 3–020
Administrative discretion 9–015
Administrative letters 3–040
Amendment of documents
  10–041
Attestation 10–034, 10–055

British Medical Association
  (BMA), lobbying by 1–016
Brussels Convention 1–019

Certiorari, writ of 9–001
Chambers of Commerce,
  lobbying by 1–016
Comfort letters 3–040
Commission *see* European
  Commission
Committee on Institutional
  Affairs of the European
  Parliament 1–014
Committee on Legal Affairs and
  Citizens' Rights 1–012
Committee on Petitions 1–010,
  1–011
  advice by 1–012
  public right to information,
    and 1–015
Committee on the Rules of
  Procedure, the Verification
  of Credentials and
  Immunities 1–016
Committees of inquiry 1–013
Community driving licence
  5–006—5–007

Community law
  breach of, remedies *see*
    Remedies
  common internal law, as 1–002
  competition rules *see*
    Competition rules
  damages, civil claims for,
    relevance in 1–007
  direct effect *see* Direct effect
  directives *see* Directives
  directly applicable *see* Direct
    applicability
  effectiveness, principle of
    5–022—5–023,
    8–003—8–006, 9-007
  English courts, and *see* United
    Kingdom
  features of 1–002
  freedom of expression and
    information 3–008
  fundamental rights *see*
    Fundamental rights
  implementation of, time limit
    for 2–002, 5–009—5–020,
    6–003, 6–005, 6–006
  indirect enforcement of 1–007
    ECHR, using 3–005
  indirect interpretation
    6–001—6–020
  international law, and 1–002,
    2–007
  legal practitioners in England
    and Wales, effect on
    1–002
  national courts, and 1–007,
    3–001—3–052,
    6–001—6–020
    damages, award of *see*
      Damages

279